RATIONALITY
AND
RELATIVISM

RATIONALITY
AND
RELATIVISM

EDITED BY

Martin Hollis

AND

Steven Lukes

Basil Blackwell

Introduction, compilation and editorial matter
Copyright © Martin Hollis and Steven Lukes 1982

First published 1982
Reprinted 1983, 1985, 1988, 1990
Basil Blackwell Ltd
108 Cowley Road, Oxford OX4 1JF, England

British Library Cataloguing in Publication Data
A CIP catalogue record for this book is available from the British Library.

ISBN 0-631-12773-9
ISBN 0-631-13126-4 Pbk

Phototypesetting by Oxford Publishing Services
Printed and bound in Great Britain
by Billing & Sons Ltd, Worcester

CONTENTS

CONTRIBUTORS

BARRY BARNES was trained in natural sciences and in sociology before moving to the Science Studies Unit, University of Edinburgh. Among his publications are *Scientific Knowledge and Sociological Theory* (1974), *Interests and the Growth of Knowledge* (1977) and *T. S. Kuhn and Social Science* (1982). He is also co-editor of two collections of readings in the sociology and social history of science, *Natural Order* (with S. Shapin, 1979) and *Science in Context* (with D. D. Edge, 1982).

DAVID BLOOR lectures in the philosophy of science at the Science Studies Unit, University of Edinburgh. He is author of *Knowledge and Social Imagery* (1976) and has just completed a book on Wittgenstein and the sociology of knowledge.

JON ELSTER is Associate Professor in Social and Historical Philosophy at the University of Oslo. His research interests include the theory of rational and irrational behaviour, Marxism and more generally the philosophy of the social sciences. His publications include *Logic and Society* (1978), *Ulysses and the Sirens* (1979) and *Explaining Technical Change* (1982).

ERNEST GELLNER has been Professor of Philosophy at the London School of Economics since 1962. He was educated in Prague and Oxford. Fieldwork on Moroccan Berbers brought him a Ph.D. in social anthropology (London, 1961) and resulted in *Saints of the Atlas* (1965) and *Muslim Society* (1981). His philosophical publications include *Words and Things* (1959), *Thought and Change* (1964) and *Legitimation of Belief* (1975). He has been a Fellow of the British Academy since 1974.

IAN HACKING is Henry Waldgrave Stuart Professor of Philosophy at Stanford University. His books include *Logic of Statistical Inference, Why does Language matter to Philosophy?* and *The Emergence of Probability*. Two forthcoming books are *Representing and Intervening*, about scientific realism and experimental science, and *One Person, Many Tongues*, a collection of essays about language.

MARTIN HOLLIS is Professor of Philosophy at the University of East Anglia. He is co-author, with E. J. Nell, of *Rational Economic Man: A Philosophical Critique of Neo-Classical Economics* (1975) and author of *Models of Man* (1977). He has also edited a seventeenth-century anthology, *The Light of Reason* (1971), and co-edited *Philosophy and Economic Theory* (with F. Hahn, 1979).

ROBIN HORTON is Professor of Philosophy at the University of Port Harcourt. He is the author of *The Gods as Guests: An Aspect of Kalabari Religious Life* (1960) and *Kalabari Sculpture* (1965) and co-editor (with Ruth Finnegan) of *Modes of Thought: Essays on Thinking in Western and Non-Western Societies* (1973). He has also published numerous papers on African traditional thought and religion.

STEVEN LUKES is Fellow in Politics and Sociology at Balliol College, Oxford. His publications include *Emile Durkheim* (1973), *Individualism* (1973), *Power: A Radical View* (1974) and *Essays in Social Theory* (1977), and he is co-editor of *The Good Society* (with A. Arblaster, 1971). He is currently writing a book on marxism and morality.

WILLIAM NEWTON-SMITH is Fairfax Fellow in Philosophy at Balliol College. He is author of *The Structure of Time* (1980) and *The Rationality of Science* (1981). Currently he is writing a book on the philosophy of W. v. O. Quine.

DAN SPERBER is *chargé de recherche* at the Centre National de la Recherche Scientifique in Paris. He is author of *Rethinking Symbolism* (1975) and numerous articles in anthropology, linguistics and Ethiopian ethnography.

CHARLES TAYLOR is Professor of Political Science at McGill University. His publications include *The Explanation of Behaviour* (1964) and *Hegel* (1975).

INTRODUCTION

The temptations of relativism are perennial and pervasive. In many fields of thought and inquiry they are openly embraced. Within social anthropology, they have been ever-present, though partially, if firmly, resisted. Recent upheavals in the philosophy of science have turned the historian or sociologist of science into something of an anthropologist, an explorer of alien cultures. It is as if scientific paradigms and theoretical frameworks were strung out in time like islands across an archipelago. Other minds, other cultures, other languages and other theoretical schemes call for understanding from within. Seen from within, they make us doubt whether there is anything universal under the sun. This doubt is also a challenge to the very idea of a single world. Is not the world, as interpreted in our scheme of things, but one of many? Are not our forms of reasoning and tests of truth as parochial as any other? This is the primrose path to relativism and it is paved with plausible contentions.

This volume is about interpretation, translation and explanation. All the contributors hold that interpretation must proceed from within and is bound up with some concept of rationality; that translation raises radical questions of interpretation; and that both challenge received ideas of explanation. All are concerned with the bearing of relativism or its denial upon proper interpretation and explanation. But not all are of one mind and the volume is part of a flourishing debate. Twelve years ago some aspects of this debate were presented in *Rationality,* a collection edited by Bryan Wilson and published by Basil Blackwell. Some of those authors are once more taking a hand. Others, who have published elsewhere on these matters, are here taking stock of their years of thought on the subject. In all but one case, their essays are specially written for this volume and to some extent take account of one another. The result is in no way intended to be definitive or comprehensive. It is, rather, a report from part of a lively and changing front. Each essay represents a distinct position and arises from a continuing exercise in reflection and debate among philosophers and social scientists.

In this introduction, we seek to sketch the main sources of contemporary relativism, the principal forms it has taken and its claims to make sense of the accumulating evidence from anthropology and the history of science. We show how these claims are made and criticized, in different ways, by our various authors who, in the process, reveal interesting subsidiary and cross-cutting differences among themselves.

SOURCES OF RELATIVISM

Romantic

Relativism has always appealed to noble and worthy sentiments. Within anthropology a need and duty have long been felt not only to understand the worlds of other cultures from within, but also to respect them: here to interpret the world is not to change it. It was easy to suppose that this implied judging other cultures only by their, not our, standards, especially in the face of the prevailing ethnocentric assumptions of nineteenth-century anthropology. So Franz Boas and his followers forged a cultural relativism which refused to see any hierarchy among peoples or an evolutionary scale linking the primitive to the modern, or early magic and religion to modern science in the manner of Frazer and Tylor. Instead, they parcelled out humanity into separate cultures, biologically and mutually irreducible, each with its own system of 'values' determining its own 'individuality'. Cultural anthropology, Herskovits argued, should lead us to see 'the validity of every set of norms for the people whose lives are guided by them, and the values they represent'.[1] This involved a double denial: first, of the claim of any culture studied that the norms governing other cultures' beliefs and practices are invalid; and second, of any such claim on our part, since, typically, 'ethnocentrism is rationalized

---

[1] M. Herskovits, *Man and his Works* (Alfred Knopf, New York, 1947), p. 76.

and made the basis of programmes of action detrimental to the well-being of other peoples'.[2]

This attitude can be construed more widely as a response to Enlightenment rationalism, with its belief in universal laws of human nature and in an all-embracing scientific method for accumulating truths, its distrust of subjectivity and arbitrariness and its serene belief in intellectual and moral progress and in the link between them. Nietzsche distilled this response into sharp question and answer:

> What then is truth? A mobile army of metaphors, metonyms and anthropomorphisms – in short a sum of human relations, which have been enhanced, transposed and embellished poetically and rhetorically, and which after long use seem firm, canonical and obligatory to a people: truths are illusions about which one has forgotten that this is what they are; metaphors which are worn out and without sensuous power; coins which have lost their pictures and now matter only as metal, no longer as coins.[3]

The mobile army is a gang of local militias, each keeping order in its own province. Nietzsche's imagery is uncommon but his theme has become a commonplace. It is a Romantic version of the thought that reality is socially constructed. For a notable recent example, compare Mary Douglas's claim that this thought 'demands an imaginative effort which has been left to artists, novelists and poets' but poses 'urgent questions . . . for the philosophy of science'. Hence her talk of 'subjective truth' and the need 'to recognise at last our cognitive precariousness'.[4]

Scientific

On the other hand, relativism may be enlisted in the service of science. A truly scientific approach, it has been argued, to the sociological study of beliefs requires it. The position is firmly stated in this volume by Barry Barnes and David Bloor, who advocate what they call a 'strong programme' in the sociology of knowledge. Relativism, they

---

[2] Ibid., p. 68.

[3] F. Nietzsche, 'On truth and lie in an extra-moral sense' (1873), a posthumous fragment included in W. Kaufman (ed.), *The Portable Nietzsche* (Viking Press, New York, 1954).

[4] Mary Douglas (ed.), *Rules and Meanings: The Anthropology of Everyday Knowledge* (Penguin, Harmondsworth, 1973), p. 10; and *Implicit Meanings: Essays in Anthropology* (Routledge & Kegan Paul, London, 1975), p. xviii.

say, 'is essential to all those disciplines, such as anthropology, sociology, the history of institutions and ideas, and even cognitive psychology, which account for the diversity of systems of knowledge, their distribution and the manner of their change'. It is 'those who oppose relativism, and who grant certain forms of knowledge a privileged status, who pose the real threat to a scientific understanding of knowledge and cognition'. Local acceptance goes with local modes of cultural transmission, of socialization and social control, of power and authority: the scientific task is to trace these links, investigating 'the specific, local causes' of beliefs being held.[5]

But a strong programme, with its accompanying relativism, can also be defended on 'hermeneutic' and 'critical' grounds, as Mary Hesse has done recently. She opposes 'those who ground their faith in universal rationality on a contingent belief that our language and science are somehow the high points of the historical evolution of ideas'. Western science is not the textbook saga of cumulative Reason, and we have much to learn from 'cross-cultural understanding and self-reflexive critique' in understanding science itself.[6] The scientific approach to our own culture, as to others, is to grasp it from within, heeding the implication that objectivity is an internal standard.

Anti-epistemological

A third motive for embracing relativism is, broadly, philosophical: namely a principled rejection of the search for the rational foundations of knowledge. Its most eloquent recent exponent is Richard Rorty,[7] who endorses what he calls 'the holistic, antifoundationalist, pragmatist treatments of knowledge and meaning which we find in Dewey, Wittgenstein, Quine, Sellars, and Davidson' and, specifically, their abandonment of 'the quest for commensuration': a 'set of rules which will tell us how rational agreement can be reached or what would settle the issue on every point where statements seem to conflict'. Rorty proposes a blessed release from the idea that 'there are foundations to serve as common ground for adjudicating knowledge claims' and that

[5] This volume, pp. 22f.
[6] Mary Hesse, 'The strong thesis of sociology of science' in her *Revolutions and Reconstructions in the Philosophy of Science* (Harvester Press, Brighton, 1980), pp. 29–60.
[7] In his *Philosophy and the Mirror of Nature* (Blackwell, Oxford, and Princeton University Press, Princeton, 1980).

the philosopher is 'guardian of rationality', indeed from the project of epistemology itself. This latter is the misguided attempt 'to see the problems of justification within normal discourse' as 'hooked on to something which demands moral commitment – Reality, Truth, Objectivity, Reason', rather than as 'practices adopted for various historical reasons and as the achievement of objective truth, where "objective truth" is no more than and no less than the best idea we currently have about how to explain what is going on'.[8]

On this view, the philosopher can obviously construct no algorithm for choice among scientific theories. But what then is he to say of the considerations advanced against the Copernican theory by Cardinal Bellarmine – namely, the scriptural description of the fabric of the heavens? Were they 'illogical or unscientific'? Rorty answers no. This was no 'black-and-white struggle between reason and superstition', but rather one between the value of 'getting the heavens right' and that of 'preserving the Church, and the general cultural structure of Europe', between different 'grids' determining the relevance of one statement to another, and specifically what sorts of evidence there could be for statements about the movements of the planets. Galileo won the argument but not because the Galilean 'grid' is more 'objective' and 'rational'. On the contrary, the Bellarmine–Galileo issue is on a par with that between Kerensky and Lenin, or the Royal Academy (circa 1910) and Bloomsbury. The value of science and rationality do not float 'free of the educational and institutional patterns of the day': Galileo was *creating* the notion of scientific value. It was a 'splendid thing he did so' but 'the question of whether he was "rational" in doing so is out of place'.[9]

FORMS OF RELATIVISM

Moral relativism

The most familiar form of relativism, though it does not appear in these pages, is moral relativism. Distinct from mere moral *diversity* or variation, and from moral *relativity* (that is the relativity of such variation to independent variables, such as cultural and social factors),

---

[8] Ibid., pp. 317, 316, 317, 385.
[9] Ibid., pp. 328–31.

this is the denial of more than local standing to the grounds of moral belief and practice. It is plausible to suppose that this is what Pascal meant when, speaking of different conceptions of the virtues, he observed that 'What is truth on one side of the Pyrenees is error on the other.'[10] Yet if, *contra* Pascal, we hold that moral judgements are not capable of truth and falsity, and moralities are human or social inventions, and there are no 'facts of the matter' or canons of discourse comparable to science to decide between conflicting judgements and theories, then the case for moral relativism may seem only to be stronger still – as distinct from the various forms of cognitive relativism that form the subject-matter of this volume.

We cannot explore this question any further here and so will just observe that this last distinction should be viewed with the greatest caution. Thought about experience can be subdivided for convenience and there are indeed modes of reasoning peculiar to some realms. But moral thought is largely discursive and human beings do not live wholly in convenient compartments. Also, scientific progress is not determined solely by the 'facts of the matter', and it may be doubted that there are such textbook determinants at all, or indeed any canonical 'method' furnishing an algorithm for theory choice. Moreover, there are many cognitive activities which it is rash to call 'science', and to define rational thought in terms of a logic of scientific thought is to court charges of parochialism. In short, the neat contrast between moral and cognitive relativism, with special arguments relating to each, is dubious in the extreme.

We will, however, for the sake of convenience, speak of cognitive relativism in the usual way (leaving aside the question of whether ethics is cognitive) and proceed to distinguish, under its wide aegis, conceptual and perceptual relativism, and relativism about truth and about reason.

Conceptual relativism

Different groups and cultures order their experience by means of different concepts. The order which they find is notoriously not given to them directly by experience. Strikingly different inventories of the world's furniture can be found by glancing across continents or over time. (As Bulmer observed, the Karam of New Guinea include under

---

[10] *Pensées*, v, 294.

the concept 'yakt' only some birds but also bats, but not cassowaries.[11]) Different schemes of classification incorporate witches and tree spirits, phlogiston and the ether, electrons and magnetic fields. Experience underdetermines what it is rational to believe about the world: schemes of concepts provide grids on which to base belief. Such schemes link the particular (witches, electrons) to more general concepts, up to the most basic, general, or abstract, which it seems natural to call categories of thought. Contemporary Westerners rely on categories of space, time, causation, number, personhood, for instance, which are not undisputed among themselves and which differ in certain ways from those elsewhere. So far, no relativist conclusion follows, but the temptation is plain, especially when it is noticed that conceptual variation is relative to social or cultural context.

That *some* concepts are relative in this way to context is undeniable. That *all* are, and more particularly the basic categories of thought themselves, is the challenging thought. The thought is that each scheme, itself relative to context or culture, *organizes* or *fits* nature or the world or reality. In short, with the idea that neither reality itself, nor men's relation to it, nor the constraints of rational thinking set limits upon the content or form of such schemes, we reach relativism in earnest.

Perceptual relativism

The earnest thesis is evoked by the suggestive but elusive formula that different communities or groups of scientists 'live in different worlds'. This formula, redolent as it is of idealism, is common to the two most influential relativisms of recent years, namely, the trans-cultural version from anthropology and the trans-theoretical version (internal, however, to our theoretical culture) from the history, sociology and philosophy of natural science.

Thus Sapir wrote:

> The 'real world' is to a large extent unconsciously built upon the language habits of the group. The worlds in which different societies live are *distinct* worlds, not merely the same world with different labels attached. We see and hear and otherwise experi-

[11] See R. Bulmer, 'Why is the cassowary not a bird?', *Man*, n.s., 2 (1967), pp. 5–25.

ence very largely as we do because the language habits of our community predispose certain choices of interpretation.[12]

There are two related ideas here. One is that what we perceive cannot be explained by the nature of the object perceived. It raises philosophical issues about perception which cannot be put in a paragraph and crop up only incidentally in this volume. The other is the specific diagnosis that language in some sense determines or constitutes what is perceived. There are, say Barnes and Bloor for instance, 'no privileged occasions for the use of terms – no "simple perceptual situations" – which provide the researcher with "standard meanings" uncomplicated by cultural variables'.[13] This has been a central strand in the debate to which this book belongs. The most robust expression of it is to be found in Peter Winch's *The Idea of a Social Science,* typified by his dictum that 'our idea of what belongs to the realm of reality is given for us in the language that we use'.[14]

As for natural science, it is embodied in Kuhn's opposition to the traditional claim that 'what changes with a paradigm is only the scientist's interpretation of observations that themselves are fixed once and for all by the nature of the environment and of the perceptual apparatus' and his conclusion that 'we must learn to make sense of' statements such as that after a revolution the scientist 'works in a different world'.[15] Any 'facts of the matter' have to be perceived and identified before they can settle disputes and by then they are already impregnated.

If perception is relative, concepts and objects do not relate as mind to matter. But the theory-ladenness of facts is not decisive, as both Newton-Smith and Horton observe below. Nor is the thought that percepts without concepts are blind. To reach relativism in earnest, more steps are needed. Certainly, however, the textbook account of

---

[12] E. Sapir, 'The status of linguistics as a science', *Language*, 5 (1929), p. 209.
[13] This volume, p. 38.
[14] P. Winch, *The Idea of a Social Science and its Relation to Philosophy* (Routledge & Kegan Paul, London, 1958), p. 15.
[15] T. Kuhn, *The Structure of Scientific Revolutions* (University of Chicago Press, Chicago, 1964), p. 120. See also pp. 93, 125, 149, 166, 169. Cf. Feyerabend: '. . . a change of universal principles brings about a change of the entire world. Speaking in this manner we no longer assume an objective world that remains unaffected by our epistemic activities, except when moving within the confines of a particular point of view': P. Feyerabend, *Science in a Free Society* (New Left Books, London, 1978), p. 70.

rationality in belief does rely on their being data of observation and a theory-neutral language with which to describe them. To relativize perception, whether to language or to paradigms, and thus reverse the priority, is a major first step.

Relativism of truth

The crucial further step is the claim to relativize truth. What is true for the Hopi is not so for us; what is true for Aristotle is not so for Galileo. But what is it whose truth-value varies so? As Newton-Smith argues below, on a traditional account of meaning and translation, linking meaning to truth-conditions, the same sentence cannot be true in one language and false in another. If s and s^1 have the same meaning, whatever conditions make s true would make s^1 true. So it is no surprise that relativists tend to favour holistic conceptions of truth and meaning, which make the primary semantic unit something more complex than the sentence. There is then a further question of whether or not there is a common stock of non-relative observational truths which serve to anchor communication. (This is what Horton in his essay terms 'primary theory', giving the world a foreground of middle-sized, enduring, solid objects, related in space and time by 'push-pull' causal links, and distinguishing objects from human beings and self from other persons.) If there is no such common stock, then there are incommensurable conceptual schemes and realities. As Davidson has noted, this version of relativism abandons 'the attempt to make sense of the metaphor of a single space within which each scheme has a position and provides a point of view'.[16] If, on the other hand, the relativist holds that there is such a common stock, then he owes us an account of how theories (scientific and otherwise) relate to the observational data and can be specified, identified as alternative and, indeed, known to be incommensurable.

One kind of answer is offered by Quine, and it is no surprise that some relativists, such as Mary Douglas, appeal to his authority.[17] On his view, theories are underdetermined by (all actual and possible) data and translation is indeterminate: different translation manuals can, in principle, predict behaviour equally well and thus be equally good, and then, on Quine's assumptions, what is said and believed is

[16] D. Davidson, 'On the very idea of a conceptual scheme', *Proceedings and Addresses of the American Philosophical Association*, 47 (1973–4), p. 17.
[17] Douglas, *Implicit Meanings*, ch. 17.

itself indeterminate. *This* kind of relativism, however, is of little use to practising anthropologists or historians of science. For *they* must surely believe that they can succeed, at least in principle, in identifying what their subjects believe. They might be prepared to swallow the idea that success in translation can only be locally judged – 'there can only be translation acceptable for practical purposes, as judged by contingent, local standards'.[18] But how can they stomach the further thought that what is to be translated is itself relative to a translation manual? In short, Quine's relativism, though it might be coherent, is too strong and too heady a brew for the purposes at hand.

Relativism of reason

The final step is to relativize what counts as a reason, or a good reason, for holding beliefs. The basic thought here is seductively plausible: that what warrants belief depends on canons of reasoning, deductive or non-deductive, that should properly be seen as social norms, relative to culture and period. At its most ambitious, this thought reaches to deductive logic itself. 'The criteria of logic,' Winch boldly declared, 'are not a direct gift from God but arise out of and are only intelligible in the context of ways of living and modes of social life.'[19] And so Barnes and Bloor proclaim that 'the compelling character of logic, such as it is, derives from certain narrowly defined purposes and from custom and institutionalized usage. Its authority is moral and social'; and they refer to alternative 'logical conventions.'[20] In upshot, what counts as a good reason may be context-dependent. Galileo consulted observation and experiment, Bellarmine the scriptures; Evans-Pritchard the available evidence of causal connections, Azande the poison oracle. Each is equally enmeshed in a web of reasons, properly woven by its own standards from within but finally incapable of support from without.

The rationalist replies by refusing to divorce reasons from objective truth. The crucial point here is not that a reason for belief is not a good reason, unless what it cites is true. (Rationalists do, admittedly, try to make this point; but it is a separate one and one which risks begging the question.) The crucial point is that the giving of reasons involves a

---

[18] This volume, p. 39.
[19] Winch, *The Idea of a Social Science*, p. 100; see also p. 126.
[20] This volume, p. 45.

claim that what is cited would, if true, be a good reason. In other words it has to be objectively true that one thing is good reason for another. Where the relativist sees only differences in these standards for rating reasons as good, the rationalist insists on ranking the standards. This marks one of the places where we, the editors of this volume, continue to disagree. Hollis takes the straight rationalist path, adding that the relativist needs an external standpoint in order to declare objectively that one culture has one standard and another culture another. Lukes is partially seduced by the thought that the goodness – the strength and relevance – of reasons for belief can depend on culture and context. So, although we agree that the obvious differences in what is cited in support of what in different cultures imply no final relativism, we still differ about the limits of intelligible contextual variation.

Some rationalists are thus willing to grant a great deal to relativism and discussion would not have to become too nuanced for an Introduction. For instance Hacking describes himself as an 'anarcho-rationalist', who preserves truth from relativization but makes a fresh and disconcerting case for a relativism of 'styles of reasoning'. We leave further pursuit to the reader both of his article and of the doubts expressed by Newton-Smith and Lukes in theirs.

Relative to what?

These are, we judge, the main strands of relativism in rough progression. Belief is relative to . . . well, what? Five answers merit a brief mention. Uncontentiously, beliefs vary with natural environment, as does the boiling point of water, and it is no surprise to find people who live in different climates taking suitable interest in their surroundings. That is no doubt why the Eskimo has thirty-eight words for snow. Secondly there is the human equipment with which we perceive and reflect and, were we concerned with the science of psychology here, we would take the matter seriously. Dan Sperber draws attention to some bearings on developmental psychology in his essay.[21] Thirdly there is social context, which has often been proposed as a source of variation in beliefs, notably when constructing a theory of ideology. The theme is developed below by Barnes and Bloor in their account of some causal relations between the social and the cognitive.

Fourthly language can be seen as prime mover, in the spirit of the

[21] Ibid., pp. 157ff.

quotations from Sapir and Winch; and, fifthly, belief can be made relative to some all-embracing context, like a form of life, as in Winch again. These two moves are suggestive enough but remain indeterminate, until it is asked whether linguistic or cognitive context is relative in its turn. If the answer is 'Yes', that leads back presumably to a previous reply. An answer of 'No' on the other hand, leads on to some species of idealism and has produced much disagreement among relativists themselves. Dispute is in part about what is finally the given in social or human life, the bedrock where explanation should cease. In part it is also about method, since idealists may reject the whole notion that one entity (a culture, say) stands to another (a social system, for instance) in external relations of cause and effect. This also, however, raises complexities beyond the scope of an Introduction.

RATIONALITY AND RELATIVISM

The essays in this collection can be seen as examining the relations between rationality and relativism through the answers they give to three questions. The first is: 'Does the rich and extensive evidence of apparently irrational beliefs adduced among others by social anthropologists and historians of science require us to accept relativism in any strong form?' In this volume, positive answers to this question come, forthrightly, from Barnes and Bloor and, more circumspectly, from the 'anarcho-rationalist' Hacking. All the other contributors offer differently accented negative answers, which essentially fall into three categories (though most answer in more than one category). Either apparently irrational beliefs really are irrational beliefs, perhaps backed by mistaken beliefs about what is really reasonable; or they are not really irrational, given the (technical or social or cultural or psychological) context; or they are not really beliefs, at least in the propositional sense meriting rational appraisal. (Hollis and Newton-Smith, in the end, stress the first, Horton and Lukes the second, and Sperber the third.)

The second and third questions are: 'In identifying beliefs, must we – indeed can we – discriminate between those which are true and rational and those which, in varying ways, are not?' and 'If so, does the kind of explanation to be sought vary with the category of belief explained or does it remain uniform and "symmetrical" throughout?' The forthright relativist answer is that there are no objective, external epistemic standpoints and that explanation is therefore symmetrical.

This is the answer of Barnes and Bloor. Our other contributors offer alternative answers, but with such differences of reasoning and nuance that the reader cannot complain of being dragooned in any one direction.

Barnes and Bloor, citing historical studies of scientific knowledge and anthropologists' work on commonsense knowledge and pre-literate cosmologies, claim that 'there is more evidence to be cited for relativism than against it'. Cognitive relativism for them starts from the observation of the variability of beliefs and the conviction that their adoption in a given situation 'depends on, or is relative to, the circumstances of the users'. To this they add a 'symmetry' or 'equivalence' postulate, to the effect that the explanation of why beliefs are held does not vary with the epistemic status of the belief.[22] As Mary Hesse has put it, 'rational norms and true beliefs in natural science are just as much explananda of the sociology of science as are non-rationality and error'.[23] Some non-relativists (among them Elster, Horton and Lukes) might be inclined to agree with this, but not with the cognitive relativist's *reason* for asserting it, which is that 'rules of argument and criteria of truth are internal to a social system', that 'truth' and 'rationality' are to be redefined as 'internal to given societies' and that where explanation is to stop is simply the point where questioning by 'the relevant local consensus' ceases.[24] In short, cognitive relativism, of the forthright sort defended by Barnes and Bloor, denies that there is any valid distinction between what is true, reasonable and explanatory and what counts as knowledge, on the one hand, and what is locally accepted as such, on the other. 'For the relativist,' they say, 'there is no sense attached to the idea that some standards or beliefs are *really* rational as distinct from merely locally accepted as such.'[25]

For Hacking, this position must qualify as 'an inane subjectivism', since it holds that 'whether *p* is a reason for *q* depends on whether people have got around to reasoning that way or not'. The relativism he carefully defends asserts rather that 'the sense of a proposition *p*, the way in which it points to truth or falsehood, hinges on the style of reasoning appropriate to *p*'. Thus 'renaissance medical, alchemical

[22] Ibid., pp. 24–5, 22.
[23] Hesse, *Revolutions and Reconstructions*, p. 56.
[24] Ibid., p. 45.
[25] This volume, p. 27.

and astrological doctrines of resemblance and similitude', for example, in specifying alternative possibilities for truth-or-falsehood, are evidence for such relativism, which, however does not imply subjectivity. Subjectivity claims that 'with different customs we could "rightly" take some propositions for true while at present we take them for false'; relativity that their very sense and their being true or false depends on how we reason about them, that alternative styles of reasoning yield other categories of truth-or-falsehood than ours, and that the rationality of a style of reasoning 'does not seem open for independent criticism, since the very sense of what may be established by that style depends upon the style itself'.[26] There is, it seems, no meta-reason justifying a style of reasoning, no external or non-circular way of assessing it.

By contrast, Hacking's 'arch-rationalist' holds that there just are good and bad reasons and these are 'not relative to anything' and 'do not depend on context' and that 'it has taken millenia to evolve systems of reasoning. By and large our Western tradition has contributed more to this progress than any other.'[27] The remaining contributors to this volume are different kinds of rationalist by which we mean, merely, that they reject the forthright relativization of truth and reason. They are, however, not all equally arch, at least as regards the context-dependence of reasoning. So, with different emphases, Taylor, Newton-Smith, Elster, Horton and Lukes all stress the impact of context upon the diverse forms that human reasoning takes.

Most arch is Hollis, who takes on the whole 'strong programme' of Barnes and Bloor. In contrast to them he uses 'the notion of a reason objectively', arguing that

> there are tests for whether a belief is objectively rational and that subjectively rational beliefs need not pass them . . . and there is a minimum score which all beliefs must attain and a maximum score which some must; and that 'good reason' is an objective term, to be applied with increasing warrant as the maximum is approached.

For Hollis the identification of beliefs – seeing the actors' world from within – requires a 'bridgehead of true and rational beliefs': successful translation, and indeed interpretation, of beliefs must presuppose

---

[26] Ibid., pp. 48f, 60, 64f, 56.
[27] Ibid., p. 52f.

'what a rational man cannot fail to believe in simple perceptual situations, organized by rules of coherent judgement which a rational man cannot fail to subscribe to'. These presuppositions are *a priori* for Hollis: they are assumed, not discovered. What Hollis infers from all the richly documented evidence of apparently irrational beliefs is not relativism but the indispensability of rationalism in order that they can be identified and then, should the appearance of irrationality be justified, explained differently from true and rationally held beliefs, for 'true and rational beliefs need one sort of explanation, false and irrational beliefs another', with 'mixed explanations for the mixed cases'.[28]

Taylor's essay focuses directly on the 'rich' concept of rationality that is in play when we compare scientific and pre-scientific cultures. It raises the issue (addressed, as we have seen, by Rorty, Winch and Hacking) of whether the opponents of Galileo, or primitive practitioners of ritual magic, along with post-Galilean scientists, each have their own form of rationality, governed by different, contextually-given, 'internal' criteria of 'success'. He answers that the first two groups must concede to the third in an argument they cannot, in a sense, avoid. It is true that the Paduan opponents of Galileo, like the Zande believers in witchcraft, have reasons for their beliefs, reasons backed by fundamental assumptions about the ordering of the cosmos, embedded in their 'atheoretical cultures', in which understanding the universe and coming into attunement with it are inseparable activities. In this sense, their activity is 'incommensurable' with our 'disengaged' search for theoretical understanding. But they cannot fail to acknowledge scientific advance and its associated increased technological control and 'out of this can arise valid trans-cultural judgements of superiority', so that 'our culture can surely lay claim to a higher, and fuller, or more effective rationality, if it is in a position to achieve a more perspicuous order than another'. There is, in short, 'a definite respect in which modern science is superior to its renaissance predecessors . . . the science which dissociates understanding and attunement achieves greater understanding *at least of physical nature*'.[29]

Newton-Smith takes issue with all the foregoing contributors. Against Barnes and Bloor's forthright relativism, he argues that, on a

[28] Ibid., pp. 69, 72–5, 85.
[29] Ibid., pp. 102ff, our italics.

traditional view of meaning, relativism of truth and of reason are incoherent: the possibility of translation entails the falsehood of relativism, and the truth of relativism the impossibility of translation. Relativism, on this account, ends by depriving the natives of trans-latable beliefs and, on any account, fails as an explanation, generating more puzzles than it solves. Against Hacking's 'muted' relativism, in which 'styles of reasoning' determine the sense and the availability of propositions, he claims it to be either innocuous (linking evidence to the determining of sense) or implausible (claiming that what is true can only be determined *within* a style of reasoning: but observational success offers a style-neutral standard). Against Hollis, he argues (with Horton) that the 'bridgehead' of low-level perceptual beliefs and logic which are needed for translation to get going is not an *a priori* presupposition but an empirical hypothesis, for which the predictions of our translation scheme give evidence. And against Taylor, he argues that Galileo's critics did not, by virtue of their incommensurable world-view, have different kinds of reasons for their beliefs: rather, *because* of their different beliefs about the conditions obtaining in the cosmos, they reasoned as we do but to different conclusions.

Elster's paper, like the Marxist theory of ideology for which it seeks to provide micro-foundations, simply assumes that 'illusion', 'bias', errors of perception, and inference, and 'distortion' are detectable by applying the normal canons of scientific method and logic. Whether there are 'adequate reasons' for a belief is decidable by correct reason-ing in the light of 'available evidence'. The question of ideology arises in the first instance where beliefs which fail by these (non-relative) cognitive standards are shown to be 'shaped in an irrational way', whether because of interest or social position. The Marxist theory, as Elster shows, commits one to the assumption that 'individuals differ systematically, e.g. in a class-related way, in the extent to which their external situation lends itself to certain kinds of fallacies, inferential errors and illusions'. On the other hand, Elster also argues that beliefs for which there are (non-relatively) good reasons may not be held for those reasons and that (*contra* Hollis) where beliefs are rationally grounded, sociological explanation of why they are held may well be appropriate. Epistemology needs history because 'whatever the ap-parent rationality of the belief, a genetic explanation of the belief may well show that it was not in fact held for those good reasons'.[30] But

[30] Ibid., pp. 137, 147.

unlike Barnes and Bloor, Elster assumes that where it *is*, this is explanatory of the beliefs and decidable in a way that is relative neither to observer nor observed.

Sperber, one of the three anthropologists represented here, spells out unfamiliar costs of the relativism often favoured by the practitioners of his discipline: in particular, what possible model of cognitive development could accord with alternative, incommensurable cognizable worlds? Sperber argues, positively, that much of the evidence that has been presented by anthropologists for relativism has been pre-cooked in that it has been presented as evidence of seemingly irrational beliefs in propositions, which fit together into a whole scheme. His case is that there is a very wide range of beliefs, which are often called 'symbolic', held in different ways, and which are not propositional but different kinds of commitment to semipropositional representations – which cannot be true or false themselves but determine a range of possible propositional interpretations. These semi-propositional representations 'give us the means to process information . . . which exceeds our conceptual capacities'.[31] Often the point of holding such beliefs is the very search for a proper interpretation. Judgements of rationality appropriate to propositional beliefs are not obviously appropriate to semi-propositional beliefs. What makes it rational to hold a representational belief of a semipropositional sort is evidence on its source. If the apparently irrational beliefs have a *propositional* content, however, then the appearance of irrationality can usually be dispelled by an intellectualist approach, treating it as an explicable failed attempt at explanation. But, says Sperber, holding a representational belief of a semi-propositional content is rational enough if all members of your cultural group hold it too.

Our other two anthropologists, Gellner and Horton, take the 'intellectualist' line that the apparently irrational beliefs of traditional or primitive thought are, whatever else they may be, in the first instance interpretable as attempted theoretical explanations of the world, and subject as such to trans-cultural standards of rational appraisal. Thus Gellner, in arguing that the conceptual unification of the world through science is a culturally specific modern phenomenon, though accessible to all, clearly implies that it is not 'just our vision' but 'the account of how things actually are', the 'correct vision or cognitive

[31] Ibid., p. 170.

style': our world is 'not *a* world; it is *the* world'. He is in no doubt that 'the atomization of information and the orderly systemization of explanation', typified by what Hacking and Taylor call 'the Galilean style', is a precondition 'of having real knowledge'. This position is implicit in the epistemology accompanying the rise of modern science and is only strengthened by its generation of 'a kind of technology which helps its adherents to prevail' and by the fact that it 'provides the single context within which we investigate and interpret all other visions', which were once its rivals. Such visions are typically package deals, self-maintaining circles of ideas, unsymmetrical and idiosyncratic, uncodified, framed in the absence of literacy and thus not necessarily consistent. It is the 'establishment and institutional underpinning of the *one* outstanding cumulative cognitive style, atomistic and symmetrical, which produces the really decisive parting of the ways'.[32] Where Hacking sees an irreducible diversity of such styles, between which no rational choice is possible, Gellner, like Taylor and Horton, sees a rational ordering of styles, marked by spectacularly differential cognitive success.

Horton's paper revisits the territory first charted by his famous paper 'African traditional thought and modern western science' published in Wilson's volume of 1970, in the light of the extensive critical responses it has generated. From reflection on these criticisms, he retains a commitment to the pertinence of comparing African traditionalism and Western modernism and to stressing their continuities as forms of the cognitive enterprise, while revising his account of their contrasts, now stressing especially those between faith in tradition and faith in progress, and between the absence and presence of inter-theoretic competition. His arguments for these rely on their being a level of thought and discourse, shared by all cultures, of 'primary theory', confined to everyday observation and push-pull causation, providing 'the cross-cultural voyager with his intellectual bridgehead'.[33] It enables him to identify the striking differences of secondary theory (also stressed by Gellner) – chiefly that between anthropomorphic African spiritualism and impersonal Western mechanism – greatly extending its causal vision, by postulating through analogies a hidden realm of hidden entities and processes, but remaining intellectually dependent upon it. On the one hand, Horton

---

[32] Ibid., pp. 187, 188, 189, 191, 194.
[33] Ibid., p. 228.

describes the syndrome of 'cognitive traditionalism': here a prevailing conservatism allows for some adaptive change, theorizing is predominantly consensual, the impact of new experience is greatly filtered, there is little systematic intellectual criticism, and theory relates to practical experience. By contrast, the syndrome of 'cognitive modernism' incorporates a progressive conception of knowledge and a competitive mode of theorizing which, in the natural sciences, yield cumulative success at explanation, prediction and control but (broadly speaking) in the social sciences merely ideological polemics and little cognitive advance. (Horton's diagnosis for this is inadequate commitment to the goals of science on the part of social scientists.) He also offers intriguing explanations of the transition from the one syndrome to the other, in terms of modes of transmission of ideas (especially the role of literacy), the pace of social change, social heterogeneity, etc.

Horton's whole argument rests on the denial of relativism and on the notion of 'a strong core of human cognitive rationality' common to the cultures of all places and times, using theory to explain, control and predict events, forging out of a shared world of common 'primary theory' dramatically different secondary theories in different economic, technological and social settings. Unlike Hollis, Horton argues (with Newton-Smith) that this is an empirically refutable assumption of the translation enterprise. Again unlike Hollis, but with the support of Barnes and Bloor, Elster and Lukes, he offers a symmetrical sociology of belief, traditional and modern. But, as against Taylor and Lukes, he holds that the relative failure of our knowledge of the social as against the physical world to manifest cumulative progress is due merely to social scientists' failure of commitment to shared goals of 'explanation, prediction and control'.

Finally, Lukes draws some conclusions from the debate, as conducted here and elsewhere, with respect to five distinct but related issues. First, as regards the assumptions required for trans-cultural and trans-theoretical understanding, he agrees with Hollis on the need to assume true beliefs in common in order to identify what is not common, but argues against Davidson's Principle of Charity (that most beliefs are correct) and for the so-called Principle of Humanity, which which advocates the minimizing of unintelligibility. This relies on a model of the agent based on the way we understand ourselves, and it helps explain why the bridgehead should be populated by the everyday observational and practical beliefs of Horton's 'primary theory'. Neither anthropologists nor historians of science have shown such beliefs to be relative, let alone incommensurable. Second, he argues for seeing the bridgehead as *both a priori* presupposition *and* empirically refutable hypothesis. *That* there must be such a bridgehead is *a priori;* but what forms it – how to gain access to an alien belief-system – is not. The entire translation enterprise *may* fail (though none do) and is, in any case, always revisable in the light of evidence. Third, he considers alternative strategies of interpreting the pragmatics of belief – 'intellectualist', 'symbolist' and 'fideist'. After commenting on the problems distinctive of each, he seeks to illustrate how a choice may be made between them, by working through a detailed anthropological example, and concludes that, though different strategies raise different explanatory problems and appeal to different evidence, argument and evidence can in principle decide between them. Fourthly, he pinpoints in what ways the explanation of beliefs may be seen as asymmetrical between truth and falsity and between rationality and irrationality. The answer here depends on just *what* it is sought to explain: simple observational beliefs and simple inferences, theoretical beliefs held on authority, or complex mixed cases; and particular beliefs, changes in belief or the outcome of such changes. And finally, he considers what survives of the case for relativism, in face of the two decisive arguments against it developed, in different forms, in this volume: the 'bridgehead' argument for necessary assumptions of interpretation, and the argument from the cognitive superiority of modern science, which has relied upon the 'absolute conception of knowledge' associated with Descartes and Galileo. Following Taylor and in criticism of Horton, he concludes by asking whether this view of knowledge is appropriate to social enquiry and answers that much of such enquiry is inherently perspectival: actors' and observers' perspectives are, for various reasons, intrinsic to its explanatory enterprise, which is, however, subject to constraints that significantly limit such relativism as they imply.

These, then, are the main and subsidiary lines of division among our various contributors. We now gladly turn the discussion over to them.

Relativism, Rationalism and the Sociology of Knowledge

Barry Barnes and David Bloor

In the academic world relativism is everywhere abominated. Critics feel free to describe it by words such as 'pernicious'[1] or portray it as a 'threatening tide'.[2] On the political Right relativism is held to destroy the defences against Marxism and Totalitarianism. If knowledge is said to be relative to persons and places, culture or history, then is it not but a small step to concepts like 'Jewish physics'?[3] On the Left, relativism is held to sap commitment, and the strength needed to overthrow the defences of the established order. How can the distorted vision of bourgeois science be denounced without a standpoint which is itself special and secure?[4]

The majority of critics of relativism subscribe to some version of *rationalism* and portray relativism as a threat to rational, scientific standards. It is, however, a convention of academic discourse that might is not right. Numbers may favour the opposite position, but we shall show that the balance of argument favours a relativist theory of knowledge. Far from being a threat to the scientific understanding of forms of knowledge, relativism is required by it. Our claim is that

---

[1] E. Vivas, 'Reiteration and second thoughts on cultural relativism' in H. Schoek and J. Wiggins (eds), *Relativism and the Study of Man* (Van Nostrand, Princeton, N.J., 1961).
[2] A. Musgrave, 'The objectivism of Popper's epistemology' in P.A. Schilpp (ed.), *The Philosophy of Karl Popper* (Open Court, La Salle, Ill., 1974), ch. 15, p. 588.
[3] K.R. Popper, *The Open Society and its Enemies* (Routledge & Kegan Paul, London), vol. 2, 1966, p. 393; H.R. Post, *Against Ideologies* (Inaugural lecture, Chelsea College, University of London, 28 Nov 1974), p. 2, for Jewish physics. Vivas also invokes the image of Belsen.
[4] S. Rose and H. Rose (eds), *The Radicalisation of Science* (Macmillan, London, 1977).

relativism is essential to all those disciplines such as anthropology, sociology, the history of institutions and ideas, and even cognitive psychology, which account for the diversity of systems of knowledge, their distribution and the manner of their change. It is those who oppose relativism, and who grant certain forms of knowledge a privileged status, who pose the real threat to a scientific understanding of knowledge and cognition.[5]

I

There are many forms of relativism and it is essential to make clear the precise form in which we advocate it. The simple starting-point of relativist doctrines is (i) the observation that beliefs on a certain topic vary, and (ii) the conviction that which of these beliefs is found in a given context depends on, or is relative to, the circumstances of the users. But there is always a third feature of relativism. It requires what may be called a 'symmetry' or an 'equivalence' postulate. For instance, it may be claimed that general conceptions of the natural order, whether the Aristotelean world view, the cosmology of a primitive people, or the cosmology of an Einstein, are all alike in being false, or are all equally true. These alternative equivalence postulates lead to two varieties of relativism; and in general it is the nature of the equivalence postulate which defines a specific form of relativism.

The form of relativism that we shall defend employs neither of the equivalence postulates just mentioned, both of which run into technical difficulties. To say that all beliefs are equally true encounters the problem of how to handle beliefs which contradict one another. If one belief denies what the other asserts, how can they both be true? Similarly, to say that all beliefs are equally false poses the problem of the status of the relativist's own claims. He would seem to be pulling

---

[5] We refer to any collectively accepted system of belief as 'knowledge'. Philosophers usually adopt a different terminological convention confining 'knowledge' to justified true belief. The reason for our preference should become clear in the course of the paper. For a full account of the ideas that form the background of this paper and a description of their implications for the sociology of knowledge, see B. Barnes, *Scientific Knowledge and Sociological Theory* (Routledge & Kegan Paul, London, 1974); B. Barnes, *Interests and the Growth of Knowledge* (Routledge & Kegan Paul, London, 1977); D. Bloor, *Knowledge and Social Imagery* (Routledge & Kegan Paul, London, 1976).

the rug from beneath his own feet.[6]

Our equivalence postulate is that all beliefs are on a par with one another with respect to the causes of their credibility. It is not that all beliefs are equally true or equally false, but that regardless of truth and falsity the fact of their credibility is to be seen as equally problematic. The position we shall defend is that the incidence of all beliefs without exception calls for empirical investigation and must be accounted for by finding the specific, local causes of this credibility. This means that regardless of whether the sociologist evaluates a belief as true or rational, or as false and irrational, he must search for the causes of its credibility. In all cases he will ask, for instance, if a belief is part of the routine cognitive and technical competences handed down from generation to generation. Is it enjoined by the authorities of the society? Is it transmitted by established institutions of socialization or supported by accepted agencies of social control? Is it bound up with patterns of vested interest? Does it have a role in furthering shared goals, whether political or technical, or both? What are the practical and immediate consequences of particular judgements that are made with respect to the belief? All of these questions can, and should, be answered without regard to the status of the belief as it is judged and evaluated by the sociologist's own standards.

A large number of examples could be provided from recent work by historians, sociologists and anthropologists which conform to the requirements of our equivalence postulate. For example, many excellent historical studies of scientific knowledge and evaluation now proceed without concern for the epistemological status of the cases being addressed. They simply investigate the contingent determinants of belief and reasoning without regard to whether the beliefs are true or the inferences rational. They exhibit the same degree and kind of curiosity in both cases.[7] Anthropologists too are increasingly

[6] These are the kinds of relativism that Popper identifies as his target on p. 387 and p. 388 of his *Open Society*, vol. 2. The claim that relativism is 'self-refuting' is thoroughly discussed and thoroughly demolished in Mary Hesse, 'The strong thesis of sociology of science', ch. 2 of her *Revolutions and Reconstructions in the Philosophy of Science* (Harvester Press, Brighton, 1980).

[7] As a selection of such work, see:
A. Brannigan, 'The reification of Mendel', *Social Studies of Science*, 9 (1979), pp. 423–54; T.M. Brown, 'From mechanism to vitalism in eighteenth-century English physiology', *Journal of the History of Biology*, 7 (1974), pp. 179–216. K.L. Caneva, 'From galvanism to electrodynamics: the transformation of German physics and its social context', *Historical Studies in the*

24 *Barry Barnes and David Bloor*

accounting for systems of commonsense knowledge and pre-literate cosmologies in the same way.[8]

On the level of empirical investigation – and concentrating on the practice of investigators rather than the theoretical commentary they may provide – there is more evidence to be cited for relativism than

Physical Sciences, 9 (1978), pp. 63–159; R.S. Cowan, 'Francis Galton's statistical ideas: the influence of eugenics', *Isis*, 63 (1972), pp. 509–28; A.J. Desmond, 'Designing the dinosaur: Richard Owen's response to Robert Edmond Grant', *Isis*, 70 (1979), pp. 224–34; J. Farley, *The Spontaneous Generation Controversy from Descartes to Oparin* (Baltimore, 1977); J. Farley and G.L. Geison, 'Science, politics and spontaneous generation in nineteenth-century France: the Pasteur-Pouchet debate', *Bulletin of the History of Medicine*, 48 (1974), pp. 161–98; P. Forman, 'Weimar culture, causality, and quantum theory, 1918–1927: adaptation by German physicists and mathematicians to a hostile intellectual environment', *Historical Studies in the Physical Sciences*, 3 (1971), pp. 1–115; E. Frankel, 'Corpuscular optics and the wave theory of light: the science and politics of a revolution in physics', *Social Studies of Science*, 6 (1976), pp. 141–84; M.C. Jacob, *The Newtonians and the English Revolution, 1689–1720* (Ithaca, 1976); J.R. Jacob, 'Boyle's atomism and the Restoration assault on pagan naturalism', *Social Studies of Science*, 8 (1978), pp. 211–33; J.R. Jacob, *Robert Boyle and the English Revolution. A Study in Social and Intellectual Change* (New York, 1977); J.R. Jacob, 'The ideological origins of Robert Boyle's natural philosophy', *Journal of European Studies* 2 (1972), pp. 1–21; D. MacKenzie, 'Statistical theory and social interests: a case study', *Social Studies of Science*, 8 (1978), pp. 35–83; D. MacKenzie, 'Eugenics in Britain', *Social Studies of Science*, 6 (1976), pp. 499–532; D. MacKenzie, *Statistics in Britain 1865–1930: The Social Construction of Scientific Knowledge* (Edinburgh University Press, 1981); D. MacKenzie, S.B. Barnes, 'Biometriker versus Mendelianer: Eine Kontroverse und ihre Erklärung', *Kölner Zeitschrift für Soziologie*, special edition 18 (1975), pp. 165–96; D. Ospovat, 'Perfect adaptation and teleological explanation: approaches to the problem of the history of life in the mid-nineteenth century', *Studies in History of Biology*, 2 (1978), pp. 33–56; W. Provine, 'Geneticists and the biology of race crossing', *Science*, 182 (1973), pp. 790–6; M.J.S. Rudwick, 'The Devonian: a system born in conflict' in M.R. House *et al.* (eds), *The Devonian System* (London, 1979); S. Shapin, 'The politics of observation: cerebral anatomy and social interests in the Edinburgh phrenology disputes' in R. Wallis (ed.), *On the Margins of Science: The Social Construction of Rejected Knowledge* (Sociological Review Monographs 27, Keele, 1979), pp. 139–78; R.S. Turner, 'The growth of professorial research in Prussia, 1818–1848: causes and contexts', *Historical Studies in the Physical Sciences*, 3 (1971), pp. 137–82; R.S. Turner, 'University reformers and professorial scholarship in Germany, 1760–1806' in L. Stone (ed.), *The University in Society* (Oxford, 1975), vol. II, pp. 495–531; Mary Winsor, *Starfish, Jellyfish and the Order of Life: Issues in Nineteenth-Century Science*

against it. It is mainly on the programmatic level that the determined opposition to relativism is to be found. Since instances of the empirical material have been marshalled and discussed elsewhere[9] the issues that will be addressed here will be of a more methodological and philosophical character.

II

If the relativist places all beliefs on a par with one another for the purposes of explanation, then we can say that he is advocating a form of *monism*. He is stressing the essential identity of things that others would hold separate. Conversely, rationalists who reject relativism typically do so by insisting on a form of *dualism*. They hold on to the distinctions between true and false, rational and irrational belief and insist that these cases are vitally different from one another. They try to give the distinction a role in the conduct of the sociology of knowledge or anthropology or history, by saying that the explanations to be offered in the two cases are to be of a different kind. In particular, many of the critics of relativism implicitly reject our equivalence postulate by saying that rational beliefs must be explained wholly or

(New Haven, 1976); B. Wynne, 'C.G. Barkla and the J Phenomenon: a case study in the treatment of deviance in physics', *Social Studies of Science*, 6 (1976) pp. 304–47; B. Wynne, 'Physics and psychics; science, symbolic action and social control in late Victorian England' in B. Barnes and S. Shapin (eds), *Natural Order: Historical Studies of Scientific Culture* (Sage, London, 1979) ch. 7. A valuable review and discussion of this and other material is S. Shapin, 'History of science and its sociological reconstruction', *History of Science*, 20, Sep 1982 (forthcoming).

[8] M. Douglas, *Implicit Meanings* (Routledge, London, 1975); see also her 'Cultural Bias', Occasional Paper 34, Royal Anthropological Institute (London, 1978); cf. also M. Cole, J. Gay, J. Glick, D. Sharp, *The Cultural Context of Learning and Thinking* (Basic Books, New York, 1969) and R. Horton, and R. Finnegan (eds), *Modes of Thought* (Faber, London, 1973).

[9] See B. Barnes, and S. Shapin, (eds), *Natural Order: Historical Studies of Scientific Culture* (Sage, London, 1979); D. Bloor, 'The sociology of [scientific] knowledge' in W. Bynum, E.J. Browne and R. Porter (eds), *Dictionary of the History of Science* (Macmillan, London, 1981); S. Shapin, 'Social uses of science' in G.S. Rousseau and R.S. Porter (eds), *The Ferment of Knowledge: Studies in the Historiography of Eighteenth-century Science* (Cambridge University Press, Cambridge, 1981) pp. 93–139.

partly by the fact that they *are* rational, whilst irrational beliefs call for
no more than a causal, socio-psychological or 'external' explanation.
For example, Hollis has recently insisted that 'true and rational beliefs
need one sort of explanation, false and irrational beliefs another'.[10]
Imre Lakatos was one of the most strident advocates of a structurally
similar view. He equated rational procedures in science with those that
accord with some preferred philosophy of science. Exhibiting the
cases which appear to conform to the preferred philosophy is called
'internal history' or 'rational reconstruction'. He then asserts that 'the
rational aspect of scientific growth is fully accounted for by one's logic
of scientific discovery'. All the rest, which is not fully accounted for, is
handed over to the sociologist for non-rational, causal explanation.[11] A
version of this theory is endorsed by Laudan.[12] Even the sociologist
Karl Mannheim adopted this dualist and rationalist view when he
contrasted the 'existential determination of thought' by 'extra-
theoretical factors' with development according to 'immanent laws'
derived from the 'nature of things' of 'pure logical possibilities'. This
is why he exempted the physical sciences and mathematics from his
sociology of knowledge.[13]

As the first step in the examination of the rationalist case let us
consider a charge that is sometimes made against the relativist. It is
said, for example by Lukes, that the relativist has undermined his own
right to use words like 'true' or 'false'.[14] Answering this charge is not a
difficult task, and it will help to bring the character of relativism, and
the shortcomings of rationalism, into sharp focus.

Consider the members of two tribes, T1 and T2, whose cultures are
both primitive but otherwise very different from one another. Within

[10] M. Hollis, 'The social destruction of reality', this volume p. 75.

[11] I. Lakatos, 'History of science and its rational reconstructions' in R. Buck
and R. Cohen (eds), *Boston Studies in the Philosophy of Science*, vol. 8 (Reidel,
Dordrecht, 1971) p. 106.

[12] L. Laudan, *Progress and its Problems: Towards a Theory of Scientific Growth*
(Routledge & Kegan Paul, London, 1977). For a critical review, see B.
Barnes, 'Vicissitudes of belief', *Social Studies of Science*, 9 (1979), pp. 247–63.

[13] K. Mannheim, *Ideology and Utopia* (Routledge & Kegan Paul, London,
1936), p. 239. For a reply to Mannheim, see D. Bloor, 'Wittgenstein and
Mannheim on the sociology of mathematics', *Studies in History and Philosophy
of Science*, 4 (1973), pp. 173–91.

[14] See, for instance, Lukes' critical reply to D. Bloor, 'Durkheim and Mauss
revisited: classification and the sociology of knowledge' in *Studies in History
and Philosophy of Science* (forthcoming).

each tribe some beliefs will be preferred to others and some reasons accepted as more cogent than others. Each tribe will have a vocabulary for expressing these preferences. Faced with a choice between the beliefs of his own tribe and those of the other, each individual would typically prefer those of his own culture. He would have available to him a number of locally acceptable standards to use in order to assess beliefs and justify his preferences.

What a relativist says about himself is just what he would say about the tribesman. The relativist, like everyone else, is under the necessity to sort out beliefs, accepting some and rejecting others. He will naturally have preferences and these will typically coincide with those of others in his locality. The words 'true' and 'false' provide the idiom in which those evaluations are expressed, and the words 'rational' and 'irrational' will have a similar function. When confronted with an alien culture he, too, will probably prefer his own familiar and accepted beliefs and his local culture will furnish norms and standards which can be used to justify such preferences if it becomes necessary to do so.

The crucial point is that a relativist accepts that his preferences and evaluations are as context-bound as those of the tribes T1 and T2. Similarly he accepts that none of the justifications of his preferences can be formulated in absolute or context-independent terms. In the last analysis, he acknowledges that his justifications will stop at some principle or alleged matter of fact that only has local credibility. The only alternative is that justifications will begin to run in a circle and assume what they were meant to justify.[15]

For the relativist there is no sense attached to the idea that some standards or beliefs are really rational as distinct from merely locally accepted as such. Because he thinks that there are no context-free or super-cultural norms of rationality he does not see rationally and

[15] It may be objected that the present argument would only apply in a world where people were divided into relatively isolated social groups and would fail in proportion to the degree that cosmopolitan uniformity prevailed – or when what Durkheim called an 'international life' emerged. This is one of the objections E. Gellner presses against Winch in 'The new idealism – cause and meaning in the social sciences' in I. Lakatos and A. Musgrave (eds), *Problems in the Philosophy of Science* (North Holland, Amsterdam, 1968), pp. 377–406, esp. p. 397. In fact in our argument the picture of the isolated tribes T1 and T2 is merely expository and not a necessary feature of the argument. The size of the context and the actual presence of alternatives is entirely contingent. The same point would apply even if there happened to be just one, homogeneous, international community.

irrationally held beliefs as making up two distinct and qualitatively different classes of thing. They do not fall into two different natural kinds which make different sorts of appeal to the human mind, or stand in a different relationship to reality, or depend for their credibility on different patterns of social organization. Hence the relativist conclusion that they are to be explained in the same way.

III

A typical move at this point in the argument is to try to contain and limit the significance of the sociology of knowledge by declaring that because it is merely the study of *credibility* it can have no implications for *validity*. Validity, say the critics, is a question to be settled directly by appeal to evidence and reason and is quite separate from the contingencies of actual belief. As Professor Flew has put it, 'an account of the sufficiently good reasons' for a belief must be distinguished from 'an account of the psychological, physiological or sociological causes of inclinations to utter words expressing this belief when appropriately stimulated'.[16] The question of the reasons for a belief and the question of its causes are quite separate sorts of issue. But having separated these two issues this critic then proceeds to shunt the sociologist and psychologist into the sidings where they can be forgotten. The rationalist is now free to operate in the realm of reason and make out its function and workings to be whatever he wishes. This is why we are told so emphatically that the sociologist of knowledge 'must be concerned with causes of belief *rather than* with whatever evidencing reasons there may be for cherishing them'.[17]

Unfortunately for the rationalist the freedom which this convenient division of labour would give him cannot be granted: the distinctions upon which it is based will not stand examination. The reason is that it would be difficult to find a commodity more contingent and more socially variable than Flew's 'evidencing reasons'. What counts as an 'evidencing reason' for a belief in one context will be seen as evidence for quite a different conclusion in another context. For example, was

[16] A.G.N. Flew, 'Is the scientific enterprise self-refuting?', *Proceedings of the Eighth International Conference on the Unity of the Sciences, Los Angeles, 1979* (New York, 1980) vol. 1, pp.34–60.
[17] Ibid.

the fact that living matter appeared in Pouchet's laboratory preparations evidence for the spontaneous generation of life, or evidence of the incompetence of the experimenter, as Pasteur maintained? As historians of science have shown, different scientists drew different conclusions and took the evidence to point in different directions. This was possible because something is only evidence for something else when set in the context of assumptions which give it meaning – assumptions, for instance, about what is *a priori* probable or improbable. If, on religious and political grounds, there is a desire to maintain a sharp and symbolically useful distinction between matter and life, then Pouchet must have blundered rather than have made a fascinating discovery. These were indeed the factors that conditioned the reception of his work in the conservative France of the Second Empire.[18] 'Evidencing reasons', then, are a prime target for sociological enquiry and explanation. There is no question of the sociology of knowledge being confined to causes *rather than* 'evidencing reasons'. Its concern is precisely with causes *as* 'evidencing reasons'.

IV

Obviously, it would be possible for the rationalist to counterattack. He could say that the above argument only applies to what are *taken* to be reasons, rather than to what *really are* reasons. Once again, the charge would be that the sociologists had conflated validity and credibility. But if a rationalist really were to insist on a total distinction between credibility and validity he would simply leave the field of discourse altogether. Validity totally detached from credibility is nothing. The sociologist of knowledge with his relativism and his monism would win by default: his theory would meet no opposition. It is because of the rationalist's desire to avoid this consequence that sooner or later, overtly or covertly, he will fuse validity and credibility. He too will treat validity and credibility as one thing by finding a certain class of reasons that are alleged to carry their own credibility with them: they will be visible because they glow by their own light.

To see how this comes about consider again the two tribes T1 and T2. For a member of T1 examining what is to him a peculiar belief

---

[18] Farley and Geison, 'Science, politics and spontaneous generation'.

from the culture of T2, there is a clear point to the distinction between the validity and the credibility of a belief. He will say that just because the misguided members of T2 believe something, that doesn't make it true. Its rightness and wrongness, he may add, must be established independently of belief. But, of course, what he will mean by 'independently of belief' is independently of the belief of others, such as the members of T2. For his own part, he has no option but to use the accepted methods and assumptions of his own group. In practice this is what 'directly' ascertaining truth or falsity comes down to.

The simple structure of the example makes it easy to see what is happening. The distinction between validity and credibility is sound enough in this case, but its real point, its scope and its focus, is entirely local. As the relativist would expect, it is not an absolute distinction, but one whose employment depends upon a taken-for-granted background. It is a move within a game, and it is with regard to the background knowledge, assumed by the move, that validity and credibility are tacitly brought together. Without this, the distinction itself could never be put to use, or its contrast be given an application.

If our imaginary tribesman was dialectically sophisticated he might realize that he is open to the charge of special pleading, and that he had, in his own case, collapsed the distinction upon which he had been insisting. How could he reply to the accusation that he had equated the validity and credibility of his own beliefs? As a more careful statement of his position he might claim that not even the fact that his own tribe believes something is, *in itself*, sufficient to make it true. But he would then have to mend the damage of this admission by adding that it just was a fact that what his tribe believed *was* true. A kindly providence, perhaps, had here united these two essentially different things.

For the sociologist of knowledge these refinements change nothing. They do not remove the special pleading, they simply elaborate upon it. But they remind us that we need to locate the point at which the rationalists of our culture make the same move. We must examine the rationalist case to find the point at which reasons are said to become visible by their own light and Reason in Action transcends the operation of causal processes and social conditions.

V

A familiar candidate to invoke for the role of Reason in Action is the class of beliefs which are supposed to be directly and immediately apprehended by experience. It may be said that some knowledge claims can be sustained, and can attract credibility purely in virtue of their correspondence with reality – a correspondence which any reasonable agent can recognize. Some things we just *know* by experience and no contingent factors, such as their support by authority or their coherence with the overall pattern of culture, are necessary for their maintenance.

Such a theory is easily recognized as a species of naïve empiricism and its weaknesses are well known. Nevertheless similar assumptions can emerge in a disguised form. For example Flew has argued that 'when it is a question of accounting for beliefs about matters of everyday use and observation, then there is nothing like so much room for sophisticated social and historical causes'.[19] The polemical force of this appeal to everyday use and observation may be gathered from the following claim which we shall assess in some detail:

> The cause of our belief that the ferry canoe is where it is on the Zaire River does not lie in the social structure of our tribe. It is to be found, instead, in certain intrusive non-social facts: that when we turn our eyes towards the right bit of the river the canoe causes appropriate sensory impressions; and that those heedlessly placing themselves in the water rather than the canoe are incontinently eaten by crocodiles.[20]

It would be possible to take exception to this passage by stressing how much more is involved in the identification of an object as 'the Zaire river ferry canoe' than turning our eyes in the right direction. All the socially sustained classifications that are involved in the process have been simply left out of account. But though such criticisms would be correct and well deserved, they would not fully meet the point being made. What is really at issue here is the status of certain skills such as our ability to navigate ourselves around our environment; avoiding falling in rivers; and remembering the location of medium-scale physical objects. The question is: how do these skills relate to a relativist sociology of knowledge? Do they provide any basis for criticism, and hence comfort for the rationalist?

The first point to notice is that the facts to be attended to are skills that individuals share with non-linguistic animals. They are a real and important part of our mentality and, as Flew has pointed out, they are not greatly illuminated by sociologists or historians. Indeed, they are

[19] Flew, 'Is the scientific enterprise self-refuting?'
[20] Ibid.

taken for granted by these disciplines. This is because they belong to the province of the biologist and the learning theorist. It is no surprise that different aspects of knowledge are divided out amongst different scientific disciplines. But it is surely no skin off the sociologist's nose that he cannot explain how a dog retrieves its buried bone.

The important point is that none of the work in cognitive psychology which might explain this order of fact is going to be sufficient to account for the problems addressed by the sociologist. These concern variations in institutionalized patterns of knowledge. The difference between knowledge as it concerns the sociologist and the kind of knowing used in the objection may be represented by an analogy: it is the difference between a *map* and an individual organism's working knowledge of a terrain. There is a qualitative difference between these two things: one is a collective, the other an individual, representation. A map is an impersonal document, not a state of mind; it is a cultural product which requires conventions of representation. (And, of course, there are an indefinitely large number of different conventions which may be agreed upon.) Information about the psychological capacities which permit individual navigation won't add up to competent answers to questions, say, about the creation, maintenance, and change of cartographic norms.

That features of animal navigation should be seen as *criticism* of the sociology of knowledge simply reveals an individualistic bias in the way that the word 'knowledge' is being construed. As an objection it trades on a muddle between social and individual accomplishments. Furthermore, the kinds of individual cognitive skills that are in question are increasingly coming under the scope of the *causal* theories produced by physiologists and psychologists. They are showing themselves to be amenable to precisely the type of explanation that, as a good rationalist, Flew was at pains to *contrast* with the operation of reason. This hardly makes them fit candidates for the role of Reason in Action which was the use to which our rationalist critic was putting them. Some of the facts about everyday use and observation may indeed provide little room for sophisticated sociological or historical explanation, but that is because they provide room for sophisticated psychological explanations. While these can happily *co-exist* with the sociology of knowledge, they directly *contradict* the claims of the rationalist critics of that discipline.[21]

[21] Of course it would be possible for the same argument, with the same monist and dualist alternatives, to be repeated on the level of psychological expla-

There is no need for a relativist sociology of knowledge to take anything other than a completely open and matter-of-fact stance towards the role of sensory stimulation. The same applies to any other of the physical, genetic or psychological and non-social causes that must eventually find a place in an overall account of knowledge. The stimulation caused by material objects when the eye is turned in a given direction is indeed a causal factor in knowledge and its role is to be understood by seeing how this cause interacts with other causes. There is no question of denying the effect on belief of the facts – that is, of the segment of *unverbalized reality* that is the focus of the beliefs in question. All that need be insisted upon is that when due allowance is made for the effect of 'the facts' it is made in accordance with the equivalence postulate. This means that the effect of 'the facts' on a believer plays the same general role whether the belief that results is a true one or a false one.

To show what is meant by this let us look at a simple, real-life case where, it may be considered, reality impinges in the same causal way on those who held true and false beliefs about it. Consider the eighteenth-century chemists Priestley and Lavoisier who gave diverging accounts of what happens during combustion and calcination. For simplicity we may say that Priestley's phlogiston theory was false and Lavoisier's oxygen theory was true. Both Priestley and Lavoisier were looking at samples of (what we would call) lead oxide and mercuric oxide. They both arranged pieces of apparatus so that they could heat

---

nation. It has been known for philosophers to insist that, in psychology, causal accounts are only appropriate for pathological phenomena, e.g. saying that, while error and illusion might be causally explicable, normal or correct perception is not a fit subject for empirical investigation and causal explanation. See D. Hamlyn, *The Psychology of Perception* (Routledge & Kegan Paul, London, 1969), ch. 2, pp. 11–13; and G. Ryle *The Concept of Mind* (Hutchinson, London, 1949), p. 326.

In contrast, for fruitful and fascinating attempts to give good causal explanations of both successful and erroneous perception, see R.L. Gregory, *Eye and Brain* (Weidenfeld & Nicolson, London, 1966). Perhaps one day the dualist account of Ryle and Hamlyn will be developed into its ultimate form, and we will be told that the operations of adding machines are causally determined only when erroneous results are produced, and that at other times such machines operate rationally in ways which require no explanation.

these substances. They then observed what happened, and recorded the behaviour of various volumes of gas given off and absorbed.

Nevertheless Priestley and Lavoisier believed totally different things: they gave sharply conflicting accounts of the nature of the substances they observed and their properties and behaviour. Indeed they asserted that quite different substances were present in the events they witnessed. Lavoisier denied that there was such a substance as phlogiston and postulated the existence of something called 'oxygen'. Priestley took exactly the opposite view. He insisted on the existence of phlogiston, identifying it with certain samples of gas agreed by both to be present in the experiment. Furthermore Priestley denied Lavoisier's 'oxygen' and characterized the gas so labelled – which he had himself discovered – by means of his own theory.[22] Clearly the effect of 'the facts' is neither simple nor sufficient to explain what needs explaining, viz. the theoretical divergence. It is because the effect of 'the facts' is so different that the sociology of knowledge has a task.

There were, indeed, some occasions when for a while the experimenters observed different things from one another, e.g. when one came across a phenomenon that the other had not yet heard about. Furthermore, it is clear that when either of them observed something new in their apparatus it evoked a response. Thus Priestley spotted the appearance of water when, as we would say, he heated lead oxide in hydrogen. (For Priestley this was 'minium' in 'phlogiston'.) But what the new observation did was to prompt the elaboration of his existing approach. Similarly, the *differential* exposure to facts merely resulted, for a while, in a slightly different degree of elaboration of their respective systems of thought.

The general conclusion is that reality is, after all, a common factor in all the vastly different cognitive responses that men produce to it. Being a common factor it is not a promising candidate to field as an explanation of that variation. Certainly any differences in the sampling of experience, and any differential exposure to reality must be allowed

[22] J.B. Conant, 'The overthrow of phlogiston theory', in J.B. Conant and K.K. Nash (eds), *Harvard Case Histories in Experimental Science*, vol. I (Harvard University Press, Cambridge, Mass., 1966). Lavoisier's 'oxygen' gas was conceived by him to be the principle of acidity plus caloric – the heat fluid. Caloric has now gone the same way as phlogiston and has been rejected as a theoretical entity, and it was later discovered that Lavoisier's 'principle of acidity' was not present in hydrochloric acid.

for. But that is in perfect accord with our equivalence postulate which enjoins the sociologist to investigate whatever local causes of credibility operate in each case. There is nothing in any of this to give comfort to the rationalist, or trouble to the relativist.

VII

Another important line of attack directed against relativism appears in a well-known sequence of papers by Martin Hollis and Steven Lukes.[23] They hold that all cultures share a common core of true beliefs and rationally-justified patterns of inference. This core is made up of statements which rational men 'cannot fail to believe in simple perceptual situations' and 'rules of coherent judgement, which rational men cannot fail to subscribe to'.[24] Elsewhere these cultural universals are described as 'material object perception beliefs' and 'simple inferences, relying, say, on the law of non-contradiction'.[25] According to Hollis and Lukes the truth of the statements in this core, and the validity of the inferences therein, are everywhere acknowledged because there are universal, context-independent criteria of truth and rationality, which all men recognize and are disposed to conform to. Without such universal criteria there would be no common core.

Clearly if there is indeed such a core, and it is sustained by context-independent criteria of truth and rationality, then relativism is confounded. But why must we accept that it exists? Interestingly, Lukes

---

[23] M. Hollis, 'The limits of irrationality', *European Journal of Sociology*, 7 (1967), pp. 265–71; and 'Reason and ritual', *Philosophy*, 43 (1967), pp. 231–47; and also this volume. See also S. Lukes, 'Some problems about rationality', *European Journal of Sociology*, 7 (1967), pp. 247–64; 'On the social determination of truth' in Horton and Finnegan, *Modes of Thought;* 'Relativism, cognitive and moral', *Supplementary Proceedings of the Aristotelian Society*, 68 (1974), pp. 165–89; 'Rationality and the explanation of belief', paper given at the Colloquium on 'Irrationality: Explanation and Understanding', Maison des Sciences de l'Homme, Paris, 7–9 Jan 1980. Note: Hollis', 'The limits of rationality' and 'Reason and ritual' and Lukes' 'Some problems about rationality' have all been reprinted in B.R. Wilson (ed.), *Rationality* (Blackwell, 1970), chs. 9, 10 and 11. Page references will be to the Wilson volume, unless otherwise stated.

[24] Hollis, this volume, p. 74.

[25] Lukes, 'Rationality and the explanation of belief', p. 8.

and Hollis make no serious attempt to describe the common core, or to mark its boundaries. Rather, they seek to show that it *must* exist, or at least that its existence must be assumed *a priori* if the possibility of communication and understanding between distinct cultures is admitted. We are asked to consider the problems facing say, an English-speaking anthropological field-worker, seeking to understand an alien culture. Such an individual must grasp the meaning of the alien concepts and beliefs, and this, we are told, requires him to *translate* them into English. This is where the common core comes in: it serves as the 'rational bridgehead' which makes translation possible. It is the basis upon which simple equivalences between two languages can be initially established so that the enterprise of translation can get off the ground. By assuming that in 'simple perceptual situations' the aliens perceive much as we do, infer much as we do, and say more or less what we would say, we can 'define standard meanings for native terms'. This then 'makes it possible to identify utterances used in more ambiguous situations', lying outside the bridgehead, in which 'supernatural' or 'metaphysical' or 'ritual' beliefs are expressed.[26] The basic point, however, is that without the rational bridgehead we would be caught in a circle. We need to translate 'native' utterances in order to know what beliefs they express, while at the same time we need to know what is believed in order to know what is being said. Without an assumed bridgehead of shared beliefs there 'would be no way into the circle', for there is, says Hollis, 'no more direct attack on meaning available'.[27]

Stated in abstract terms this argument has a certain plausibility. And if it were to prove correct it would certainly bolster the rationalist case and run counter to our equivalence postulate. The beliefs belonging to the rational bridgehead will be those whose enduring presence is explicable simply in virtue of the untrammelled operation of universal reason. Their credibility will be of a different sort from the diversity of beliefs that are peculiar to different cultures. The credibility of this latter class will have to be explained by special local causes, whilst the former 'simply are rational'.[28] The fact is, however, that the bridgehead argument fails as soon as it is measured against the realities of language learning and anthropological practice.

[26] Hollis, 'The limits of irrationality', pp. 215, 216, and 'Reason and ritual', p. 221.
[27] Hollis, 'The limits of irrationality', p. 208.
[28] Lukes, 'Some problems about rationality', p. 208.

Notice how the whole argument hinges on the supposed role of translation: there is 'no more direct attack on meaning available'. But the fact is that translation is *not* the most direct attack on meaning that is available. It was not available, nor did it play any part at all, in the first and major attack that any of us made upon meaning when we acquired language in childhood. First language acquisition is not a translation process, and nothing that is absent here can be a necessary ingredient in subsequent learning. To understand an alien culture the anthropologist can proceed in the way that native speakers do. Any difficulties in achieving this stance will be pragmatic rather than *a priori*. There is, for instance, no necessity for the learner to assume shared concepts. Such an assumption would be false and would have nothing but nuisance value.

To see why this is so consider what is involved when a child learns an elementary concept like 'bird'. Such learning needs the continuing assistance of culturally competent adults. A teacher may gesture towards something in the sky and say 'bird'. Given the well-known indefiniteness of ostension a child would probably glean very little information from this: is it the object or the setting that is intended? But after a few acts of ostension, to different birds in different settings, he would begin to become competent in distinguishing 'birds' from 'non-birds', and might perhaps himself tentatively point out and label putative birds.

Suppose now that the child labels a passing aeroplane a 'bird'. This would be a perfectly reasonably thing to do given the points of resemblance between aeroplanes and birds. Of course, there are noticeable differences too, but there are such differences between every successive instance of what are *properly* called 'birds'. All the instances of empirical concepts differ in detail from one another and we can never apply such concepts on the basis of perfect identity rather than resemblance. What the child is doing, in effect, is judging the resemblances between the aeroplane and the previous instances of 'bird' to be more significant than the differences. The general form of his judgement, with its balancing of similarities and differences, is identical to those which lead to proper or accepted usage. It is only his knowledge of custom which is defective.

What happens in the case of the child is that he is overruled. 'No, that is an aeroplane.' This correction is at once an act of social control and of cultural transmission. It helps him to learn which of the possible judgements of sameness are accepted by his society as relevant to the use of 'bird'. In this way the particulars of experience are ordered into clusters and patterns *specific to a culture*.

The significance of this point becomes even more clear when we see how the things we call 'birds' are dealt with in other cultures. When the anthropologist Bulmer visited the Karam of New Guinea he found that many of the instances of what we would call 'bird' were referred to as 'yakt'. He also found that instances of bats were included amongst the 'yakt', while instances of cassowaries were scrupulously denied admittance to the taxon. Objects were clustered in different ways, and the analogies that it is possible to discern amongst phenomena were channelled along different paths. Nevertheless, it was not too difficult to learn 'yakt': the task simply involved noting what the Karam pointed out as 'yakt' until it was possible to pick them out as well as the Karam did.[29]

What these examples show is that even empirical terms like 'bird' do not constitute a special core of concepts whose application depends only upon an unconditioned reason. Learning even the most elementary of terms is a slow process that involves the acquisition from the culture of specific *conventions*. This makes apparently simple empirical words no different from others that are perhaps more obviously culturally influenced. There are no privileged occasions for the use of terms – no 'simple perceptual situations' – which provide the researcher with 'standard meanings' uncomplicated by cultural variables. In short, there is no bridgehead in Hollis' sense.[30]

Because there are no 'standard meanings' there is no question of using them to provide a secure base from which to advance towards more ambiguous cases whose operation is to be understood in a qualitatively different and derivative way. All concepts and all usages stand on a par: none are intrinsically 'unambiguous' or intrinsically 'ambiguous' any more than some are intrinsically 'literal' or intrinsically 'metaphorical'. Furthermore, there is no telling in advance

[29] R. Bulmer, 'Why is the cassowary not a bird?', *Man*, n.s., 2 (1967), pp. 5–25.

[30] For a fuller development of these points, see M. Hesse, *The Structure of Scientific Inference* (Macmillan, London, 1974), chs 1 and 2. Their sociological significance is explored in B. Barnes, 'On the conventional character of knowledge and cognition', *Philosophy of the Social Sciences*, 11 (1981), pp. 303–33. D. Bloor, 'Durkheim and Mauss revisited: classification and the sociology of knowledge', *Studies in History and Philosophy of Science* (forthcoming) – a German version of this paper appeared in *Kölner Zeitschrift für Soziologie*, special issue, 23 (1980), pp. 20–51.

which are the 'problematic' cases where an alien culture will deviate from ours. For example, Bulmer could not have predicted in advance what the Karam would call bats or cassowaries, simply because of the initial identity of usage he discerned between the Karam 'yakt' and our 'bird'. Similarly, no one could predict on the basis of past usage what the Karam would do with a hitherto unknown case such as, say, a barn-owl. Existing usage is only a precedent defined over a finite number of particular instances. It does not fix the proper handling of new cases in advance. Diverse developments are possible, and even where cultural diversity is not present it could emerge at any moment by a revision of the existing sequence of judgements of sameness and difference.

It might be objected, none the less, that the 'rational bridgehead' was invoked to account for the possibility of translation, and translation is a *possible* mode of understanding alien culture, even if it is not a *necessary* mode. How is translation possible? Might not an anti-relativist argument be based simply upon the possibility of successful translation?

The way to proceed here is to assume nothing about translation in advance, least of all that it is successfully carried out. Instead we should ask what is implied for translation by the little empirical knowledge we possess of the simpler aspects of semantics and language learning. One clear implication arises from the character of concepts as arrays of judgements of sameness. Every such array, being the product of a unique sequence of judgements, is itself unique. No array in one culture can be unproblematically set into an identity with an array from another culture. Hence perfect translation cannot exist: there can only be translation acceptable for practical purposes, as judged by contingent, local standards. And this is a conclusion which fits well with what we know of the extremely complex procedures and activities which constitute translation as an empirical phenomenon.

Thus the rational bridgehead, the alleged common core of belief shared by all cultures, turns out to be a purely imaginary construct with no empirical basis at all. It is not difficult, however, to perceive its origins in the received culture of epistemologists. It is an old philosophical dualism dressed in a new garb. The distinction between the parts of a culture that belong to the rational core, and the parts that are specific and variable is just another version of the idea that observational predicates are qualitatively different from theoretical predicates. The bridgehead argument is a plea for a single pure observation language. Of all the dualisms of epistemology this must be the most discredited.[31] Surely, we now all recognize that although we may well all share the same unverbalized environment, there are any number of equally reasonable ways of speaking of it.

VIII

Hollis' and Lukes' argument includes the claim that there are simple forms of inference which all rational men find compelling. Among the instances offered here is 'p, p implies q, therefore q'. Hollis introduces this under the logicians' name of *modus ponens* and represents it by using the usual symbol for material implication, $(p . (p \rightarrow q)) \rightarrow q$.[32] It is noticeable, however, that Hollis and Lukes do not even begin to make their case. In particular they offer no relevant empirical evidence for their claim. None the less it is interesting to explore what follows if men do indeed evince some general disposition to conform to *modus ponens* and to other simple patterns of inference. It then becomes necessary to ask *why* men are disposed in favour of these forms of inference. What might account for the existence of such alleged universals of reason?

According to the rationalists there are two distinct issues here, and two ways of approaching the question. We can either search for the causes of the phenomenon, or we can seek to furnish reasons for it. Naturally a rationalist will want to provide the sufficiently good reasons that are at work, and hence show that deductive intuitions are explicable in rational terms. The aim will be to show that deductive forms of inference can be shown to be rationally justified in an absolute and context-free sense. Unfortunately for the rationalist there is little that he can offer by way of reasoned argument in favour of adherence to deductive inference forms. We have reached the end-point at which justification goes in a circle.

The predicament is neatly captured in Lewis Carroll's story of what the Tortoise said to Achilles. Presented by Achilles with premises of the form '$p \rightarrow q$' and 'p' the tortoise refuses to draw the conclusion 'q' until the step has been justified. Achilles obliges by formulating the rule according to which the tortoise is to proceed. The rule makes

---

[31] Cf. Hesse, *The Structure of Scientific Inference*.
[32] Hollis, 'Reason and ritual', p. 232.

clear the grounds upon which the step to 'q' may be taken. Given the rule 'when you have "$p{\to}q$" and "p" conclude "q" ' and given both '$p{\to}q$' and 'p', will you *now* conclude 'q'? he asks. Unfortunately the tortoise is able to point out that when the justifying premise has been added the new inference is again dependent on a step of the type that has been called into question: so he asks for yet another premise to be formulated, and so on. The attempt at justification therefore fails, and Achilles finds that he cannot use logic to force the tortoise to draw the desired conclusion.[33]

The basic point is that justifications of deduction themselves presuppose deduction. They are circular because they appeal to the very principles of inference that are in question.[34] In this respect the justification of deduction is in the same predicament as the justifications of induction which tacitly make inductive moves by appealing to the fact that induction 'works'. Our two basic modes of reasoning are in an equally hopeless state with regard to their rational justification.[35]

---

[33] L. Carroll, 'What the Tortoise said to Achilles', *Mind*, n.s., 4 (1895), pp. 278–80. Carroll, of course, does not use bare ps and qs but begins with a simple proposition from Euclid.

[34] It has been argued that there are technical defects in Carroll's paper and that the tortoise shifts his ground with regard to what has to be justified at different stages in the regress. See J. Thomson, 'What Achilles should have said to the Tortoise', *Ratio*, 3 (1960), pp. 95–105. Nevertheless the basic thrust of Carroll's argument is correct. Circularity emerges whenever an attempt is made to ground our most general notions of validity. See W. Quine, 'Truth by convention' in his *Ways of Paradox* (Random House, New York, 1966). See also J. McKinsey, *Journal of Symbolic Logic*, 13 (1948) pp. 114–15; and S. Kleene, ibid., pp. 173–4. These points are fully discussed in Susan Haack, 'The justification of deduction', *Mind*, 85 (1976), pp. 112–19. In particular Haack shows that appeals to the truth table definition of material implication in order to justify *modus ponens* itself uses that principle (p. 114).

[35] Haack, in 'The justification of deduction' exhibits the similarity between the scandal of induction and the scandal of deduction. Needless to say, an *inductive* justification of deductive inference-forms and contradiction-avoiding rules is useless in the battle against relativism. If these rules and forms are favoured and institutionalized only where they prove profitable in discourse, then their incidence becomes intelligible in terms of contingent local determinants just as sociological relativism requires. And, conversely, all the deviations from the rules and forms are likely to become *equally* justified in the same way. This will show them to be just the same kinds of phenomena as the rules and forms themselves. Consider all the familiar locutions we find of pragmatic value in informal speech which appear to do violence to formal logical rules: 'Yes and no', 'It was, and yet it wasn't', 'The

As with induction a variety of attempts have been made to evade the circularity of justification.[36] Perhaps the most fully developed attempt at justification has been to say that the validity of inferences derives simply from the meaning of the formal signs or logical words used in them. For instance, the meaning of '$\rightarrow$' is given by 'truth table' definitions or the rules of inference of the logical system of which it is a part, and the validity of the inferences in this system derives from these meanings. This is the theory of 'analytic validity'. Unfortunately for the rationalist this theory has been completely devastated by the logician A.N. Prior.[37]

Prior develops his argument by taking the case of the very simple logical connective 'and'. Why is 'p and q, therefore q' a valid inference? The theory of analytic validity says that it is valid because of the meaning of 'and'. What is the meaning of 'and'? This is given by stating the role that the term has in forming compound propositions, or conjunctions, and drawing inferences from them. 'And' is defined by the rules that (i) from any pair of statements 'p' and q', we can infer the statement 'p and q', and (ii) from any conjunctive statement 'p and q', we can infer either of the conjuncts. As an antidote to the seductive power of this circular procedure Prior shows that a similar sequence of definitions would permit the introduction of connectives that would justify the inference of any statement from any other. Consider, he says, the new logical connective 'tonk':

> Its meaning is completely given by the rules that (i) from any statement P we can infer any statement formed by joining P to

---

whole was greater than its parts', 'There is some truth in that statement', 'That statement is nearer to the truth than this one', 'A is a better proof than B', and so on. All these locutions, indeed everything in discourse which Lukes identifies as needing elucidation by 'context-specific' rather than 'universal' rules, become identical in character to 'universally-rational' forms of discourse. The dualism essential to the anti-relativist position disappears.

[36] For instance, it may be said that justifications of deduction are 'superfluous' and that it is a mistake to concede that they are necessary. Critics of Lewis Carroll have taken this line, e.g. W. Rees, 'What Achilles said to the Tortoise', *Mind*, n.s., 60 (1951), pp. 241–6. But judgements about what is, or is not, superfluous are highly subjective. In the present type of case we may suspect that they will derive their credibility entirely from their convenience for the purposes in hand, namely evading the problem that justifications are circular.

[37] A.N. Prior, 'The runabout inference ticket', *Analysis*, 21 (1960), pp. 38–9.

any statement Q by 'tonk' (which compound statement we hereafter describe as 'the statement P-tonk-Q'), and that (ii) from any 'contonktive' statement P-tonk-Q we can infer the contained statement Q.[38]

Hence we can infer any Q from any P.

What Prior's paper shows is that appeal to rules and meanings cannot by itself justify our intuitions about validity, because these rules and meanings are themselves judged according to those intuitions, e.g. intuitions to the effect that 'and' is defined by acceptable rules, whereas 'tonk' is not. The theory of analytic validity invites us to run to meanings to justify our intuitions of validity, but then we have to run back again to our intuitions of validity to justify our selection of meanings. Our preference for the 'right' rules which define 'acceptable' connectives reveals the circularity of the intended justification. The intuitions are basic and the problem of justification set by the tortoise is the end-point after all. Like the good relativist that he is, the tortoise awaits a reasoned justification of deduction, confident that none will be forthcoming.[39]

IX

What else is there to do then but to turn to causes for an answer to the question of the widespread acceptance of deductive inference forms and the avoidance of inconsistency? A plausible strategy is to adopt a

---

[38] Ibid., p. 38.

[39] Prior's paper has been discussed by N. Belnap, 'Tonk, Plonk and Plink', *Analysis*, 22 (1962), pp. 130–4; J.T. Stevenson, 'Roundabout the runabout inference ticket', *Analysis*, 21 (1962), pp. 124–8; and Susan Haack, *Philosophy of Logics* (Cambridge University Press, Cambridge, 1978), p. 31.

None of these commentators address the main point in Prior's argument. They all treat his paper as if it posed the question of how we should define logical connectives, rather than the question of the source of the validity of the inferences containing them. Thus their response takes the form of saying that *properly* chosen meanings accomplish valid inferences. The point, then, is to locate the source of propriety for these choices, and this reintroduces our intuitions of validity again. Belnap explicitly invokes these intuitions but, despite his appreciation of Prior's paper, appears not to see that he is supporting rather than correcting him.

Hollis' paper 'A Retort to the Tortoise', *Mind*, 84 (1975), pp. 610–16, is simply another attempt to reify 'meaning' and impute to it the power to solve basic problems of validity.

form of nativism: the disposition arises from our biological constitution and the way the brain is organized. Such a move, needless to say, gives no comfort to rationalism: epistemologically, to invoke neuronal structure is no better than to invoke social structure; both moves seek explanations rather than justifications. And for this very reason nativism is perfectly compatible with relativism. At whatever point it is found necessary, the explanation of credibility may swing from social to biological causes. Our empirical curiosity swings from asking how our society is organized to asking how the brain is organized. Our general cognitive proclivities become subject to empirical enquiry just as are the cognitive proclivities of other species. The empirical scientific investigation of human cognition, its manifest structure and its physiological basis, is, of course, a lengthy task. At any given time our overall understanding of the matter, and in particular our verbal accounts of it, will be provisional and liable to change. They are subject to the same fluctuations and redescriptions as are found in the study of any other empirical phenomenon.

This consideration reinforces an important point: no account of our biologically-based reasoning propensities will justify a unique system of logical conventions. Just as our experience of a shared material world does not itself guarantee shared verbal descriptions of it, so our shared natural rationality does not guarantee a unique logical system. Hollis and Lukes make the same mistake in dealing with logic as they do with descriptive predicates. They fail to keep what belongs to unverbalized reality separate from what belongs to language. Just as they conflated the two with their doctrine of a universal observation language; now they take the plausible belief that we possess deductive dispositions and render it, without a second thought, into the abstract and highly conventionalized notion of material implication. To combat this confusion we need to remember the gap between the varied systems of logic as they are developed by logicians and the primitive, biologically based, informal intuitions upon which they all depend for their operation. Hollis and Lukes' conflation soon takes its revenge on them: *modus ponens* for material implication, which they confidently take to be a rational universal, has been explicitly deemed to fail, and is rejected, in some interesting systems of logic.[40]

---

[40] A.R. Anderson, and N. Belnap, 'Tautological entailments', *Philosophical Studies*, 13 (1961), pp. 9–24. This paper develops some of the consequences of demanding that the entailment relation satisfy conditions of 'relevance'

Logic, as it is systematized in textbooks, monographs or research papers, is a learned body of scholarly lore, growing and varying over time. It is a mass of conventional routines, decisions, expedient restrictions, dicta, maxims, and *ad hoc* rules. The sheer *lack* of necessity in granting its assumptions or adopting its strange and elaborate definitions is the point that should strike any candid observer. Why should anyone adopt a notion of 'implication' whereby a contradiction 'implies' any proposition? What is compelling about systems of logic which require massive and systematic deviation from our everyday use of crucial words like 'if', 'then', and 'and'?[41] As a body of conventions and esoteric traditions the compelling character of logic, such as it is, derives from certain narrowly defined purposes and from custom and institutionalized usage. Its authority is moral and social, and as such it is admirable material for sociological investigation and explanation. In particular the credibility of logical conventions, just like the everyday practices which deviate from them, will be of an entirely local character. The utility of granting or modifying a definition for the sake of formal symmetry; the expediency of ignoring the complexity of everyday discourse and everyday standards of reasoning so that a certain abstract generality can be achieved: these

between premise and conclusion. This is one of the plausible intuitive requirements that are violated by the 'Lewis Principle', that a contradiction entails any statement: '*P* and not *P* entails *Q*', regardless of whether or not *Q* 'has anything to do with' *P* or its negation. The Lewis Principle is a theorem of the axiom system sometimes called the system of tautological implication. To challenge the theorem means rejecting, for instance, the disjunctive syllogism which is equivalent to *modus ponens*. This is what Anderson and Belnap do on grounds of relevance. The result is a perfectly consistent axiom system: the four-valued logic of De Morgan implication. See Haack, *Philosophy of Logics*, pp. 200–1; D. Makinson, *Topics in Modern Logic* (Methuen, London, 1973), ch. 2.

It is ironic that logicians, who expose with admirable ruthlessness how problematic, variable and difficult to ground patterns of inference are, and who freely confess how very little is agreed upon by the totality of practitioners in their field, are turned to again and again to provide constraints upon the possibilities of rational thought. Just as there is always a certain demand for iron laws of economics, so there seems always to be a demand for iron laws of logic.

[41] For a careful documentation of the relation between ordinary and technical usage, see P. Strawson, *Introduction to Logical Theory* (Methuen, London, 1952).

will be the kinds of justification that will be offered and accepted or disputed by specialists in the field.

The point that emerges is that if any informal, intuitive reasoning dispositions are universally compelling, they are *ipso facto* without any reasoned justification. On the other hand, any parts of logic which can be justified will not be universal but purely local in their credibility. The rationalist goal of producing pieces of knowledge that are both universal in their credibility *and* justified in context-independent terms is unattainable.[42]

There is, of course, a final move that the rationalist can make. He can fall back into dogmatism, saying of some selected inference or conclusion or procedure: this just *is* what it is to be rational, or, this just *is* a valid inference.[43] It is at this point that the rationalist finally plucks victory out of defeat, for while the relativist can fight Reason, he is helpless against Faith. Just as Faith protects the Holy Trinity, or the Azande oracle, or the ancestral spirits of the Luba, so it can protect Reason. Faith has always been the traditional and most effective

---

[42] For an extension of this argument from logic to mathematics, see D. Bloor, *Knowledge and Social Imagery* (Routledge & Kegan Paul, 1966). chs 5–7. Here a modified empiricist theory of mathematics is defended against Frege. See also Bloor, 'Polyhedra and the abominations of Leviticus', *British Journal for the History of Science*, 11 (1978), pp. 245–72. This provides a sociological reading of I. Lakatos, *Proofs and Refutations* (Cambridge University Press, Cambridge, 1976).

[43] Although dogmatic assertions are perhaps the most common ways in which philosophers indicate the end-points at which they revert to faith, there are other ways. Quine for example explicitly takes for granted currently accepted scientific knowledge. Similarly, logicians often set out the points where they allow 'intuition' to decide for them which of different arguments they will accept.

Equally widespread, if less defensible, is the decision to reject an argument because of its consequences. If a series of inferences leads to solipsism, or scepticism, or relativism, it is assumed, simply by that very fact, that the series must contain an error. Thus, H. Putnam describes how one of his papers is designed to 'block' a perfectly good, but inconvenient, inductive inference: '[There is] a serious worry . . . that eventually the following meta-induction becomes overwhelmingly compelling: *just as no term used in the science of more than 50 . . . years ago referred, so it will turn out that no term used now . . . refers.*

It must obviously be a desideratum for the Theory of Reference that this meta-induction be blocked . . . ('What is realism?, *Philosophical Papers* (Cambridge University Press, Cambridge, 1975), vol.2).

Finally, of course, there is the occasional quite straightforward profession

defence against relativism. But if at this point the relativist must retire defeated, to gaze from some far hilltop on the celebratory rites of the Cult of Rationalism, he can nevertheless quietly ask himself: what local, contingent causes might account for the remarkable intensity of the Faith in Reason peculiar to the Cult?[44]

---

of faith, which scorns any disguise. I.C. Jarvie, for example, is disarmingly frank when he opposes relativism by suggesting: 'Perhaps, when we do science, and even more so mathematics, we participate in the divine . . . [It is] awe at the transcendental miracle of mathematics and science that has moved philosophers since Ancient Greece' ('Laudan's problematic progress and the social sciences', *Philosophy of the Social Sciences*, 9 (1979), p. 496).

[44] A plausible hypothesis is that relativism is disliked because so many academics see it as a dampener on their moralizing. A dualist idiom, with its demarcations, contrasts, rankings and evaluations is easily adapted to the tasks of political propaganda or self-congratulatory polemic. *This* is the enterprise that relativists threaten, not science. See notes 1–4 above. If relativism has any appeal at all, it will be to those who wish to engage in that eccentric activity called 'disinterested research'.

Language, Truth and Reason

Ian Hacking

I wish to pose a relativist question from within the heartland of rationality. It is not about the confrontation between science and alien cultures, for it comes out of our own scientific tradition. It does not rehearse the Kuhnian stories of revolution, replacement and incommensurability, but speaks chiefly of evolution and accumulation. Its sources are not hermeneutics but the canonical writings of positivism. Far from invoking 'the dogman of the dualism of scheme and reality' from which, according to Donald Davidson, 'we get conceptual relativity', it may well learn a trick from Davidson himself.[1]

I start from the fact that there have been different styles of scientific reasoning. The wisest of the Greeks admired Euclidean thought. The best minds of the seventeenth century held that the experimental method put knowledge on a new footing. At least part of every modern social science deploys some statistics. Such examples bring to mind different styles of reasoning with different domains. Each has surfaced and attained maturity in its own time, in its own way.

An inane subjectivism may say that whether p is a reason for q depends on whether people have got around to reasoning that way or not. I have the subtler worry that whether or not a proposition is as it were up for grabs, as a candidate for being true-or-false, depends on whether we have ways to reason about it. The style of thinking that befits the sentence helps fix its sense and determines the way in which it has a positive direction pointing to truth or to falsehood. If we continue in this vein, we may come to fear that the rationality of a style of reasoning is all too built-in. The propositions on which the reason-

---

[1] Donald Davidson, 'On the very idea of a conceptual scheme', *Proceedings and Addresses of the American Philosophical Association*, 47 (1974), pp. 5–20.

ing bears mean what they do just because that way of reasoning can assign them a truth value. Is reason, in short, all too self-authenticating?

My worry is about truth-or-falsehood. Consider Hamlet's maxim, that nothing's either good or bad but thinking makes it so. If we transfer this to truth and falsehood, this is ambiguous between: (*a*) Nothing, which is true, is true, and nothing, which is false, is false, but thinking makes it so: (*b*) Nothing's either true-or-false but thinking makes it so. It is (*b*) that preoccupies me. My relativist worry is, to repeat, that the sense of a proposition *p*, the way in which it points to truth or falsehood, hinges on the style of reasoning appropriate to *p*. Hence we cannot criticize that style of reasoning, as a way of getting to *p*, or to not-*p*, because *p* simply is that proposition whose truth value is determined in this way.

The distinction between (*a*) and (*b*) furnishes a distinction between subjectivity and relativity. Let (*a*, be subjectivism: by thinking we might make something true, or make it false. Let (*b*) be the kind of relativity that I address in this paper: by thinking, new candidates for truth and falsehood may be brought into being. Many of the recent but already classical philosophical discussions of such topics as incommensurability, indeterminacy of translation, and conceptual schemes seem to me to discuss truth, where they ought to be considering truth-or-falsehood. Hence bystanders, hoping to learn from philosophers, have tended to discuss subjectivity rather than relativity. For my part, I have no doubt that our discoveries are 'objective', simply because the styles of reasoning that we employ determine what counts as objectivity. My worry is that the very candidates for truth or falsehood have no existence independent of the styles of reasoning that settle what it is to be true or false in their domain.

STYLES OF REASONING

It is not the case that *nothing's* either true or false but thinking makes it so. Plenty of things that we say need no reasons. That is the core of the discredited philosophical doctrine of observation sentences, the boring utterances that crop up in almost any language, and which make radical translation relatively easy. Translation is hard when one gets to whole new ranges of possibility that make no sense for the favoured styles of reasoning of another culture. It is there that ethnographers begin to have problems. Every people has generated its own peculiar styles. We are no different from others, except that we can see, more clearly from our own written record, the historical emergence of new styles of reasoning.

I take the word 'style' from the title of a forthcoming book by A.C. Crombie: *Styles of Scientific Thinking in the European Tradition*.[2] He concludes an anticipatory paper with the words:

> The active promotion and diversification of the scientific methods of late medieval and early modern Europe reflected the general growth of a research mentality in European society, a mentality conditioned and increasingly committed by its circumstances to expect and to look actively for problems to formulate and solve, rather than for an accepted consensus without argument. The varieties of scientific methods so brought in to play may be distinguished as,
> (1) the simple postulation established in the mathematical sciences,
> (2) the experimental exploration and measurement of more complex observable relations,
> (3) the hypothetical construction of analogical models,
> (4) the ordering of variety by comparison and taxonomy,
> (5) the statistical analysis of regularities of populations and the calculus of probabilities, and
> (6) the historical derivation of genetic development.
> The first three of these methods concern essentially the science of individual regularities, and the second three the science of the regularities of populations ordered in space and time.[3]

Coincidentally, at the same conference to which Crombie read these works, Winifred Wisan announced another forthcoming work, *Mathematics and the Study of Motion: Emergence of a New Scientific Style in the 17th Century*.[4] Both Crombie's and Wisan's papers were about Galileo, who has long been a favourite candidate for advancing a new style of thought. Sometimes words more dramatic than 'style' are

[2] Clarendon Press, Oxford, forthcoming.
[3] A.C. Crombie, 'Philosophical presuppositions and shifting interpretations of Galileo' in J. Hintikka, D. Gruender and E. Agazzi (eds), *Theory Change, Ancient Axiomatics and Galileo's Methodology, Proceedings of the 1978 Pisa Conference on the History and Philosophy of Science* (Reidel, Dordrecht, 1981), vol. I p. 284 [numerals (1)–(6) inserted].
[4] W.L. Wisan, 'Galileo and the emergence of a new scientific style', ibid., pp. 311–39.

used, as when Althusser writes of Thales opening up a new continent, that of mathematics, Galileo opening up the continent of dynamics and Marx that of history.[5] But often the word 'style' is chosen. It is to be found in Collingwood. Stephen Weinberg, the theoretical physicist, recalls Husserl speaking of a Galilean style for 'making abstract models of the universe to which at least the physicists give a higher degree of reality than they accord the ordinary world of sensation'.[6] Weinberg finds it remarkable that this style should work, 'for the universe does not seem to have been prepared with human beings in mind'. The linguist Noam Chomsky picks up this remark in his most recent book, urging that 'we have no present alternative to pursuing the "Galilean style" in the natural sciences at least'.[7]

Like T.S. Kuhn's 'paradigm', the word 'style' serves my four contemporary authors to point to something general in the history of knowledge. There are new modes of reasoning that have specific beginnings and trajectories of development. Even these four will surely not agree in carving up histories into styles. The historian will find many styles where Chomsky sees only one. Doubtless the very word 'style' is suspect. It is cribbed from art critics and historians, who have not evolved a uniform connotation for the word. Nor would all their remarks about style tidily transfer to modes of reasoning. That is a problem that Wisan's paper begins to address. The success of the word 'style', as an analytic term for the history of science, may depend on the reception of Crombie's immensely learned historical analysis. Use of a borrowed word needs detailed examples to flush it out. Despite these reservations I shall take the fact that these recent writers employ the word in similar ways as an excuse for not attempting my own exegesis here.

ARCH-RATIONALISM

The existence of styles of reasoning does not immediately suggest relativism. Before elaborating the relativist worry sketched at the

---

[5] Louis Althusser, *Politics and History* (New Left Books, London, 1972), p. 185.
[6] Stephen Weinberg, 'The forces of nature', *Bulletin of the American Academy of Arts and Sciences*, 29 (1976), p. 28.
[7] Noam Chomsky, *Rules and Representations*, (Columbia University Press, New York, and Blackwell, Oxford, 1980), p. 9.

beginning of this paper, I shall first state a rationalist position informed by a proper respect both for history and for the idiosyncracies of ourselves and others. I shall call it arch-rationalism. (I, too, am an arch-rationalist most of the time.)

The arch-rationalist believes what right-thinking people have known all along. There are good and bad reasons. It has taken millennia to evolve systems of reasoning. By and large our Western tradition has contributed more to this progress than any other. We have often been narrow, blinkered and insensitive to foreign insights. We have repressed our own deviant and original thinkers, condemning many to irretrievable oblivion. Some of our own once-favoured styles of reasoning have turned out to be dead ends and others are probably on the way. However, new styles of reasoning will continue to evolve. So we shall not only find out more about nature, but we shall also learn new ways to reason about it. Maybe Paul Feyerabend's advocacy of anarchy is right. To compel people to reason in approved ways is to limit us and our potentialities for novelty. Arch-rationalism is convinced that there are good and bad reasons, but since it does not commit us to any specific regimentation like that of formal logic or Sir Karl Popper, it is fairly receptive to Feyeraband's imitation anarchy.

My arch-rationalist thinks that there is a fairly sharp distinction between reasons and the propositions they support. Reasons merely help us find out what is the case. The arch-rationalist wants to know how the world is. There are good and bad reasons for propositions about nature. They are not relative to anything. They do not depend on context. The arch-rationalist is not an imperialist about reason. Maybe there could be people who never reason nor deliberate at all. They tell jokes, make and break promises, feign insults and so forth, but they never reason. Just as statistical reasons had no force for the Greeks, so one imagines a people for whom none of our reasons for belief have force. On the other hand the arch-rationalist is an optimist about human nature. We who value truth and reason do imagine that a truthless and unreasoning people would, if left alone, evolve truth and reason for themselves. They would in their own way acquire a taste for speculation about the diagonal of a square, for motion on the inclined plane, for the tracks of the planets, for the inner constitution of matter, the evolution of the species, the Oedipus complex and amino acids.

The arch-rationalist not only grants that our kinds of truth and reason may not play as great a role in the life of other peoples as in our own culture; he may also be a romantic, hankering after a simpler, less reason-impregnated life. He will grant that our values are not inevitable, nor perhaps the noblest to which our species can aspire. But he cannot escape his own past. His admission of the historicity of our own styles of reasoning in no way makes it less objective. Styles of reasoning have histories and some emerged sooner than others. Humankind has got better at reasoning. What ground for relativism could there be in all that?

Instead of challenging the assumptions of the arch-rationalist, I shall extract a hint of incoherence from his heartland, which is, in the end, positivism.

POSITIVISM

Positivism is commonly taken to be a hard-headed antagonism to all forms of relativism. I shall create a question for the arch-rationalist from three aspects of positivism itself. I draw them from Auguste Comte, Moritz Schlick and Michael Dummett, i.e. the original positivist of the 1840s, the leader of the Vienna Circle in 1930, and the most gifted present exponent of one among that family of doctrines.

Comte. He was an historicist. His epistemology is a massive and almost unreadable account of human knowledge, a narrative of the human mind in which each intellectual innovation finds its own niche. One of his ideas is that a branch of knowledge acquires a 'positivity' by the development of a new, positive, style of reasoning associated with it. He is none too clear what he means by 'positive'; he sometimes says he chose the word chiefly because it had overtones of moral uplift in all European languages. A positive proposition is one that is by some means befitting the branch of knowledge to which it belongs. We may pun on his word: a positive proposition is one that has a direction, a truth value. It is no distortion to say that for Comte a class of positive propositions is a class of propositions that are up for grabs as true-or-false.

There are many aspects of Comte's thought from which one hastily withdraws – I refer both to questions of ideology and to issues of interest to analytic philosophers of science (e.g. his analysis of causation) I draw attention only to the idea of a historical evolution of different styles of reasoning, each bringing in its train its own body of positive knowledge. Each finds its place in great tabular displays of the sciences that serve as pull-outs from his gigantic epistemological text, the *Cours de philosophie positive*. Comte did not think that the evolution of styles and of positive knowledges had come to an end. His life goal was the creation of a new positive science, sociology. This would require a new style of reasoning. He ill foresaw what this style would be, but his meta-conception of what he was doing was sound.

Schlick. One of the more memorable statements of logical positivism is Moritz Schlick's, 'the meaning of a sentence is its method of verification'.[8] Those words could not stand unmodified, because the Vienna Circle had succumbed to Gottlob Frege's dictum that meanings are definite, objective and fixed. Schlick's maxim would imply that a change or advance in a method of verification would change the meanings of a sentence. Rather than give up the idea of meanings handed down from generation to generation, tranquil and unmodified, logical positivists revised Schlick's maxim again and again, although with no satisfactory outcome.[9] But for Comte, or any other of those fortunate writers of 1840 not yet infected by Fregean theories of meaning, Schlick's statement would be just fine. It is precisely, for Comte, the methods of verification – the ways in which the positive truth values are to be established – that determine the content of a body of knowledge.

Dummett. In logic, a proposition that has a definite truth value, true, or false, is called *bivalent*. Dummett's work has made philosophers think closely abiout bivalence.[10] It was first inspired by a philosophical reconstruction of some of the thoughts behind intuitionist mathematics. In what is called a non-constructive proof, one cannot exhibit the mathematical objects that are proved to exist. (So one might have a step in which one asserts that there is a prime number with a certain property, but be unable to say which prime number it is.) Non-constructive proofs may also assume of a proposition that it is either true or false, without being able to show which truth value it has. Some philosophical mathematicians, including Dummett, have doubted whether such non-constructive proofs are admissible.

Dummett is attracted to the following basis of his doubt. Whether or not a proposition is bivalent must depend upon its meaning. He

---

[8] Moritz Schlick, 'Meaning and verification', *The Philosophical Review*, 46 (1936), p. 261.
[9] For an account of repeated failures, see Ian Hacking, *Why Does Language Matter to Philosophy?* (Cambridge University Press, Cambridge, 1975), ch. 9.
[10] Michael Dummett, *Truth and Other Enigmas* (Duckworth, London, 1976), *passim*.

wonders how we can confer meanings on statements in non-constructive mathematics – meanings in virtue of which the statements are bivalent, although there is no known way to settle the truth values. It is we who through our linguistic practices are the sole source of the meanings of what we say. How then can we confer a meaning on a statement, such that it is bivalent, when nothing we know how to do bears on the truth or the falsehood of the statement? Maybe statements of non-constructive mathematics acquire bivalence only as we perfect means of determining their truth values or exhibiting the mathematical objects of which they speak?

Although this subtle question arose in sharp form in the intuitionist critique of classical mathematics, Dummett extends it to other forms of discourse. Many statements about the past cannot now be settled by any practicable means. Are they bivalent? Might bivalence recede into the past as historical data become irrevocably erased? Dummett does not claim that his worries are conclusive, nor does he expect parallel answers for every kind of discourse. One might, on reflection, come out for bivalence in the case of history, but reject it for non-constructive mathematics.

Positivity and bivalence. I have spoken of being true-or-false, and have used Comte's word 'positive'. Is this the same idea as bivalence? Not as I shall use the words. Being positive is a less strong characteristic than bivalence. Outside mathematics I suspect that whether a statement is bivalent or not is an abstraction imposed by logicians to facilitate their analysis of deductive argument forms. It is a noble abstraction, but it is a consequence of art, not nature. In the speculative sciences that concern me in this paper, the interesting sentences are the ones that are up for grabs as true or false – ones for which we believe we have methods that will determine the truth values. The applications of these methods may require as yet unimagined technological innovation. Moreover we find out more about the world, we find out that many of our questions no longer make sense. Bivalence is not the right concept for science. Allow me a couple of examples to point to the distinction required.

At the time of Laplace it was very sensible to think that there are particles of caloric, the substance of heat, that have repulsive forces that decay rapidly with distance. On such an hypothesis Laplace solved many of the outstanding problems about sound. Propositions about the rate of extinction of the repulsive force of caloric were up for grabs as true or false and one knew how to obtain information bearing on the question. Laplace had an excellent estimate of the rate of extinction of the repulsive force, yet it turns out that the whole idea is wrongheaded. I would say that Laplace's sentences once were 'positive'. They were never bivalent. Conversely, Maxwell once said that some propositions about the relative velocity of light were intrinsically incapable of determination, yet a few years after he said that Michelson had invented the technology to give precise answers to Maxwell's questions. I would say that the sentences of interest to Maxwell had positivity when he uttered them, but were bivalent only after a transformation in technology – a transformation whose success depends on delicate experimental details about how the world works.

In short, Comte's 'positive' is drawing attention to a less demanding concept than Dummett's 'bivalent'. Yet the two are connected and so are the thoughts of both writers. Dummett says: not bivalent unless we have a proof of the truth value, or a known sure-fire method for generating the proof. Comte says: not positive, not in the running for being true-or-false, until there is some style of reasoning that will bear on the question.

Comte, Schlick and Dummett are no more relativist than Crombie or Chomsky. Yet a positivist train of thought, combined with an emphasis on styles of reasoning, has the germ of relativism. If positivity is consequent upon a style of reasoning, then a range of possibilities depends upon that style. They would not be possibilities, candidates for truth or falsehood, unless that style were in existence. The existence of the style arises from historical events. Hence although whichever propositions are true may depend on the data, the fact that they are candidates for being true is a consequence of an historical event. Conversely the rationality of a style of reasoning as a way of bearing on the truth of a class of propositions does not seem open for independent criticism, because the very sense of what can be established by that style depends upon the style itself.

Is that a nasty circle?

I shall proceed as follows. First, I observe that by reasoning I don't mean logic. I mean the very opposite, for logic is the preservation of truth, while a style of reasoning is what brings in the possibility of truth or falsehood. Then I separate my idea of style of reasoning from the incommensurability of Kuhn and Feyerabend, and from the indeterminancy of translation urged by Quine. Then I examine Davidson's fundamental objection to the supposition that there are alternative ways of thinking. He may refute subjectivity, as I understand it, but not relativity. The key distinction throughout the following discussion is the difference between truth-and-falsehood as opposed to truth. A second important idea is the looseness of fit between those propositions that have a sense for almost all human beings regardless of reasoning, and those that get a sense only within a style of reasoning.

INDUCTION, DEDUCTION

Neither deductive logic nor induction occur on Crombie's list. How strange, for are they not said to be the basis of science? It is instructive that no list like Crombie's would include them. The absence reminds us that styles of reasoning create the possibility for truth and falsehood. Deduction and induction merely preserve it.

We now understand deduction as that mode of inference that preserves truth. It cannot pass from true premises to a false conclusion. The nature of induction is more controversial. The word has been used in many ways. There is an important tradition represented alike by the philospher C.S. Peirce and the statistician Jerzy Neyman: induction is that mode of argument that preserves truth most of the time.

Deduction and induction were important human discoveries. But they play little role in the scientific method, no more than the once revered syllogism. They are devices for jumping from truth to truth. Not only will they give us no original truth from which to jump, but also they take for granted the class of sentences that assert possibilities of truth or falsehood. That is why they do not occur in Crombie's list. In deduction and induction alike truth plays the purely formal role of a counter on an abacus. It matters not what truth is, when we employ the mechanics of the model theory of modern logicians. Their machine works well so long as we suppose that the class of sentences that have truth values is already given. (Or, in the case of intuitionist logic, one supposes that the class of sentences that may, through proof, acquire truth values is already given.) Induction equally assumes that the class of possible truths is predetermined. Styles of reasoning of the sort described by Crombie do something different. When they come into being they generate new classes of possibilities.

INCOMMENSURABILITY AND THE INDETERMINANCY OF TRANSLATION

Philosophers have recently given us two doctrines that pull in opposite directions. Both seem to use the idea of a conceptual scheme, a notion that goes back at least to Kant but whose modern nominalist version is due to Quine. He says that a conceptual scheme is a set of sentences held to be true. He uses the metaphor of core and periphery. Sentences at the core have a kind of permanence and are seldom relinquished, while those on the periphery are more empirical and more readily given up in the light of 'recalcitrant experience'.

My talk of styles of reasoning does not mesh well with Quine's idea of a conceptual scheme.[11] In his opinion two schemes differ when some substantial number of core sentences of one scheme are not held to be true in another scheme. A style of reasoning, in contrast, is concerned with truth-or-falsehood. Two parties, agreeing to the same styles of reasoning, may well totally disagree on the upshot, one party holding for true what the other party rejects. Styles of reasoning may determine possible truth values, but unlike Quine's schemes are not characterized by assignments of truth values. It is to be expected, then, that Quine's application of the idea of a conceptual scheme will not coincide with my idea of styles of reasoning.

Quine's most memorable thesis is the indeterminancy of translation. Let L and M be languages spoken by two truly disparate communities. Quine holds that there are indefinitely many possible but incompatible translations between L and M. No matter how much speakers of L and M might converse, there is in principle no way of settling on a definitely right translation. This is not a matter of settling on nuances; Quine means that you could take a sentence s of L and translate it by one system of translation into p of M, and translate it by another system into q of M, and p and q would, in M, be held to be incompatible.

As we shall see in the next section, Donald Davidson has noticed that the notion of conceptual scheme does not ride well with the indeterminancy of translation. For how are we to say that speakers of L have a scheme different from we who speak M? We must first pick out the true sentences from the core of the scheme of L, and show that many of these translate into sentences of M that we who speak M hold

---

[11] W.V. Quine, *Word and Object* (Wiley, New York, 1960), ch. 2.

to be false. But what is to assure that this is the right translation? When translating there is a strong instinct to render central doctrines of *L* as main truths of *M*. Once you focus on truth rather than truth-or-falsehood, you begin a chain of considerations that call in question the very idea of a conceptual scheme.

The thesis of indeterminacy of translation pulls in one direction and the idea of incommensurability pulls in another. We owe incommensurability to Kuhn and Feyerabend.[12] The idea is that disparate systems of thought are not mutually expressible. Kuhn has tended to make the idea fit commonplace situations while Feyerabend emphasizes the extreme. Thus Feyerabend's favourite example of incommensurability is the break between the cosmologies of archaic and classical Greece. Kuhn, in contrast, comes back to the idea of 'no common measure' in the original meaning of the word, and applies it to more everyday 'advances' in knowledge. When there has been a scientific revolution the new science may address new problems and employ new concepts. There is no way of settling whether the new science does its job better than the old one because they do different jobs. Kuhn finds this sort of incommensurability in all sorts of revolutions that strike the outsider as minor, while Feyerabend focuses on big shifts in human thought. Both writers once suggested that incommensurability should be understood in terms of schemes and translation. Incommensurability meant that there would simply be no way of translating from one scheme to another. Thus this idea pulls in a direction exactly opposite to Quine's. Indeterminancy says there are too many translations between schemes, while incommensurability says there are none at all.

Would either the Kuhnian or the Feyerabendian idea of incommensurability apply if styles of reasoning were to supersede each other? The Kuhnian 'no common measure' does not apply in any straightforward way because when we reason differently there is no expectation of common measure of the sort that successive Kuhnian paradigms invite. Hence it is to the more extreme, Feyerabendian, use of the term that we must look. That is surely the popular conception of incommensurability: the inability of one body of thought to understand another.

I do admit that there is a real phenomenon of disparate ways of

[12] For one version of this famous idea, see Paul Feyerabend, *Science in a Free Society* (New Left Books, London, 1978), pp. 65–70, 1970–1.

thinking. Some styles of reasoning have been so firmly displaced that we cannot even recognize their objects. The renaissance medical, alchemical and astrological doctrines of resemblance and similitude are well-nigh incomprehensible. One does not find our modern notions of evidence deployed in those arcane pursuits. There is very little truth in all that hermetic writing, and to understand it one cannot search out the core of truth that meshes with our beliefs. Yet that stuff may not be best described as incommensurable with our modern chemistry, medicine and astronomy. It is not that the propositions match ill with our modern sciences, so much as that the way propositions are proposed and defended is entirely alien to us. You can perfectly well learn hermetic lore, and when you do so you end up talking the language of Paracelsus, possibly in translation. What you learn is not systems of translation but chains of reasoning which would have little sense if one were not re-creating the thought of one of those magi. What we have to learn is not what they took for true, but what they took for true-or-false. (For example, that mercury salve might be good for syphilis because mercury is signed by the planet Mercury which signs the marketplace, where syphilis is contracted.)

Understanding the sufficiently strange is a matter of recognizing new possibilities for truth-or-falsehood, and of learning how to conduct other styles of reasoning that bear on those new possibilities. The achievement of understanding is not exactly a difficulty of translation, although foreign styles will make translation difficult. It is certainly not a matter of designing translations which preserve as much truth as possible, because what is true-or-false in one way of talking may not make much sense in another until one has learned how to reason in a new way. Understanding is learning how to reason. When we encounter old or alien texts we have to translate them, but it is wrong to focus on that aspect of translation that merely produces sentences of English for sentences of the other language. With such a limited focus one thinks of charitably trying to get the old text to say as much truth as possible. But, even after Paracelsus is translated into modern German, one still has to learn how he reasoned in order to understand him. Since the idea of incommensurability has been so closely tied to translation rather than reasoning, I do not use it here.

The indeterminacy of translation is an equally wrong idea. It is empiricially empty, because we know that unequivocal translation evolves between any two communities in contact. It is the wrong theoretical notion because it starts from an idea of truth-preserving matching of sentences. In fact the possibilities available in one language are not there in the other. To get them into the second language one has to learn a way of reasoning and when that has been done there is no problem of translation at all, let alone indeterminacy.

There is perfect commensurability, and no indeterminacy of translation, in those boring domains of 'observations' that we share with all people as people. Where we as people have branched off from others as a people, we find new interests, and a looseness of fit between their and our commonplaces. Translation of truths is irrelevant. Communication of ways to think is what matters.

CONCEPTUAL SCHEMES

In his famous paper, 'On the very idea of a conceptual scheme', Donald Davidson argues more against incommensurability than indeterminacy, but he is chiefly against the idea of a conceptual scheme that gives sense to either. [13] He provides 'an underlying methodology of interpretation' such that 'we could not be in a position' to judge 'that others had concepts or beliefs different from our own'. He makes plain that he does not reach this result by postulating 'a neutral ground, or a common coordinate system' between schemes. It is the notion of a scheme itself to which he is opposed. He rejects a 'dogma of dualism between scheme and reality' from which we derive the bogey of 'conceptual relativity, and of truth relative to a scheme'.

Davidson distinguishes two claims. Total translatability between schemes may be impossible, or there may be only partial untranslatability. Even if we do not follow the intricacies of his argument, nor even accept its premises, we can, like Davidson, dismiss the idea of total untranslatability. As a matter of brute fact all human languages are fairly easily partially translatable. The fact is closely connected with what I said earlier, that there is a common human core of verbal performances connected with what people tend to notice around them. But I said that there is a looseness of fit between that broad base of shared humanity and the interesting things that people like to talk about. That looseness leaves some space for incommensurability. It is

---

[13] Davidson, 'On the very idea of a conceptual scheme'. For a systematic explanation of Davidson's programme, see Ian Hacking, *Why Does Language Matter to Philosophy?* (Cambridge University Press, Cambridge, 1975), ch. 12.

not only the topics of discussion that may vary from group to group, but what counts as a point of saying something. Yet Davidson counters there too, and mounts a magnificent attack against even the notion of partial untranslatability between groups of people. Since in fact even partial untranslatability is chiefly a matter of coming to share the interest of another, and since lots of travellers are pretty sympathetic people, interests do get shared, so we should welcome an argument against partial untranslatability too. Yet since Davidson's argument may seem founded upon a lack of concern for alternative interests, we may fear his premises while we accept his conclusions. My diagnosis is that, like Quine, he assumes that a conceptual scheme is defined in terms of what counts as true, rather than of what counts as true-or-false.

TRUTH VERSUS TRUTH-OR-FALSEHOOD

Davidson concludes his argument against relativity with the words, 'Of course the truth of sentences remains relative to a language, but that is as objective as can be.' Earlier he rightly states what is wrong with the idea of making a sentence true:

> *Nothing,* makes sentences and theories true: not experience, not surface irritations [he there alluded to Quine], not the world . . . *That* experience takes a certain course, that our skin is warmed or punctured . . . these facts, if we like to talk that way, make sentences and theories true. But this point is better made without mention of facts. The sentence 'my skin is warm' is true if and only if my skin is warm. Hence there is no reference to a fact, a world, an experience, or a piece of evidence.[14]

Davidson's example, 'my skin is warm', serves me well. I urge a distinction between statements that may be made in any language, and which require no style of reasoning, and statements whose sense depends upon a style of reasoning. Davidson writes as if all sentences were of the former class. I agree that 'my skin is warm' is of that class. When I once looked for the best example of a sense-datum sentence to be actually published in the annals of real science, I hit upon precisely this sentence, or rather, 'my skin is warmed'. It begins Sir William Herschel's investigations of 1800 which are said to commence the

---

[14] Davidson, 'On the very idea of a conceptual scheme', p. 16.

theory of radiant heat. (He noticed that using filters of some colours his skin was warmed, while using other colours he had much light but little heat.)[15]

Herschel went on to pose a theory of invisible rays of heat, a theory that we now call correct, although his own experiments made him give it up. In the course of this reasoning he abandoned the following sentence, 'The heat which has the refrangibility of the red rays is occasioned by the light of those rays.' We can certainly write out a truth condition of the form '*s* is true if and only if *p*' for this sentence. But there arises a problem for the sufficiently foreign translator. It is not that words like 'ray' and 'refrangible' are mildly theoretical and the translator may have no such notions in his vocabulary. If another culture has acquired the styles of reasoning enumerated by Crombie it can perfectly well learn Herschel's physics from the ground up – that is just what I do in making sense of Herschel's text. The problem is that the sufficiently foreign person will not have Herschel's kind of sentence as the sort of thing that can be true-or-false, because the ways of reasoning that bear on it are unknown. To exaggerate the case, say the translator is Archimedes. I do not choose him at random, for he wrote a great tract on burning mirrors and was a greater scientist than Herschel. Yet I say he would not be able to effect a translation until he had caught up on some scientific method.

I should repeat my opposition to usual versions of incommensurability. It is not that Herschel's science had some Newtonian principles about rays and refrangibility that determine the meaning of sentences in which those words occur, and so those sentences could not have the same meaning in another theory. On the contrary, Herschel's sentences were fairly immune to change in theory. They were up for grabs as true or false in 1800; Herschel thought first that a crucial sentence is true and later held it to be false; many years later the world agreed on the truth of the sentence. Herschel, then, first grabbed the right end of the stick and then grabbed the wrong one. My claim about a translator less well placed than Archimedes is that until he learns how to reason more like Herschel, there are no ends of a stick to grab.

[15] For discussion and references, see Ian Hacking, 'Spekulation, Berechnung und die Erschaffung von Phänomenen' in P. Duerr (ed.), *Versuchungen: Aufsätze zur Philosophie Paul Feyerabends* (Suhrkamp, Frankfurt, 1981), pp. 126–58.

SCHEMES WITHOUT DOGMA

'Truth of sentences', writes Davidson, 'remains relative to a language, but that is as objective as can be.' I claim that for part of our language, and perhaps as part of any language, being true-or-false is a property of sentences only because we reason about those sentences in certain ways. Subjectivists put their worries in the form of saying that with different customs we could 'rightly' take some propositions for true while at present we take them for false. Davidson has dealt sharply with all such formulations. But he has left a space for a relativist fear. The relativist ought to say that there might be whole other categories of truth-or-falsehood than ours.

Perhaps I am proposing a version of the conceptual scheme idea. Quine's conceptual schemes are sets of sentences held for true. Mine would be sets of sentences that are candidates for truth or falsehood. Does such a notion fall into the 'dogma of scheme and reality' that Davidson resents? I do not think so. The idea of a style of reasoning is as internal to what we think and say as the Davidsonian form, '*s* is true and only if *p*' is internal to a language. *A style is not a scheme that confronts reality*. I did speak earlier of styles of reasoning being applied to data and to the formation of data. But data are uttered and are subject to Davidsonian treatment. There is much to be said about the neglected field of study, experimental science, but it has nothing much to do with scheme/reality. My own present work on the subject tries to show how experiment has a life of its own unrelated to theories or schemes.

ANARCHO-RATIONALISM

This paper makes two assertions and draws some inferences from them. Each assertion and every inference is in need of clarification. To list them is to show how much more must be done.

(1) There are different styles of reasoning. Many of these are discernible in our own history. They emerge at definite points and have distinct trajectories of maturation. Some die out, others are still going strong.

(2) Propositions of the sort that necessarily require reasoning to be substantiated have a positivity, a being true-or-false, only in consequence of the styles of reasoning in which they occur.

(3) Hence many categories of possibility, of what may be true or false, are contingent upon historical events, namely the development of certain styles of reasoning.

(4) It may then be inferred that there are other categories of possibility than have emerged in our tradition.

(5) We cannot reason as to whether alternative systems of reasoning are better or worse than ours, because the propositions to which we reason get their sense only from the method of reasoning employed. The propositions have no existence independent of the ways of reasoning towards them.

This chain of reflections does not lead to subjectivity. It does not imply that some proposition, with a content independent of reasoning, could be held to be true, or to be false, according to the mode of reasoning we adopt. Yet this defeat of subjectivity seems hollow because the propositions that are objectively found to be true are determined as true by styles of reasoning for which in principle there can be no external justification. A justification would be an independent way of showing that the style gets at the truth, but there is no characterization of the truth over and above what is reached by the styles of reason itself.

Can there not be a meta-reason justifying a style of reason? Can one not, for example, appeal to success? It need not be success in generating technology, although that does matter. Nor is it to be success in getting at the truth, for that would be circular. There can, however, be non-circular successes in truth-related matters. For example, following Imre Lakatos, one might revamp Popper's method of conjecture and refutation, urging that a methodology of research programmes constantly opens up new things to think about.[16] I have quoted Chomsky giving a similar meta-reason. On his analysis of the Galilean style, it has not only worked remarkably well, but also, in the natural sciences, at least, we have no alternative but to go on using that style, although, of course, in the future it may not work. Although Chomsky does not make the distinction, his meta-reason is less that Galileo's style continues to find out the truth about the universe than that it poses new kinds of probing and answering. It has produced an open-ended dialogue. That might terminate in the face of a nature that ceased to participate in ways that the Galilean can make sense of. We

---

[16] Imre Lakatos, *The Methodology of Scientific Research Programmes* (Cambridge University Press, Cambridge, 1978), chs 1 and 2.

know it might cease to cater to our interests, but at present (says Chomsky) we have no alternative.

Chomsky is saying that if we want to engage in certain pursuits (call them the natural sciences or even the pursuit of truth in our tradition), we must reason with our reasons. Other styles of reasoning may occur; some are current. Other people may have other interests. We ought at least to be cautious, in the social sciences, in looking for other styles of reasoning (that is the problem for other contributors to this collection). Such considerations may lead the arch-rationalist to be a stick-in-the-mud, but since relativity does not imply subjectivity, he can carry on doing what we do with few qualms.

Some arch-rationalists may even find themselves agreeing that an anarcho-rationalism I have learned from Feyerabend is appealing. Our overall interests in truth and reason may well be served by letting other styles of reason evolve in their own ways, unfettered by a more imperial kind of rationalism. But that does not mean to say that I, as anarcho-rationalist, will take up something so recently killed off in our own tradition as homoeopathic medicine and its appeal to similitudes. That is for others (though if they look healthier than me, I might join up). Anarcho-rationalism is tolerance for other people combined with the discipline of one's own standards of truth and reason. The anarcho-rationalist is at home with the sentiment expressed by Sartre in his last interview:

> C'est ça ma tradition, je n'en ai pas d'autre.
> Ni la tradition orientale, ni la tradition juive.
> Elles me manquent par mon historicité.[17]

---

[17] *Le Nouvel Observateur*, 10 March 1980, p. 93.

The Social Destruction of Reality

Martin Hollis

It is evident that all the sciences have a relation, greater or less, to human nature; and that, however wide any of them may seem to run from it, they still return back by one passage or another. Even *Mathematics, Natural Philosophy* and *Natural Religion* are in some measure dependent on the science of MAN; since they lie hid under the cognisance of men and are judged by their powers and faculties.

D. Hume, Introduction to *A Treatise of Human Nature*

That the final determinants of belief are human, yet not intellectual, is an idea as old as scepticism. But it need not be a sceptical idea. Hume, for instance, saw in it the grounding of a new science, which would explain the human understanding as the work of custom and imagination. He was sceptical about Reason but confident about science and the tracing of our beliefs to custom and imagination was to be a scientific project. Philosophers have not, on the whole, taken kindly to his proposal, except recently in the philosophy of natural science, but sociologists of knowledge have carried it a great way. Of late a 'strong programme' has crystallized, intended to deprive Reason of all her traditional autonomy and to place the study of the social world on a thoroughly scientific footing. I find this a most instructive exercise, less for its results – witness my title – than for what it reveals about the understanding of beliefs. It forces friend and foe alike to think hard

My long-standing debt to Steven Lukes has been increased by his helpful criticisms of earlier drafts. I would also like to thank Richard Bernstein for perceptive comments and David Bloor for responses, which, although unrepentant, I respect and appreciate.

about the social world, the mental life of social actors and the very idea of a social science.

Traditionally 'knowledge' has been regarded as belief which has passed an objective test and is held because it has passed the test. 'Reason' is the portmanteau name for the rules of proof, which aid the mind in securing *a priori* knowledge, and for the canons of empirical evidence, used in judging the truth of beliefs against the facts of an independent world; both for Mathematics and for Natural Philosophy. (It has also included whatever intuition is deemed needful to ground the first inferences.) Hence we have knowledge, only if we follow Reason; custom and imagination are never enough. So, traditionally, there is a basic asymmetry about the explanation of belief. A man who knows believes because he knows; a man whose beliefs can be explained by custom or imagination does not know. A 'strong programme' in the sociology of knowledge rejects this distinction root and branch.

It is commonly a four-point programme:

(i) *Causality*. The programme seeks the causal conditions which bring about beliefs (or knowledge), treating beliefs as effects, after the manner of any object of scientific study.

(ii) *Impartiality*. It is impartial between true and false beliefs (as between rational and irrational or any other epistemic classification). All beliefs are equally grist to the mill.

(iii) *Symmetry*. Explanation, since it does not vary with the epistemic status of the belief explained, can be dubbed symmetrical.

(iv) *Reflexivity*. The programme makes no exception in its own case. It applies reflexively to itself and the beliefs held by sociologists of knowledge are, in turn, objects for scientific study.

The four points are non-committal between imagination and custom (psychology and sociology), although a sociologist of knowledge of course opts for custom. But they are committed squarely to the side of science against the autonomy of Reason. There is nothing special about the beliefs which constitute knowledge. 'Knowledge for the sociologist is whatever men take to be knowledge. It consists of those beliefs which men confidently hold to and live by.'[1]

In what follows I shall take the four points in turn, raising queries

---

[1] David Bloor, *Knowledge and Social Imagery* (Routledge & Kegan Paul, London, 1976), p. 2. See also his summary of the programme on pp. 4–5, which I have heeded gratefully in this paragraph.

and suggesting revisions. The programme is meant to rot away the props of a familiar notion of objectivity and I shall resist by defending Reason. My aim is constructive. It is to clear the way for a sociology of knowledge helpful to an actionist theory of the social world as human handiwork. So I distinguish two kinds of rot spread by the programme. One is, so to speak, wet rot – a determinist picture of the shaping of beliefs by social conditions, which leaves small place for human agency as a motor concept. The snag lies in the Causality clause, partly in its making causation one-way and more in its separation of intellectual from social. The other is a lethal dry rot – a relativism implied in the other clauses, laudably meant to make us see the social world from within but resulting, I allege, in the social destruction of reality. By way of cure I shall argue for an asymmetry in the explanation of beliefs, with those true and rationally held treated differently from those false and irrationally held and with mixed explanations for the mixed cases. Reason thus advises a blend of charity and judgement in the understanding of social life and hence a damp-proof course for the sociology of knowledge too.

CAUSALITY AND BELIEF

The programme looks tempting in at least some areas of thought. Natural Religion, for example, has lost the place which Hume gave it in the citadel of the sciences and has long seemed a suitable candidate. This is not to say that a strong programme seeks to convict religious believers of some kind of global error by showing the ground of belief in God to be not God but society. For, even if, thanks initially to Comte's theory of progress and to anthropological interest in primitive religions, there has been some such tendency in the past, the programme need not endorse it. The idea is to tackle religious beliefs, like all others, without prejudice to their truth. The most ardent believer can agree that religion takes different forms in different social conditions and can profit from sociological help in applying the parable of the sower. The causality clause must then be read not as asserting a brute social determinism but as seeking necessary and sufficient causal conditions and this I take to be its intention.

There is no good reason, however, to insist that causation is all one-way. Beliefs helped to shape the Church, whose power extended to the social conditions which in turn helped to shape it and its beliefs.

More generally a strong programme is entitled to whatever a theory of ideology has to offer; and there ideas are commonly given work to do, for instance in masking and so perpetuating social forms. Perhaps the explanations of the last resort must be held to lie in social (or economic) facts, but meanwhile there can be interplay. Indeed the four points of the programme, taken together, demand it. For, we shall find, the attack on the autonomy of Reason is not meant to abolish all considerations of rationality. How the actors conceive their world is still important to understanding that world, even if their conceptions are rational by varying criteria, which finally have social determinants. Presumably then, the Causality clause permits causation both ways.

That is merely to extend the scope of the programme, at least provided that beliefs are never the explanations of the last resort. Deeper problems are set by the presumption that social and intellectual systems can be separated and then related as cause and effect. This seems to me a dangerous piece of rot. Ideas cannot, I submit, be described in isolation from the social world, which they let actors describe to themselves; nor can the social world be furnished without the aid of the actors' ideas. There is fusion in the identities of the actors, who can be treated neither as walking beliefs, nor as bipeds whose beliefs are accidents. Consider, for instance, Catholicism, both as an intellectual system of doctrines, interpretations and precepts and as a system of social positions within the Church, affecting the everyday lives of Catholics. The distinction is real enough but it is got by abstracting in two different ways from the same charivari. No doubt the beliefs and the social life of priests (or of laymen) vary systematically between New York, Dublin and Warsaw. Yet a priest is not essentially the occupant of a social position who just happens to hold Catholic beliefs. Nor is he a universal believer who just happens to live somewhere. His flock have social relations with their father confessor and his spiritual journey takes him through the streets and offices of a social world.

Each abstraction can itself be made in different ways. Sometimes it is useful to abstract a unitary Catholic view on say, contraception, sometimes it is more useful to emphasize the discord. Whichever is done, the beliefs are those of social actors and the converse point can be made about abstracting to the political influence of the Church. Hence the units, which a strong programme connects, are each doubly abstracted from what the actors themselves usually manage to live as a single life. To treat beliefs as units, or even as properties of actors, is no doubt a proper and useful device. But it is a device and it should not lead us into thinking of intellectual systems as entities. Conversely social relations are partly ideal, in that norms and rules are real only given actors who regard (at least some of) them as real. They are external to each actor but only because they are recognized. They genuinely enable and constrain in the familiar way; but only because enough actors rely on them to enable and constrain. No doubt there are material conditions upon the shape of norms and latent material consequences of norms. But social systems are detected by a double abstraction and to treat them as objects is also a device.

I cannot argue here for this view of social life as the life of actors with two aspects each identified with the aid of elements from the other. I introduce it simply to put the Causality clause in question. What relation is meant by 'Causality'? The reference is certainly to nothing so crude as the impact of billiard balls or movement of levers. The underlying notion cannot be simply production or correlation. At any rate, if an advocate of a strong programme were to treat the explanation of beliefs in a mechanical or statistical way, it would be easy to object. But I presume that he would have no duty to be so simple-minded. It should be possible to admit the interpenetration of ideas and things in the furnishing of the social world without abandoning the programme. In that case, however, we are owed more on the nature of Causality than I find to hand. Equally it should be possible to hang on to a notion of agency, instead of losing the actors in the interplay of the intellectual and the social. But there too an account of agency is owing. So I end this brief section with a query over the Causality clause. Read simple-mindedly, it seems to me to fall at once, partly because there has to be causation both ways and more because intellectual and social cannot be isolated. How then should it be read? With this question in mind for later, I turn to Impartiality.

IMPARTIALITY AND IDENTIFICATION

The second point of the programme is Impartiality, the refusal to confine itself to false beliefs or to irrational beliefs or to any other epistemic category. It is much bound up with the third point, Symmetry, but I find it convenient to take them separately. Impartiality has to do with what essential distinctions should be drawn among beliefs to be studied and I shall link it with the matter of how we are to identify the beliefs which people hold. Symmetry concerns the explanation of why they hold them. For both I shall be asking what kinds of judgement an enquirer must make, in order to understand a system of beliefs. I take there to be understanding, when he knows what his subjects believe (identification) and why they believe it (explanation). But let no one forget that the two go together, lest we propose a canon for explaining beliefs, which would make it impossible to have identified them.

To clear the ground, some simplifying assumptions are needed. I assume that a society, culture or group holds a belief, if enough of its members do. (Thus I shall ignore questions of numbers, authority and the gap between publicly asserted and privately held belief.) I assume that beliefs can be ascribed to persons, as predicates to subjects, without first discussing intentionality, opacity and other issues in philosophical logic. I assume that a system of beliefs differs from a list inasmuch as there are connections in the minds of the holders. These connections can be regarded as beliefs about beliefs, marking out some as the reasons for holding others. Thus I assume a subjective rationality in the idea of a system and I take it that not even the strongest programme will object to this much. I assume, in short, just enough common ground to get argument going.

A belief can be warrantably ascribed to someone, I shall contend, only as an element of a system, some of whose members are held because they are true, some because there is good reason for holding them and none without some reason. Here the notion of a reason is being used objectively. In the previous paragraph I assumed that beliefs are rational from the actor's point of view, since he can always cite some other belief or an alleged fact, which, by some rule of justification, seems to him to warrant any belief. I shall contend that there are tests for whether a belief is objectively rational and that subjectively rational beliefs need not pass them; that there is a minimum score which all beliefs must attain and a maximum score which some must; and that 'good reason' is an objective term, to be applied with increasing warrant as the maximum is approached.

Yet much of what is believed is surely false or suspect. Mankind could hardly survive without beliefs which are incoherent, unlikely, disconnected or daft. Life is too short for constant Cartesian monitoring, even supposing that to be possible in principle. Social life often runs better on some false or at least unquestioned beliefs. Language cannot be understood solely as if all utterances were assertions or all assertions sincere. None the less I do contend that the identification of beliefs requires a 'bridgehead' of true and rational beliefs. This metaphor is borrowed from an attempt on the problem which I have made elsewhere[2] and shall not repeat in detail. But the nub of it can be put quite briefly.

An enquirer ascribes a belief to an actor. He does so by interpreting evidence. The evidence can, it seems, only be what the actor and others say and do. Their sayings and doings must have been rightly understood. Hence, apparently, every interpretation requires a previous one. So how is identification possible? A tempting reply is that the air of paradox is spurious; each interpretation is provisional and subject to confirmation; a later interpretation can overturn an earlier one; so the need for a previous interpretation is genuine but harmless. But, I retort, there are two reasons why there has to be more to it than the pragmatic assembling of a jigsaw. One is that even this pragmatic work presupposes internal relations among the beliefs – if you like, the existence of both a picture on the face of the jigsaw and a geometry to the shapes of the pieces – which are not discovered by the confirming process. The other is that, in addition to internal relations, there must be an external determinant which is also presupposed and not discovered. It would foreclose on a long dispute to call this simply 'the world' and I prefer to regard it as an *a priori* guarantee of overlap between the perceptual judgements of the enquirer and his informants. Putting internal and external constraints together, I submit that the enquirer must presuppose shared percepts, judgements, concepts and rules of judgement in the making of his empirical discoveries about beliefs. So, although some individual interpretations are adjustable later, adjustment cannot be so thorough as to overthrow the bridgehead of interpretations it relies on.

Formally speaking, to know on evidence e that S believes p involves knowing that, on evidence e, it is more likely that S believes p than that S believes anything inconsistent with p, and that e can be relied on. This requires fixed rules for judging between rival interpretations and, if e depends in turn on e', requires that e' (or whatever e' depends on) be secure too. In upshot there has to be some set of interpretations

---

[2] 'Reason and ritual', *Philosophy*, 1968, reprinted in B. Wilson (ed), *Rationality* (Blackwell, Oxford, 1970) and in A. Ryan (ed.), *The Philosophy of Social Explanation* (Oxford University Press, Oxford, 1973); also 'The limits of irrationality', *European Journal of Sociology*, 1967, reprinted in Wilson, *Rationality*.

whose correctness is more likely than that of any later interpretation which conflicts with it. The set consists of what a rational man cannot fail to believe in simple perceptual situations, organized by rules of coherent judgement, which a rational man cannot fail to subscribe to. All interpretation thus rests on rationality assumptions, which must succeed at the bridgehead and which can be modified at later stages only by interpretations which do not sabotage the bridgehead.

To take the last paragraph more slowly, consider the case where the enquirer and his subjects speak different languages. To be justified in claiming that beliefs expressed in the source language are those held by speakers of the target language, the enquirer must be justified in his translations. For instance it must be more likely that 'Das Gras ist grün' means 'The grass is green' and that S believes the grass is green than that it means something else incompatible with this but expressing what S actually believes. Sometimes, however, S will express what he does not in fact believe, for instance when he is confused, secretive, polite or deceitful. Here it has to emerge as more likely that 'Die Königin ist wunderschön' means 'The Queen is marvellous' and that S does not believe it than that it means something which S does believe. This option is open sometimes, only if it is not open always. If the enquirer is to strike a balance of probabilities for the translation of 'q', there must be some 'p' of which he cannot report: 'I know what 'p' means but I do not know whether S believes 'p'.' Here 'p' belongs to the bridgehead. If 'Das Gras ist grün' is an example, and if, *per impossibile*, S in fact believed the grass to be red, the translation would still have to be 'The grass is green' and the enquirer would have to emerge convinced that S believed the grass to be green. For, whatever particular divergences can be absorbed, translation depends ultimately on insisting that S would say in the enquirer's language what the enquirer does say.

What is *per impossibile* here is not – or not without long argument – that S might see as red what the enquirer sees as green. It is, rather, the idea that translation can occur without there being the same facts of the world described in the two languages. Equally the moral is not so much that there is a single, objective and neutral world as that translation needs to presuppose one. Whether or not the world is a fact, it is an indispensable presupposition. If expressions from two languages are to be rightly equated, any conditions for one meaning what it does in its language are conditions for the other in its language. Conditions for meaning should not, in general, be confused with conditions for reference; but, in the special case of defining without interdefining, understanding relies on a species of naming.

That the case is both special and crucial can be seen by asking how the enquirer can ascribe false and irrational beliefs to S. No doubt there are other options to try first – that S is lying, for example, or has unobvious but good reasons for the belief – but sometimes there is nothing else for it. Now the enquirer must decide whether it is likelier that S is at fault or that the translation is. He can never come down in favour of the translation, unless he is sure of other translations, embodying identifications of other beliefs. It is crucial then that meanings can sometimes be established by ascribing true and rational beliefs. Such 'bridgehead' cases are, however special, since otherwise false and irrational beliefs could not be ascribed at all. Falsity and irrationality need to be *prima facie* but not conclusive evidence against a translation.

The conclusion, which I shall draw in the end, is that some beliefs are universal among mankind. There are, because there have to be, percepts and concepts shared by all who can understand each other, together with judgements which all would make and rules of judgement which all subscribe to. If understanding is to be possible, there must be, in Strawson's phrase, 'a massive central core of human thinking which has no history'.[3] But the conclusion will come better after the next two sections and it is enough for the moment that good sense is prior to bad. If Impartiality is a refusal to distinguish good sense from bad, it leaves us without reason for preferring one translation to other. In ascribing beliefs, we must be able to start by discerning the true and rational and to end with the false and irrational.

SYMMETRY AND EXPLANATION

The strong programme seems to me wholly wrong about symmetry and I shall contend that true and rational beliefs need one sort of explanation, false and irrational beliefs another. The intermediate cases – false and rational, true and irrational – will be taken up at the end, with non-rational beliefs ruled out altogether.

That there is some asymmetry seems patent, offhand. In one of

[3] D.P.F. Strawson, *Individuals* (Methuen, London, 1959), p. 10.

James Thurber's *Fables for Our Time* a man finds a unicorn browsing among the tulips in his garden.[4] He informs his wife, who, remarking with scorn that the unicorn is a mythical beast, summons the police and a psychiatrist, to have him certified. She tells them what he said and they ask him to confirm it. 'Of course not,' he replies, 'the unicorn is a mythical beast.' So they shut her up in an institution and the man lives happily ever after. It seems patent that the truth of the various beliefs makes all the difference. If there actually was a unicorn in the garden, his belief is not certifiable. If he actually said that there was, her belief that he did needs no psychiatrist to explain it. The psychiatrist intervenes only where beliefs are false or irrational. A strong programme which contests this patent asymmetry can surely be convicted of rot?

When we try to generalize the story, however, we find little to embarrass the strong programme. No doubt there are obvious facts of experience whose denial is a sign of mental disorder. But it is not true in general that beliefs about reality refer to the obvious contents of an independent realm. So, if we build on an apparent asymmetry for obvious commonsense, we would pay for it, when we came to beliefs whose objects were not obvious or of some other character. What of the beliefs of those engaged in Mathematics, Natural Philosophy and Natural Religion? I think it is important to treat these engagements as continuous with everyday life and certainly not as peculiar in the ontological status of their objects of reference. Otherwise a bridgehead in commonsense will be no basis for advance. It would be an exaggeration to say that all beliefs express the holders' understanding of reality. But those which do are the enquirer's road into unknown territory.

It might seem that my line relies on there being facts of the world independent of all theory. If so, a proof of the theory-dependence of facts might count in favour of the strong programme and against making appeal to objective judgements. (It might also, incidentally, subvert the kind of objective Causality which the Causality clause asserts.) But, to my mind, nothing said about a bridgehead forces me to settle the question of theory-dependence and it does not spoil Thurber's story, if unicorns and tulips are theory-dependent. The

---

[4] 'The Unicorn in the Garden', also reprinted in *The Thurber Carnival* (Hamish Hamilton, London, 1945 and Penguin Books, Harmondsworth, 1975).

world, I said carefully, is an overlap rather than a fact. Presumably a strong programme is not intended to make it a matter of indifference whether to send for a psychiatrist or a zoo-keeper. So there is a distinction of reality from illusion, which the programme needs as much as anyone. When I argue later that the programme ends with the social destruction of reality, it will not be because it insists on the theory-dependence of facts. I see no threat, therefore, from treating commonsense beliefs as easy cases for whatever method is appropriate in general, rather than as a theory-free starting-point.

The asymmetry in explanation, which I claim to detect, stems from elsewhere. It arises because beliefs are woven into a system by actors' beliefs about their beliefs. These are the actors' own reasons for belief and so their own explanations of why they believe what they do. Schematically someone, who cites p as his reason for believing q, believes not only p and q but also that p is good enough reason to believe q. One of the enquirer's tasks is to discover these connections, not merely because his list of actors' beliefs will be incomplete without them, but also because his list must add up to a system. But he must also produce his own explanation of why the actors believe what they believe. In doing so, he cannot fail to endorse or reject the actors' own reasons or, where the actors are not of one mind, to side with some against others. I shall argue next that endorsing and rejecting are not symmetrical.

Suppose a disciple of C. B. Macpherson is investigating the thought of Thomas Hobbes and (uncontentiously) ascribes these four beliefs to the author of *Leviathan*:

(1) that men are best served by absolute government;
(2) that (1) can be established, granted an essential egoism in men;
(3) that men are truly egoists in the sense required;
(4) that Hobbes believed (1) because he believed (2) and (3).

Now suppose that the disciple himself explains Hobbes' belief in absolute government by reference not only to *Leviathan* but also to a prevalent ideology of possessive individualism. He presents Hobbes as the voice of a new bourgeoisie, frustrated under existing government and well suited by Hobbes' ideas. This is not yet to say that these factors are meant to explain the text itself, rather than its acceptance by some readers and rejection by others. But, to keep the example short and neat, suppose they are also meant to explain why *Leviathan* reaches its famous conclusions. There are now two explanations and, however their relation is treated, asymmetry emerges.

At first sight the two explanations conflict, Hobbes claiming to have given sufficient reason to any rational person and the enquirer claiming a further element. If so, the citing of the social context is a criticism of the text. It says, in effect, either that Hobbes' conclusion cannot be reached from his premises or that the premises are at fault. For, to grant that Hobbes knowingly had sufficient reasons for the conclusions is to admit (4) that Hobbes believed (1) because he believed (2) and (3). In other words, it is to endorse Hobbes' own account. A rival explanation has to lock on to a flaw in the text; otherwise it is merely a wrong explanation. In so far as the actors' reasons are good reasons, they explain what the actor takes them to explain. A rival explanation is confined to what is defective in the actor's own. All depends on what the enquirer endorses or rejects and the results are asymmetrical.

But does a strong programme offer rival explanations? It does not always do so. For instance the occasion for writing *Leviathan* may lie uncontentiously in the social history of the period and, in general, there is much to say about the fact of ideas without touching the actors' view of their merit. But a strong programme is not just a set of platitudes. It proposes a contentious theory of the relation between context and belief. The theory purports to explain belief (and utterance) and is thus committed to a contentious view of human identity and agency. Imprecise though it may be, it is certainly not shared by all actors. Indeed it is not fully shared by any, except for those who happen to subscribe fully to the programme. So (almost) every actor would reject some beliefs held by the enquirer. The enquirer cannot fail to reject some beliefs of any actor who rejects some beliefs of the enquirer. Nor can the enquirer pretend not to judge, out of respect for the actor. The only way for the enquirer to respect actors' beliefs which imply that the enquirer is wrong is to treat those beliefs as false (or else to abandon the programme). Thus, in so far as social context yields even a supplementary explanation of the actors' system, the enquirer is no more by-passing the actors' account than he would be if the actors had explicitly considered and rejected the enquirer's account.

Those unconvinced by the last paragraph may perhaps be relying on one of two (tempting but incompatible) notions of rationality in belief. One is that rationality is a purely formal property, solely to do with the relation between premises and conclusion. If so, the enquirer seems to have his by-pass, partly because no one holds beliefs solely because they are coherent and partly because actors and enquirer can all hold coherent beliefs. But, I reply, the enquirer is also interested in intellectual disagreements among actors. Such disputes are rarely battles in formal logic. They concern the content of the belief-system and what, in context, it is rational to accept. Coherence comes into them but so also do other tests of sound judgement. For instance a historian of science will distinguish not only between the beliefs of Copernicans and Ptolemeans but also between leaders and the hacks within each camp.[5] The reasons earlier requiring more than tests of coherence in order to establish a bridgehead apply also to establishing the contents of any belief system. The actors' own notion of rationality in belief involves more than coherence and that fact alone should suffice to establish that judgement cannot be confined merely to the actor's passage from premises to conclusion.

The same fact also invites us to adopt another notion of rationality, a contextual one. There seems plainly to be a relativity about what counts as a good reason for belief among different groups. If so, the enquirer has his by-pass, because he makes no judgement on these different rules of the game. To say that a reason is good in its context is not to endorse it; and thus the enquirer can arrive at a system of beliefs (rather than a mere list) without passing judgement. But, I reply, the enquirer must still decide what is *explanandum* and what is *explanans*. Which, for example, is the fact that Hobbes could cite the bulk of *Leviathan* as good reason for the conclusions? If *explanans*, then the beliefs of his critics, who rejected his conclusions, must be explained in some other way. If *explanandum*, then there is no need to explain why the critics disagreed. Even if rationality is somehow relative to context, the enquirer still has to decide which of conflicting beliefs are rational in their context. He still has to endorse or reject the actors' claims to be rational men.

Weber's recipe for the writing of history bids us ask what it would have been rational for an actor to do and then, when needed, to explain why he did not do it. Where the actor did the rational thing because it was the rational thing, that ends that particular question. The recipe works equally well for a contextual notion of rationality, provided that it is not confused with a subjective notion which would guarantee vacuously that all actors were always rational. There is no risk of that, where actors in the same context differ in what they believe and in their

---

[5] John Dunn kindly pointed this out to me.

own explanations of their own beliefs. Admitedly the historian will not always know what would have been rational, neither absolutely nor even in context. But in that case he must lay his bets. He does so by issuing probable explanations, subject to revision. In issuing an explanation, he is in effect comparing the rationality of discrepant actors with reference to his own reckoning of what would have been rational. In revising it, he is redistributing marks either between himself and the actors or among the actors. He need not claim to be omniscient but he cannot avoid laying bets and this need stands, whether the notion of rationality involved is absolute or contextual.

In sum a strong programme is forced into judging between itself and the actors. The scope of enquirer's explanations, which conflict with an actor's own, either is or is not limited by how rationally the actor holds his beliefs. If it is, then the actor's own explanation stands, when it passes a test of rational criticism and falls when it does not; and there is asymmetry. If it is not, then the actor's own explanation stands when, for good reason or bad, it coincides with the enquirer's and falls when it does not; and there is again asymmetry. Asymetry results not from imposing an absolute notion of rationality but from the fact that actors justify their own beliefs to themselves in ways which often conflict with the metaphysics of a strong programme.

None of this puts the sociology of knowledge out of business. Where beliefs are not rationally held, there is scope for the usual structural accounts. More to the point, even where beliefs are rational, there are further questions to ask about social conditions. Why, for instance, was Holland a centre of scientific advance in the seventeenth century? There are, no doubt, social conditions favourable to the spread of knowledge and it is a valuable task to unearth them. I insist only that they differ relevantly from conditions which favour the spread of ignorance. There is not just one study, the spread of belief, treated as if it were like the spread of anthrax; and the enquirer must not only see the actors' world from within but also judge it. There can be a sociology of knowledge as well as a sociology of ignorance. But, while the social conditions of intellectual failure explain the failure, those of intellectual success do not explain why beliefs are held.

REFLEXIVITY AND RELATIVISM

I come, finally, to the promised fiasco, the social destruction of reality. There is an old paradox about a strong programme. If there is to be the same impartial and symmetrical style of explanation for all beliefs, it should, presumably, apply to the beliefs of those who advocate a strong programme. Yet these beliefs lay claim to a scientific status, which the programme dare not forfeit and dare not assert, since both would subvert the programme. The paradox, I hasten to add, has never stopped the sociology of knowledge in its tracks. Just as Hume saw nothing self-referentially absurd in the scientific reduction of science to custom and imagination, so too the traditional discipline has refused to blush for its canons of objectivity. But, equally, the traditional discipline has not included Reflexivity.

The reason, no doubt, is that older approaches relied on a stout distinction between relationalism and relativism. Relationalism merely introduces a notion akin to perspective. Just as the perceptual character of an object can be said to depend on perspective without impugning the objectivity of the relations involved, so too the sociologist was credited with a bird's-eye view of beliefs, social facts and the causal relations between them. Admittedly critics were not slow to complain that a bird's-eye view is strictly for the birds, since there is nowhere for a free-floating intelligence to perch in discerning these objective relations. But sociologists of knowledge were unselfconscious about making a perch for Reason, so that first-order accounts would not self-destruct at the second-order. In any event, this attitude illustrates the previous section. The beliefs of the sociologist were exempt from the general search for social causes of belief, because they were warranted by Reason. That is a nice example of asymmetry.

The recent addition of Reflexivity, however, is not prompted just by honesty. Older approaches are strongly deterministic. Even if the social world is identified from within the actors' consciousness, it is explained from without and the actors have no initiative. The Durkheimian version is not materialist; yet there the important fact about norms is less than they are internal to all actors collectively than that they are external to each. That evocative phrase 'the social construction of reality' refers to a deterministic process whereby things collectively defined as real are real in their consequences. Self-reference is an embarrassment, not a selling-point. Recently, however, the sociology of knowledge has been harnessed to a search for an action sociology. Here 'the social construction of reality' refers to human handiwork. The actors create social, indeed perhaps all, facts. The social world is both seen from within and explained from within. When a strong programme is harnessed to this sort of view of social life, it cannot avoid reflexivity and relativism, even if it wished.

Nor does it wish. The upshot of Impartiality and Symmetry is to insist that the actors' beliefs are always rational, when properly understood. This is guaranteed partly by making the criteria for rational belief relative to the conceptual scheme and social context in which they occur, and partly by making reality whatever a social group who share a conceptual scheme take to be real. Belief is rational, if it is a legitimate interpretation of experience and legitimacy is a matter of coherence and consensus. The same applies to scientific beliefs, which can be studied in the sociology of science. So science, including sociology, is taken off the gold standard of truth and treated as a floating currency – or, rather, truth drops out and is replaced with a guaranteed rationality. The treatment meted out to Natural Religion earlier is extended to Mathematics and Natural Philosphy.

Old and new approaches coexist and our four-point strong programme does not decide between them. The difference lies in whether social constructions determine individual consciousness, with the actors' striving after rational order a matter of their adjusting their beliefs to what they are expected to believe, or whether norms and collective representations are the outcome of negotiations among rational actors. Either way there will need to be more said about the meaning and implications of the Causality clause. But, for reasons of space, I confine myself to Reflexivity, in the context of an actionist sociology of knowledge. Here Reason is dethroned but not abandoned. The idea is to treat rationality as variable and to make it an axiom of method that the social world is always rational from within. The sociology of knowledge becomes the study of internally rational social transactions. It is in many ways a liberating development but I fear that it spreads a dry rot too vicious for anyone's comfort.

The snag is that there are now too many ways of making the actors' world rational from within. It is not as if the ascription of belief and desire were at least constrained by given criteria of rationality. For the dethroning of Reason must make it a contingent matter what criteria are in use among what groups of actors. Nor is it still as if there were objective furniture of the social (or indeed of the natural) world. Now the furniture is accessible only through the actors' beliefs and can therefore be constituted in whatever way helps the final account hang together. Both ontology and epistemology are relative to shared belief and, in principle, variable without constraint, beyond that of overall coherence. Since the criteria of coherence are themselves included in epistemology, it ought to follow, that there are no constraints at all. Indeed it does follow, I maintain, and only failure of nerve stops anyone who has gone this far drawing the conclusion. Moreover, since other cultures are, epistemologically, merely a case of Other Minds, there will no longer be any constraint on any interpretation of one person's beliefs and desires by another. What set off as an insight into the construction of social objects ends as the sceptical destruction of reality.

I can myself see only two ways of stopping the rot. One is to retrieve the given, to restore the independence of facts, to let there be at least an independent and objective natural world. With the present state of upheaval in the philosophy of natural science, this is easier said than done; but the reasons for wanting to attempt it are patent. Even if it can be done for the natural world, however, there is still a generic difficulty for the interpretation of belief. Behaviourism aside, there is no easy way round the 'double hermeneutic', which arises when the objects of study are themselves interpretations. Whether or not there is a veil of perception, there is assuredly a veil of thought. So I myself accept the reasons for refusing a social ontology independent of human beliefs and wish to retain some thesis about the construction of social reality. But the 'bridgehead' argument still stands and the need for it arose just because not enough was given in perception to set standards of judgement for choosing between rival understandings of systems of belief. Empiricism cannot now be smuggled back in.

The other way, then, is to place an *a priori* constraint on what a rational man can believe about his world. On transcendentalist grounds there has to be that 'massive central core of human thinking which has no history' and it has to be one which embodies the only kind of rational thinking there can be. The 'massive central core' cannot be an empirical hypothesis, liable in principle to be falsified in the variety of human cultures but luckily in fact upheld. Otherwise, as Sextus Empiricus remarked in ancient praise of scepticism, 'In order to decide the dispute which has arisen about the criterion, we must first possess an accepted criterion by which we shall be able to judge the dispute; and in order to possess an accepted criterion, the dispute about the criterion must first be decided.'[6] To escape Sextus, the

---

[6] *Outlines of Pyrrhonism*, II.e.xx (Loeb edition).

existence of a core must be taken as a precondition of the possibility of understanding beliefs. There has to be an epistemological unity of mankind.

The plain snag here is that such reflections yield at most an existence proof. What has to be in the core? Notoriously not everything which Kant said about the categories of human thought has remained intact. Not only does the core not include all categorial thinking (since, indisputably, cultures do vary in their ways of categorizing experience) but there is also a distinction between what must be universal and what merely is universal (in the sense that, although it is not found only in some cultures, it might be). It is tempting to respond by making the core all form and no content, by assigning to it only the formal properties of coherent belief, and leaving all particular beliefs about what there is to empirical enquiry. But this line of division between the necessary and the contingent does not give enough to stop the rot. The enquirer needs a guarantee in advance that the actors' world makes basic sense to both enquirer and actors. The guarantee is expressed in the proposition that men are rational. It has to go beyond the assertion that the rational man makes rational inferences from the unvarnished news supplied by the senses. For, even if there is such news, it brings with it neither categories nor principles of categorial organization. Hence the plain snag remains. Without specifying the core, I cannot make this paper cogent. But neither can I make it short. So I simply enter a plea for metaphysics.

Meanwhile there are still the false-but-rational and true-but-irrational. I have argued that the sociology of knowledge must distinguish the true-and-rational from the false-and-irrational. Without the former there is no entry into a system of beliefs and the actors' world cannot be seen from within. Without the latter, there is no accounting for intellectual change. Thus the sociology of knowledge advocated here starts with beliefs which are held for the good reason that they are true and advances by identifying beliefs which are held for the fairly good reason that others are true. It is then ready to deal with beliefs held for the indifferent reason that others are held. Thence it enters the realm of beliefs held when there was better reason not to hold them; and a fresh form of explanation is needed. With false beliefs irrationally held the divorce between identification and explanation is complete; they are identified on the pretence that they are true and rational and explained in the recognition that they are neither. The two missing classes thus require a mixed explanation, from within to the degree to which they resemble one ideal type and from without for the rest.

If there are to be two forms of explanation for beliefs, I must state the scope of each. Explanation from within is complete where the actor believes because he knows. Explanation from without is residual. The size of the residue varies from case to case, with the restriction that the explanation must not overturn the identification of the belief explained. Mixed cases are those where the actor has incomplete reasons and the two forms of explanation coexist. Epistemologically, this makes correct explanation a function of the enquirer's omniscient judgement and I wish to forestall the obvious objection that enquirers are human. Methodologically, the enquirer is trying to strike a balance of probability between rival interpretations. Since he is fallible, he can only give his own reasons for his balance and must be ready to revise in the face of better reasons. But he has to stake his judgement and, epistemologically, this requires a reference to objective truth. Without one, there is no balance to strike.

By way of summary, I revert to the four points of the original strong programme. The Causality clause must be amended to allow causation both ways but its troubles go deeper. It relies on a distinction between social and intellectual which I cannot endorse and is fatally silent about the nature of social agency. All might be well in the end on a determinist reading of the social construction of reality. But the livelier enterprise of shaping the sociology of knowledge in the service of displaying the social world as a human construction depends on making actors for the most part rational. This sets a larger question mark over Causality than I have had space for. The Impartiality clause makes the identification of beliefs impossible and I suggest that the sociology of knowledge needs to pass epistemic judgements, although it remains true that all beliefs are grist to its mill. The Symmetry clause yields to a wholly crucial asymmetry, with one kind of explanation for the true-and-rational, another for the false-and-irrational, and mixed explanation for the mixed cases. With Reason restored, the Reflexivity clause is no longer an embarrassment and the social destruction of reality is off the agenda. In all I urge an account of social knowledge and social action which pivots on the concept of rationality and takes the side of judgement against that of charity.

Martin Hollis

This is an old but, I hope, durable line and the nub of it was well put by Vico two centuries ago:

> There must in the nature of human institutions be a mental language common to all nations, which uniformly grasps the substance of things feasible in human social life and expresses it with as many diverse modifications as these same things may have diverse aspects.[7]

There must indeed!

---

[7] *New Science*, sec. II ('On Elements'), para. 161.

Rationality

Charles Taylor

I

What do we mean by rationality? We often tend to reach for a characterization in formal terms. Rationality can be seen as logical consistency, for instance. We can call someone irrational who affirms both p and not-p. By extension, someone who acts flagrantly in violation of his own interests, or of his own avowed objectives, can be considered irrational.

This can be seen as a possible extension of the case of logical inconsistency, because we are imputing to this agent end E, and we throw in the principle: who wills the end wills the means. And then we see him acting to prevent means M from eventuating, acting as it were on the maxim: let me prevent M. Once you spell it out, this makes a formal inconsistency.

Can we then understand the irrationality in terms of the notion of inconsistency? It might appear so for the following reason: the mere fact of having E as an end and acting to prevent M isn't sufficient to convict the agent of irrationality. He might not realize that the correct description of his end was 'E'; he might not know that M was the indispensable means; he might not know that what he was now doing was incompatible with M. In short, he has to know, in some sense, that he is frustrating his own goals, before we are ready to call him irrational. Of course, the knowledge we attribute to him may be of a rather special kind. He may be unable or unwilling to acknowledge the contradiction; but in this case, our imputation of irrationality depends on our attributing unconscious knowledge to him.

Thus logical inconsistency may seem the core of our concept of irrationality, because we think of the person who acts irrationally as having the wherewithal to formulate the maxims of his action and objectives which are in contradiction with each other.

Possibly inconsistency is enough to explain the accusations of irrationality that we bandy around in our civilization. But our concept of rationality is richer. And this we can see when we consider the issue that many of us have been raising in this book: are there standards of rationality which are valid across cultures? Can we claim that for instance, peoples of a pre-scientific culture, who believe, let's say, in witchcraft or magic, are less rational than we are? Or at least that their beliefs are less rational?

This is the question discussed by Peter Winch in his celebrated article 'Understanding a primitive society'.[1] He takes as the basis of his discussion Evans-Pritchard's study of witchcraft among the Azande, and he vigorously rebuts the suggestion that we can condemn Azande beliefs about witchcraft and oracles as irrational.

One might think that this imputation was pretty hard to rebut when Evans-Pritchard seems to catch Azande in what looks like a flagrant contradiction. Post-mortem examination of a suspect's intestines can reveal or fail to reveal 'witchcraft substance', and hence show conclusively that he was/wasn't a witch. Now this belief, together with beliefs about the inheritance of witchcraft, ought to make the test sufficient to show that all members of the suspect's clan were/were not witches. A very few post-mortem results scattered among the clans ought to settle the question for everyone for all time. But the Azande apparently do not draw this conclusion. They go on treating the question as an open one, whether X or Y is a witch. Are they irrational?

Winch argues against this conclusion. The above just shows that the Azande are engaged in a quite different language game: 'Zande notions of witchcraft do not constitute a theoretical system in terms of which Azande try to gain a quasi-scientific understanding of the world.'[2] So it is a misunderstanding to try to press Zande thought to a contradiction here.

I can't help feeling that this answer is insufficient as it stands. Even if the Azande are not interested in building a theoretical understanding of the world, it surely matters to them if their whole system for imputing witch status lands them in a contradiction. Their whole practice seems to imply that there is very much a fact of the matter whether X is a witch, and it is this which would seem to be threatened

---

[1] P. Winch, 'Understanding a primitive society', *American Philosophical Quarterly*, 1 (1964), pp. 307–24.
[2] Ibid., p. 315.

if the criteria were to yield contradictory results.

But in fact the Azande were probably quite justified on their own terms in brushing off Evans-Pritchard's objections. If one wanted to derive a theoretical defence from what is implicit in their judgements and practice, it might not be hard to do so. One might say something of the kind: witch power is mysterious; it doesn't operate according to the exceptionless laws that you Europeans take as the basis of what you call science. But only if you assume this does the contradiction arise.

But of course, no such answer was forthcoming. And here we come to what is perhaps the crucial difference for our question between Zande society and ours: we have this activity of theoretical understanding which seems to have no counterpart among them.

What is theoretical understanding? The term goes back, of course, to the Greek expression which we translate as 'contemplation' (theōria). And however far the modern usage has strayed from the original, there is a continuity. This consists in the fact that a theoretical understanding aims at a disengaged perspective. We are not trying to understand things merely as they impinge on us, or are relevant to the purposes we are pursuing, but rather grasp them as they are, outside the immediate perspective of our goals and desires and activities. This is not to say that a theory may not have a big pay-off in practical or productive terms; nor even that the motivation for engaging in theoretical enquiry may not be this expected pay-off. But it remains the case that the understanding itself is framed in terms of a broader perspective, and it gives us a picture of reality which is not simply valid in the context of our goals. The paradox of modern scientific practice is the discovery that such detached understanding has a much higher eventual pay-off.

The original idea of 'contemplation' carried the sense of this disengaged perspective; and although there has been a battle in our civilization as to what this entailed, and most notably a sharp discontinuity in the scientific revolution of the seventeenth century, about which more below, we are still recognizably the heirs of those who coined this Greek term. This kind of activity implies two connected things: that we come to distinguish this disengaged perspective from our ordinary stances of engagement, and that one values it as offering a higher – or in some sense superior – view of reality. We don't find these things in every culture, and this makes for an immense difference in the things we think and say.

Now theoretical understanding is related to rationality, since the beginning of our intellectual culture. The Greek word we translate as 'reason' is of course *logos*, which has a large range of related meanings, including 'word', 'speech', 'account' as well as 'reason'. Reason is taken by both Plato and Aristotle as a condition of really knowing something.

For Plato in the *Republic*, to have real knowledge of something (*epistēmē*) is to be able to 'give an account' of it (*logon didōnai*). This seems to involve being able to *say* clearly what the matter in question is. Rational understanding is linked to articulation.

This offers a possible interpretation of 'rational' which we might see as very important in our tradition: we have a rational grasp of something when we can *articulate* it, that means, distinguish and lay out the different features of the matter in perspicuous order. This is involved when we try to formulate things in language, which is why the Greek philosophical vocabulary marks this inner connection between speech and reason, even though at the time not very much was made of language itself as an object of philosophical enquiry.

But if this is so, then theory and rationality are connected. The best articulation of something is what lays it out in the most perspicuous order. But for those matters amenable to theoretical understanding, the most perspicuous order will be that from the disengaged perspective. This offers a broader, more comprehensive grasp on things. Thus one might say: the demands of rationality are to go for theoretical understanding where this is possible.

We have to add this last rider, because not everything may be amenable to theory. For instance, Aristotle thought that moral matters were not, in which he saw himself as disagreeing with Plato. But it may be possible to be more or less rational in these matters as well, as indeed Aristotle believed we could be. There may be a kind of perspicuous articulation which can't be theoretical, e.g. because disengagement doesn't make sense here as a demand, but attaining which constitutes being rational.

But the connection between rational and theoretical is none the less close, if theoretical understanding is the most rational kind in its field, even if it isn't the whole of rationality.

I think that we who live in a theoretical culture tend to find some view of this kind plausible. And so we are tempted to judge other, atheoretical cultures as *ipso facto* less rational. This is quite a distinct question from finding them contradictory or inconsistent.

Indeed, the above understanding of rationality can show how consistency can be a key criterion, without exhausting the force of the term. To strive for rationality is to be engaged in articulation, in finding the appropriate formulations. But it is a standard intrinsic to the activity of formulating that the formulations be consistent. Nothing is clearly articulated with contradictory formulations (unless one wants to claim that being is itself subject to contradiction, a view which has well-known defenders). So consistency is plainly a necessary condition of rationality.

But within the context of our theoretical culture, there are more than these formal criteria of rationality. Someone who flagrantly violates the canons of theoretical discourse (or what are understood to be such), while claiming to talk about things and describe how things are, seems also to be sinning against rationality. Of course, if the agent concerned is a member of our culture, we can interpret this as contradictory behaviour. For we assume that one among us who opens his mouth to describe understands his own activity as falling under the appropriate canons; to violate them is to frustrate his own ends.

But the judgement of irrationality, or at least of lesser rationality, doesn't depend on contradiction. For we are tempted to judge as less rational members of atheoretical cultures who plainly don't accept our canons – or at least may not, for it may not be at first sight as plain as all that what canons they do accept.

This brings us back to the Azande. We can't jump to the conclusion that they're irrational on the grounds that we have caught them in a contradiction which they persist in disregarding; but this is not because they are playing some language game in which contradiction doesn't matter. There may be such, but I find it hard to see how witchcraft imputation could be one. Rather it is plausible that the apparent contradictions could be ironed out if the peculiar nature of witches and witchcraft were to be given theoretical description. We already have a hint of this in the Azande sense that it all adds up somehow, which must underlie their unconcern when Evans-Pritchard points to the seeming contradictions. But of course, they are quite uninterested in working this out for Evans-Pritchard or anyone else, as might the members of some theoretical culture – the kind of thing that some of our cleverest ancestors did who went along with the witch craze of early modern Europe. (And some of the intellectual techniques are already in evidence in Zande in attempts to explain inconsistent poison oracle results.)

But their very disinterest creates an imputation of lesser rationality in our minds. From our point of view, we feel like saying of them that they aren't interested in how things really are, outside how things function for them in their world of social practices. They aren't interested in justifying what they say and believe from this broader perspective; from which perspective, were they to adopt it, we believe that some of their central tenets would collapse (and perhaps even from inner contradiction in some cases).

This is the imputation which Winch rejects, on the grounds, if I can put it my way, that it is wrong to judge an atheoretical culture by the standards of a theoretical one. And wrong in the sense of being a mistake, though there is undoubtedly some arrogance involved here as well. The activities engaged in are different, and it would be wrong to assess them in the same way.

Others have argued that this thesis of incommensurable activities is wrong-headed, and that the problem of rationality can't be side-stepped in this way. This is the issue I would like to take up. Thus Winch in the article quoted above goes on to take Alasdair MacIntyre to task for claiming to be able to apply standards of rationality cross-culturally. This would allow us to judge in certain cases that the practices of another culture were deficient in rationality relative to the analogous ones in our culture; and the practices of witchcraft would be a paradigm target for this kind of judgement.

Winch argues against this that standards of rationality may differ from culture to culture; and that we have to beware of applying our standards for a foreign practice where they may be entirely inappropriate. What lies behind the difference in standards of rationality is the difference in activities. Something quite different is probably afoot in a primitive society's practice of magic. There has been a tendency among modern Western thinkers to understand magic as a kind of proto-technology, an early attempt to get control over nature by less effective means than scientifically-informed technique. The primitive practice naturally suffers from the comparison, and can even be made to look irrational in its resistance to refutation by the standards of modern science.

Sir James Frazer offers the classical formulation of a view of this kind. And although his Victorian confidence in his categories now seems to us flat-footedly ethnocentric, it is not entirely clear that we manage to avoid more sophisticated variants of the same basic error. So Winch seems to argue here: 'MacIntyre criticizes, justly, Sir James Frazer for having imposed the image of his own culture on more primitive ones; but that is exactly what MacIntyre himself is doing here.'[3]

We should consider more seriously the possibility that we have quite failed to understand what the point of the activity is. Zande magic may not be just 'a (misguided) technique for producing consumer goods'.[4] Rather the rites may constitute a 'form of expression' through which the possibilities and dangers inherent in life 'may be contemplated and reflected on – and perhaps also thereby transformed and deepened'. The rites 'express an attitude to contingencies', while at the same time 'they are also fundamental to social relations'.

The judgement of lesser rationality seems to be based on a misunderstanding. It is not just itself mistaken; it is based on an approach which will never allow us to achieve an adequate account of the foreign society studied. The very nature of human action requires that we understand it, at least initially, in its own terms; that means that we understand the descriptions that it bears for the agents. It is only because we have failed to do that that we can fall into the fatal error of assimilating foreign practices to our own familiar ones.

Now I am attracted by this Winchian argument, but I think there is something still inadequate about it as it stands. Somehow the contrast doesn't quite come off. It may sound convincing that the Azande are among other things 'expressing an attitude to contingencies' in their magical rites. But can we say that they are doing this *as against* trying to control certain of these contingencies? It would seem not. And Winch himself makes this point: the rites have a relation to consumption; they are undertaken to make the crops grow free of the hazards that threaten them. Winch's thesis is that they *also* have this other dimension which he stresses.

That is why the position Winch criticizes always will have a certain plausibility. We can all too easily find analogies between primitive magical practices and some of our own, because they *do* overlap. Thus a lot of what Robin Horton says in his 'African traditional thought and Western science'[5] concerning the analogies between African religious thinking and Western scientific theory is very convincing: both bring unity out of diversity, place things in a wider causal context, and so on.

But this is beside the point which is really at issue. Only if the claim

[3] Ibid., p. 319.
[4] Ibid., p. 321.
[5] In R. Wilson (ed.), *Rationality* (Blackwell, Oxford, 1970), pp. 131–71.

were that primitive religion and magic comprised a set of activities clearly distinct from and contrasted to those involved in modern science would the very useful and illuminating points of the kind made by Horton constitute a valid objection. Sometimes people who inveigh against ethnocentric interpretations sound as though they're making a claim of this kind. For instance, J. Beattie ('On understanding ritual')[6] distinguishes practical from symbolic or expressive activity, and argues that we ought to understand ritual mainly as concerned with the second.

But to make this kind of clear contrast is, paradoxically, to be insufficiently radical in our critique of ethnocentricity. For it describes the difference between the two societies in terms of a contrast between activities that makes sense to us in virtue of our form of life, but would be unintelligible to the people whose form of life we are trying to understand. It is a feature of our civilization that we have developed a practice of scientific research and its technological application from which the symbolic and expressive dimensions have been to a great extent purged. The seventeenth-century revolution in scientific thought rejected previously dominant scientific languages in which what one can call an expressive dimension had an important part. This was the case, for instance, with the language of 'correspondences', in which elements in different domains of being could be thought to correspond to each other in virtue of embodying the same principle.

We have an example of this kind of thinking in a passage like the following, which is an early seventeenth-century 'refutation' of Galileo's discovery of the moons of Jupiter:

> There are seven windows given to animals in the domicile of the head, through which the air is admitted to the tabernacle of the body, to enlighten, to warm and to nourish it. What are these parts of the microcosmos: Two nostrils, two eyes, two ears and a mouth. So in the heavens, as in a macrocosmos, there are two favourable stars, two unpropitious, two luminaries, and Mercury undecided and indifferent. From this and from many other similarities in nature, such as the seven metals, etc., which it were tedious to enumerate, we gather that the number of planets is necesarily seven.[7]

[6] In Wilson, *Rationality*, pp. 240–68.
[7] S. Warhaft (ed.), *Francis Bacon: A Selection of his Works* (Toronto, 1965), p. 17.

The argument seems ludicrous to us today, and we are likely to remember the scene in Berthold Brecht's *Galileo,* where the Paduan philosophers refuse to look through his telescope, preferring to show by argument from Aristotle that the moons couldn't be there. What could be more irrational from our point of view?

But of course the argument would make sense if we could be confident that the world order was actually put together in such a way as to embody the same set of principles in its different domains: just as when we enter an airline washroom and see 'No Smoking', 'Ne pas fumer', and some inscription in Japanese, we feel entitled to suppose that any account of how those letter marks got there would have to incorporate some reference to the speech act of instructing users to refrain from smoking.

But why should people feel confident of this? I think we can understand this if we reach back into the past of our own civilization, to which after all this kind of reasoning belongs, and note the quite different boundaries that were then drawn between activities: why must the universe exhibit some meaningful order, in terms of which the contours of the parts could be explained? I think this becomes understandable if we see understanding the universe and coming into attunement with it as inseparable activities.

To see what this might involve, let's look at one of the interpretations of Plato which was extremely influential in the development of the mode of thought which underlies the above passage. Presented over-simply, we could say that it gives us a view of man as a rational animal; and rationality as the capacity to grasp the order of being. To say that man is a rational animal is to say that this is his telos, the goal he implicitly is directed towards by nature. To achieve it is to attain happiness and well-being. Not to have attained it, or worse, not even to be endeavouring to do so, is to be in misery and confusion. There must be confusion, because properly understood our nature can only turn us towards our proper goal. To know it is to love it; consequently, to have anything else as a goal is to have imperfect knowledge of our own nature, and hence of the order of things of which it is a part.

But then there is a close connection between understanding the order of things and being in attunement with it. We don't understand the order of things without understanding our place in it, because we are part of this order. And we cannot understand the order and our place in it without loving it, without seeing its goodness, which is what I want to call being in attunement with it. Not being in attunement with it is a sufficient condition of not understanding it, for anyone who genuinely understands must love it; and not understanding it is incompatible with being in attunement with it, since this presupposes understanding.

For anyone with this outlook there is a strong temptation to believe in a meaningful order, or at any rate an order of things such that it could be loved, seen to be good, an order with which we could be attuned. If this were not the case, then there couldn't be a kind of understanding inseparable from attunement; and this seems to threaten the close connection between understanding the world and the wisdom of self-knowledge and self-reconciliation. Those who see the world-order purely in terms of accident and chance are not thereby led to love it more or to be happier with themselves; and this means they must be wrong, if knowlege and wisdom are closely linked.

I am not here trying to reconstruct an *argument* of an influential pre-modern tradition of thought, let alone of Plato's. I am just trying to point to a close connection between a certain view of the universe as meaningful order and a conception of the close link between understanding and attunement, or knowledge and wisdom. These stand in a relation of mutual support. And if one stands inside an *epistēmē*, to use Foucault's term, which links them together, it becomes not at all strained or unnatural to argue along the lines of the above passage.

I may seem to have wandered a bit far in discussing a controversy three centuries old, but all this relates closely to the main issue. For first it allows us to see how the breaking of the connection between understanding and attunement was an essential part of the modern revolution in science.[8] The conception of the universe as meaningful order, as a possible object of attunement, was seen as a projection, a comforting illusion which stood in the way of scientific knowledge.

[8] This is in important ways an oversimplification. It can be argued that one of the motives of the rejection of the conception of the universe as meaningful order was theological. This can be seen to some extent in Bacon's language – his talk of 'Idols' for instance, – or with Mersenne. As was already evident earlier with nominalist thinkers in the later Middle Ages, some saw a conception of the universe as self-justifying order as incompatible with the sovereignty and transcendence of the creator. To see reality 'without superstition or imposture, error or confusion', in Bacon's phrase (*Novum Organum*, Book I, CXXIX), was to help to put oneself back in tune with *God*. But this meant dissolving the identity between scientific understanding of the world and wisdom.

Science could only be carried on by a kind of ascesis, where we discipline ourselves to register the way things are without regard to the meanings they might have for us.

And this discipline has become central to the norms and practice of modern science. Our civilization is full of admonitions to avoid the facile path of projecting on to the world the order of things which we find satisfying or meaningful or flattering, with criticism for those who follow this, and much self-congratulation on the part of those who believe they don't. We are given early and often the edifying stories of Darwin or Freud, who had the courage to face truths allegedly shattering to our comforting images of cosmic hierarchy and our place in it, and they are sometimes placed in a Trinity with Copernicus (or Galileo) for this reason.

So it comes quite naturally to us to distinguish sharply between scientific study of reality and its accompanying technological spin-off, on one hand, and symbolic activity in which we try to come to terms with the world on the other. This kind of contrast is one that has developed out of our form of life. But exactly for this reason, it is probably going to be unhelpful in understanding people who are very different from us. It certainly wouldn't help to say, for instance, that ritual practices in some primitive society were to be understood simply as symbolic, that is, as being exclusively directed at attunement and not at all at practical control; or that the body of religious beliefs was merely expressive of certain attitudes to the contingencies of life, and not also concerned with giving an account of how things are. To this kind of position (if anyone really holds it), arguments like those of Horton are a sufficient answer.

But it is still insufficiently helpful to say something to the effect that ritual practices somehow combine the practical and the symbolic. This may not be flatly untrue, but it is putting the point in ethnocentric language. Somebody might try to combine the two in our civilization, and we could describe his attempt in these terms because we distinguish them clearly. But the point about quite different societies is that the question at least arises whether this distinction has any sense for them.

Here's where the example of the earlier phase of our civilization may help. Within the bounds of that *epistēmē* understanding and attunement cannot be separated. You can't know the order of things without loving it, nor the other way around. The very attempt to identify separate activities here, two different goals, would have to be based on a confusion. The difference between the two phases is not that they have made different selections or combinations out of the same catalogue of activities, but that their very catalogues are different and, what is more, incommensurable.

I use this latter term to point to the fact that the activities are not just different but incompatible in principle. Two activities are incompatible in practice when as a matter of fact you couldn't carry on both at the same time. This is a case for football and chess, for instance. The impossibility is merely *de facto*. We could imagine some incredibly athletic genius who could be figuring out how to put his opponent in check at the same time as he feints to get around the defence man and shoots for the goal. But when we come to soccer and rugby football, we have two activities which are incompatible in principle. For the rules which partly define these games prescribe actions in contradiction to each other. Picking up the ball and running with it is against the rules of soccer.

Something like this kind of relation holds between pre- and post-Galilean science. Giving an account in terms of the correspondences just isn't a valid move for modern science. Nothing has been accomplished which can be recognized as an explanation. Presented as an account of how things are, it's a 'foul', a violation of the canons of science. But plainly it was meant to be taken as just such an account. Galileo's opponents above were arguing that the moons of Jupiter couldn't exist on the basis of the order of things of which they would have to be a part. This would only make sense if the order explained how things are as they are. Because the order of things expressed by the correspondences is explanatory, we conclude that the number of planets *must* be seven. It is because we know what underlies and explains what is that we know what is.

Now the difficult thing about the relation of ritual magic in primitive societies to some of the practices of our society is that it is clearly not identical with any of our practices, nor is it simply different, as other of their practices – their games, for instance – might be. Rather they are incommensurable. They are different, yet they somehow occupy the same space.

If we focus just on the second aspect, at the expense of the first, we will see the primitive practice as the same as one of ours; and then we'll be tempted to judge it as inferior, perhaps irrational. And so to avoid ethnocentric arrogance, we may be tempted to seize on the first aspect and forget the second. But then we have just as false a picture, e.g., of practitioners of magic as engaged in an exercise of pure symbolic expression, rather as we do when we sing the national anthem. And *au fond*, we will probably still be guilty of ethnocentricity, since we will be projecting on to them one of the things *we* do, which *we* have distinguished from science or technology: this kind of pure symbolic activity, which isn't meant to *effect* anything, is a quintessentially modern thing.

The real challenge is to see the incommensurability, to come to understand how their range of possible activities, that is, the way in which they identify and distinguish activities, differs from ours. As Winch says, 'we do not initially have a category that looks at all like the Zande category of magic';[9] but this is not because their magic is concerned with ends quite foreign to our society, but rather because the ends defined in it cut across ours in disconcerting ways. Really overcoming ethnocentricity is being able to understand two incommensurable classifications.

What does this mean for our main issue, whether we can make judgements of rationality cross-culturally? Winch's argument seemed to be that such judgements were likely to be very dubious, because standards of rationality can differ greatly. And they differ because the activities concerned are different. But when we look at the key cases that interest us, like primitive magic, we find that the activities are not simply different, but rather that they are incommensurable. And this seems to be Winch's view too, because he is far from subscribing to the simple view that primitive magic is some purely expressive activity. If it were, we would already have a category for it, for *we* have lots of purely expressive rituals: singing anthems, striking the flag, etc.

But realizing this threatens to undermine Winch's conclusion. For incommensurable activities are rivals; their constitutive rules prescribe in contradiction to each other. Only where two activities are simply different is there no question of judging one to be an inferior version of the other, and perhaps in some cases inferior in rationality. That is what is tempting to the anti-imperialist liberal conscience, wary of ethnocentrism, in a view which assimilates magic to pure symbolic activity. It takes the heat off; we no longer have to judge whose way of life is superior. Or if any judgements are to be made, pre-technological societies seem to come off better because their symbolic activity is so much richer than ours.

[9] Winch, 'Understanding a primitive society', p. 319.

But incommensurable ways of life seem to raise the question insistently of who is right. It's hard to avoid this, since anyone seriously practising magic in our society would be considered to have lost his grip on reality, and if he continued impervious to counter-arguments, he would be thought less than fully rational. How do you keep this judgement from extending to the whole way of life in which magic fits?

One answer might be to argue that even though incommensurable, the activities still have their distinct internal criteria of success; that therefore each is bound to come off best by its own standards; and hence that one cannot make any non-ethnocentric judgements of relative superiority.

If I can be permitted to revert once more to my example comparing two phases of our theoretical culture, in order to cast light on comparisons between theoretical and atheoretical cultures, we can see what this would mean. The science of the High Renaissance which Galileo and others pulverized was concerned both with explaining how things are and with wisdom. The Renaissance sage had a different ideal from the modern scientific researcher's. From our point of view within this culture, we may want to argue that our science is clearly superior. We point to the tremendous technological spin-off it has generated in order to silence many doubters.

But a defender of relativism might retort that this begs the question. We are the ones who value technological control; so to us our way is clearly superior. But the sage didn't value this, but rather wisdom. And this seems to be a quality we're rather short of, and very often seem shortest of in precisely those societies where technological control is at its greatest. So we still don't seem to have a reason why a Renaissance sage, should one still exist, ought to listen to us. He would still be scoring higher by *his* criteria, even as we are by ours. Each would be invulnerable to the others.

Now as a matter of fact, this argument seems historically inaccurate, since many of the figures of high Renaissance sciences, like Giordano Bruno, for instance, or John Dee, seemed to have very far-reaching ambitions of technological achievement, of which producing gold out of baser metals is merely the most notorious. It is true that these achievements were also seen as having a spiritual dimension quite lacking in our modern goal of technological control, but that is just the standard difference between the two outlooks.

But this objection might seem of no great significance in principle, since there certainly were earlier phases of Western history in which the ideal of the sage had no close connections with that of the magus, or wonder-worker. The in-principle point about the impossibility of non-ethnocentric judgements of superiority would go through even though it might break down adventitiously in this case.

But the point in fact bites deeper. It is not just an accident that there are no more Renaissance magi among us. There is an inner connection between understanding the world and achieving technological control which rightly commands everyone's attention, and doesn't just justify our practices in our own eyes.

I realize I am running up against a widely held contemporary view. For instance, Mary Hesse in her 'Theory and value in the social sciences'[10] speaks of prediction and control as 'pragmatic' criteria – as though we could have chosen to assess our sciences by other ones! But I don't see how this could be. To make a really convincing rebuttal is probably beyond my powers in any circumstances, and certainly it is in the space I have here. But let me say a few things in defence of my view.

Our ordinary, pre-scientific understanding of the world around us is inseparable from an ability to make our way around in it, and deal with the things in it. That is why so much of our pre-scientific language identifies the objects surrounding us by their standard functions and uses in our lives. This goes, for instance, for our words for most of our artefacts, and for many of the distinctions we mark among natural objects – for instance, between the edible and the non-edible, and so on.

In these circumstances, it is difficult to understand how an increase in scientific knowledge beyond pre-scientific common sense could fail to offer potential recipes for more effective practice. Once we see what properties lie behind and explain edibility, how can we fail to notice that the distinction applies also in ways we hadn't suspected? Once we understand the principles underlying our ability to lift heavy objects in certain stances and not in others, viz., those of leverage, how can we fail to see that we can also apply them to lift objects with other objects? And so on. The basic point is that given the kind of beings we are, embodied and active in the world, and given the way that scientific knowledge extends and supersedes our ordinary understanding of things, it is impossible to see how it could fail to yield further and more far-reaching recipes for action.

[10] In C. Hookway and P. Pettit (eds), *Action and Interpretation* (Cambridge University Press, Cambridge, 1979), p. 2.

But further and more far-reaching recipes for action, when applied, are what we call increased technological control. And this means that the protagonist of modern science has an argument which the Renaissance magus must listen to. One can almost put it in the form of a *modus tollens:* there is no scientific advance without increased technological applicability; but in your case, we see no increased technological application; so you are making no advance. This is of course not a fully conclusive argument, among other reasons because we had to shift from 'applicability' to 'application' in moving from the first premise to the second. The opponent could retort that he wasn't concerned about these applications, unlike our degenerate consumer society, but that the recipes were being generated none the less. (Once again, I repeat that this unconcern was not in fact true of the magus, but this doesn't affect the argument.) But assuming that this loophole could be plugged, or at least the opponent placed under challenge to show what these recipes were, we have a *prima facie* convincing argument in favour of the superiority of modern science.

Of course, the argument could break out at another level, around in just what superiority had been proved. Certainly not in the way of life as a whole. Perhaps, after all, it's better all things considered to live as a Renaissance magus. But surely one could say that modern science represents a superior understanding of the universe, or if you like, the physical universe. Let's suppose even that the retort comes back, say from a Platonist, that the physical universe is hardly an important thing to understand, so why make all this fuss? We don't consider people who have collected a great deal of insignificant knowledge as being scientific tyros; for instance a man who knew how many flies there were in Oxfordshire. Surely we could then reply that Platonic reasons for finding this kind of knowledge without signficance are themselves belied by the success of our science. The realm of the material was meant to be that of the flux; the stable reality which can be grasped in truly universal propositions was supposed to lie beyond. But the very technological success of a science of the material based on general laws shows this view to be in serious need of revision.

In short, there is a definite respect in which modern science is superior to its Renaissance predecessor; and this is evident not in spite of but because of their incommensurability. The issue can be seen in this way. One view ties understanding nature to wisdom and attunement, the other dissociates them. In this they have incompatible norms. This is what makes the incommensurability. But precisely because they are not simply different, but are in principle incompatible, we can assess one as superior to the other. One can see, in this case, that the science which dissociates understanding and attunement achieves greater understanding at least of physical nature. And the interlocutor is forced to recognize that something has been achieved here which at least creates a presumption against him and in favour of the new science.

This is not to say that there is some common criterion by which one is proved inferior to the other, if that implies some criterion already accepted by both sides. The whole dimension of technological pay-off may have been profoundly depreciated and considered irrelevant, as it was in the Platonist tradition. But once a spectacular degree of technological control is achieved, it commands attention and demands explanation. The superiority of modern science is that it has a very simple explanation for this: that it has greatly advanced our understanding of the material world. It's not clear what traditional Platonism could say about this phenomenon, or where it could go for an explanation.

What we have here is not an antecedently accepted common criterion, but a facet of our activity – here the connection between scientific advance and technological pay-off – which remains implicit or unrecognized in earlier views, but which cannot be ignored once realized in practice. The very existence of the technological advance forces the issue. In this way, one set of practices can pose a challenge for an incommensurable interlocutor, not indeed in the language of this interlocutor, but in terms which the interlocutor cannot ignore. And out of this can arise valid transcultural judgements of superiority.

Of course, I must repeat, there is no such thing as a single argument proving *global* superiority. The dissociation of understanding of nature and attunement to the world has been very good for the former. Arguably it has been disastrous for the latter goal. Perhaps the critics are right who hold that we have been made progressively more estranged from ourselves and our world in technological civilization. Maybe this could even be shown as convincingly as the scientific superiority of moderns.[11]

But even if it were, it wouldn't refute this scientific superiority. It

[11] And certainly the natural science model dissociating understanding and attunement has wreaked havoc in its successive misapplications in the sciences of man in the last few centuries. But this again says nothing about its validity as an approach to inanimate nature.

would just mean that we now had two transcultural judgements of superiority; only unfortunately they would fall on different sides. We should be in a cruel dilemma when it came to choosing the proper human form of life. This may be really our predicament. Or it might be that we are superior in both respects. Or some third alternative might be the case. But wherever the final global verdict falls, it doesn't invalidate but rather depends on such transcultural judgements.

What does this mean for transcultural judgements of rationality between theoretical and atheoretical societies? It means, it seems to me, that such judgements can be made. They can arise precisely where there are incommensurabilities, such as between the set of beliefs underlying primitive magic, for instance, and modern science.

Both offer articulations, they lay out different features of the world and human action in some perspicuous order. In that, they are both involved in the kind of activity which I have argued is central to rationality. But one culture can surely lay claim to a higher, or fuller, or more effective rationality, if it is in a position to achieve a more perspicuous order than another.

It seems to me that a claim of this kind can be made by theoretical cultures over against atheoretical ones. If one protests and asks why the theoretical order is more perspicuous transculturally, granted the admitted difference between the aims of the activities compared, and granted that the two cultures identify and distinguish the activities differently, the answer is that at least in some respects theoretical cultures score successes which command the attention of atheoretical ones, and in fact invariably have done so when they met. A case in point is the immense technological successes of one particular theoretical culture, our modern scientific one.

Of course, this particular superiority commands attention in a quite non-theoretical way as well. We are reminded of the ditty about nineteenth-century British colonial forces in Africa: 'Whatever happens We have got The Gatling gun, And they have not.' But as I have argued above, technological superiority also commands attention for good intellectual reasons. And it is not only through Gatling guns that theoretical cultures have impressed others in time with their superiority, and hence become diffused. They were spreading well before the explosion of modern technology.

Once again, it may be that considerations which we in theoretical cultures can no longer appreciate so overweight the balance in favour of the pre-theoretical ones as to make them offer the overall superior form of life. But even if this were so, it wouldn't invalidate the transcultural comparisons we do make; and in particular the claim to a higher rationality. It would just overweight these judgements with other more important ones which told in the other direction.

What does this argument make of Winch's plurality of standards of rationality? In a sense, I entirely agree that we must speak of a plurality of standards. The discourse in which matters are articulated in different societies can be very different; as we can see in the Azande disinterest in explaining away the paradox Evans-Pritchard put to them in witchcraft diagnosis. The standards are different, because they belong to incommensurable activities. But where I want to disagree with Winch is in claiming that plurality doesn't rule out judgements of superiority. I think the kind of plurality we have here, between the incommensurable, precisely opens the door to such judgements.

But does this mean that I have to say Azande are irrational? This seems a foolish as well as an arrogant thing to say. And so it is, because we naturally make the difference between someone who is in violation of the basic standards governing articulation in his own culture, and people of another culture where the standards are different, even if inferior. The terms 'irrational' we reserve for the first kind of case. That is why I argued in the first section that inconsistency lies at the basis of most of the accusations of irrationality which we trade in our society.

But the concept of rationality is richer than this. Rationality involves more than avoiding inconsistency. What more is involved comes out in the different judgements we make when we compare incommensurable cultures and activities. These judgements take us beyond merely formal criteria of rationality, and points us toward the human activities of articulation which give the value of rationality its sense.

Relativism and the Possibility of Interpretation

W. Newton-Smith

I THE INCOHERENCE OF RELATIVISM

In recent years various historians, sociologists and philosophers of science have espoused relativism attracted in part by its apparent explanatory power. The relativist is impressed by the variation in belief and in reasoning from age to age and from social group to social group. This variation, the more extreme relativist tells us, arises from the fact that the differing ages or groups live in different worlds. Different things are true for them. That is why variation in belief is to be expected. Relativism has the additional attraction of appearing to be charitable. For instance, for a relativist there can be no question of negatively evaluating the capabilities of a primitive tribe to deal with the world – our world. They have their own world and can be imagined to be doing just as well with it on their own terms as we are doing with our world on our terms.

In this paper I argue that relativism is not a successful explanatory hypothesis. There is, of course, a problem in advancing this bold, negative claim without qualification. For relativists rarely make clear the content of their thesis. Consequently I begin by offering a formulation of the central relativist idea. It will be seen in the first section of this paper that on the formulation offered relativism is incoherent. In the second section of the paper I set this conclusion aside and examine the alleged explanatory force of relativism. It will be shown that not only does the thesis not explain anything, it generates puzzles and mysteries. Arguments unfortunately have to have premises and the conclusions of sections I and II depend on the viability of certain assumptions about meaning. It is assumed that the notion of meaning is legitimate and that however we analyse that notion it makes sense to talk of determinate translation (at least in certain contexts). If my arguments have force it should not be surprising that those who are hard on meaning (i.e. Quine or Hacking) will be soft on relativism. Consequently I explore in the third section of the paper the possibility of defending an interesting version of relativism given that one has abandoned a traditional approach to meaning. The most forceful recent attack on this tradition depends on Quine's thesis of the indeterminacy of translation. It will be shown that indeterminacy does entail a form of relativism. However, while the indeterminacy thesis generates a form of relativism which is at least not obviously incoherent, it deprives relativism of any explanatory force. Thus this version of relativism is one which undermines its attractiveness. Some who describe themselves as relativists have in mind weaker doctrines than considered in sections I, II and III. As an illustration of an attempt to develop a more muted relativism I consider in the final section, section IV, Hacking's relativism.

Relativist theses have been advanced in regard to truth, reason and ethics. This paper deals only with truth and reason, beginning with truth. The central relativist idea is that what is true for one tribe, social group or age might not be true for another tribe, social group or age. If that were so, it would appear to license one to talk about the different tribes, social groups or ages as inhabiting different world, as relativists have been notoriously prone to do. Schematically expressed the relativist thesis is:

something, s, is true for ψ and s is false for ϕ.

But what is the something? The trick is to find some one thing the truth of which can vary giving us an interesting version of relativism without lapsing into incoherence. Clearly it is just boring to take the something as a sentence. The sentence 'grass is good to smoke' is false in the ideolect of my farming friends in Wales but true in the ideolect of some communes in my neighbourhood. We can understand how this happens and while the Welsh hill farmers and hippies live in different worlds they do not do so in any substantial metaphysical sense. The truth of a sentence depends on both what it means and on how the world is. A sentence can vary in truth-value from group to group in view of variation in the former without any variation in the latter. Alternatively one might say in the interest of avoiding triviality that it is propositions and not sentences that vary in truth-value. But this is to take the short road to incoherence. For propositions are individuated in terms of truth-conditions. It is just incoherent to suppose that the same proposition could be true in ψ and false in φ.

Since this is bound to seem too slick, it is instructive to pose the problem in a slightly different form. Suppose we encounter some social group, call them the Herns, who produce a sentence *s* in a context in which we would hold a sentence *s'* to be true. We may be saying the same thing as the Herns or we may be saying different but complementary things, or we may be saying incompatible things. We cannot adjudicate between these alternatives without a translation of *s* into our language. That is, we have to find a sentence of English which has the same meaning that *s* has in Hernish. It is a necessary (but not sufficient) condition of two sentences having the same meaning that they have the same truth-conditions. If *s''*, is a sentence which we hold to be the translation of *s*, then, *ex hypothesi* we are committed to saying that *s* has for them whatever truth-value *s''* has for us. If we hold *s''* to be false and they hold that *s* is true we are committed to saying that they are just plain mistaken. There is no question of coherently saying that *s* is true for them and its translation, *s''*, is false for us. Assuming it to be legitimate to employ a traditional concept of meaning and translation, what the relativist maintains as a possibility with regard to truth is no such a thing. It is just incoherent.

If we cannot be relativists about truth could we none the less be relativists about reason? Consider first deductive reasoning. *Prima facie* relativism about deductive reasoning is problematic. For given the close relationship between valid deductive inferences and tautologies, it is hard to see how there could be variation in patterns of valid reasoning if there cannot be variation in truth. For patterns of inference are representable by sentences which are logically true. In fact the best way to view logic is as the representation of truth-preserving transformations. This means that if truth cannot vary, neither can deductive logic.

It is instructive to ask what would ever justify us in construing the Herns as assenting to a claim which we would reject by appeal to logic. Consider the law of non-contradiction which has been much discussed in this context. Could the Herns have a system of reasoning in which it is legitimate to assert something which we would translate as being of the form '*p* and not-*p*'? If we are to have an interesting case we have to set aside situations in which this happens through stupidity or carelessness. We have also to exclude the case where a contradiction is articulated for ritualistic mystification as is done in the Christian church. The problem is: how could we justify the claim that we have a correct translation? The constraint on translation is that it be part of a successful attempt to explain the behaviour of the Herns. Thus ascribing to them a sincere, knowing belief in a contradiction is a dubious move. In fact it is worse than that. Suppose the Herns assert '*p* and not-*p*' but refuse, for instance, to assert '*q*' for arbitrary '*q*'. In which case they do not mean what we mean by 'and' and 'not'. For there are simple rules partly constitutive of the meaning of these terms that justify this inference. [1] Thus if they reject the consequence of asserting what we translate as '*p* and not-*p*' either they are too stupid to see this (in which case their assertion of '*p* and not-*p*' is no more interesting than assertions of that by very stupid people in our culture) or they do not mean what we mean by 'and' and 'not'. In this case they do not believe what we express by '*p* and not-*p*'. If on the other hand they do assert '*q*' for arbitrary '*q*', the situation is even worse. If they believe everything (i.e. any sentence and its negation) the task of explaining their behaviour by reference to their beliefs and goals is doomed. And, furthermore, it would be difficult to maintain that they were even asserting if they are so indiscriminate in the sentences they assent to. This argument does not show *a priori* that there can be no variation in logic across languages. My claim is only that the assumption of the invariance of logic is the best initial working hypothesis. The discussion of the law of non-contradiction illustrates that one cannot simply imagine another group rejecting a law we accept without imagining far-reaching differences between them and us. It is not *contradictions* which they accept unless they accept any arbitrary sentence. And if they do accept any arbitrary sentences then the translation which attributes to them the acceptableness of contradictions is in point of fact likely to preclude the possibility of finding any reasonable explanation of their behaviour. That in turn means we should explore translation schemes that do not involve attributing to them sincere and explicit beliefs in contradictions.

I have argued for the invariance of logic as a working hypothesis. But even if the argument is convincing the achievement is modest. For

---

[1] The proof is:

    (1) *p* and not-*p*.
    (2) Therefore, *p*.
    (3) Therefore, *p* or *q*.
    (4) Therefore, not-*p*. (from line 2)
    (5) Therefore, *q*. (from lines 3 and 4).

deductive logic is but a poor thing, being merely a tool for achieving consistency. Rationality requires more than consistency. It requires having good reasons for one's beliefs. If relativism held with regard to reason even if it failed with regard to truth and logic, this would be a victory for the Kingdom of Darkness. The relativist thesis about reasons can be schematically characterized as follows:

> R is a reason for holding that p is true for ψ while R is not a reason for holding that p is true for ϕ.

Obviously the relativist is not merely claiming that R is taken as a reason by, say, the Herns and not by us. He is claiming that R really is a reason for the Herns and is really not a reason for us. In considering this alleged possibility, care must be taken to avoid trivialization. For instance, care must be taken that the contexts are relevantly similar. Otherwise such cases as the following would count the relativism of reason. If someone says 'I promise' that is a reason for thinking that a promise has been made in some contexts. In others, such as play-acting or practising the declination of the verb 'promise', it is not.

Given that we are comparing relevantly similar contexts can reason vary with context? That fact that truth cannot vary across such contexts precludes the possibility that reason should vary. R is a reason for believing that p just in case there is an appropriate truth linking R and p. That my typewriter case looks white to me is a reason for thinking that it is white just because things that look white in the sort of circumstances that obtain at the moment are or tend to be white. That the litmus paper has turned red is a reason for thinking that the liquid in which it has just been submerged is an acid just because it is true that acid causes litmus paper to turn red. That Jones smokes and has smoked for over twenty years at least forty cigarettes a day is a reason for thinking that he will get cancer just because it is true that those who do this generally get lung cancer. Whether R is conclusive reason for p or merely a fallible indicator of p, whether R is semantically or contingently connected to p it remains true that R is a reason for p just in case there is a truth of the appropriate kind linking R and p. Thus, if relativism about truth is incoherent, relativism about reason is incoherent.

Having accused the relativist of making an elementary error the onus is on me to explain how this has come about. To this end consider as a case of an apparently relativity of reason the early seventeenth-century 'refutation' of Galileo's discovery of the moons of Jupiter discussed by Taylor in this volume. In the passage quoted, that there are seven 'windows' of the head is cited as a reason for thinking that there are seven planets. This is so remote from what we would regard as a reason for a hypothesis about the number of planets that it is tempting to make a relativistic move. We are disinclined to regard it as a simple mistake for we do not see how anyone would even take it seriously as a candidate for being a reason. The relativist appears to explain the difference from us of those who took it as reason without condemning them as irrational. For, he says, this is a reason for them. That is the difference between them and us. They have not made a simple mistake, they simply operate with a system in which different things are reasons.

This relativistic move has only the appearance of being an explanation. For the substantive question remains: what is it about them and us that gives rise to different things being reasons? Not only is the relativist move only apparently explanatory, it is methodologically deficient. For a relativist orientation inclines one to assume all too easily that there is some brute intractable difference between ourselves and other social groups and ages. A non-relativist will probe deeper. In the particular case being considered he will find a web of belief which renders the particular claim intelligible to us. God created a harmonious universe. Harmony involves a mirroring of man and cosmos. Hence facts about men can be reasons for hypotheses about the cosmos. The difference between them and us is seen on reflection not to be so extreme. We can see that if these conditions did obtain, that there were seven 'windows' would be a reason for thinking there were exactly seven planets. The difference between them and us is not a difference in what is a reason for something but a difference as to whether the conditions in question obtain. This fact which I will call the *conditionalization of reason* shows the reason is not relative and explains why it can appear to be so. We should not simply assume that different things are reasons for others. We should consider their web of belief. We are likely to find that difference is explicable in terms of difference in beliefs about what conditions actually obtain. This means that if we shared their beliefs about what conditions obtained we would tend to share their beliefs about which beliefs are reasons for which beliefs. That is, we are assuming that there is a similarity in how we reason about beliefs. On the relativist alternative we assume diversity at two levels: beliefs about the world and beliefs about the relation between beliefs. And methodologically this is not promising. For the greater the difference we posit between us and them, the greater will be the difficulty in rendering their behaviour intelligible. Assuming that their non-deductive reasoning processes are similar to ours is likely to be the most fruitful starting-point for constructing a theory which is explanatory of their behaviour.

Taylor uses the example discussed above to illustrate what he calls 'incommensurable activities'; that is, activities the constitutive rules of which preclude one from simultaneously participating in both. The incommensurability, Taylor argues, raises the question of which is superior, a question which is problematic since there may be no criterion of success common to both activities. According to Taylor the pre-Galileans were involved in the activity of both understanding the world (i.e. discovering truths about it) and becoming attuned to it. However, even for us to describe the activity in this way is to give a distorted account of it. For the distinction between understanding and attunement which we make could not be drawn in their form of life. A similar point is made by Taylor about descriptions of the behaviour of primitive tribes as symbolic. The sense of 'symbolic' discourse for us depends on the contrast with literal fact-stating discourse. Since this distinction is not drawn in the form of life of the tribe the description is distorting. It might seem then that the articulation of a non-relativist thesis about truth commits one to giving a distorted account of those groups in regard to which it is articulated. For the articulation of that thesis depends on distinctions we draw that the groups in question may not draw. However, the relativist is himself guilty of this distortion. For he describes the tribe as using truth-claiming discourse and then gives a particular construal of the notion of truth involved. In view of Taylor's argument a careful anti-relativist should formulate his claim as follows: in so far as it is reasonable to describe the discourse of a group in terms of a notion of truth-claiming, the notion of truth cannot be construed relativistically. Thus the non-relativist can give content to his thesis even granting Taylor's claim that there are 'incommensurable activities'. One should also note that relativistic theses have been advanced with regard to groups involved in the same activity, in which case Taylor's notion of 'incommensurable activities' does not apply. For instance, Kuhn's claim[2] that scientists with

---

[2] T.S. Kuhn, *The Structure of Scientific Revolutions* (University of Chicago Press, Chicago, 1970), 2nd ed, p. xxx.

different paradigms live in different worlds is meant to apply to twentieth-century physicists and Bloor[3] has advanced relativistic claims about mathematics over the last two centuries.

II RELATIVISM AND THE POSSIBILITY OF INTERPRETATION

It is unseemly to dismiss ideas of great longevity with nothing more than a brisk *reductio ad absurdum* argument. What is more, it is dialectically ineffectual. One's opponent is likely to remain unconvinced, muttering that there is some mistake, he knows not what, in the argument. A fully satisfactory treatment must uncover what makes relativism attractive. Having done so it must show why relativism cannot deliver these apparently attractive goods. The relativist hypothesis is a genuine explanation only if it solves more puzzles than it creates. That it does this is not clear. For instance, consider the question of the construal of truth in the relativist thesis. If we assume a correspondence notion of truth, we get a plurality of worlds. One world to make each system of 'truths' true. These 'incompatible' worlds (remember that the sets of truths characterizing them are incompatible) all exist. What then is the relationship between them? An answer has not been forthcoming. We must beware of explanatory hypotheses that give rise to unanswerable questions. If on the other hand we construe truth in a coherence sense the situation is no less problematic. If truth just is a matter of membership of some internally coherent web of sentences why should there be any common core to beliefs? Even the most extreme relativist allows some invariance at the observational level. This means that the 'worlds' have parts in common. Just how the divergent parts are relative to one another is no small mystery. It is massively implausible to suppose (and no relativist does suppose) that there is not a common observational core of perception and belief. But on a coherence construal, that there is this common core is totally mysterious. This argument is not meant to be a knock-down *reductio ad absurdum*. It is designed only to show that *prima facie* the thesis is a bad bet from the explanatory point of view because of its puzzle-generating character. This might be compen-

[3] D. Bloor, *Knowledge and Social Imagery* (Routledge & Kegan Paul, London, 1976), ch. 5.

sated for if it explained anything. Unfortunately not only does it not explain, it excludes any explanation of human behavior as I show below.

It was argued that if translation of Hernish is possible, no substantial relativist thesis (applied to us and the Herns) is coherent. That is, the possibility of translation entails the falsehood of relativism. By contraposition, the truth of relativism entails the impossibility of translation. This result is to be expected. It is a necessary but not sufficient condition of a translation being correct that it match sentences with regard to truth-conditions. If truth becomes a mess, so does translation. One wonders what principles a relativist supposes do in fact govern translation. On what basis does he match sentences? Sameness of length? Sameness of sound? The fact that relativists do translate displays that they do not believe in their own thesis.

We can now see that relativism, far from being explanatory, actually precludes the possibility of rendering intelligible the behaviour of Herns. For if no translation is possible, we cannot ascribe particular beliefs and desires to them – excepting such beliefs (if any) and desires that we can properly ascribe to non-linguistic creatures. Hence we can neither describe their behaviour as constituting particular actions nor explain their actions as we standardly do by showing how beliefs and desires fit together to produce actions. In this argument it is not supposed that translation is a self-contained activity which we can undertake before turning to the description of beliefs and desires and the description of behaviour as action. Meaning, belief and action form a hermeneutical triangle. If translation lapses so does the ascription of beliefs and the explanation of behaviour in action terms.[4]

On the above picture of translation one will begin by hypothesizing a similarity between oneself and the Herns in regard to basic desires, low-level perceptual beliefs, and logic. If on this basis one is able to come up with a translation scheme which enables one to successfully predict Hern behaviour that will be evidence for both the translation and the initial assumption. Hollis in this volume writes as if the initial assumptions had an *a priori* status. All interpretations, according to him, rest on rationality assumptions consisting of 'what a rational man cannot fail to believe in simple perceptual situations, organized by

---

[4] For further discussion of the relation between meaning and belief see D. Davidson, 'Belief and the basis of meaning', *Synthese*, 27 (1974), pp. 309–23.

rules of coherent judgement which a rational man cannot fail to subscribe to', assumptions which have to be presupposed, not discovered. But there is no reason to elevate reasonable *a posteriori* conjectures into *a priori* presuppositions. We gain evidence for Hollis' 'bridgehead' by discovering that the theory of translation based on that conjectured bridgehead gives us a better predictive theory of Hern behaviour than any other theory. Hollis seems to think that there must be some privileged set of interpretations to be appealed to in obtaining evidence for and against other interpretations. If we were to assess each interpretation by reference to other interpretations there would indeed have to be some privileged interpretations to break what would otherwise be a circle of infinite regress. But the ultimate test of a particular interpretation is whether it is part of the overall scheme of translation and interpretation which has the greatest predictive power. The overall scheme gives evidence for each particular interpretation including those in Hollis' bridgehead.

Not only is relativism not explanatory, it is not charitable either. It started off with the aim of giving a charitable construal of the diversity of belief and in the end deprives the Herns of any beliefs at all. The relativist wants to stop us using 'philosophical B-52s' (Hacking's phrase) to read our truth, logic and rationality on to the Herns. In the end we cannot give them any truth, logic or rationality at all. It will not do for the relativist to take refuge in the thought that the Herns have language, beliefs and desires which we cannot get at. This is no more plausible than supposing that snails have beliefs, we know not which. His thesis was supposed to explain the diversity of beliefs. And by this desperate move he has withdrawn the claim that there is a diversity of belief.

Before turning to explore the possibility that relativism may be coherently explicated and rendered plausible within a Quinean framework, I want to guard against a possible misinterpretation. It is not claimed that relativists would be doomed as translators if they were abandoned on a South Sea island with the Herns. They would translate. They would match sentences via truth-conditions. But in so doing they would be acting on the assumption that their own relativist thesis was false. Further, in elaborating the consequence of not being able to translate I am drawing attention to the fact that they cannot set translation aside as something problematic for a relativist while going on to talk about beliefs and actions as if these notions would remain unproblematic.

III INDETERMINACY

To this juncture the argument depends crucially on certain old-fashioned assumptions about meaning. To wit, that is legitimate to employ a notion of meaning on which one can talk of sentences across language as being or not being the same in meaning and further that sameness of meaning requires (but is not exhausted by) sameness of truth-conditions. In this section I explore the consequences of treating meaning like phlogiston; that is, proscribing all use of it and its dependent cognates. The most reasoned attack on meaning is that of Quine. This depends on his thesis of the indeterminacy of translation and that generates a version of relativism that is at least not obviously incoherent. However, this route to relativism is an explanatory dead-end.

The thesis of indeterminacy is the combination of two theses. First, it presupposes the thesis of the *underdetermination of translation* (hereafter cited as *UT*). That is, it is claimed that with regard to, say, Hernish there will be more than one translation manual which fits equally well the behaviour of the Herns. That is, on any one of these manuals one will be able to predict equally well the linguistic and non-linguistic behaviour of the Herns. Secondly, it involves what I call the *thesis of the essential accessibility of facts* (hereafter cited as *TEAF*). That is, it is assumed that there is no content to the supposition that a matter of fact is at stake if there is no way in principle of getting at the supposed matter of fact.

Quine is a behaviourist. For him equal predictive power comes down to equal predictive power with regard to bodily movements (including linguistic behaviour). To avoid all the untenable assumptions involved in such crude behaviourism we can rephrase the thesis of the underdetermination of translation as follows. For any social group there will be more than one system of triads of meaning, belief and action (based on different translation manuals) all of which render the group's behaviour intelligible. On this underdetermination thesis this will remain so, no matter how much information we collect about the flora and fauna of Hern social life.

Putting these together we have, schematically, the following situation. Translation manual M_1 assigns to Hernish sentence H the English sentence S_1 and manual M_2 assigns S_2. Underdetermination means that there is no way of deciding which is the correct translation. (I assume for ease of exposition that there are only two manuals.) The traditionalist holds that there is a matter of fact at stake. That is, one of the sentences of English matches H in meaning and the other does not. Under the assumption of underdetermination the traditionalist holds that it is simply impossible to us to find out which matches H in meaning. But given the thesis of *TEAF* there is no content to talk of *the* meaning of H. Because there is no way of finding out what the meaning of H is, there is no content to the supposition that there is *the* meaning of H. This is the crux of the thesis of the *indeterminacy of translation* (hereafter cited as *IT*).

We cannot conclude from *IT* that relativism holds in the form considered in section I above. It is not that we have found a Hernish sentence which means what an English sentence means but differs in truth-conditions. We have found that there is nothing determinate said by a Hern. Each translation manual gives a different saying. This applies equally to speakers of English. If we use M_1 to translate a sentence of English S_1 into the Hernish sentence H, we can use M_2 to translate H into a different English sentence S_2. This permuting of English sentences means that I can treat you as meaning by S_1 what I think I mean by S_1 or as meaning what I think I mean by S_2. Since there is, *ex hypothesi* (under *IT*) no matter of fact at stake with regard to what you mean by S_1, you say nothing determinate in saying that S_1 is true.

Given *IT* we can no longer attach sense to how the Herns say the world is. There are different equally viable ways of construing their discourse which involve the ascriptions of different theories about the world. There is no fact of the matter at stake with regard to the question of which theory they believe. How the Herns describe the world is to be relativized to an ascription of meaning by us, an ascription which is ultimately arbitrary. Thus, *IT* gives rise to a kind of relativism. The relativism rejected as incoherent in section I was connected with extreme incommensurability. For that relativism meant that no translation was possible. This relativism gives rise to too many translations. There are too many ways of making things commensurable.

On what I called the traditional approach to meaning, translation involved matching sentences by reference to truth-conditions. Quine offers us a different conception of translation. Translation is a matter of matching sentences so as to maximize predictive power *vis-à-vis* Hern behaviour. Underdetermination means that there is no unique maximum. If we define translation in this way, we will find, according to Quine, equally good manuals, M_1 and M_2, one of which takes the Hernish sentence S into the English sentence S_1 and the other into the English sentence S_2 where S_1 and S_2 can have different truth-conditions. A Quinean framework with its different conception of translation offers some hope of articulating an interesting relativist thesis which is not obviously incoherent. If the relativist chooses not to follow Quine, the onus is on to him to articulate some third conception of translation if he is to avoid the incoherence involved in combining relativism with a traditional approach to meaning.

Is this relativism? The relativist picture with which we began and which was found to be incoherent was the picture of some things being true for one social group and false for another. On this picture the question as to who is right simply lapses: both parties are right on their own terms. Analogously, IT has the consequence that the question of what was really said lapses. Different translation manuals lead to the ascription of different sayings and there is no question (within the limits of UT) as to which translation manual is correct. Thus what is said is relativized to a manual.

The argument deployed does not show that every sentence of a language suffers from indeterminacy of meaning. For it might be that every viable translation manual from Hernish into English is in agreement on some sub-set of sentences of Hernish. Call this the *invariance set*. Sentences in the invariance set will say something determinate unlike those not in the set. If the invariance set were empty, nothing determinate about the world could be said in Hernish. To the extent that it is not, determinate things can be said. For Quine the invariance set is never empty. For Quine holds that there is a dichotomy between observation and theoretical language and that observational language always admits of determinate translation. Indeterminacy arises at the theoretical level.

Before turning to consider whether we should accept IT it will be fruitful to extend this notion of an invariance set from translation as a special type of theory to theories in general. Let T_1 and T_2 be two scientific theories. The invariance set of T_1 and T_2 is the (possibly empty) set of sentences the members of which are consequences of both T_1 and T_2. If T_1 and T_2 are theories underdetermined by the data, the observational consequences of the theories will be in the invariance set. At least some theoretical consequences will not be in the invariance set.

Why should we adopt IT? We have seen that it follows from UT and

TEAF. I have argued elsewhere that we should adopt *TEAF* and will not discuss that claim further in this paper.[5] Quine argues for *UT* on the basis of his claim that all theories are underdetermined by the data. Many have doubted the very intelligibility of this thesis. In the work referred to above I have argued that while it is intelligible and probably holds in some cases Quine has not shown that it holds for all theories. In what follows I will explore the consequences of adopting the thesis of underdetermination as a general hypothesis about theories. Let T_1 and T_2 be rival theories for some subject matter. Given *TEAF* we cannot adopt a realist conception of the sentences which are not in the invariance set for T_1 and T_2. That is, we cannot assume that there are facts about the world that makes these sentences true or false. To do so would be to admit the existence of facts which would, *ex hypothesi*, be inaccessible. Thus while we can be realist about the invariance class we will have to take an instrumentalist construal of the sentences not in this class.

A very limited instrumentalism would be harmless enough. However, the extent of indeterminancy of translation will be a function of the extent of underdetermination. That is, we cannot argue for the existence of a signficantly large set of sentences not in the invariance class in the case of translation except of the assumption of a significantly large set of sentences not in the invariance class of theories in general. This means that we will not get an exciting indeterminacy of translation thesis unless it is appropriate to adopt an extensive instrumentalism with regard to theories in general.

Extensive instrumentalism is extremely implausible as the following argument shows. The history of a mature science like physics is marked by an impressive increase in the predictive power of theories. Why is it that contemporary scientific theories are better in this regard than their predecessors? The best explanation of this phenomenon is the realist hypothesis that theories are capturing more and more theoretical truth about the world. On an instrumentalist construal of theories this increase in predictive power is simply a total mystery. This means that the hypothesis of massive underdetermination is not a good explanatory bet. For it precludes the possibility of offering an explanation of the phenomenon of increasing predictive power of scientific theories.[6]

---

[5] 'The underdeterminaton of theory by data', *Proceedings of the Aristotelian Society*, Suppl. Vol., 1978.
[6] This argument is developed in detail in my *The Rationality of Science*

The only way in which we have been able to give sense to relativism involves adopting a general framework within which the concept of meaning is jettisoned. Indeterminacy of translation provides such a framework. However, that framework, depending as it does on the underdetermination of theories, precludes the possibility of adopting a realist construal of scientific theories.[7] This means that we should not adopt the thesis of underdetermination as an explanatory hypothesis. Consequently we have to reject indeterminacy. Thus the sort of Quinian relativism we have been considering has nothing going for it as an explanatory hypothesis. In addition it lapses as an explanation of the phenomena that a sociologist or an anthropologist might actually meet. For their starting-point is the discovery of diversity of belief. But on the sort of relativism that comes out of *IT* there is no sense attached to any unqualified notion of diversity of belief, for that presupposes a notion of determinacy of translation. It does not say: they believe different things because they inhabit a different world, use a different logic and so forth. It says: what they believe is not determinate. Furthermore, the sense that Quine gives to diversity is a purely theoretical one and not a diversity that any anthropologist is actually going to meet. Thus that *IT* is true cannot be offered as an explanatory hypothesis to be invoked in the face of actual anthropological findings. The whole Quinean approach means that all propositions must be assessed in the way we think of science as assessing hypothesis (in terms of explanatory and predictive power). But on scientific grounds *UT* and *IT* have nothing going for them.

IV MUTED RELATIVISM

While truth and reason do not vary, something does; and Hacking has sought to give sense to a form of relativism by arguing that what can

---

(Routledge & Kegan Paul, London, 1981), ch. VIII.

[7] Quine has sought to maintain a realist conception of scientific theories notwithstanding underdetermination. However he has failed to give any convincing argument for admitting inaccessible facts in physics but not in translation. I have argued elsewhere that his own favoured response to underdetermination in the case of physics is in fact incompatible with realism and commits him to a form of relativism. See my 'Trans-theoretical truth without transcendent truth' in A. Koch (ed.), *Veroffentlichungen der Internationalen Hegel-Vereinigung* (1982, forthcoming).

vary from age to age or from social group to social group is the availability of propositions. That is, a proposition which is for us a candidate for being true or false may be a proposition which the Herns cannot even entertain. The reason for this, according to Hacking, is that the sense of a non-observational proposition is in part fixed by the style of reasoning used in relation to the proposition. Given that styles of reason change, as Hacking argues, one cannot grasp the sense of a sentence used in one style of reasoning without grasping the style of reasoning. Archimedes could not understand Herschel's sentence 'The heat which has the refrangibility of the red rays is occasioned by the light of those rays' unless he mastered the changes in styles of scientific reasoning.

I have described Hacking's relativism as muted. For he is not advancing the strong claim that there is no way, say, that Archimedes could have understood Herschel. The claim is the more modest one that in order to understand he has to grasp the style of reasoning. With this claim I do not dissent for it is a form of the general claim that evidence plays a role in the determination of sense. There is nothing particularly relativistic about this claim. However, Hacking then proceeds to give an account of styles of reasoning which generates an exciting relativism. Hacking's claim is that 'the propositions that are objectively found to be true are determined as true by styles of reasoning for which in principle there can be no external justification. A justification would be an independent way of showing that the style gets at the truth, but there is no characterization of the true over and above what is reached by the styles of reason itself' (this volume, p. 65).

Hacking considers whether one could offer a meta-reason to justify a style of reason by appeal, for example, to success. He notes that it could not be success in getting at the truth for that would be circular. He notes that there may be a possibility of non-circular truth-related criteria. It is not clear to me whether in the end Hacking thinks that there are external justifications for styles of reasoning. If he agrees that there is, then his exciting relativism lapses. And, agree he should for, as I argue below, there are in fact external justifications.

Let us agree with Hacking that some propositions have a sense partially determined by the style of reasoning associated with them. Hacking agrees that there are other propositions, the humble non-theoretical sort, the sense of which is largely independent of the style of reasoning. In this case we can avoid circularity in using success in assessing styles of reasoning if our criterion can be formulated in terms of those low-level propositions. Then it is in principle open to us to take each of the styles of reasoning considered by Hacking and look to their observational successes over time. Not only does this give us a style-independent way of assessing styles, but taken in conjunction with the arguments used above it gives us a reason for supposing that deliverances of successful styles have some truth in them. That is, as a bonus we have fallible indicators of truth which are independent of the actual style in which the propositions in question have their sense. Consequently we have to conclude that Hacking has failed to articulate a viable interesting form of relativism.

The full specification of a relativist thesis concerning truth and/or reason will involve a theory of meaning and translation. On a traditional approach to meaning there is no coherent thesis. A Quinean approach to meaning gives a version of relativism which is not obviously incoherent. However the framework within which the thesis is developed is one in which it has no explanatory power. For it in fact makes the entire scientific enterprise a mystery. One who is inclined to be relativistic will have to develop some yet different approach to meaning. Since the prospects for this are not promising he would be advised to gain what he can from Taylor's 'incommensurable activities' or Hacking's variation in 'styles of reasoning'. Interesting as these are they do not go any way to vindicating the relativistic picture of the world as a product of our language or culture.

Belief, Bias and Ideology

Jon Elster

An ideology is a set of beliefs of values that can be explained through the (non-cognitive) interest or position of some social group. I shall mainly discuss ideological beliefs, though at some points reference is also made to ideological value systems. Ideological beliefs belong to the more general class of biased beliefs, and the distinction between interest and position explanations corresponds to the more general distinction between distortion and illusion as forms of bias. In recent work in social psychology the distinction has also been captured by the opposition between 'hot' and 'cold' causation of beliefs, or between 'psychodynamics' and 'psychologic'.[1]

The goal of my essay is to provide micro-foundations for the Marxist theory of ideological belief. I believe that this theory is potentially of great importance, and that its underdeveloped state is mainly due to misguided notions of what kinds of evidence and explanation it requires. Some have been content to impute causal connection between beliefs and social structure on the basis of 'structural homologies', a solemn name for whatever arbitrary similarities the writer in question can think of.[2] Others have explained beliefs through their

I am grateful to G. A. Cohen and Martin Hollis for their comments on an earlier draft of this essay.

[1] For the first opposition, see R.P. Abelson, 'Computer simulation of hot cognition', in S. Tomkins and S. Messick (eds), *Computer Simulation of Personality* (Wiley, New York, 1963), pp. 277–98. For the second, see R. Nisbett and L. Ross, *Human Inference: Strategies and Shortcomings of Social Judgment* (Prentice-Hall, Englewood Cliffs, N.J., 1980), ch. 10.

[2] See J. Elster, *Leibniz et la Formation de l'Esprit Capitaliste* (Aubier-Montaigne, Paris, 1975), ch. 1, for a comment on the methodological problems of this structuralist approach to the history of ideas.

accordance with class interest, without pausing to define the terms (long-term or short-term interest? interest of the class members or of the class as a whole?) or to sketch plausible mechanisms by which the interests can bring about their own fulfilment. Against these approaches I would like to insist on the need for an understanding of the psychological mechanisms by which ideological beliefs are formed and entrenched. This in turn is part of a broader argument that Marxist theory will prove incapable of fruitful development without an explicit espousal of methodological individualism.[3]

I should briefly mention the two traditions that I draw most heavily on in the following pages. First, there is the recent work in cognitive psychology by Amos Tversky and others, recently and admirably synthetized by Richard Nisbett and Lee Ross. I shall have some critical remarks to offer on the more speculative of their arguments, but these do not detract from the solid achievements of their empirical work. These advocates of the 'cool' approach to irrational beliefs have set a standard for theoretical and experimental rigour that their 'hot' opponents should certainly try to emulate, even though by the nature of the case this may prove more difficult.

Secondly, I have learned much from some outstanding case studies in intellectual and political history. Joseph Levenson's analysis of China's confrontation with the West shows unforgettably how varied and subtle are the reactions of the human mind to a state of acute dissonance, in this case traditional Chinese assumption of superiority set on collision course with perceived military inferiority. And Paul Veyne's study of civic giving in classical antiquity argues convincingly that the subjects' ideological adaptation to their state of submission was endogenous, and not only did not require, but would have been incompatible with, deliberate ideological manipulation by the rulers. He thus provides a theoretical alternative to Gramsci's notion of hegemony that for a generation has dominated Marxist thought on the subject. In fact, Veyne's study offers a whole system of philosophical anthropology, inspired in approximately equal parts by Hegel, Focqueville and Festinger. As I have argued elsewhere, his is a path-breaking contribution to the theory of micro-foundations of political institutions that all social theorists henceforward ignore at their peril.[4]

---

[3] See my forthcoming 'Marxism, functionalism and game theory' *Theory and Society* (1982) for a more sustained argument to this effect.

[4] See J. Elster, 'Un historien devant l'irrationel: Lecture de Paul Veyne',

In the first part below, I sketch in broad outline a view of human irrationality, including irrational beliefs. In the second part I deal with the illusionary beliefs that are faulty because shaped by defective cognitive processes. The third part then looks at the distorted beliefs that arise when belief-formation is shaped by wants or preferences. The discussion is largely typological and conceptual, not because I do not value causal analysis, but because I believe there is a need to find out which way the grain runs before you cut.

I

It is generally agreed that in the genesis of human behaviour both beliefs and values (which I shall call interchangeably also desires, wants and preferences) are involved. I shall follow Donald Davidson and assume that beliefs and wants are causes of actions. This implies that action may be irrational in two cases: either it is caused in a wrong way by the desires and beliefs causing it, or it is caused by beliefs and desires that have themselves been caused in a wrong manner. Davidson has mostly studied the first variety of irrational behaviour.[5] Here I shall survey some mechanisms of the second kind, with the purpose of locating bias and ideology on the map of irrational mental phenomena.

Some cases of irrational formation of mental states are also formation of irrational mental states. In some cases, that is, we can tell from the desires and beliefs alone that they are irrational, without any need

Social Science Information, 19 (1980), 773–804, for an introduction to Veyne's thought. My 'Sour grapes', in A. K. Sen and B. Williams (eds), *Utilitarianism and Beyond* (Cambridge University Press, Cambridge 1982), is a companion-piece to the present essay, in which I attempt to spell out some of the broader implications of Veyne's theory of preference formation, paralleling the ideas offered here on belief formation.

[5] Thus weakness of will occurs when a reason is a cause of an action without being a reason for it: D. Davidson, 'How is weakness of the will possible?' in J. Feinberg (ed.), *Moral Concepts* (Oxford University Press, Oxford, 1969), pp. 93–113. Davidson also explains elsewhere how non-standard internal causal chains may lead to a reason causing the action for which it is a reason, but causing it in the wrong way: 'Freedom to act', in T. Honderich (ed.), *Essays on Freedom of Action* (Routledge & Kegan Paul, London, 1973), pp. 136–56.

to study their genesis. If there is such a thing as self-deception, it must be detectable independently of the past mental history, but this need not be the case for wishful thinking. Similarly, we can tell that intransitive preferences are irrational from their structure alone, but to be able to say the same about what I elsewhere have called adaptive preferences ('sour grapes')[6] we typically need to know how they were shaped. In this survey I am mainly concerned with beliefs that do not have irrationality written on them for all to read. I am concerned with beliefs that satisfy the Hintikka criterion for defensibility, i.e. beliefs such as there exists a possible world in which they are true and also believed.[7] In fact, the belief may be true in the actual world and still be irrational, if it is not well grounded in the available evidence. Even more important, they may be well grounded (false or true, it does not matter) and still be irrational, because shaped in an irrational way. This will prove of central importance in Part III.

I have distinguished between two varieties of mental states, cognitive and affective. Similarly we may distinguish between two ways in which irrational mental states may be brought about, by a faulty cognitive structure or by some affective drive. This gives us altogether four possibilities. Let me explain them through some examples, not intended to be exhaustive of the respective classes (which themselves are not thought to be exhaustive of the larger universe of irrational mental processes).[8]

Adaptive preference is the adjustment of wants to possibilities, not the deliberate adaptation favoured by Stoic, Spinozistic or Buddhist philosophy, but a causal process taking place 'behind the back' of the individual concerned. The driving force between such adaptation is the often intolerable tension and frustration ('cognitive dissonance') of

[6] See my 'Sour grapes'.

[7] J. Hintikka, *Knowledge and Belief* (Cornell University Press, Ithaca, N.Y., 1961). Why not simply say that a belief-system is consistent if there is some possible world in which it is true? Hintikka shows that the presence of higher-order beliefs imposes the need for a more complex criterion. See also Elster, *Logic and Society* (Wiley, Chichester, 1978), ch. 4.

[8] In particular, irrational emotions and their formation falls outside the scope of the present typology. For some comments on this intriguing problem see A. Rorty, 'Explaining the emotions', *Journal of Philosophy*, 75 (1978), pp. 139–61; and R. de Sousa, 'The rationality of emotions', in A. Rorty (ed.), *Explaining the Emotions* (University of California Press, Berkeley and Los Angeles, 1980), pp. 127–52.

having wants that one cannot possibly satisfy. I use the term 'drive' rather than 'desire' of this force, to convey that it is not a question of something that guides your choice, but of something that shapes what guides your choice.[9]

Preference change by framing means that the relative attractiveness of options change when the choice situation is reframed in a way that rationally should have no impact on the preferences. It has been extensively studied by Amos Tversky and Daniel Kahneman, who cite an example from L. J. Savage of 'a customer who is willing to add £X to the total cost of a new car to acquire a fancy car radio, but realizes that he would not be willing to add £X for the radio after purchasing the car at its regular price'. And the authors add: 'Many readers will recognize the temporary devaluation of money that makes new acquisitions unusually attractive in the context of buying a house.'[10] They refer to such phenomena as akin to perceptual illusions.

Wishful thinking is the shaping of beliefs by wants so as to produce a belief that a desired state actually obtains or will obtain. A desire for promotion may bring about the belief that promotion is imminent. Like adaptive preference formation this is a 'hot' rather than a 'cold' process, but unlike adaptive preference formation the end-result is a set of beliefs, not of desires.

Inferential error is the cold way to irrational beliefs. The varieties of such errors have been extensively surveyed by Nisbett and Ross, who conclude that the 'intuitive scientist' is prone to a depressingly large number of unfounded judgements and inferences stemming from defects in the cognitive apparatus. Such errors are like framing shifts in preferences with respect to their causes, and like wishful thinking with respect to their effects. A typical example is that 'an individual judged *very* likely to be a Republican but rather *unlikely* to be a lawyer

---

[9] Need I say that this is a nebulous and difficult opposition? The reality of, and the need for, some such distinction can be brought out by considering the case of 'counter-adaptive preferences', as when a person prefers living in Paris over London when in London and vice versa. Here there is a self-destructive *drive* that shapes the person's *desire* so that it is never satisfied. By contrast, it is harder to distinguish the drive from the desire when the drive is for the satisfaction of the desire. In my 'Sour grapes' I discuss some criteria that may help us distinguish drives from meta-desires.

[10] A. Tversky and D. Kahneman, 'The framing of decisions and the rationality of choice', *Science*, 1981. See also D. Kahneman and A. Tversky, 'Prospect theory', *Econometrica*, 47 (1979), p. 263–91.

would be judged *moderately* likely to be a *Republican lawyer*[11] as if the probabilities were additive and not multiplicative.

There is no need here to discuss the relative importance of cold versus hot factors in the formation of irrational desires and beliefs. Common sense tells us that both must be important, and science presumably will be able to tell us when the one or the other mechanism is at work. Let me make a polemical remark, however, that may bring out some important conceptual points. This remark is addressed to Nisbett and Ross, who argue that the hot motivational factors have been over-stressed in the analysis of bias, and the cold cognitive factors underestimated. Two of their arguments go as follows. First, they say that 'self-serving motivational factors need not be introduced to explain most of the fundamental inferential or judgmental biases discussed in this book. In fact, as we shall see, the erroneous judgements, predictions and causal assessments reached by the intuitive psychologist – far from being self-serving – often undermine self-esteem and limit the individual's capacity to satisfy personal needs'.[12] This I read as an argument that since beliefs shaped by interests typically also serve them, beliefs that undermine interests cannot have been shaped by them. But the premise of this inference is wrong, as I argue below. Beliefs born of passion tend to betray it, not to serve it.

Secondly, towards the end of the book the authors seem to recognize this fact, when they write that the '*costs* of willy-nilly distortions in perception are simply too high to make them a cure-all for the disappointed or threatened perceiver'.[13] But then, curiously, they seem to reverse their earlier reasoning and use this observation as an argument against the motivational theory of bias. They invoke in passing natural selection, which 'must surely deal harshly with such unrestrained subservience of reality to wishes'.[14] They do not, however, ask the analogous question about inferential error, except for some brief references to the idea that such error may be an inevitable by-product of rational meta-strategies for problem-solving.[15] What-

---

[11] Nisbet and Ross, *Human Inference*, p. 146.
[12] Ibid., p. 13.
[13] Ibid., p. 234.
[14] Ibid.
[15] The authors refer to A. Goldman, 'Epistemics: the regulative theory of cognition', *Journal of Philosophy*, 75 (1978), pp. 509–24; but the idea has been current among economists for some time. D. North actually argued that ideologies may be a rational response to the problem of costly information:

ever may be the value of this approach,[16] I cannot see why it might not work as well for such hot phenomena as self-deception and weakness of will.[17] There does not seem to be any difference between hot and cold errors in that (i) they are likely to get you into trouble, and (ii) that they may turn out to be lesser evils compared to the lack of the meta-strategies of which they are by-products.

Often, in a state of dissonance, there are two functionally equivalent ways of achieving consonance, by adaptive preferences or by wishful thinking. This is reflected in the way in which we talk about these phenomena. Thus in the original French version the fox disliked the grapes because they were too *green*, a perceptual distortion, not because they were too sour. Similarly, a well-known self-destructive mechanism is proverbially rendered either by 'Forbidden fruit is sweet' or by 'The grass is always greener on the other side of the fence'. The first achieves dissonance by changing the preferences, the second by changing the perception. In such cases the distinction between beliefs and values is tenuous. In other cases the two mechanisms, while equivalent, can be clearly distinguished from each other. Thus Levenson explains how the spectrum of Chinese reaction to Western superiority included both wishful thinking, through the belief that China could adopt Western techniques while retaining the Chinese essence; and 'sour grapes' through the argument that Western techniques were not worth having anyway, and that they in fact represented an option that China had rejected long ago.[18] In complex ideological phenomena the two strands of distorted beliefs and of adaptive preferences are nearly always found together, but we know little of the mechanisms that determine the relative importance of the one and the other. The

---

'Institutional change and economic growth', *Journal of Economic History*, 31 (1971), pp. 118–25.

[16] The idea obviously has some attractions, but it could be vindicated only by showing that the actual amount of error is close to the optimal one (i.e. part of an optimal package). And I cannot see how one could even make a start at this demonstration.

[17] Rorty offers an argument to this effect, relying on the idea that *habit* is the important feature of human life that both makes for integrity *and* for self-deception and weakness of will: 'Self-deception, akrasia and irrationality', *Social Science Information*, 19 (1980).

[18] J. Levenson, *Confucian China and its Modern Fate* (University of California Press, Berkeley and Los Angeles, 1968), vol. 1, ch. IV, and *passim*.

practical difference between the two is enormous, for through adaptive preference change some durable peace may be found, whereas wishful thinking more often than not only postpones the confrontation.

II

I first explore some of the modes of ideological thought that are due to cognitive sources: illusions that stem from the position of the observer in the social structure. Let me state at the outset the first of a series of negative propositions that form an important part of my argument:

> *First proposition:* There is no reason to suppose that beliefs shaped by a social position tend to serve the interests of the persons in that position.

In particular, ideas shaped by class position need not serve class interest. This insight is also formulated by Leszek Kolakowski:

> [When] Engels says that the Calvinistic theory of predestination was a religious expression of the fact that commercial success or bankruptcy does not depend on the businessman's intention but on economic forces, then, whether we agree with his statement or not, we must regard it as asserting a merely causal connection: for the idea of absolute dependence on an external power (viz. the market in the 'mystified' shape of Providence) does not seem to further the businessman's interest, but rather to set the seal on his impotence. [19]

The context shows the Kolakowski is not quite clear in his mind on this point, as he only makes a distinction between causal and teleological determination of beliefs, and not the further distinction between hot and cold causation. He seems to believe, wrongly in my opinion, that the phrases 'beliefs are caused by the interests of the class in question' and 'beliefs are what they are because of the situation of the class' are synonymous. In fact, the two distinctions between causal and teleological explanations of beliefs and between position and interest explanations cut across each other, giving a total of three

[19] L. Kolakowski, *Main Currents of Marxism* (Oxford University Press, 1978), vol. I, p. 342.

rather than two possible cases: causal position explanations, causal interest explanations and the teleological interest explanations (or functional, as I shall say here).

This ambiguity means that Kolakowski's observation could also be seen as an instance of my third proposition (Part III). But the example he cites from Engels clearly falls under the first proposition. The example is of interest also from a substantial point of view. It says, roughly, that agents in a competitive market tend to generalize the economic fact that their behaviour cannot influence prices, so as to believe that they are equally powerless with respect to non-material elements that are important to them. (Weber, on the other hand, stressed that his analysis of the relation between capitalism and Calvinism was valid only for the early stage of capitalism, when religion had to provide the element of compulsion that later was realized through the competitive market.)[20] a corollary would be that imperfectly competitive capitalism should foster an 'illusion of control', so that agents that are more than quantity-adjusting price-takers should also come to believe that their actions make a difference for their salvation. This may or may not be the case: it could be interesting to find out. More generally, perfect, imperfect and strategic markets might tend to develop, respectively, attitudes of dependence, control and interdependence that might be less justified in other arenas.

A particularly important case backing the first proposition is the tendency of the oppressed and exploited classes in a society to believe in the justice of the social order that oppresses them. This belief, perhaps, is mainly due to distortion, i.e. to such affective mechanisms as rationalization. But there is also an element of illusion, of bias stemming from purely cognitive sources. As brilliantly explained by Paul Veyne, it was obvious to any dependent man in classical antiquity that he owed his living and his security to his master: 'c'est à ce patron de droit divin que je dois de manger et d'exister, car que deviendrais-je, si lui-même n'existait pas, ni ce vaste domaine où je vis et dont il est le propriétaire?'[21] This may be called a micro-political illusion, corresponding to what Veyne elsewhere calls the micro-economic illusion

---

[20] M. Weber, 'Die protestantische Ethik und der Geist des Kapitalismus', in *Gesammelte Aufsätze zur Religionssoziologie* (Mohr, Tübingen, 1920), vol. I, p. 203. It might prove worth while to pursue this comparison between causal and functional theories of the relation between Calvinism and capitalism. See also Elster, *Leibniz*, ch. V.

[21] P. Veyne, *Le Pain et le Cirque* (Seuil, Paris, 1976), p. 554.

and which is the belief that the economic mechanisms that are valid for the individual, at the margin, also are valid for the whole.[22] Since I would be worse off without my master, it follows that a society without masters would be intolerable, for who would then provide employment and protection? A similar optical illusion may account for the theories that explain feudalism as a voluntary exchange between the serfs and the lord, the latter providing protection and receiving goods and labour services in return.[23] The illusion of a voluntary and rational arrangement disappears when one observes that the lord provided protection mainly against other lords, much as a gangster can justify his protection racket by pointing to the threat from rival gangsters. Feudalism may have been a Nash equilibrium, in the sense that for each agent feudal behaviour was optimal given that everybody else behaved feudally. But there may have been other Nash equilibria as well, and in any case a Nash equilibrium may well be severely suboptimal. And even a Pareto-optimal Nash equilibrium may be unjust on criteria of distributive justice.

The same illusion, I believe, underlies the neoclassical theory of exploitation under capitalism[24] and, more generally, all theories that argue that workers should be paid according to what each of them produces in circumstances that, logically, have no place for all of them. Neoclassical theory says that labour is not exploited if paid according to marginal product, i.e. if each worker is paid as if he were the last to be hired, or, more to the point, the first to be fired. With individual wage negotiations, each worker can be made to see himself in this light, but of course each cannot be the last. Similarly Marx argued that the capitalist could reap the profit from co-operation by paying each worker according to what he could make by himself before entering into co-operation with other workers:

> Being independent of each other, the labourers are isolated persons, who enter into relations with the capitalist, but not with

[22] Ibid., p. 148 ff. For the logical structure of this fallacy, see also Elster, *Logic and Society*, p. 97ff.

[23] D. North and R. Thomas, 'The rise and fall of the manorial system: a theoretical model', *Journal of Economic History*, 31 (1971).

[24] See, for a brief exposition and references, Elster, 'Exploring exploitation', *Journal of Peace Research*, 15 (1978), pp. 3–17.

[25] K. Marx, *Capital*, vol. I (1867) (International Publishers, New York), p. 333.

each other . . . Because [the productive power developed by the labourer when working in co-operation] costs capital nothing, and because, on the other hand, the labourer himself does not develop it before his labour belongs to capital, it appears as a power with which capital is endowed by Nature.[25]

These examples have shown that because of their place in the social and economic structure, the dependent, oppressed and exploited may have beliefs that do not serve their interests. But, correspondingly, these beliefs certainly serve the interests of their masters. And there is indeed an important strand in the theory of ideology that argues for a systematic correlation between the belief systems in a society and the interest of the ruling classes. Against this I advance my

Second proposition: There is no reason to suppose that beliefs shaped by a social position tend to serve the interest of the ruling or dominant group.

In particular, there is no reason to believe that ideas shaped by the position of the dominant class itself serve the interest of that class. The example from Engels cited by Kolakowski illustrates this point. Another example shows that the capitalist can fall victim to an optical illusion similar to the worker's. Marx argues that the confusion between money and capital, characteristic of mercantilist economic thought, is explained by the equivalence of the two for the practical capitalist: 'He has the choice of making use of his capital by lending it out as interest-bearing capital, or of expanding its value on his own by using it as productive capital, regardless of whether it exists as money-capital from the very first, or whether it still has to be converted into money-capital. But to apply [this argument] to the total capital of society, as some vulgar economists do, is of course preposterous.'[26] And of course this preposterous argument, which was the theoretical foundation of many mercantilist policies and according to Heckscher was still employed by German economists during the First World War,[27] was in no way favourable to the interest of the dominant class out of whose position it emerged. For a third example consider George

[26] Marx, *Capital*, vol. III (1894) (International Publishers, New York), p. 377.
[27] E. Heckscher, *Mercantilism* (Allen & Unwin, London, 1954), rev. edn, vol. II, p. 202; also Elster, *Leibniz*, pp. 115ff., 169ff.

Katona's argument that a manufacturer, when asked about the probable incidence of a general tax increase on the general price level, may answer wrongly that prices will rise, because in his limited sphere of experience a tax increase is just like a wage increase in the effect on cost and pricing. [28] But if this view of the practical capitalist was made into a policy foundation, it would certainly have bad consequences for the capitalist class. In fact, no extended arguments are needed for the case that an illusionary perception of reality will in general not be conducive to an efficient manipulation of reality.

Another kind of backing for the second proposition would be provided by cases, if such could be found, in which the social position of an oppressed class generated illusions that actually served its interest, and therefore went counter to that of the dominant class. But, as just observed, this is not likely to happen. Nisbett and Ross point out, however, that 'unrealistically positive self-schemas or other illusions about the self, together with the processing biases they can engender, may be more socially adaptive than are totally accurate self-perceptions'. [29] Similarly, Kolakowski writes of Lenin:

> After 1917 he expected a European revolution any day, and thought he could run the Russian economy by means of terror. But all his misjudgements were in the direction of expecting the revolutionary movement to be stronger and to manifest itself earlier, than it actually did. They were fortunate errors from his point of view, since it was only on the basis of false estimates that he decided on an armed insurrrection in October 1917. His mistakes enabled him to exploit the possibilities of revolution to the full, and were thus the cause of his success. [30]

In other words, 'fortunate errors' of perception may raise the level of aspiration and mobilize energy that would have lain dormant with a more realistic understanding of the situation. Such errors need not stem from a cognitive bias. They are perhaps more likely to arise out of wishful thinking, or even be deliberately nurtured by some agent manipulating the situation. [31] But on the abstract level one may well

---

[28] G. Katona, *Psychological Analysis of Economic Behavior* (McGraw-Hill, New York, 1951), pp. 45ff. The classical example of this line of reasoning is Adam Smith's statement: 'What is prudence in the conduct of every private family can hardly be folly in that of a great kingdom.'

[29] Nisbett and Ross, *Human Inference*, pp. 189–99.

[30] Kolakowski, *Main Currents of Marxism*, vol. II, p. 525.

[31] As in the notion of 'optimal tautness of plans', see, e.g., M. Keren, 'On the tautness of plans', *Review of Economic Studies*, 39 (1972), pp. 469–86.

imagine that an oppressed class can be led by its situation to form illusionary beliefs that also serve its interests in some way. Still there is, I believe, a *presumption* that illusions are inefficient, and therefore the second proposition is false if we restrict ourselves to the positions of the oppressed classes.

I want to dwell somewhat on the notion of illusions that are either useful or conducive to truth. Nisbett and Ross offer some interesting, though partly ambiguous, observations on this 'dangerous notion'. First, as already mentioned, they stress that illusions may actually benefit the individual having them, by the effect on motivation. Secondly they observe, but without distinguishing this case from the preceding one, that such illusions may be good from the overall social point of view: 'We probably would have few novelists, actors or scientists if all potential aspirants to these careers took action based on a normatively justifiable subjective probability of success.'[32] Observe that this way of 'rationalizing the irrational' – a favourite pastime of the modern social scientist – differs from the alternative way, already referred to, which is that of seeing illusions as inevitable by-products of the rational allocation of time to problem-solving. Saying that illusions are actually conducive to success differs from saying that they are the necessary cost of success, just as saying that luxury is an indispensable means to welfare (through the effect on employment) differs from saying that luxury is an inevitable but regrettable side-product of welfare.[33]

Thirdly, and passing now from utility to truth, the authors observe that some illusions may even be conducive to truth, either by correcting another illusion or by substituting for correct inference. For example, people seem to have great difficulties in understanding or applying the simple notion of regression to the mean, e.g. in seeing that extreme observations are likely to prove atypical. This defect can lead to such harmful practical conclusions that punishment is more effective than reward in training, because on the average good performances (even when rewarded) will be followed by less good, while bad performances (even when not punished) will be followed by less

---

[32] Nisbett and Ross, *Human Inference*, p. 271.
[33] Cf. Elster, *Leibniz*, pp. 194–5, for brief remarks on the historical antecedents of these two rationalizations of the irrational, corresponding on the theological level to Leibniz and Malebranche respectively and on the secular level to Mandeville and Leibniz respectively.

bad. [34] Nisbett and Ross then point to no less than three mechanisms that, by compensation or substitution, may enable us to make correct predictions. (1) By diluting the information that leads to wrong predictions with additional *irrelevant* information, subjects are enabled to improve their score. (2) The irrational gambler's fallacy, when interacting with the equally irrational 'fundamental attribution error', may give a net result of rational regression. (3) As in other cases, [35] a causal interpretation of what is essentially a sampling effect may give a correct result, as when the baseball trainer argues that the brilliant first-year player will be spoiled by all the attention he gets and not live up to his performance in the next season.

The important question here is whether the beneficial consequences of the illusions can serve to *explain* them. No one, I believe, would argue that all illusions are beneficial and to be explained by their benefits, though some might want to say that they are part of an optimal meta-strategy in the sense indicated above. But one might want to argue that when an illusion is systematically beneficial, the question should at least be raised whether it cannot be explained as a compensating or substituting device. Both natural selection and psychological reinforcement might conceivably serve as mechanisms underlying this functional explanation. [36] This holds for the cases in which the illusions are beneficial for the person having them. Much more controversial is the idea that illusions could be explained by consequences beneficial for other persons. I find it hard to imagine a

[34] See A. Tversky and D. Kahneman, 'Judgment under uncertainty', *Science*, 185 (1974), pp. 1124–30.

[35] See W. Feller, *An Introduction to Probability Theory and its Applications* (Wiley, New York, 1968), 3rd edn, vol. 1, p. 122, for the distinction between real after-effects and effects of sampling. But even though the two procedures may give roughly similar predictions, they may lead to very different evaluations. Given the statistical observation that the longer a person has been unemployed the greater the chances that he will not find employment in the next period, it may not make much difference for prediction whether the underlying mechanism is taken to be mover–stayer or cumulative inertia – see R. Boudon, *Mathematical Structures of Social Mobility* (Elsevier, Amsterdam, 1973) – but in the former case we may consider the unemployed as inherently lazy and in the latter as unfortunate victims of a process that hits them. Bias is seldom totally innocent.

[36] P. van Parijs makes a persuasive case for reinforcement as one mechanism capable of sustaining functional explanations in 'Functional explanation and the linguistic analogy', *Philosophy of the Social Sciences*, 9 (1979), pp. 525–43.

mechanism by which the illusions of an oppressed class could be explained by their beneficial consequences for the ruling class. There are good reasons for thinking that the oppressed classes often will be victims of a kind of myopia that prevent them from seeing the injustice of their situation – and it is clear that this is good for the ruling class; but even a systematic correlation would not by itself warrant an explanatory statement. And it is even less plausible that illusions could be explained, as suggested by Nisbett and Ross, by their good effects on 'society', because this does not give us the kind of actor required for the monitoring of a feedback process. If beneficial consequences of an illusion shall serve to explain it, they must be, I think, beneficial for the individual subject to the illusion (or for his close relatives through kin selection). Some additional considerations on functional explanations of ideologies are offered in Part III.

A final remark on the topic of illusions answers a question that some readers may have put to themselves: Is there not an inconsistency when I attribute illusions both to features of the situation and to the cognitive apparatus of the subject? In the Marxist theory of ideologies class position is central, but in cognitive psychology the stress is laid on the internal psychic mechanism of the subject, and so it might seem strange to seek in the latter micro-foundations for the former. This, however, is an artificial opposition. For illusions to occur both the external situation and the internal processing must come into play. It is consistent with cognitive psychology to assume that individuals differ systematically, e.g. in a class-related way, in the extent to which their external situation lends itself to certain kinds of fallacies, inferential errors and illusions. And one could also speculate, though I would be more sceptical as to the value of the outcome, that differences in social origin generate differences in the internal apparatus and thus in the liability to illusions (keeping the external situation constant).

III

Beliefs often are distorted by interest, mainly perhaps through wishful thinking (of which rationalization is a subspecies), but also by pessimism, conformism and related mechanisms. I shall here limit my attention to wishful thinking, the tendency to form beliefs when, and because, I prefer the state of the world in which they are true to states in which they are false. Let me sharply distinguish this phenomenon from that of believing at will, a deliberate choice rather than a causal process. Believing at will, supposing it to be at all possible,[37] is related to wishful thinking, as is deliberate character-planning to adaptive preferences.[38] The decision to believe is guided by a conscious desire, wishful thinking is shaped by a non-conscious drive. Or perhaps (I have little confidence in my ability to see clear in these muddy waters) we should argue that in wishful thinking my conscious desire is the cause of my belief, with the proviso that it causes the belief in a wrong or non-standard way. (And if I am right in thinking that believing at will is impossible, there is no right way.)[39]

Similarly, wishful thinking should be distinguished clearly from self-deception, supposing the latter to be at all possible. Many writers use these terms interchangeably, and 'rationalization' as synonymous with both.[40] But I believe that the notion of self-deception as commonly understood involves paradoxes that are absent from that of wishful thinking. Self-deception or bad faith involves two inconsistent beliefs, a fact that in itself does not make it impossible.[41] But there is also the peculiar feature that the self-deceiver intentionally hides one of his beliefs from himself and professes the other as his official view. The idea of (successful) self-deception therefore raises two closely related questions: How do you manage to *forget intentionally* what you really know or believe? And how can you *believe at will* something which you know that there are inadequate grounds for believing? The decision to forget is in itself paradoxical and inconsistent, in that the harder you try to carry it out, the harder it is to succeed; it is like an

[37] For various arguments to the effect that it is not possible to believe at will, in various senses of that phrase, see: B.A.O. Williams, 'Deciding to believe', in his *Problems of the Self* (Cambridge University Press, Cambridge, 1973), pp. 136–51; J. Elster, *Ulysses and the Sirens* (Cambridge University Press, Cambridge, 1979), ch II.3; B. Winters, 'Willing to believe', *Journal of Philosophy*, 76 (1979), pp. 243–56.

[38] For the relation between adaptive preferences and character planning, see my 'Sour grapes'.

[39] Wishful thinking would be even more irrational than weakness of will if this account is accepted. In weakness of will, on Davidson's argument, the action is caused by reasons that *are* reasons for acting that way, and it is irrational only because these reasons defeat the stronger reasons for acting differently. But given the premises of the text, a desire could *never* rationalize a belief.

[40] E.g. Kolakowski, *Main Currents of Marxism*, vol. III, pp. 89, 116, 82; Levenson, *Confucian China*, vol. 1, pp. 59ff., 70.

[41] Elster, *Logic and Society*, ch. 4.

attempt to create darkness by light. And I have already suggested that believing at will may be a feat beyond human abilities.

However, as in the related case of weakness of will, the theoretical objections simply seem to evaporate in the case of massive clinical, fictional and everyday experience attesting to the reality of the phenomenon. And so there is a need for a theoretical analysis of self-deception: *wie ist es überhaupt möglich?* Among the better-known attempts to provide an answer are those of Freud, Sartre, Fingarette and Schafer. [42] In my view none of them are convincing, as they all tend to reproduce the basic paradox in ever-subtler forms. I would rather suggest a diversified strategy, explaining different cases of what is usually called self-deception along different lines. [43] First, some cases may be unsuccessful *attempts* at self-deception, and so no more paradoxical than other attempts to realize contradictory goals. Secondly, some cases can be understood through a distinction between higher-level and lower-level beliefs, so that I can deliberately choose not to acquire the lower-level beliefs that would give substance to my higher-level belief and thus make it less tolerable. ('I do not want to know the details.') Thirdly, some cases may be understood as unsuccessful attempts at character-modification, when I exploit the leeway in the description of my character in order to change it. ('I am *not* afraid.') Fourthly, I may now bring it about that I believe something at a later time, if I can also bring about forgetfulness of the process itself. And fifthly, there is wishful thinking.

The argument for a distinction between wishful thinking and self-deception is that the former, unlike the latter, can arrive at beliefs that are not only true (which is irrelevant) but well grounded in the available evidence. Consider again the man who wishes to be promoted. We might speak of self-deception if he 'really' (somehow, somewhere) believes that he is not going to be promoted, but nevertheless hides this knowledge from himself and believes promotion to be imminent. But it might also be the case that the man had very good

---

[42] H. Fingarette, *Self-Deception* (Routledge & Kegan Paul, London, 1969) also includes useful accounts of Freud and Sartre. Elster, *Ulysses and the Sirens*, ch. IV.4, has a brief discussion of R. Schafer, *A New Language for Psychoanalysis* (Yale University Press, New Haven, Conn., 1976).

[43] The following is a brief résumé of Elster, *Ulysses and the Sirens*, ch. IV.4, itself an excessively brief and programmatic account that cannot claim to have solved the problem of self-deception or given an adequate refutation of rival views.

grounds for believing himself about to be promoted, but that he arrived at this belief in another way, viz. through wishful thinking. Here there is no duality, no opposition between the reality principle and the pleasure principle. There is no question here of hiding from oneself an unpleasant truth or well-grounded belief, for the well-grounded belief is also the one which the believer wants to be true and indeed believes because he wants it to be true. He has good reasons for believing it, but does not believe it for those reasons. [44]

I believe, moreover, that this abstract possibility has many embodiments in everyday life. Surely we have all met persons basking in self-satisfaction that seems both to be justified and not to be justified: justified because they have good reasons for being satisfied with themselves, and not justified because we sense that they would be just as satisfied were the reasons to disappear. In other words, distortion is not like a 'force', because it cannot be measured by its effects. There may be a strong tendency to distort, and yet zero distortion. The point is well made by Levenson: 'To speak of apologetics is not to suggest that Chinese thinkers, in vindicating the worth of Chinese culture against Western pretentions, were saying anything untrue. What is true is no less true because apologists insist on it. But apologists are no less apologetic because what they insist upon is true; it is the insistence that counts.'[45] In other words, wishful thinking cannot be detected simply by looking at the ideas involved, nor by comparing the beliefs with the evidence available. We have to get knowledge about the way in which the belief was actually shaped.

I believe this shows irrefutably that in some cases at least wishful thinking does not involve self-deception: the cases, namely, in which the belief born of desire is also borne out by the evidence. But then, why should not the same be true in other cases? Why could it not be the case that the wishful believer goes directly for the pleasant belief, instead of going through the four-step process of (1) arriving at the well-grounded belief, (2) deciding that it is unpalatable, (3) suppressing it, and only then (4) adhering to another and more tolerable belief? Or again, why should the repellent force of an unpleasant belief have explanatory privilege over the attracting force of a pleasant belief? I

---

[44] The Davidsonian flavour of this phrase is obvious, but see note 39 for a difference between this case and the non-standard causal chains in Davidson, 'Freedom to act'.

[45] Levenson, *Confucian China*, vol. 1, 73–4.

suggest that in the absence of specific arguments to the contrary, wishful thinking is a more parsimonious explanation than self-deception. Indeed, I believe that the substitution of wishful thinking for self-deception is a major step towards the elimination of Freudian unconscious as a theoretical entity – an elimination that is highly desirable not only because of the paradoxes of self-deception (defence and repression), but also because of the incoherence of the notion of unconscious intentions.[46] My own half-shaped view is that in order to understand the irrational side of human behaviour we shall do better by appealing to *inconsistent intentions backed by wishful thinking* than by invoking unconscious intentions backed by self-deception.

Paralleling the first proposition above, I now argue for a

Third proposition: There is no reason to suppose that beliefs shaped by interests tend to serve these interests.

On general grounds, distorted beliefs cannot be expected, any more than illusionary beliefs, to be very helpful for goal achievement. If out of wishful thinking I form a belief that I am about to be promoted, my subsequent display of unwarranted self-confidence may destroy once and for all my chances of promotion. The Lysenko affair showed how disastrous may be the result when scientific beliefs are formed by wishful thinking, an attitude unforgettably captured in *The First Circle*. Blatant apologetics, while often shaped by interest, do not serve them very well, precisely because they are so blatant.[47] And, referring again to Paul Veyne,[48] the exploited and oppressed classes may be led by rationalization into believing that their fate is just and proper – a belief that may indeed give short-term gratification, but

[46] Very briefly put, the notion is incoherent because intentional action is action conducted in terms of something physically absent, viz. a future, as yet unrealized goal. But for the absent to make a difference for action in the present, it must be re-presented in some way, and I believe that consciousness is nothing but a medium for such re-presentation of the absent. The unconscious would at most be capable of some local climbing along a pleasure gradient.

[47] See E. Genovese, *The World the Slaveholders Made* (Pantheon, New York, 1969), on George Fitzhugh's attempt in 1857 to justify Southern slavery by a series of arguments that may have done more harm than good to the cause he defended: G. Fitzhugh, *Cannibals All* (Harvard University Press, Cambridge, Mass., 1960).

[48] Veyne, *Le Pain et le Cirque*, pp. 298ff.

cannot be said to serve the interest of these classes well at all.

Let us make some distinctions here, as not all the examples just cited can be reduced to a single formula. First, the tendency to engage in wishful thinking is in itself liable to get you into trouble, independently of the actual beliefs. The promotion example can be modified to include the previously used assumption that the belief in promotion is well-grounded, and yet the chances for promotion may be destroyed if the good reasons for believing in it are not what causes the belief. ('He would be promoted were he not so infernally confident that he will be promoted.') Secondly, it may be the actual belief that is relevant for the question of interest. A belief about instrumental means–end relationship, if true, is no less efficient because it is arrived at by wishful thinking. But of course instrumental beliefs shaped by interest will serve interest only by a fluke. Thirdly, the relevant question may be whether the belief is generally accepted rather than whether it is true. A belief system that, if accepted, would have the consequence of legitimating a system of social inequality, may not be accepted by the lower classes if it is too obviously tailor-made to, and shaped by, the interest of the upper classes. Self-serving theories of the need for inequality are rarely self-serving. The interest of the upper class is better served by the lower classes spontaneously inventing an ideology justifying their inferior status. This ideology, while stemming from the interest of the lower classes in the sense of leading to dissonance reduction, is contrary to their interest because of a tendency to overshoot, resulting in excessive rather than in proper meekness.[49] And in addition what is proper meekness in the short run may well be excessive in the long, and therefore contrary to interest in another sense as well.[50]

But lucidity about self may also be contrary to interest. In his study of Chinese reactions to Western superiority, Levenson discusses at some length what he calls the '*t'i-yung* rationalizers', a group of thinkers who thought it possible to reconcile Chinese *t'i* (essence or substance) with Western *yung* (function). But of course, 'Chinese learning had come to be prized as substance because of its function, and when its function was usurped, the learning withered.'[51] The

---

[49] Ibid., p.313; also my forthcoming 'Sour grapes' for a tentative explanation of this overshooting.

[50] See Elster, *Logic and Society*, pp. 119ff., for an analysis of the temporal Prisoner's Dilemma involved here.

[51] Levenson, *Confucian China*, vol. 1, p. 61.

reactionary traditionalists, as may be imagined, had no difficulty in denouncing the fallacy. 'Nevertheless, although the reactionaries might well plume themselves for sensing the logical inadequacies of that particular rationalization for innovation, their conclusion – that the innovation must be stopped, rather than the rationalization changed – was unsound. For they were obscurantist in failing to realize that innovation was inevitable, and that some rationalization, logical or not, was a psychological necessity.'[52] Wishful thinking, that is, may be as efficient as illusionary beliefs in setting up a bootstrap operation by which something becomes possible because it is thought to be possible. But as in the case of illusionary beliefs, self-serving wishful thinking must be the exception.

Conversely, I would like to argue for a

Fourth proposition: There is no reason to suppose that beliefs that serve certain interests are also to be explained by those interests.

I deliberately use the language of explanation instead of that of causation, because interest may explain beliefs in other than causal ways. In a straightforward causal explanation, interest shapes belief and thereby explains it. It follows from what has already been said that there is no reason to suppose that a belief serving a given interest will also have been shaped by that interest, although this may happen by fluke. But there is also a possible functional explanation, to the effect that a belief may be explained by the interest it serves. When Marx says that the social principles of Christianity, among many other things, 'preach the necessity of a ruling and an oppressed class, and for the latter all they have to offer is the pious wish that the former may be charitable',[53] we may well wonder whether this is not also offered as an *explanation* of Christianity in class societies. The phrase 'opium of the people' has similar explanatory overtones. As observed above, for a consequence to explain its cause there must be some underlying feedback mechanism, which in the present case is hard to imagine. But in other cases it is not difficult to conceive of ways in which beliefs persist because they serve certain interests. Theories in the social

---

[52] Ibid., p. 77.
[53] K. Marx, 'The Communism of the *Rheinischer Beobachter*' (1847) in K. Marx and F. Engels, *Collected Works* (Lawrence & Wishart, London), vol. 6, p. 231.

sciences often are hard to falsify by testing, and so there is some scope for interest to determine which of several contending theories shall receive economic support and be enabled to survive.[54] But the mere fact that a belief system has beneficial effects for some social class, e.g. by legitimating its rule, does not in itself create a presumption that these effects can explain the persistence of the system.

Two additional remarks on this point may be in order. First, I think it is important to stress that the ambiguities of the notion of an ideology are in fact common to the whole Marxist notion of the superstructure. For example, when Marxists argue that the state in capitalist society is also a capitalist state, i.e. is to be explained by the interest of the capitalist class, they can and do mean two radically different things. Some political institutions are to be explained (à la Cohen) through their stabilizing *effect on* the economic structure, others as *effects of* that structure. An example of the first according to Marx is nineteenth-century England, in which property was distributed so that capitalists had much, landowners had some and workers had none, while political power was distributed so that the capitalists had little, landowners virtually all and workers none. Marx argued that the second distribution had to be explained in terms of its stabilizing consequences for the first, because the political struggle of the workers against the government would then weaken their economic struggle against the capitalists.[55] Accepting for the sake of argument that this explanation is corrrect, it does not follow that the power structure was an effect of the economic structure. More plausibly the power structure was a remnant from feudalism that was retained because it had these effects on the structure. An example of the second explanation-type would be Marx's analysis in the *18 Brumaire* of the naked class rule of the bourgeoisie before Bonaparte's *coup d'état*. This regime represented an unequal distribution of power that directly grew out of, and was causally explainable in terms of, the unequal distribution of property, and yet it had a destabilizing effect on the property

---

[54]　T. Stang-Dahl, *Barnevern og Sammfunnsvern* (Pax, Oslo, 1977), shows how the contrast between French and Italian criminology was decided not on scientific grounds (both were essentially worthless), but because the Italian school was too deterministic to appeal to the judges and penologists whose co-operation was needed. Punishment requires a modicum of free will to make sense.

[55]　See Marx's article 'The Chartists', *New York Daily Tribune*, 10 August 1852.

structure.[56] Political regimes shaped by economic interest may turn out to be disastrous for those interests.

The second observation concerns some theoretical problems of scientific explanation. To my argument that the subjects spontaneously invent an ideology justifying their oppression, so that there is no need to explain the ideology in terms of the interest of the ruling class which it in fact serves, two objections may be raised. The first[57] is that the ruling class, being in control of the means of education, could have corrected the distorted (and illusionary) beliefs of the subjects had it so chosen; therefore the fact that it did not so choose makes it co-responsible for the ideology. To this I have three brief replies. First, moral responsibility cannot be used as grounds for imputing causal responsibility (one cannot infer 'is' from 'ought'), and it is with the latter exclusively that I deal here. Secondly, acts of omission cannot normally serve as causes (though they may serve as a basis for ascribing moral responsibility). And thirdly, the objection presupposes that the ruling class does not share the distorted beliefs, e.g. that the Roman emperors did not themselves believe in their divine nature. But this, as argued by Veyne, is a total misunderstanding of religious psychology. The subjects will believe only in the superiority of rulers who never stoop to prove their superiority. (Which is why no Soviet citizens believe in the superiority of the Soviet leadership.)

The second objection[58] is the following. Given that the legitimation was spontaneously invented by the oppressed, can we not reasonably assert that in the absence of such an ideology (e.g. in the presence of a rebellious ideology) the rulers would have cracked down on the subjects by violent repression? (In fact, Veyne does not assert that the spontaneous ideologies are indispensible for the stability of class rule, and again we may look to the Soviet Union to see that they are not.) And if this is granted, can we not then argue that in class societies the rule of the dominant class will be stabilized *by some mechanism*, be it an endogenous and spontaneous belief in the natural superiority of the superiors, or a harshly repressive system? And from this, does it not follow that we can explain functionally, at high level of generality, the

[56] K. Marx, *The Eighteenth Brumaire of Louis Bonaparte* (1852) in Marx and Engels, *Collected Works* (Lawrence & Wishart, London), vol. 11, pp. 142–3.
[57] This objection was raised both by G. A. Cohen and by Martin Hollis in their comments on an earlier draft of this essay.
[58] This objection was raised by G. A. Cohen in his comment on the earlier draft.

presence of such mechanisms? That there is *some* mechanism can be explained in terms of the stabilizing effect, even though other arguments may be needed to explain why this or that mechanism is realized. I have not made up my mind as to the general validity of this somewhat counter-intuitive idea, that when asked 'Why is it there?' one may answer: 'Because if it had not been there, something else with the same consequences would have been there.' For the present purposes, however, it suffices to observe that if we are trying to explain *ideologies*, the explanation must not be at a level of abstraction at which it is impossible to distinguish between ideological and political facts. Whatever the relevance of the functional explanation for whatever it is trying to explain, it seems obvious that the purely causal explanation of belief formation does indeed have explanatory force.

The four propositions argued above have been directed towards a facile Marxist theory of ideologies, that concludes unthinkingly from the fact that an idea is shaped by class position to the proposition that it also serves class interest; or that assumes that class interests served by an idea automatically also explain it. More generally, there has been in Marxist thought an obsession with the social significance of ideas and institutions – a tendency to impose arbitrary patterns on events so as to make them guided by the invisible hand of history. (Actually two hands have been postulated, each of which can be invoked when the other will not do – one that makes everything come out in the interest of the capitalist class, and one that makes everything into a precondition for the communist revolution.) To say this is not to advocate that we abandon Marxism, but that we firmly retain the causal mode of Marxist explanation and equally firmly reject the functional mode. Even if Cohen's attempt to salvage functionalist Marxism proved to be successful, his criteria for a valid functional explanation are so strict that almost no actual theories would satisfy them.[59] If, then, we retain Marxism together with methodological individualism and causal

---

[59] Let me briefly sum up some salient aspect of the problem. We are dealing with cases in which there is no known feedback mechanism from consequence to cause. With such a mechanism the functional explanation is explicitly reduced to a causal one, and so the problem disappears. Cohen then argues that even without the knowledge of a feedback mechanism, we can back the functional explanation by a consequence law, mirroring the ordinary causal laws used to back causal explanations: *Karl Marx's Theory of History: A Defence* (Oxford University Press, Oxford, 1978) ch. IX. One objection then is that such consequence laws would not distinguish between real and spurious

explanation, the foundation is laid for a satisfactory theory of socially grounded belief. The scope of this theory is much wider than has been argued by some recent writers, who have focused exclusively on the relation between beliefs and evidence. Against this I would like to advance a

Fifth proposition: There is no reason to believe that if a belief is rationally grounded in the available evidence, the search for a genetic explanation is misguided.

In particular, this goes against what Larry Laudan has called the *arationality assumption:* 'whenever a belief can be explained by adequate reasons, there is no need for, and little promise in, seeking out an alternative explanation in terms of social causes.'[60] We have seen repeatedly that this is not correct. A belief may be illusionary, and yet be well grounded in the available evidence, if it stems from the two compensatory errors or from an error that in some type of context can substitute for correct inference; or justified belief and wishful thinking may coincide simply by fluke. Why did Malthus believe that unproductive consumption was required for economic growth? Because good economic reasons made him think so (Keynes)? Or because he had a desire to justify the existence of the unproductive classes to which he himself belonged (Marx)? The mere fact that there were adequate reasons for the belief is not sufficient to decide in favour of the first answer. Whatever the apparent rationality of the belief, a genetic explanation may show that it was not in fact held for those good reasons. Since epistemology deals with the rationality of

---

correlation. To this Cohen replies that one could in principle do this by suitable experiments and comparisons. To this I counter that in practice, and perhaps in principle as well, such corrective procedures could not dispense with knowledge of the mechanism. There may be more to be said about the problem, but it is at any rate clear that there has perhaps not been a single example in the history satisfying the austere criteria that Cohen lays down for a successful functional explanation backed exclusively by consequence laws. More detailed discussion of these issues is found in the exchanges between Cohen and myself in *Political Studies* (1980) and in *Theory and Society* (1982), and in my review of his book in *Annales: Economies, Sociétés, Civilisations* (1981).
[60] L. Laudan, *Progress and its Problems* (University of California Press, Berkeley and Los Angeles, 1977), p. 203.

beliefs, and since the rationality of a belief can neither be read off it straight away nor be assessed by comparing the belief with the evidence, we must conclude that epistemology needs history.[61]

---

[61] This conclusion parallels the conclusion of my 'Sour grapes': 'Adaptive preference formation is relevant for ethics, and it is not always reflected in the preferences themselves, and so it follows that ethics needs history.'

Apparently Irrational Beliefs

Dan Sperber

INTRODUCTION

Extract from my field diary:

> [*Dorze, Southern Ethiopia*]
> *Sunday 24 viii 69*

. . . Saturday morning old Filate came to see me in a state of great excitement:

'Three times I came to see you, and you weren't there!'
'I was away in Konso'.
'I know. I was angry. I was glad. Do you want to do something?'
'What?'
'Keep quiet! If you do it, God will be pleased, the Government will be pleased. So?'
'Well, if it is a good thing and if I can do it, I shall do it.'
'I have talked to no one about it: will you kill it?'
'*Kill?* Kill what?'
'Its heart is made of gold, it has one horn on the nape of its neck. It is golden all over. It does not live far, two days' walk at most. If you kill it, you will become a great man!'

And so on . . . It turns out Filate wants me to kill a dragon. He is to come back this afternoon with someone who has seen it, and they will tell me more. . .

> *Monday 25 viii*

Good weather.
The old man with his dragon did not come back. A pity. . .

I had respect and affection for Filate. He was a very nice, very old man. He was not senile, however; and he was too poor to drink. His excitement on that day was caused by what he had come to tell me, rather than the other way around. All this makes it even more bewildering: how could a sound person believe that there are dragons, not 'once upon a time', but there and then, within walking distance? How am I to reconcile my respect for Filate with the knowledge that such a belief is absurd?

This is of course just a concrete instance of a much discussed general problem: how to account for apparently irrational beliefs?[1] One approach consists in claiming that these beliefs are genuinely irrational and the product of some pre-rational mental processes. I have discussed this old-fashioned view elsewhere.[2] Another approach consists in claiming that people of other cultures 'live in other worlds', so that what is rational in their world may well appear irrational in ours. This view, known as cognitive relativism, is supported by many anthropologists and philosophers. It has in part superseded, in part encompassed two other approaches: intellectualism and symbolism. In this paper, I want to discuss relativism, and to argue for a rationalist alternative.

The paper has three parts. In the first part, I present what I think is the best possible case for relativism from an anthropological point of view.[3] In the second part I present psychological arguments against relativism. In the third part I present the rationalist approach I am advocating.

---

[1] Among recent discussions, see B.R. Wilson (ed.), *Rationality* (Blackwell, Oxford, 1970); R. Finnegan and R. Horton (eds), *Modes of Thought* (Faber, London, 1973); E. Gellner, *Cause and Meaning in the Social Sciences* (Routledge & Kegan Paul, London, 1973); J. Skorupski, *Symbol and Theory: A Philosophical Study of Theories of Religion in Social Anthropology* (Cambridge University Press, Cambridge, 1976); C. Hookway and P. Pettit (eds), *Action and Interpretation: Studies in the Philosophy of the Social Sciences* (Cambridge University Press, Cambridge, 1978). In the background of most of the discussions W.V. Quine's *Word and Object* (MIT Press, Cambridge, Mass., 1960) looms large.

[2] D. Sperber, 'Is symbolic thought prerational?' in M.L. Foster and S.M. Brandes (eds), *Symbol a Sense: New Approaches to the Analysis of Meaning* (Academic Press, New York, 1980), pp. 25–44.

[3] Another line of argument for relativism is based on philosophical scepticism (e.g. Quine, *Word and Object*). It is irrelevant, however, to the assessment of relativism as a theory in the empirical sciences, and hence to my present perspective.

I ANTHROPOLOGICAL ARGUMENTS

The limits of the intellectualist and the symbolist approaches

That people of different cultures live in different worlds is an unclear assumption, but it is clearly intended as a strong one. Could the intellectualist or the symbolist approach make such an assumption unnecessary?

According to the intellectualist approach, apparently irrational beliefs are less irrational than mistaken. They are part of attempted explanations of the world which are developed in a rational way, but on the basis of poor evidence, inadequate patterns of argumentation, lack of awareness of alternatives, etc.

In many societies, the earth is held to be flat: it is easy to see how this belief could be mistaken rather than irrational. And there are plenty of cases, including modern Western ones, for which a similar explanation is straightforward. Robin Horton, by drawing attention to the existence of apparent paradoxes in Western science, has shown how less obvious cases could be described in intellectualist terms. For instance:

> There are striking resemblances between psychoanalytic ideas about the individual mind as a congeries of warring entities, and West African ideas, about the body as a meeting place of multiple souls.[4]

In other cases, however, an intellectualist interpretation would seem much overextended. To take but one example, the Fataleka of the Solomon islands studied by Remo Guidieri maintain not only that the earth is flat, but also that it is the fifth of nine parallel strata among which various entities are distributed: a person's reflection is in stratum three, flutes are in stratum four, crocodiles in stratum seven, stratum eight is empty, etc. Could this be a *mistake?* The anthropologist moreover reports:

> In all the comments I could gather, the nine strata of the universe are described without the relationship between them and between the entities that inhabit them being made explicit.[5]

[4] R. Horton, 'African traditional thought and Western science', *Africa*, 37 (1967), pp. 50–71, 155–87, reprinted in Wilson, *Rationality*, pp. 131–71, see p. 139. See also his 'Destiny and the unconscious in West Africa', *Africa*, 31 (1961), pp. 110–16.

[5] R. Guidieri, *La Route des Morts* (Seuil, Paris, 1980), p. 47.

It seems that rather than explaining the world, this stratigraphy itself begs – in vain – for an explanation. Similarly, the world is hard enough to explain without golden-hearted single-horned dragons. It is unclear how, by adding them to the scene, the Dorze would have made the task easier.

So instead of showing how Filate's beliefs turn out to be rational, all the intellectualist has to offer is the meagre comfort of a *petitio principii:* if we had all the data . . .

According to the symbolist approach, myths and rituals are irrational only when taken at a superficial literal level. They should be viewed as an indirect expression of cosmological observations, or metaphysical concerns, or classificatory schemas, or moral values, or social relationships, etc. . . (here authors differ).

Clearly, if an indirect, rationally accepted meaning is the one intended, then the problems raised by literally absurd beliefs are no greater than those raised by literally absurd metaphors. In both cases, the absurdity could be accounted for as a means to signal that a non-literal interpretation is intended. The use of such indirect forms of expression should not throw suspicion on the user's rationality.

The pertinence of the symbolist approach is nicely illustrated by the well-known statement of the Bororo of Central Brazil: 'We are red macaws.' Reported by Von den Steinen in 1894, it became a favourite example of the primitive's departure from Western commonsense rationality.[6]

It is a good thing, then, that Christopher Crocker was able to reinvestigate the matter in the field. It turns out that (1) only men say 'we are red macaws'; (2) red macaws are owned as pets by Bororo women; (3) because of matrilineal descent and uxorilocal residence, men are in important ways dependent on women; (4) both men and macaws are thought to reach beyond the women's sphere through their contacts with spirits. 'In metaphorically identifying themselves

---

[6] It has been discussed, among others, in E. Durkheim and M. Mauss, *Primitive Classification*, trans. from French by Rodney Needham (University of Chicago Press, Chicago, 1963); L. Lévy-Bruhl, *Les Fonctions Mentales dans les Sociétés Inférieures* (Alcan, Paris, 1911); E Cassirer, *The Philosophy of Symbolic Forms*, vol. 2: *Mythical Thought*, trans. from the German by Ralph Manheim (Yale University Press, New Haven, Conn., 1955); L.S. Vygotsky, *Thought and Language*, trans. from the Russian by Eugenia Haufmann and Gertrude Vakar (MIT Press, Cambridge, Mass., 1962); C. Geertz, *The Interpretation of Cultures: Selected Essays* (Basic Books, New York, 1973).

with red macaws, then, the Bororo . . . seek . . . to express the irony of their masculine condition.'[7] So, the enigmatic subject-matter of so many learned discussions turns out to be but an indirect form of expression well within the bounds of commonsense rationality. No doubt, many other puzzling cases around the world could be handled in similar fashion.

Crocker's argument, however, cuts both ways and illustrates also the limits of the symbolist approach. In the course of etablishing that 'we are red macaws' is a metaphor, he shows how it differs from superficially similar, literally absurd Bororo statements which are not meant figuratively, and how the 'red macaws' metaphor is itself based on a belief in real contacts with spirits.

Apparently irrational beliefs which believers insist are literally true are found everywhere. Symbolist analyses attribute hidden meanings to these beliefs. Yet, when these meanings are, for all we know, hidden from the believers themselves, the suspicion of irrationality remains.

I am afraid no hidden meaning was indended in Filate's request. What he was asking me to do was to kill a dragon, not to decipher a cryptic message.

Relativism at its scientific best

Once the intellectualist and the symbolist approaches have been applied wherever they seem to work, a large number of cases remain unaccounted for. The attraction of relativism, on the other hand, is that it seems to solve (or dissolve) the problem in each and every case.

Not all versions of relativism are worth discussing. A relativism which claims that all beliefs are not only rational but also valid in their cultural context gives itself the stamp of validity in its own cultural context and forsakes any claim to universal validity. Mary Douglas, for instance, argues for 'a theory of knowledge in which the mind is admitted to be actively creating its universe'[8] in the following terms:

> The present concern is focused on subjective truth . . . This is a
> generation deeply interested in the liberation of consciousness

[7] J.C. Crocker, 'My brother the parrot' in J.D. Sapir and J.C. Crocker (eds), *The Social Use of Metaphor: Essays on the Anthropology of Rhetoric* (University of Pennsylvania Press, Philadelphia, 1977), pp. 164–92, see p. 192.

[8] M. Douglas, *Implicit Meanings: Essays in Anthropology* (Routledge & Kegan Paul, London, 1975) p. xviii.

from control . . . It is part of our culture to recognize at last our cognitive precariousness . . .[9]

In other words, relativism is good for us. She then admits, or rather boasts, that her approach 'eschews a solid anchorage'.[10]

Relativism can also be formulated so as to be of interest to one who belongs to the scientific rather than to the hermeneutico-psychedelic sub-culture and who is concerned with objective knowledge and well-grounded theories. The formulation I shall propose makes, I think, the best possible sense of relativism. It is not, however, a generally accepted formulation. On the contrary, its implications are likely to put off most relativists. But then, I would argue, the onus is on them to show how a scientifically orientated relativist could avoid these implications.

The relativist slogan, that people of different cultures live in different worlds, would be nonsense if understood as literally referring to physical worlds. If understood as referring to cognized worlds, it would overstate a very trivial point. Of course, worlds as cognized by people of different cultures differ. They even differ in the same person from one moment to the next.

If, however, the worlds referred to are *cognizable worlds*, then the claim need be neither empty nor absurd. Beings with qualitatively different cognitive abilities do live in different worlds in this sense. Such is trivially the case of animal species with different sensory abilities.

Even when sensory abilities are similar, the capacity to synthesize sensory inputs and to abstract from them may still vary. Two species might perceive the same range of phenomena but select different sets of features on the basis of which to build their inner representations. Or they might perceive and pay attention to the same features and still organize them in radically different ways. Contrast, for instance, our usual notion of a thing based on visible spatio-temporal continuity, with that of a hypothetical species for which basic things would be smells having light and sound patterns as peripheral properties. Even if it shared our environment, and had a sensory equipment similar to ours, such a species would definitely live in a cognizable world different from ours.

[9] Ibid., pp. xvii, xviii.
[10] Ibid., p. xix.

Do cross-cultural differences in cognitive abilties determine, as do cross-species ones, different cognizable worlds? This is an empirical question with no obvious answer – in any case the same answer is not obvious to everyone.

Most anthropologists take for granted that human cognitive abilities are culturally determined. To a limited extent, this is certainly the case: pastoralists acquire an inordinate ability to perceive features of their cattle, together with a large *ad hoc* vocabulary. People with telescopes may know of many more celestial bodies. Writing provides an unbounded external memory, etc. By developing specific tools and skills, cultural groups extend the cognizable worlds of their members in different directions. These extensions, however important and interesting[11] are no evidence for relativism. They do not explain apparently irrational beliefs. Filate's dragon, for instance, could not very well be claimed to result from his possessing – or lacking – some culture-specific cognitive skill.

To be of relevance, relativism must maintain that not only opinions, interests and skills, but also fundamental concepts, meanings and, possibly, postulates used in human cognition are culturally determined.[12] Thus the development and differentiation of cognitive abilities, achieved in other species through genetic evolution, would be, in humans, taken over and pushed much further by cultural transmission.

From a relativist point of view, then, all conceptualized information is cultural. What we think of as the sky, birds, eyes, tears, hunger, death, fall, in other cultures, under concepts which differ from our own, and are therefore perceived differently.

Propositions that can be entertained, expressed, asserted are, according to relativists, language- and culture-specific. Hence it would be unreasonable to expect translations to preserve propositional content across languages. The aim of translation should be more modest:

> One general scheme of translation is better than another to the extent that it is simpler, preserves dispositions to accept sen-

---

[11] See for instance J. Goody, *The Domestication of the Savage Mind* (Cambridge University Press, Cambridge, 1977).
[12] It has been suggested that even logical rules might be culture-specific, but no one has ever worked out what this might involve empirically.

tences under analysis [i.e. propositions] in response to observation, and preserves similarity in usage.[13]

On this view, when alien beliefs appear irrational, difficulties of
translation are generally to blame: in their original formulation these
beliefs were acceptable to rational beings; the translation has failed to
preserve this acceptability. It is not surprising, in particular, that the
theoretical assumptions of another culture (e.g. the existence of a
witchcraft substance or of spirit possession) should quite often seem
irrational: such assumptions relate to actual observations through
implicit inferential steps which it is easy for members of the culture
and generally impossible for aliens to reconstruct. Without this background, no translation could preserve the acceptability of these theoretical assumptions, hence no good translation is possible.

Furthermore, it can be argued that the acceptability of propositions
does not rest on observations and inference alone, but also on a
number of general *a priori* beliefs, or postulates. Such postulates
determine a 'world-view' within which the rationality of beliefs is to be
assessed. If these postulates are culture-specific, as a strong relativist
would claim, it is unclear how they might be translated at all.[14]

Within such a relativist framework, the fact that some beliefs held in
another culture seem irrational is no evidence that they are. It is
evidence rather of how poor our understanding of that culture is. The
general problem raised by apparently irrational beliefs dissolves into
so many ethnographic issues.

Thus we find belief in dragons irrational because we take for granted
that things such as a heart of gold cannot occur in nature. This could be
a cultural postulate of our own. If so, Filate may have been too
trusting, but not irrationally credulous, in accepting a report that a
dragon had been spotted.

Relativism so understood is doubly attractive to ethnographers.
First, it gives them some guidance in interpreting their data: beliefs
must be interpreted in the context of world-views, and world-views
must be reconstructed so as to dispel the appearance of irrationality of
particular beliefs. Second, relativism makes ethnographic data
relevant to general anthropological issues: each well-interpreted belief

---

[13] G. Harman, *Thought* (Princeton University Press, Princeton, 1973),
pp. 107–8.
[14] See J. Skorupski, 'The meaning of another culture's beliefs', in Hookway
and Pettit, *Action and Interpretation*, pp. 83–106.

is a piece of evidence as to the degree and manner in which human cognition is culturally determined. Moreover, while relativism displaces intellectualism and symbolism as *solutions* to the problem of apparently irrational beliefs, it provides a framework where the intellectualist and symbolist *models* have an increased applicability: each cultural world has its own criteria of rational explanation and its own range of possible metaphors; there are no universal constraints on either.

So, why not just adopt relativism and live happily ever after?

II PSYCHOLOGICAL ARGUMENTS

The cost of relativism

Some of the implications of relativism are unwelcome. To begin with, a relativist in earnest should be either quite pessimistic about the possibility of doing ethnography at all or extraordinarily optimistic about the abilities of ethnographers.

It is a commonplace that we cannot intuit what, say, cats think. It takes the subtlest handling of rich ethological observations to arrive at simple well-grounded hypotheses in the matter. If members of other cultures live in different cognizable worlds and if one thing we can take for granted is that these worlds are much more complex than that of cats, how can we get to know them? Shouldn't we conclude, with Rodney Needham, that 'the solitary comprehensible fact about human experience is that it is incomprehensible'?[15]

Ethnographers feel, however, that after some months of fieldwork, they are in a position to provide a reasonable if incomplete account of an alien culture. Most of them modestly refrain from explaining this feat. Others attribute it to some mysterious human capacity of comprehension – or better-sounding *Verstehen* – which somehow transcends the boundaries of cognizable worlds.[16] Philosophers in the hermeneutic tradition have extensively discussed this alleged capacity. But ultimately it would fall to psychologists to describe and explain it. At present, explaining comprehension *within* a single cog-

---

[15] R. Needham, *Belief, Language and Experience* (Blackwell, Oxford, 1972), p. 246.
[16] For a more sober view of what is involved in ethnographic understanding, see my 'L'Interprétation en anthropololgie', *L'Homme*, 21 (1981). pp. 69–92.

nizable world seems a great enough task.

Relativism should cause a more immediate and even greater problem for developmental psychology.[17] Cognitive development (whether of the mind as a whole or of each distinct cognitive ability) can be viewed as series of states from an initial one at birth to a mature state. The task of developmental psychology is to describe and explain the passage from one state to another, and, globally, from the initial to the mature state. Relativism implies that the distance between the initial and the mature states is much greater than is usually assumed: it implies that the first stage of cognitive development consists not in acquiring knowledge in an essentially predetermined cognizable world, but, rather, in establishing in which world knowledge is to be acquired. Of course, the greater the distance between the initial and the mature state, the heavier the task of the developing organism, and of psychology.

On the whole, relativists show little concern or even awareness of the psychological implications of their views. Worse, they tend to misconceive them. Relativism is generally thought to be consonant with or even to lend support to an anti-innatist view of the human mind. But, I shall argue, this is quite mistaken.

In explaining how the mind develops from state n into state $n+1$, the psychologist can invoke two classes of factors: internal and environmental. Internal factors comprise all the cognitive abilities that the mind possesses in state n. Environmental factors comprise all the input information which is accessible to the mind while in state n and which contributes (in little-understood ways) to its moving to state $n+1$. In the initial state, at least, the internal factors are essentially innate.

What little understanding we have at present of internal factors is almost entirely speculative. Environmental factors, on the other hand, are open to observation and experimentation: we have some rough idea of what input is accessible to the child at various stages. One

---

[17] The following discussion is in part inspired by N. Chomsky, *Reflections on Language* (Pantheon, New York, 1975); N. Chomsky, *Rules and Representations* (Columbia University Press, New York and Blackwell, Oxford, 1980); J. Fodor, *The Language of Thought* (Crowell, New York, 1975). See also my 'Contre certains *a priori* anthropologiques', in E. Morin and M. Piatelli-Palmarini (eds), *L'Unité de l'Homme: Invariants Biologiques et Universaux Culturels* (Seuil, Paris, 1974), pp. 491–507.

generally accepted point about this input is that it is more chaotic than the knowledge developed on the basis of it. This well-known discrepancy between experience and knowledge is the main source of evidence for speculation about internal factors.

Now, relativists are bound to consider that the information accesible in the initial stage of cognitive development is even more chaotic than a non-relativist would hold, since it is not bound by the constraints of a predetermined cognizable world. If one wants to take this up seriously, one must then assume that the initial state is rich enough to exploit this hyper-chaotic initial input in order to develop a structure of the appropriate cognizable world.

Imagine an organism capable of developing the cognitive abilities of either the cat or the dog, depending, say, on whether it was raised among cats or among dogs. For this, it would need to possess innate abilities sufficient to match those of either species, plus some extra device capable of determining in which of the two cognizable worlds it had landed. It takes richer innate capacities to learn to be a cat or a dog than to be either. In the case of humans (as seen by relativists) the surplus of innate capacities required in order to determine the right cognizable world would be incommensurably greater since there are not two, but an infinity of profoundly different accessible worlds, each of a great complexity.

As far as I am aware, no relativist model of cognitive development has ever been seriously worked out or even outlined. Cross-cultural cognitive psychology is generally not relativist. [18] Anthropological and philosophical relativists seem to have lost track of the development of psychology since the heyday of behaviourism. But one does not need a worked-out model to assess some of its difficulties and implications. A relativist model of development would have to represent a much more complex process and, *ceteris paribus*, to rely more heavily on innatist hypotheses than a universalist one. The usual argument against universalism, that it implies unnecessary assumptions about innate mechanisms, should actually weigh – and quite heavily – against relativism.

Once the cost is realized, the attraction of relativism should fade. But then anthropologists can ignore this cost since it falls not on them but on psychologists (who just shrug it off, it seems). If, however, we

---

[18] See for instance M. Cole and S. Scribner, *Culture and Thought: A Psychological Introduction* (Wiley, New York, 1974).

forgo the protection of interdisciplinary ignorance, we cannot remain happy relativists any more. We have good reasons now to take a second, hard look at the original evidence for relativism: how compelling is it? Is there really not alternative approach to apparently irrational beliefs?

The evidence reconsidered

The evidence for relativism is twofold: studies of some alien categories show them to be culture-specific; interpretations of apparently irrational beliefs show them to 'make sense' in the context of culture-specific world-views.

Suppose an anthropologist were to study contemporary British culture. Some of the words he would pay attention to lend support to the view that meanings are culture-specific. They include:

(a) Words the meaning of which involves (but is not exhausted by) definite reference to particular people, places, times, etc., e.g. 'cockney', 'Marxism', 'Victorian'.

(b) Words with fuzzy meanings, e.g. 'love', 'faith', 'leftism', 'sport'.

(c) Words referring to socio-cultural institutions, e.g. 'church', 'doctorate', 'debutante'.

(d) Words the definition of which is linked to an explicit theory or norm, e.g. 'sin', 'misdemeanour', 'molecule', 'Oedipus complex'.

A considerable encyclopaedic background is necessary to understand these words. Hence, in practice, they cannot be properly translated but at best rendered with much gloss and approximation.[19]

The study of these words provides fairly strong evidence against the claim that the meanings of all words except proper names are built up exclusively from a universal stock of basic concepts. On the other hand it provides only very weak evidence for relativism proper. The question indeed arises: do these words exhibit with particular clarity the true nature of meaning in general? Or are their culture-specific semantic properties peripheral additions to a universal stock? To answer this question, the evidence should come from a systematic study of whole lexicons, or, short of that, from the study of unfuzzy words lacking cultural salience. If these turned out to have thoroughly culture-specific meanings too, relativism would be vindicated.

Quite understandably, words without cultural salience have

---

[19] See my 'L'Interprétation en anthropologie'.

received little attention on the part of anthropologists. Recently however, there have been systematic studies of various semantic fields such as colour, botanical or zoological taxonomies. [20] Most of them do not corroborate a relativist view.

One striking example in this respect is the now well-known study of basic colour terms by Berlin and Kay. [21] Colour terms were a favourite case for relativists: the colour continuum was said to be partitioned freely and hence most of the time differently in each language. A more thorough and sophisticated study of the evidence shows, on the contrary, that a universal small stock of basic colour categories underlies superficial differences in terminology. [22]

This suggest a more general remark: relativists rightly insist that resemblances across cultures may well be superficial; failure to understand this leads to poor ethnography. More neglected (except by structuralists) is the fact that cross-cultural differences may also be superficial, hence they provide no direct evidence for relativism.

Semantics is not a well-developed field nor is meaning a well-understood phenomenon. Cross-cultural semantic studies cannot be expected at this stage to provide conclusive evidence although they tend to weigh against relativism. [23] We are left then with the indirect but allegedly decisive evidence provided by the study of apparently irrational beliefs.

It is a truism – but one worth keeping in mind – that beliefs cannot be observed. An ethnographer does not perceive that the people believe this or that; he infers it from what he hears them say and sees them do. His attributions of beliefs are therefore never incontrovertible. Both the way in which the content of a belief is rendered and the description of the people's attitude as one of 'belief' are open to challenge.

It is on the basis of translations of individual statements and speculations about the motives of individual or collective actions that the

[20] For a review and discussion, see B. Berlin, 'Ethnobiological classification' in E. Rosch and B. Lloyd (eds), *Cognition and Categorization* (Lawrence Erlbaum Associates, Hillsdale, N.J., 1978), pp. 9–26.

[21] B. Berlin and P. Kay, *Basic Color Terms* (University of California Press, Berkeley, 1969).

[22] For a discussion of Berlin and Kay's work from a relativist point of view, see M. Sahlins, 'Colors and cultures', *Semiotica*, 16 (1976), pp. 1–22.

[23] Cf. E. Rosch, 'Linguistic relativity' in A. Silverstein (ed.), *Human Communication: Theoretical Perspectives* (Lawrence Erlbaum Associates, Hillsdale, N.J., 1974), pp. 51–121.

content of a people's beliefs is inferred. These translations and speculations could in principle be discussed and evaluated. In most anthropological works, however, the reader is directly presented with an elaborate interpretation in the form of a consolidated, complex, and coherent discourse (with just occasional translations of native statements and descriptions of anecdotes by way of illustration). Such interpretations are related to actual data in poorly understood, unsystematic and generally unspecified ways. They are constrained neither by standards of translation nor by standards of description. They resemble the more indirect and freer forms of reported speech, where the utterances or thoughts reported can be condensed, expanded, coalesced, fragmented, pruned, grafted and otherwise reworded at will.[24]

Anthropological interpretations serve to convey part of the experience of and the familiarity with an alien culture gained in the course of fieldwork. They are not primarily intended as evidence for factual or theoretical claims and their use as such is limited and generally unconclusive.

It may well be that anthropological (and historical) literature suggests by its very bulk and drift that people of other cultures hold beliefs which are irrational by Western standards. It does not warrant, however, more specific or more explicit claims on the issue. In particular no single properly spelt out proposition can be claimed to be believed by a given people. At best, the anthropologist may have grounds to suppose that a particular individual (e.g. Filate) holds some version of a particular belief (e.g. there are gold-hearted single-horned creatures), or that members of some group believe various propositions that resemble the anthropologist's rendering and one another.

Anthropological evidence does not warrant either the assumption that particular beliefs are integrated into coherent, all-embracing culturally transmitted world-views. This assumption plays a major role in relativism. For relativists, the rationality of particular beliefs can only be assessed within the world-view to which they belong; furthermore, there is no supracultural framework in which the rationality of the world-views themselves could ever be assessed.

Anthropological accounts of belief are usually written in the world-view format. But is this more than an expository device, a way to order

---

[24] See my 'L'Interprétation en anthropologie'.

and organize generally heterogeneous and scattered data? Godfrey Lienhardt, for instance, remarked in conclusion to his account of Shilluk cosmology:

> Shilluk cosmological ideas . . . are not systematized by the people themselves, who reveal them only by their sayings and their behaviour. It is impossible to give an account of them without abstracting them from the reality, formulating them as ideas with a certain degree of coherence between them, and thus constructing a system which has no exact counterpart in the thought of the Shilluk themselves.[25]

On the other hand, there are cases where the people themselves, or rather knowlegeable individuals such a the Dogon Ogotemmeli,[26] the Hamar Baldambe[27] or, in more complex societies, church-appointed specialists, hold a systematic cosmological discourse. Thus the world-view format is not just the anthropologist's expository device. It can also be the native's. However, even the most elaborate cosmological discourse expresses only a small systematized sub-set of the speaker's beliefs. Does this cultural discourse characterize the cognizable world of the speaker? Or is it itself but an element of that world? This crucial question is not answered by the available anthropological evidence.

The assumption that culturally determined world-views constitute the general framework of people's beliefs is a psychological assumption and should be evaluated as such. It is about patterns of human cognition and, more specifically, about the organization of memory. This is a domain where, at present, even the better-worked-out hypotheses remain highly speculative and where available evidence is at best suggestive.[28] The fact that anthropologists find it feasible and useful to convey what they have understood of some people's beliefs in

[25] G. Lienhardt, 'The Shilluk of the Upper Nile' in D. Forde (ed.), *African Worlds: Studies in the Cosmological Ideas and Social Values of African People* (Oxford University Press, Oxford, 1954), pp. 138–63, see p. 162.
[26] M. Griaule, *Dieu d'Eau* (Editions du Chêne, Paris, 1948).
[27] J. Lydall and I. Strecker, *The Hamar of Southern Ethiopia*, vol. II: *Baldambe Explains* (Klaus Renner Verlag, Hohenschäftlarn, 1979).
[28] For examples of recent discussions, see D.G. Bobrow and A. Collins (eds), *Representation and Understanding: Studies in Cognitive Science* (Academic Press, New York, 1975); C.N. Cofer (ed.), *The Structure of Human Memory* (Freeman, San Francisco, 1975); P.N. Johnson-Laird and P.C. Wason (eds), *Thinking: Readings in Cognitive Science* (Cambridge University Press, Cambridge, 1977).

the form of an integrated discourse is suggestive too, but not more than, say, the fact that modern encyclopaedias are organized in alphabetically ordered entries. Neither the discursive nor the alphabetical order seems a very plausible model for the organization of memory, while both the idea of integration and that of autonomy of entries seem relevant but vague.

There is worse. A proposition can be paradoxical, counter-intuitive or self-contradictory, but, in and by itself, it cannot be irrational. What can be rational or irrational is what one does with a proposition, for instance asserting it, denying it, entertaining it, using it as a premise in a logical derivation, etc. Thus to decide whether some belief is rational we need to know not only its content but also in which sense it is 'believed'. Now, anthropologists do not use a technical concept of 'belief' but the ordinary English notion, which does not correspond to any well-defined concept.

Clifford Geertz remarked:

> Just what does 'belief' mean in a religious context? Of all the problems surrounding attempts to conduct anthropological analyses of religion this is the most troublesome and therefore the most often avoided. [29]

Rodney Needham, who has produced the only thorough anthropological discussion of the notion of belief, argued:

> The notion of a state or capacity of belief . . . does not discriminate a distinct mode of consciousness, it has no logical claim to inclusion in a universal psychological vocabulary, and it is not a necessary institution for the conduct of social life. Belief does not constitute a natural resemblance among men. [30]

Now, if the notion of 'belief' used by anthropologists is at best vague and at worst empty, then reports of apparently irrational beliefs have little or no value as evidence for relativism.

At this point a relativist might want to retort: 'You are being unduly fussy. Anthropologists use "belief" to refer objectively to what, from a subjective point of view, is just knowledge. When it is reported, for instance, that the Zande believe that there are witches, what is meant is

[29] C. Geertz, 'Religion as a cultural system' in M. Banton (ed.), *Anthropological Approach to the Study of Religion* (Tavistock, London, 1966), pp. 1–46, repr. in Geertz, *The Interpretation of Cultures*, pp. 87–125, see p. 109.
[30] Needham, *Belief, Language and Experience*, p. 151.

that the Zande hold this as true just as they hold as true that there are cows, trees and stars. They would assert it or assent to it as a matter of course. How exactly 'belief' should be defined is for psychologists to discover. But even without a full characterization, some of the necessary conditions for a belief to be rational can be specified. A belief is not rational unless it is self-consistent and consistent with other beliefs held simultaneously. Now, many of the beliefs reported by anthropologists seem, by Western standards, to be self-contradictory or in contradiction with commonsense knowledge, hence irrational. This is evidence for relativism. It may lack psychological polish and scientific precision but these are no sufficient grounds to dismiss it.'

The relativist's retort rests on one unwarranted empirical assumption, namely that religious and other apparently irrational beliefs are not epistemologically distinguished in the believer's mind from ordinary knowledge. [31] It is generally harder to establish that something (here a psychological distinction) does not exist than to establish that it does. Even if the subjects failed to report a difference between their views on witches and their views on cows, even if they asserted both views in similar fashion, it would not follow that they hold them in the same way. Other tests might elicit a discrimination, whether a conscious or an unconscious one. However, even such weak evidence is generally lacking from works that assert the subjective equivalence of belief and knowledge. Most accounts of beliefs are written as if the utterances of so-called informants should all be taken on the same level, irrespective of whether they are produced in answer to the ethnographer's queries, during ordinary social intercourse, on ritual occasions, in judicial proceedings, etc. All native utterances get distilled together; their quintessence is then displayed as an homogeneous world-view where, indeed, no epistemological differentiation of beliefs occurs. This, however, is a fact of ethnography, not of culture.

When a statement is aimed at informing, when an idea is retained as part of one's knowledge, then consistency may well be a condition for rationality. However, the history of religious ideas, ethnographical

---

[31] For recent statements of this commonly held view, see J. Pouillon, 'Remarques sur le verbe "croire"' in M. Izard and P. Smith (eds), *La Fonction Symbolique: Essais d'Anthropologie* (Gallimard, Paris, 1979); P. Jorion, 'Why do *we* know and *others* believe?', *Philosophy of the Social Sciences*, forthcoming.

studies of verbal behaviour[32] and plain introspection strongly suggest that statements can be made with quite different purposes and with a great variety of degrees and types of commitment, ideas can be entertained and held to be true in a variety of ways, criteria of rationality may vary with types of statements and classes of 'beliefs'.

Thus there are two ways of describing apparently irrational beliefs. According to the traditional description, their apparent irrationality comes from the fact that we initially assess them in the inappropriate framework of a modern Western world-view. According to the alternative description, they appear irrational because they are wrongly taken to belong to a class of 'beliefs' for which consistency is a criterion of rationality. Anthropological literature is written *as if* the traditional description were correct, hence it provides no evidence for it. That, for all we know, the alternative description might be the correct one is enough to undermine the empirical basis of relativism.

Far from illuminating new areas and solving more problems than those which suggested its adoption in the first place, relativism, if taken seriously, should make ethnography either impossible or inexplicable, and psychology immensely difficult. It is the kind of theory that any empirical scientist would rather do without. If, as I have now argued, the evidence for relativism is weak and leaves us free to reject it, then we certainly should.

III A RATIONALIST APPROACH

Propositional and semi-propositional representations

Relativism will not be given up merely on the ground that it is theoretically unappealing and empirically insufficiently supported. Is there, it will be asked, an alternative with greater explanatory power and better evidence in its favour? In *Rethinking Symbolism*[33] I put forward what I believe is such an alternative. There, however, I was primarily concerned with establishing its superiority over various

---

[32] E.g. R. Bauman and J. Sherzer (eds), *Explorations in the Ethnography of Speaking* (Cambridge University Press, Cambridge, 1974); M. Bloch (ed.), *Political Language and Oratory in Traditional Society* (Academic Press, London, 1975).

[33] Trans. from the French by Alice Morton (Cambridge University Press, Cambridge, 1975).

symbolist approaches. Here, I shall redevelop this rationalist approach in contrast to relativism.

'Believe' is standardly described as a verb of propositional attitude (Russell's phrase) along with 'know', 'suppose', 'regret', 'hope', etc. These verbs typically take as object a sentence introduced by 'that' (e.g. 'Paul assumes that Bill will come') and specify the mental attitude (here *assuming*) of the subject (*Paul*) to the proposition expressed by the sentential object (*Bill will come*). As already suggested, there is no reason to expect that these ordinary language notions would be retained by a well-developed psychological theory. But what of the more abstract notion of a propositional attitude? Is the problem just that 'believe', 'know', etc., provide too vague and arbitrary a classification for propositional attitudes, or is it, more radically, that there is no place in scientific psychology for a category of propositional attitudes at all, nor *a fortiori* for its sub-categories, however defined?

The recent development of cognitive psychology involves a shift back from the radical behaviourist rejection of all mental concepts to a more traditional view of the matter:

> Cognitive psychologists accept . . . the *facticity* of ascriptions of propositional attitudes to organisms and the consequent necessity of explaining how organisms come to have the attitudes to propositions they do.
>
> What is *un*traditional about the movement . . . is the account of propositional attitudes that it proposes . . . having a propositional attitude is being in some *computational* relation to an internal representation. [34]

This framework for psychological research, to which, at present, there is no genuine alternative, is however, neither without problem [35] nor immune from revisions. I would like to suggest one emendation which, when it comes to the study of apparently irrational beliefs, has far-reaching consequences.

The phrase 'propositional attitude' is misleading: it obscures the fact that we can have such 'attitudes' to objects other than propositions in the strict sense. Propositions are either true or false. Sets of propositions are either consistent or inconsistent. Propositions, as opposed to sentences or utterances, cannot be ambiguous and hence

---

[34] Fodor, *The Language of Thought*, p. 198.
[35] See D.C. Dennett, *Brainstorms: Philosophical Essays on Mind and Psychology* (Harvester Press, Hassocks, 1978); and Fodor himself.

true in some interpretations and false in others. Yet some of our so-called beliefs have several possible interpretations and we can hold them without committing ourselves to any of their interpretations.

A first example: Bob hears on the news

Stagflation has recently become the main problem of Western economies

and he 'believes' it (as he would say himself). However, Bob is not quite sure what 'stagflation' means. What is it, then, that Bob believes? It could not be the proposition expressed by the journalist, since Bob is not capable of building the corresponding mental representation. It is not just the utterance, because Bob is capable of stating his belief by paraphrasing this utterance rather than merely quoting it; moreover Bob believes many of its implications (e.g. that Western economies have a new important problem). There is, however, one expression that Bob cannot paraphrase and the implications of which he cannot compute, namely 'stagflation'. What Bob believes, then, seems to be a representation which combines several concepts with one unanalysed or incompletely analysed term.

Or consider, as a second example, the relativist slogan:

People of different cultures live in different worlds

I tried earlier on to fix its propositional content as charitably as I could, but the really charitable thing to do would have been not to fix its content at all, which is the attitude of most relativists. They take for granted that this slogan literally expresses a true proposition, but finding out which proposition exactly they see as an aim rather than as a precondition of relativist research. Relativists claim the right to select which of the apparent implications of their belief they will be committed to, and which of its apparent paraphrases they will acknowledge. This attitude is made easier by the vagueness of *different* and the fact that *worlds* in the plural has no fixed meaning at all in ordinary language. The object of the relativist belief, then, is neither a mere formula nor a real proposition: it is a conceptual representation without a fully fixed propositional content.

There are countless similar examples, which tend to show that the objects of our 'propositional attitudes', the ideas we hold or otherwise entertain, are not always strictly propositional in character. Just as it would be mistaken to define 'speaking' in terms of 'uttering sentences', it is mistaken, I suggest, to define thinking as an attitude to propositions: many of our utterances do not match sentences but semi-grammatical strings; similarly, many of our thoughts are what we might call semi-propositional. They approximate but do not achieve propositionality.

In order to clarify the notion of a semi-propositional representation, a comparison might be of help: a person's address is intended to identify one and only one domicile. To do so it must be complete. If, for instance, the street number is lacking, the domicile is approximately localized, but not fully identified. Similarly, a conceptual representation is intended to identify one and only one proposition. However it may fail to do so by being conceptually incomplete, i.e. by containing elements the conceptual content of which is not fully specified. A conceptual representation that succeeds in identifying one and only proposition I shall call a *propositional representation*. A conceptual representation that fails to identify one and only one proposition, I shall call a *semi-propositional representation*. [36]

An address in which the street number is lacking can be completed in as many ways as there are numbers in the specified street: one of these ways must be the proper one. Similarly a semi-propositional representation can be given as many *propositional interpretations* as there are ways of specifying the conceptual content of its elements. In principle, one of these interpretations is the proper one: it identifies the proposition to which the semi-propositional representation is intended to correspond. Suppose, for instance, that Bob thinks that 'stagflation' means either *a stagnant inflation* or *a combination of inflation and stagnation*, without being sure which; then the utterance 'stagflation has recently become the main problem of Western economies' has two possible propositional interpretations for Bob, one of which, he will assume, is the proper one, i.e. corresponds to the proposition that the journalist who produced the utterance was intending to convey.

Notice, though, that some semi-propositional representation may in fact lack a 'proper' interpretation. There is some utterance, for

---

[36] Note that saying that there are semi-propositional representations does not commit one to the existence of 'semi-propositions' (just as saying that there are incomplete addresses does not commit one to the existence of 'semi-domiciles').

instance the relativist slogan, which I do not seem fully to comprehend; the best I can do is construct a semi-propositional representation of it. I imagine that one of the possible interpretations of this representation is the proper one, i.e. corresponds to the proposition that the speaker was trying to convey. However, the speaker might have uttered something which he himself does not understand so well, and of the content of which he too has a semi-propositional representation. If so, then it is the semi-propositional representation that I have constructed, rather than any one of its propositional interpretations, which corresponds to what the speaker actually intended to convey.

Why do we entertain semi-propositional representations? Is it just some defectiveness of our cognitive system or does it play a positive role? The latter, I shall argue.

Our capacity to form semi-propositional representations gives us the means to process information – and in particular verbal information – which exceeds our conceptual capacities. A semi-propositional representation enables us to store and process as much as we understand; it determines a range of possible propositional interpretations; holding, moreover, that the proper interpretation has to be a true and relevant one, may help to select it on the basis of what was already known and what is thereafter learned. Thus a semi-propositional representation can serve as a step towards full comprehension. This of course is a common experiene of childhood, when so many lexical meanings are not fixed in our minds. It recurs throughout life in learning situations.

Inversely, if one finds oneself holding two mutually inconsistent ideas and reluctant to give up either, there is a natural fallback position which consists in giving one of them a semi-propositional form. This occurs, for instance, in scientific thinking when counter-evidence causes one, instead of rejecting the theory at stake, to search for a new interpretation of it by making some of its terms open to redefinition. As long as this search is going on, the theory is in a semi-propositional state.

Semi-propositional representations do not only serve as temporary steps towards, or back from, full propositional understanding. The range of interpretations and the search through that range, as determined by a semi-propositional representation, may be of greater value than any one of these interpretations in particular. The relativists' slogan, the teaching of a Zen master, the philosophy of Kierkegaard, and, generally, poetic texts are cases to the point. Their content is semi-propositional from the start. The speaker's or author's intention is not to convey a specific proposition. It is to provide a range of possible interpretations and to incite the hearer or reader to search that range for the interpretation most relevant to him. The ideas that come as by-products of this search may suffice to make it worthwhile, even, or, rather, particularly when no proper interpretation is ever arrived at.

Well-behaved computers of today just turn down information which does not come in a required format. Human beings, on the other hand, need not and cannot afford to be so choosy. Rather than reject information which they cannot represent propositionally, they try to salvage it by using semi-propositional representations. These play a role not only as temporary steps towards full propositionality but also as sources of suggestion in creative thinking. This, I shall argue, is a crucial part of the psychological background against which the rationality of 'beliefs' is to be assessed.

Factual beliefs and representational beliefs

In a cognitive framework, it is trivial to assume that the human system of internal representations (unlike, perhaps, that of other species) can serve as its own meta-language; in other words, it allows for the representation of representations. From this assumption and the hardly less trivial assumption that conceptual representations can be propositional or semi-propositional, important consequences follow. To expound some of these consequences, I shall make a distinction between 'factual beliefs' and 'representational beliefs'.[37]

Subjectively, factual beliefs are just plain 'knowledge', while representational beliefs would be called 'convictions', 'persuasions', 'opinions', 'beliefs', and the like. In both cases, what is being processed is a mental representation, but in the case of a factual belief there is awareness only of (what to the subject is) a fact, while in the case of a representational belief, there is awareness of a commitment to a representation.

---

[37] A comparable, though not identical, distinction has been suggested by R. de Souza, 'How to give a piece of your mind: or the logics of belief and assent', *Review of Metaphysics*, 25 (1971), pp. 52–79; and developed by Dennett, *Brainstorms*, ch. 16. See also Skorupski, 'The meaning of another culture's beliefs'.

Let us assume (again, a trivial assumption in a cognitive framework) that a human mind contains an encyclopaedic memory (i.e. a memory for conceptual representations, what most psychologists call, rather infelicitously, a 'semantic' memory) and an inferential device. A representation may be stored in the memory either independently or as part of a wider representation. For instance, in a well-read person's memory, 'Shakespeare wrote *Hamlet*' could be stored independently, while 'Hamlet saw the ghost of his father' should be stored in the context 'In Shakespeare's play . . .'. The inferential device uses conceptual representations as premises and derives conceptual representations that logically follow from the premises.[38]

We may now define: a subject's factual beliefs are all the independently stored representations that the subject is capable of retrieving from his encyclopaedic memory and all the representations that, by means of his inferential device, he is capable of deriving from his stored factual beliefs.

Holding a factual belief is rational when it is consistent with, and warranted by the other factual beliefs of the subject. This however could not constitute a necessary condition for the rationality of factual beliefs: making sure of their full consistency is not a psychologically realistic goal. A plausible necessary condition for rationally holding a factual belief is that it should be consistent with all beliefs of closely related content, i.e. with those beliefs in the context of which it is likely to be relevant and which are likely to provide evidence for or against it.

Given this, it can never be rational to hold a semi-propositional representation as a *factual* belief since some of the implications of its proper interpretation cannot be derived and hence their consistency with related factual beliefs cannot be ascertained (leaving aside formal exceptions of no empirical import). On the other hand, as I shall now argue, semi-propositional representations easily make rational *representational* beliefs.

Unlike factual beliefs, representational beliefs are a fuzzy set of related mental attitudes few of which are truly universal.

A representation R is a representational belief of a subject if and only if the subject hold some factual belief about R such as he may sincerely state that R.

---

[38] See D. Sperber and D. Wilson, *Language and Relevance*, forthcoming.

In particular R is a paradigmatic example of representational belief when the subject hold a factual belief of the form:

The proper interpretation of R is true

When R is propositional, there is no difference in rationality between holding that the proper interpretation of R is true and holding that R. On the other hand, when R is semi-propositional it may be quite rational to believe factually that the proper interpretation of R is true – and hence to believe R representationally – although it would be quite irrational to believe R factually.

What may make it rational to hold a representational belief of semi-propositional content is evidence on its source. Suppose I have plenty of evidence that my parents are truthful, and they tell me that the diviner is truthful but cryptic. Is it not rational, then, for me to believe factually that the diviner speaks the truth, to believe representationally what I understand him to say, and to interpret what he says in accordance with these beliefs? Or suppose that my teachers tell me that people of different cultures live in different worlds. It does sound silly. Yet my teachers could not be silly, could they? So what they say must be profound. Profound: another word for semi-propositional.

One may be strongly committed to a representational belief of semi-propositional content, but then it is a strong commitment to a very weak claim. The wider the range of possible interpretations of R, the weaker the claim that its proper interpretation is true. Furthermore, rather than believing factually that the proper interpretation of R is true, the subject may, with similar results, believe (factually or representionally) that:

R is what we were taught by wise people.
R is a dogma in our Church.
R is a holy mystery.
R is deemed to be true.
Marx (Freud, Wittgenstein . . .) convincingly argued for R.
Only heathens (fascists, people from the other side of the mountain. . . .) would deny R.

Accepting any of these claims has little to do with the content of R and yet it would be enough to make the subject express R in an assertive form, invoke it freely, object to its being questioned, explore its possible interpretations, in short behave as a 'believer'.

Would we want to say, though, that in all these cases, the subject holds R as a representational belief? The question has less pertinence than it might seem, since, in any case, there is little reason to expect representational beliefs to constitute a well-defined natural class. They differ in this respect from factual beliefs. If humans have a capacity for factual beliefs, i.e. for constructing, storing and deriving representations of facts, it is much more plausible that it be part of the equipment which makes acquisition possible than part of what is acquired. The same holds for the capacity to construct and process representations about representations. Once we have assumed this much, we have no need, and indeed we have no ground to further assume that there is a distinct innate capacity for representational beliefs.

An organism capable of holding all sorts of factual beliefs about representations can thereby develop or acquire an indefinite range of attitudes to representations going (among other dimensions) from absolute commitment to absolute rejection. It may be convenient to divide this range of 'representational attitudes' into a few broad categories but there is no reason to expect these to have much psychological significance. 'Representational beliefs' is such a category. How much should be included, where the line should be drawn, is a matter of expediency rather than of truth.

For my present purpose, a broad category of representational beliefs, including all kinds of strong commitments to a representation, is the most convenient. It has the advantage of matching anthropologists' own vagueness while clarifying what it is that they are being vague about. Anthropologists are vague as to what exactly is the attitude of the people to their beliefs, beyond its being one of commitment.[39] There is some justification for this vagueness, since there is no reason to suppose that people expressing the same belief all have exactly the same attitude to it.

Anthropologists, then, use 'belief' with a vagueness suited to their data. Philosophers discussing relativism[40] generally take for granted

---

[39] See J. Favret-Saada, *Deadly Words*, trans. from the French by Catherine Cullen (Cambridge University Press, Cambridge, 1980) for a remarkable exception.

[40] E.g. S. Lukes, 'Some problems about rationality', *Archives Européennes de Sociologie*, 8 (1967), repr. in Wilson, *Rationality*.

as a matter of mere definition that beliefs are 'propositions accepted as true', i.e. in my terms that all beliefs are (or are logically equivalent to) factual beliefs.

If people of different cultures did hold apparently irrational *factual* beliefs, then it might be acceptable to try and reformulate the content of these beliefs so as to establish their rationality, even at the cost of having to imagine different cognizable worlds. But there is no reason, either theoretical or empirical, to assume that the apparently irrational beliefs reported by anthropologists and historians are factual beliefs. No theoretical reason: the very fact that, when assumed to be factual, these beliefs appear irrational is reason enough to assume, on the contrary, that they are representational beliefs with a semi-propositional content, thereby avoiding the costs of relativism. No empirical reason: look in the literature for evidence as to the exact attitude people have toward their 'beliefs'; what little evidence there is supports the view that the beliefs we are dealing with are representational and have a semi-propositional content.

That beliefs reported by anthropologists are representational is rather obvious: they are *cultural* beliefs, i.e. representations acquired through social communication and accepted on the ground of social affiliation. Anthropologists learn about these cultural beliefs by recording ritualized expressions of traditional wisdom or by specifically questioning informants about the traditions of their people rather than about their own cogitations. So, what people take for a fact is the truth or the validity, the wisdom, the respectability, the orthodoxy, etc., of a representation, i.e. they believe this representation representationally.

Again, that apparently irrational beliefs have a semi-propositional content is, to say the least, what the available evidence strongly suggests. In a few cases such as that of 'mysteries' in the Catholic doctrine, the natives explicitly say so: the meaning (i.e. the proper propositional interpretation) is beyond human grasp. More often, the semi-propositional character of cultural beliefs is implicitly acknowledged in one of two ways. In some cases people offer exegeses of their beliefs, and, while sharing beliefs, wonder, argue or even fight about interpretations. In other cases, when you ask the people what their cultural beliefs mean, what they imply, how they fit with everyday facts, etc., they beg off, saying: 'It is the tradition', 'Our ancestors knew', or something to that effect. Whether the proper interpretation is considered a secret lost or a secret to be discovered (or both), a clear if implicit distinction is made between holding a belief and knowing how to interpret it. This distinction only makes sense if these are semi-propositional beliefs.

This is not to say, obviously, that all culturally transmitted beliefs are semi-propositional. But then not all of them should appear irrational either. For instance many culturally transmitted technical beliefs are clearly rationally held factual beliefs. More generally, I would expect that when culturally transmitted beliefs have a genuinely propositional content, whatever appearance of irrationality they may give can be dispelled by an intellectualist approach.

But aren't there counter-examples, evidence that apparently irrational beliefs (not explainable in intellectualist terms) are just facts to those who hold them? There are, at least, alleged counter-examples. Here is a well-known and typical one: Evans-Pritchard reported that the Nuer hold 'that a twin is a bird as though it were an obvious fact, for Nuer are not saying that a twin is like bird but that he is a bird'.[41] But, then, Evans-Pritchard warns that we should not take Nuer statements about twins 'more literally than they make and understand them themselves. They are not saying that a twin has a beak, feathers, and so forth . . .'.[42]

Well, there is no such thing as a non-literal fact. Hence if we pay close attention to the whole of Evans-Pritchard's report, we can no longer maintain that for the Nuer it is a fact that twins are birds. It is, rather, a commonplace representational belief of semi-propositional content. Generally speaking, when anthropologists assert that R is a fact for the So-and-So, their evidence is that the So-and-So tell and are told R without batting an eyelid. Hardly overstating the case, this is what all the evidence for relativism ultimately boils down to.

Anthropologists and philosophers have been carrying on only the semblance of a dialogue. Anthropological data does not have the easy theoretical relevance that relativism would endow it with. Relativism is a sophisticated solution to a problem which, as stated, does not even arise. If apparently irrational beliefs falsely appear to be irrational, it is not because their content is misrepresented, it is because in the first place they falsely appear to be beliefs in the philosopher's sense, i.e. propositions accepted as true. The problem is not one of poor trans-

[41] E.E. Evans-Pritchard, *Nuer Religion* (Oxford University Press, Oxford, 1956), p. 131.
[42] Ibid.

lation (though, of course, poor translations are common), it is one of poor psychology.

I have suggested that we should make two psychological distinctions: between propositional and semi-propositional representations, and between factual and representational beliefs. Then, all we need in order to dispel the appearance of irrationality of cultural beliefs is to establish that they are representational beliefs of semi-propositional content. Indeed, when all the members of your cultural group seem to hold a certain representational belief of semi-propositional content, this constitutes sufficiently rational ground for you to hold it too. [43]

That cultural beliefs are representational is almost tautologous; that they are semi-propositional is implicit and even sometimes explicit in the way people express and discuss them. There are many implications to this view of cultural beliefs[44] but only one concerns us here: relativism can be dispensed with.

CONCLUSION: BEWARE OF THE DRAGON

And what about old Filate? It may have been like this: One of the traders who came to Dorze on market days told him about the dragon. Was the trader in earnest? Where had he himself heard the story? It does not matter. Filate was enthralled. In his youth, he too had travelled and fought and hunted strange animals in the wilderness. Now he was too old. But he had to tell the people. They would prepare, they would go. And when they came back with the trophy, they would thank him and include his name in their boasting songs.

Perhaps he had already taken his lyre and was about to give way to his emotion, as I had seen him do several times, singing himself to tears, when he realized what would actually happen: the people would not go, they would not sing, indeed, they would mock him. They would say: if a strange beast had been spotted, wouldn't we already have heard? No, had Filate told them that he had seen, with his own

---

[43] Of course, if your aim is knowledge and if you want not just to achieve but to maximize rationality, you should not trust easily and you should be wary of semi-propositional representations with no proper interpretation in sight; but doing so might be at the expense of rationality in social relations.

[44] Sperber, *Rethinking Symbolism;* and 'Is symbolic thought prerational?'.

gummy eyes, a stray wart-hog on the path from Ochollo, they might have gone and looked. But he had been *told* that there was a dragon, *he* had been told . . .

Yet it had to be true. He felt it. He could bet on it. Such great news and no one would listen! Better keep quiet, he must have told himself dejectedly. But then it occured to him: the *forenj*, the white man who had arrived just a few months ago, he might listen. Yes, Filate now remembered, *forenj* went for big game, they even had special equipment. If anybody could kill a dragon, a *forenj* could. The *forenj* would be grateful. He would give Filate money and clothes.

And so he came to me.

What if I had expressed doubts that such an animal exists? He would have told me what he knew: they were golden all over; whether it was real gold or just the way they looked, he didn't know. Yes, their heart was of gold, real gold. How should he know if a heart of gold could beat? He was merely quoting what people who had killed these animals were reported to have said, and they knew better than any of us. Surely I must see that.

Though I will never know what really went on in Filate's head, I do not need to invoke a difference in cognizable worlds in order to conceive of plausible hypotheses.

What I eventually found more intriguing is the way in which I responded to Filate's request, and the fact that I left it out of my diary. Once I had understood that the old man was asking me to kill a dragon, my only worry became to turn down his request without hurting his feelings or appearing a coward.

'Kill a dragon!', I said, 'I don't know if I could.'

'What are you saying?', he retorted angrily, 'I thought *forenj* knew how to kill dragons.'

'Oh, well, yes, I see, yes, ah, but . . . I don't have a gun!'

'Couldn't you get one?'

I thought then of the French vet in the nearby town of Arba Minch; he might be interested and could procure a gun.

'Yes, I suppose I could get a gun. But I wouldn't know how to find the dragon. We *forenj* may be good at killing dragons, but not at tracking them.'

This is when he said he would come back the next day, and left. So, I hadn't managed to refuse, only to delay. But why in the first place had I been so eager to refuse? Was I afraid I would have to confront the dragon? Didn't I know that dragons don't exist? Sure I knew, but still . . . [45] I could have accepted without risk, I could have postponed the answer and asked appropriate ethnographic questions, but no, my purpose had been to extricate myself from a non-existent predicament, while, at the same time, toying with the idea of going ahead.

The next day, when reporting Filate's visit in my diary, I must have felt somewhat embarrassed, since I omitted the second half of the dialogue, the part that gives me away.

Thinking again about the episode (as I have done a few times over the years), I am now not so much puzzled by my response to Filate's request as by my embarrassment and my omission. Being asked to slay a dragon is a rare experience; it nevertheless evokes many shared memories, fears and dreams. Why not, then entertain the idea and enjoy it?

It must have been like this. There I was, a trained anthropologist on his first real field trip, and a native came and asked me to kill a dragon. In the first second I knew that I had hit on a great piece of data: a wise old man believing in an actual dragon, the cultural gap illustrated in a vignette! Yet, one second later, there I was, a reluctant dragon-killer staggering on the other side of the unbridgeable gap. At that point, the difference between Filate's thought-processes and mine was that he knew how to enjoy them and make the pleasure last.

When I became my scholarly self again, taking scholarly notes, I re-created the alleged gap by conveniently omitting the embarrassing part of the episode, and I was left with a choice piece of evidence in favour of relativism.

The full story, then, is really a piece of evidence against relativism, but, more important, it is a piece of evidence *on* relativism. Several anthropologists[46] have stressed to what extent people will go in order to maintain or establish all kinds of conceptual gaps and boundaries between natural kinds, types of activity, the sexes, and, most important, between 'we' and 'they'. In pre-relativist anthropology, Westerners thought of themselves as superior to all other people. Relativism replaced this despicable hierarchical gap by a kind of cognitive apar-

---

[45] 'Je sais bien, mais quand même . . .', the basic formula of believers, argued O. Mannoni in a now classic paper, *Clefs pour l'Imaginaire ou l'Autre Scène* (Seuil, Paris, 1969), ch. 1.

[46] In particular, C. Lévi-Strauss, *The Savage Mind* (trans.) (Chicago University Press, Chicago, 1966); M. Douglas, *Purity and Danger: An Analysis of Concepts of Pollution and Taboo* (Routledge & Kegan Paul, London, 1966).

theid. If we cannot be superior in the same world, let each people live in its own world.

The best evidence against relativism is, ultimately, the very activity of anthropologists, while the best evidence for relativism seems to be in the writings of anthropologists. How can that be? In retracing their steps, anthropologists transform into unfathomable gaps the shallow and irregular cultural boundaries that they had found not so difficult to cross, thereby protecting their own sense of identity, and providing their philosophical and lay audience with just what they want to hear.

Relativism and Universals

Ernest Gellner

A spectre haunts human thought: relativism. If truth has many faces, then not one of them deserves trust or respect. Happily, there is a remedy: human universals. They are the holy water with which the spectre can be exorcized. But, of course, before we can use human universals to dispel the threat of cognitive anarchy, which would otherwise engulf us, we must first *find* them. And so, the new hunt for the Holy Grail is on.

The underlying and interconnected issues, as I see them, are these: just what is the problem of relativism, or rather, what *are* the problems of relativism? How are they related to the issues of human uniqueness or the existence of human universals? What are the general features of explanation of human conduct which are pertinent to this? What are the influential themes in recent thought which provide the terms and assumptions in which they are likely to formulate both questions and answers?

There are (at least) two problems, but those two problems are absolutely fundamental: is there but one kind of man, or are there many? Is there but one world, or are there many? These two questions are *not* identical; but they are not unconnected either. But it is quite wrong to identify or confuse the two questions, as is sometimes done. The second problem – one world or many – can also be formulated as: are there many truths or one?

The preoccupation with the issue of human or social 'universals' is in effect a concern with whether there is but one kind of man, or

Reprinted from B. Lloyd and J. Gay (eds), *Universals of Human Thought: Some African Evidence*. (Cambridge University Press, Cambridge, 1981).

whether there are many kinds of men; or alternatively, what shared features unite all men or all human societies. This the unity of *man*, rather than the unity of *worlds*, which is in the foreground of the discussion. Yet behind this, one senses a concern with relativism.

The two issues are of course intimately connected, as indeed is visible from the occasions at which the discussion strays from one to the other: if man is not one but many, then will not each kind of man also make his own kind of world, and if so, how can we choose amongst them? What happens then to the uniqueness and objectivity of truth? Our moral intuitions tend to impel us in different directions at this point. Liberalism, tolerance, pluralism, incline many to find pleasure in the idea of a multiplicity of men and visions; but the equally reputable and enlightened desire for objectivity and universality leads to a desire that at least the world and truth be but one, and not many. (The tolerant endorsement of human diversity becomes very tangled if one realizes that very many past and alien visions have themselves in turn been internally exclusive, intolerant and ethnocentric; so that if we, in our tolerant way, endorse *them*, we thereby also endorse or encourage intolerance at second hand. This might be called the dilemma of the liberal intellectual.) By contrast, extreme leftists are sometimes addicted to the thesis of the plasticity or malleability of man. This tends, especially in the case of Marxists, to form part of a polemic against the alleged habit of their opponents of turning the conceptual artefacts of one particular social order into a human universal, so as to discourage any questioning of that social order.

The pursuit of universals, of the unity of man, is also on occasion inspired by the desire to underwrite the brotherhood and equality of man. Whether indeed our values are or should be so directly at the mercy of scholarly findings may well be doubted. I do not anticipate that on the day of the publication of a generative grammar of colloquial Bongo-Bongo, definitely establishing the absolute uniqueness of Bongo-Bongo syntax, I shall promptly conclude that the discriminatory measures imposed on the Bongo-Bongo by hostile authorities are henceforth justified.

But it is, I believe, profoundly significant that by and large, whilst the ultimate motive of the enquiry may be the establishment of an unitary world, the method employed is the pursuit of the unity of *man*. Yet the unity of the world seems at the same time tacitly *assumed* within the enquiry, as providing the framework within which it is carried on (even though one also senses the tacit hope that it will also in turn be demonstrated, *through* the unity of man).

I believe this to be significant twice over. It tells us something about the current intellectual climate: we are fairly sure about which world we inhabit, and that there is but one, though we are much less sure about the foundations of this conviction, or its precise definition. We flirt with relativism, which we then try to refute by showing mankind to be one, by means of an enquiry nevertheless carried on within a unitary, unrelative world . . . We are less sure about the unity of man, or precisely what it would mean. This also constitutes a clue, to my mind, concerning the only solution to which the problem of relativism is really susceptible.

Relativism is basically a doctrine in the theory of knowledge: it asserts that there is no unique truth, no unique objective reality. What we naîvely suppose to be such is but the product – exclusively, or in some proportion, which varies with the particular form the relativism takes – of the cognitive apparatus of the individual, community, age or whatever. (Relativisms differ in many respects, including the identification of the units to which the relativity is meant to apply.) If this is inherently and necessarily so, then perhaps no sense attaches to speaking about a unique, absolute or objective truth, but only of a truth or reality relative to the unit or cognitive apparatus in question. Notoriously, there is no room for the assertion of relativism itself, in a world in which relativism is true. The previous sentences have sketched out a world; but if they did succeed in painting a relativist world, do they not at the same time willy-nilly say something absolute about it? This difficulty should not be overstressed. It does not inhibit our intuitive capacity for visualizing a relativist world; and to use this difficulty as a reason for treating the fear of relativism as groundless seems to me facile and superficial. Despite all the problems which attach to articulating the idea of a plurality of worlds and truths, intuitively this notion does make sense, and I believe this intuition to be justified.

Note however that such relativism is perfectly compatible with the existence of any number of, so to speak, *de facto* or contingent human 'universals'. In a world unbounded by any unique truth, it might still be the case, by accident, that all human languages had a certain grammatical structure, that chromatic perception was identical in all cultures, that all societies proscribed certain relations as incestuous, etc., etc. *A priori* one would perhaps have less reason in such a world to expect that these universals or constants should obtain. This is so because *one* reason, but one reason only, for this expectation would be absent in a 'relative' world: this reason being the direct constraint by objective truth. 'Objective truth' being absent, it could no longer constrain anyone. But *other* constraints could still operate.

If, on the other hand, in objective and unique truth, or in independent reality, colours 'really' are such and such, and if certain types of relationships 'really' are wrong and incestuous, etc., then, *in so far as* the human mind also apprehends the unique and rational truth, it will be canalized into a unique, universal and constant mould. Diversity of perception or opinion could then only spring from the presence of *error*. But truth is only one factor influencing the mind, amongst other possible ones, and incidentally not always a powerful one: so despite the uniqueness of truth, some societies might still be under the sway of chromatic, moral or other error. In fact, societies have often believed this about each other, and sometimes about their own past.

On the other hand, whilst not necesarily led to a unique position by Reason – which notoriously holds but a feeble sway over the human spirit – men might *still* be led to a unique position which was *not* the 'right' one, and by *other* and possibly less praiseworthy factors. There might be non-rational constraints of a neurological, social or other kind, compelling mankind to remain within some moral, linguistic or other universal, even though objectively this single path was not unique – or possibly not even correct at all.

So it is conceivable that relativism be true, and yet human universals obtain; and equally, it is possible that relativism be false, and yet no universals obtain (or only trivial ones) . . . There seems nothing, at least intuitively or *prima facie* absurd about a uniquely determined universe, available in principle for cognition in one correct form only; but one such that, within it, inside such a metaphysically well-favoured and attractive universe, it should so happen that grammatical, conceptual, kinship, moral, etc., systems were so highly variegated that comparative grammarians, anthropologists etc., had to despair of ever finding any universal traits. A God outside this universe would know how its variegated sub-systems all successfully operated within one total system, without any one of them embracing the totality and without any being mutually translatable. In so far as this diversity extended to all aspects of life, things might indeed become very difficult. First of all, if the cognitive equipment of cultures varies so much in such a unique-truth universe, it follows that all their cultures (with at most one exception) must be cognitively in error, at least in some measure; and their inability to grasp the *others* must make them, at best, incomplete. There is nothing absurd, or at least nothing unusual, in such a supposition. More difficult still, if the cognitive equipment of societies differs radically, there may be some difficulty in the practice of intercultural anthropology *at all*, for obvious reasons.

It is an interesting fact about the world we actually live in that no anthropologist, to my knowlede, has come back from a field trip with the following report: *their* concepts are *so* alien that it is impossible to describe their land tenure, their kinship system, their ritual. . . . As far as I know, there is no record of such a total admission of failure. Perhaps sanctions applied by anthropology departments are too severe? Perhaps such anthropological failures do not present their theses, or even report back from field work at all. This doesn't prove, of course, that it has never occurred; and if it had occurred, it would not prove that it was due to the inherent inaccessibility of the material, as opposed to the deficiencies of the particular investigator. What one does quite often hear is admissions of partial failure of comprehension: 'I simply cannot imagine what the so-and-so, a West African tribe, mean they they speak of washing their souls'; 'I thought I knew the Himalayan hill folk well, having lived amongst them for a considerable time, but when a death occurred in the family, I saw from their reactions that I did not understand anything'; etc. Such partial in-comprehensions are common, but they have not, to my knowledge, prevented the drawing-up of an account of at least large parts of the social life, language, etc., of the community in question. I have heard an anthropologist who had come back from a but-recently discovered group in New Guinea say that they really were 'very very distant' in their way of thinking, and implying that the strenuousness of his effort had had to be much greater than on his other field experiences with 'closer' cultural communities; but he did not report *failure*.

I think all this is significant, and indicates something (at worst, it could indicate complacency and a misguided supposition that we understand when in fact we do not); but on the often rather *a priori* reasoning of relativist philosophers, who start out from doctrines such as the ultimacy and self-sufficiency of 'forms of life', we might have expected such failure to be much more common. It is *success* in explaining culture A in the language of culture B which is, in the light of such a philosophy, really puzzling. Yet shelves groan with the weight of such books.

So, the truth of the matter seems to me this: the issues of relativism, and that of the existence of human universals, are *not* one and the same issue. The problem of relativism is whether there is one and one only world, in the end; whether all the divergent visions of reality can in the end be shown (leaving out cases when they are simply mistaken) to be diverse aspects of one and the same objective world, whose diversity can itself be explained in terms of the properties or laws of that world. There are some reasonably persuasive, if not formally compelling, reasons for holding the belief in such unique reality.

But this is not the same question as that concerning whether or not man is one and unique, whether in basic features humanity is internally alike, and perhaps also externally unique (whether all men are alike, and unlike everything non-human). Not only are the two questions about whether there is one world, and whether all men are alike, not identical, but the widely diffused assumption that a positive answer to the first depends on a positive answer to the second seems to me quite mistaken. In my view, the reasons for which will be given, the reverse relationship obtains: the positive answer to the first hinges on a negative answer to the second. The uniqueness of the world hinges on the diversity, the non-universality of man. There is one world only, there are many men; and just because there are many kinds of men, there is one world. For the unique world is the achievement of *some* men only; and had men and cultures not been diversified, the single world might never have emerged, for social forms would not have differed enough to hit on this special one; and all this is of the essence of the thing. But this paradoxical claim requires clarification and defence.

It is, as stated, a striking feature of the explorations – one is tempted to say, flirtations – with the idea of the diversity of man, of radical differentiation in the human conceptual or other equipment, that is carried out in the context of *one unitary world*. The assumption, if it becomes conscious and explicit as a result of challenge, can, I suppose, be defended as follows: but what else do you wish us to do? Where else, other than in the shared and assumed common world of the scientific and scholarly tradition in which we were trained, do you want us to carry out our investigation into the Diversity of Men? This doesn't mean that we necessarily grant that shared world more than a kind of interim status. If our researches lead us to conclude that man is irreducibly diverse, and that each kind of man has his own kind of world, then we shall accept and endorse that kind of plurality of men, visions, worlds, and refuse to endow the unique world, within which our enquires were initially conducted, with any kind of special status. It was the door through which we entered the many-chambered mansion, but once safely within it we see that it is not a unique or privileged door. This ladder we may throw away when we have ascended. . . .

Perhaps such an attitude is possible. But I doubt it. I believe that our attachment to the unique world, within which alone the enquiries into the diversity of man and hence the diversity of his visions is carried out, is far deeper and more significant than that. It is not *a* world; it is *the* world.

Before discussing why this should be so, it may be essential to consider, as briefly and schematically as possible, what this world – *the* world – is like: what are its general traits?

This one privileged world is a public and symmetrical world: symmetrical in that it contains within itself no privileged places, times, individuals or groups, which would be allowed to exempt cognitive claims from testing or scrutiny. On the contrary, all claims and all evidence are deemed to be ultimately equal: some of course are treated with respect due to past distinction, and some with derision; in intellectual matters as in social, equality is far from complete. But an idea is an idea for a' that: and their status differentiation is not absolute, total and eternal. Reality is not ranked and stratified in dignity and availability for scrutiny, as it is in other and more traditional kinds of vision. Amongst civilized members of the republic of the mind, it is recognized that in principle no idea is so silly as not to deserve any hearing at all, and none so elevated as to be exempt from discussion. All must submit to the same base-line of evidence. Quite literally, this means that nothing is sacred. Decent cognitive comportment, the observance of proper epistemological rules, cast a secularized world as their own inescapable shadow. Evidence in turn is broken up into small packages, and is not allowed exemption from scrutiny. Practice may not fully live up to this ideal, but it does not altogether violate it either.

Equality of ultimate civic rights of all ideas and evidence, so to speak, is not the only feature of this shared and unique world of ours. It also has traits which seem to attach more directly to the stuff of the world rather than to the ideas about it (though this distinction may itself be questioned). What are these substantive traits? A kind of orderliness of behaviour: it is assumed that like causes will have like effects, thereby making generalization and theory-building possible. This feature used to be given names such as the Regularity of Nature or the Principle of Sufficient Reason, and no doubt others.

The orderliness of the world is also assumed to be systematic: not only are there regularities to be discovered, but they also form a system, such that, if we are successful in our enquiries, the more specific regularities turn out in the end to be corollaries of more general ones. Ideally, the system might even one day turn out to possess an apex, an all-embracing theory. In the meantime, the fragments of it which we do possess seem to point towards such an apex, and seem to urge us on in the pursuit of it.

What reasons have we to believe in such a world – and in its unique validity – over and above the contingent and in itself plainly inconclusive and indeed suspect fact that it happens to be the vision within which, at least in office hours, most of us think and work? This is the one world, *within which* we enquire whether mankind is unitary. Yet it is itself the world of *some* men only (including *us*). Is it more than just our vision, is it the account of how things actually are? And if so, why?

There is of course no non-circular way of establishing this Single World or Unique Truth. (Other visions validate themselves by their own rules, and will not play according to ours. Hence any move which eliminates them also breaks their rules, and is consequently question-begging.) But there are at least partially non-question-begging ways of supporting this position, and these are probably all we can ever have. *If* it were the case that there existed a number of centres of consciousness or knowledge, each as it were plugged into a different cosmic programme, which in turn remained unrelated to each other, then that would be that, and there would be nothing we could do about it. (I leave aside the intriguing question whether in such a universe, the above sentence would not nevertheless contain a unique *and* all-embracing truth, relating the centres and their experiences to each other precisely by the assertion that they are not congruent.) But that does not seem to be our world. What reasons can we adduce in support of such a conviction?

There are two converging arguments, the epistemological and the sociological. They need to be sketched out briefly.

The epistemological. Here we start out with the minimum of assumptions, so as to beg no questions. Initially *anything* may be true. We ask: how can we pick out the correct option of belief, seeing that we have no prior indication of what it may be? The answer is contained in the epistemological tradition which has accompanied the rise of modern science, at first to help it along, and later so as to exlain its miraculous success.

The answer is, in rough outline: eliminate all self-maintaining circular belief systems. As the main device of self-maintaining systems is the package-deal principle, which brings about the self-maintaining circle of ideas, break up information into as many parts as possible, and scrutinize each item separately. This breaks up the circles and destroys the self-maintenance. At the same time, assume nevertheless the regularity of nature, the systematic nature of the world, not because it is demonstrable, but because anything which eludes such a principle also eludes real knowledge; *if* cumulative and communicable knowledge is to be possible at all, then the principle of orderliness must also apply to it. . . . The inherently idiosyncratic has no place in a corpus of knowledge. Unsymmetrical, idiosyncratic explanations are worthless – they are not explanations. Unconvertible currencies are not suitable for trade, and ungeneralizable explanations are useless for a practical and cumulative body of knowledge. If like conditions did *not* produce like effects, then the experimental accumulation of knowledge would have no point and would not be feasible. Only theories built on the assumption of symmetry and orderliness can be negotiated and applied. Material not amenable to treatment within this assumption is worthless, and must either be reinterpreted or discarded.

In brief: the atomization of information and the orderly systematization of explanation are imperative. Neither of them is established except as a *precondition* of having real knowledge at all. But, *ex hypothesi*, they do generate a unique world, one subject to a unique set of laws only. Information is atomized and thus obliged to shed excessive and covert theoretical loading; and theories are systematized and thus incoherences and putative idiosyncrasy are eventually eliminated.

The sociological. In our actual and shared world, diverse cultures, though not sharing their beliefs, nevertheless seem to have little trouble in communicating with each other. The world contains many communities, but they visibly inhabit the same world and compete within it. Some are cognitively stagnant, and a few are even regressive; some, on the other hand, possess enormous and indeed growing cognitive wealth, which is so to speak validated by works as well as faith: its implementation leads to a very powerful technology. There is a near-universal consensus about this, in deeds rather than in words: those who do not possess this knowledge and technology endeavour to emulate and acquire it.

As it happens, the cognitively cumulative and powerful communities apply, in their serious intellectual life, an epistemology roughly of the kind singled out previously in the specification of the epistemological argument. Powerful technology is based on a science which in turn seems to observe the rules of an information-atomizing enquiry, and of symmetrical and orderly theory-construction.

The epistemological argument is abstract and, on its own, shares all the weaknesses of abstract arguments. The history of thought must contain countless specimens of abstract arguments which sound plausible enough but which either failed to carry conviction or were eventually shown to be false or both. The sociological argument on the other hand is crude and pragmatic to the point of meretricious opportunism.

Moreover the conjunction of the two is extremely inelegant. The epistemological one deliberately starts from scratch with the absolute minimum of assumptions, whilst the sociological one makes itself a present of the world which we think we live in, of our shared and often unexamined views of what is going on in it, and incidentally of some rather crass earthy values prevailing in it. Thus, a totally impractical abstraction, an argument beyond all contexts, excogitated in a putative 'cosmic exile', is fused with a meretriciously crude and all-too-worldly consideration based on greed for wealth and scramble for power. What strange bedfellows! – but they do point one and the same way, and jointly constitute the grounds we have for choosing and accepting the unique world we think and live in.

Thus, for all the inelegance of their juxtaposition, the incongruity of this bizarre marriage of convenience, and for all their great faults taken singly, this conjunction and its two elements are the best we have, the most we shall probably ever have, and they do, infact, jointly carry conviction and – I am myself tempted to add – rightly so. But perhaps that adds nothing (other than complacency) to the preceding statement.

But if it be accepted that it is by this kind of reasoning that we have

attained a Single World and Unique Truth, then the somewhat paradoxical conclusion follows that a Single World, and Single Man, do *not*
go together at all. On the contrary: for the particular thought style
which alone generated this unique, converging, cumulative world, as
the object of human cognition, was *not* universally dispersed amongst
men. On the contrary, it was but one tradition amongst many, and a
very untypical one. It prevailed, *and* we hold it to be valid. Within it,
and on its terms, we carry out investigations into the other visions
which were once its rivals. *It* provides the single context, within which
we investigate and interpret all other visions. We do not hold it to be
valid only because it has prevailed, but the fact that it generates a kind
of technology which helps its adherents to prevail also indisputably
constitutes *a* consideration.

This position differs from pragmatism in a number of important
ways. For one thing, practical success is but one consideration, as
indicated. This view asserts that a given vision is valid *and* therefore is
practically effective, but it does not identify validity and effectiveness.
There is in fact no reason to suppose that effective science does
increase the survival-prospect of the species which carries it. The
self-destruction of humanity, through nuclear or other war or ecological disaster, is perfectly possible and perhaps probable in the post-
scientific age, whereas previously mankind did not possess the power
to destroy itself, and, owing to its dispersal, was virtually certain not to
face destruction by any outside force. So if truth were equated with
that which increases the probability of survival, then science would
certainly be untrue.

But perhaps philosophically the most significant and profound
difference hinges on the fact that pragmatism, like various related
strands in the evolutionist and Hegelian thought-styles, believed the
true cognitive vision, or rather practices, to be something ever-present
in history (including, for pragmatism, *biological* history), only becoming ever more effective and manifest with the progress of time. In one
famous formulation of this kind of view, the amoeba and Einstein use
the same method, which is the key to all real knowledge (namely, trial
and error). On the view which is here advocated, and presented as the
(only) way in which we have overcome relativism, or can ever do so,
this is not so at all: the correct vision or cognitive style appears at *a*
definite point in time, and thus introduces a radical *dis*continuity in
history. Just as it is not universal in space – it characterizes *some* men,
not *all* men – so it is also not universal in time. Pragmatists and

Hegelians believed in a kind of Permanent Revolution; the valid thought-style or its underlying ultimate principle was confirmed by eternal repetition, and its authority reinforced by such reiteration. On the present view, no such reiteration occurs to underwrite the One True Vision. This difference is the crucial difference between the nineteenth- and twentieth-century philosophical uses of history. The twentieth-century version has not yet been properly formulated philosophically.

So the Singleness of Man is *not* required for the Uniqueness of the World or of Truth. These were initially carried only by an eccentric minority, and they are not underwritten either by human universality or by permanence in time. This vision is underwritten – if valid at all, as I hold it to be – in quite a different manner which was briefly sketched out.

So the universality of a single model of man, so to speak, is not required for the philosophical purpose (the overcoming of relativism) for which it is, I suspect, often introduced. But, whether or not required for this end, it also has an inherent intrinsic interest, and deserves consideration for its own sake. So, what is the state of play with respect to the Universality of a Single Human Model?

There are (at least) two ways of approaching this: first, by asking whether there are manifest and, if you like, surface similarities in men; and secondly whether there are underlying identities or similarities in explanatory principle or mechanism. Furthermore, of course, each of these questions can be asked separately for various aspects of human activity and experience, and the answers may vary from field to field. [1]

A proper survey of the phenomena in each field could only be carried out by competent specialists in that field. None the less, it may be useful for a non-specialist to give a general impressionistic overview of what the findings suggest, when such surveys are completed.

In fields such a sensory sensibility and motor performance, differences do exist but are not very striking or extensive. It appears harder to locate them than it is to locate intercultural or inter-ethnic similarities in these fields. Moreover, when they do occur, it seems quite

---

[1] Cf. for example an excellent survey of this problem in connection with the perception and conceptualization of colour: *Voir et Nommer les Couleurs*, Laboratoire d'Ethnologie et de Sociologie Comparative (Serge Tornay, Nanterre, 1978).

reasonable to expect differences to be explained by the impact of, for example, climatic or social environment on basically similar underlying physiological equipment. So, differences are not striking and furthermore, they tend to become eliminated at the next explanatory level. To put this in another way: men seem to move and act in pretty much the same world and with much the same physical equipment.

Truly enormous intercultural differences, on the other hand, occur in certain other areas, where societies, as one is tempted to say, are free to indulge their fantasy: mythology, cosmology, metaphysics, and in some measure, in social, political, ritual organization. The profound and radical differences in world vision between sophisticated cultures are reasonably evident: when they translate their doctrines in each other's language, the resulting translations sometimes sound very odd indeed. Yet the translations are widely recognized as reasonably accurate by bilingual or bicultural persons. In this area, the view that the oddity enters only through mistranslation is implausible and difficult to sustain.

The situation is somewhat different and complex when it comes to identifying and interpreting the 'world-view' of 'primitive' peoples, i.e. those which have no script and no clerical class to codify that view. Here, the interpretation and systematization is carried out by outsiders (or those who were trained by outsiders), and the view that the oddity lies in the translation, and not in the view translated, acquires some plausibility. In what sense, for instance, can a tribesman who is no theologian, and whose society does not have theologians, be credited with a theology which seems implicit to the outsider in his ritual or myths? This question is highly pertinent to the once fashionable attribution of a distinctive 'primitive mentality' to populations living in simple societies; but it is equally pertinent to the more recent revival of the attribution to them of the scientific and experimental spirit. The issue is open and methodologically difficult. Just how different one finds the savage seems to hinge largely on whether one goes by what he *does* (which is not strange – he acts in the same world as we do, and in a similar way), or by what he says (very odd by most translations), or by functionalist interpretations of what he says (not odd after all), or whether in the end one is swayed by the thought that though odd the statement is context-bound in ritual (hence also not odd). And yet, its impact on him of the ritual hinges on it sounding odd *to him as well*, if interpreted in parallel with daily ordinary statements – and so it is odd after all. As far as I can see, you can pick and choose as to which of these levels of sophistication you select as your resting-place, and hence which conclusion you reach.

So to sum up: minor and so to speak explicable differences at sensory and motor level; very great differences at the level of self-conscious, codified civilization with codified criteria of valid belief – though interestingly a very good measure of translatability exists at the same time, which facilitates the highlighting of this divergence. (Translatability does not seem to mean agreement.) There are all kinds of 'translatability' – from giving equivalents which are acceptable in one's own language, to declaring 'they say such-and-such, combining what seem to be equivalents of such-and-such notions in our language, in a way which makes no sense to us but does appear to make sense to them.' In between these extremes, dealing with societies which do not themselves codify their own views, one is not clear what one should say: the answer appears to hinge on just how *we* codify *their* views for them.

But the really significant difference is between what may be called validation systems: the procedures and principles employed for extending and deciding the acceptance of new items. Primitive societies do not codify these, and they can only be extracted from their practice, which need not be consistent. Literacy, by creating a norm outside custom, or rather, providing the means for stabilizing such a norm, is supremely important. In the end, however, it is the establishment and institutional underpinning of the *one* outstanding cumulative cognitive style, atomistic and symmetrical, which produces the really decisive parting of the ways. It is then that the practice of *some* men finally generates *one* world.

Such, roughly, are the intersocial differences at the phenomenological or descriptive level. What about the explanatory or structural level?

The Chomskian theory of language may serve as a useful base-line, precisely because it is so very clear on the issue both of the universality and uniqueness of man. If that theory is correct, then human linguistic competence is explained by an innate equipment which is identical in all men, but which is not shared by any other organism. The argument for the identity of this equipment is simple and important: the evidence available to language-learning children is so very fragmentary and feeble that the transition from it to internalizing the complex grammatical rules involved in the generation of an indefinite class of utterances, as employed by mature language-users, constitutes a truly tremendous leap. But infants of any genetic background appear able to make this transition to whatever language they are exposed to: hence not only *is* there a tremendous leap, inexplicable without hidden (innate) aid, but it also appears to be the *same* leap which is made by all mankind. If a hidden key (which is not seen, but which is inferred from our amazing linguistic competence), opens a multitude of doors, we may conclude that the locks are identical.

The theory claims the leap is towards one and the same underlying linguistic structure. Hence the acquisition of familiarity with the *idiosyncratic* traits of individual languages must somehow be explicable as a consequence of the reiterated use of the same shared innate principles, as identical bricks can be used to erect different structures, or alternatively, as something requiring only very small and hence perhaps less mysterious 'leaps', which might consequently be explicable without any recourse to the assumption of special innate linguistic equipment. To a non-specialist, this seems a difficult programme: the idiosyncratic aspects of languages *also* seem most complex, over and above the complexities which they share, and the prospects of explaining them all in the manner indicated, dubious. I doubt whether the argument for innate equipment loses its force even with the *tiniest* 'leaps'. But we can leave that problem with structural linguists. Our present use of this theory is a kind of yardstick, and does not actually require that theory to be true or demonstrated.

Whilst postulating a pan-human shared mechanism as the explanation of human linguistic competence, the theory at the same time insists on the radical discontinuity between human language and animal systems of communication. Thus, on this theory, in the field of linguistic phenomena, *one* mechanism explains all men, and *nothing* but men. The situation can be represented diagrammatically (Figure 1), where horizontal shading covers humanity, and vertical shading is that which is covered by the theory.

If *B* indicates the apex or genus, so to speak, covering all living or

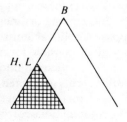

Figure 1

biological phenomena, and H and L cover human and linguistic phenomena respectively, then the areas covered by H and L are congruent, and jointly constitute a single segment of the biological. More simply: the class of men and that of proper language-users are the same class.

The thesis of the uniqueness of man, or of the existence of 'human universals', presumably means that such a congruence does hold, in the fields of linguistic and other behaviour. Schematically, it means that if, once again horizontal shading covers humanity, and vertical shading cover the field of application of some explanatory theory, then one might require that situations should not arise which can be schematized as in Figure 2.

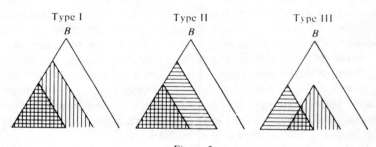

Figure 2

But it seems obvious that non-congruence of type I *does* occur: mankind obviously shares physiological mechanisms with other organisms. One's inclination is to say that these mechanisms explain aspects of behaviour which are not characteristically or distinctively human. But if only behaviour which is 'distinctively human' needs to be explained by distinctively human explanatory mechanisms, then the uniqueness-hypothesis clearly risks becoming tautological.

Non-congruence of type II raises more complex issues, as does type III. In a sense, it is obvious that explanatory mechanisms or structures of type II also occur. Suppose a political anthropologist or a political scientist develops a theory of all possible forms of political organization, by isolating the elements which go into state-formation, and then deducing all the possible forms generated by their various combinations. This theory – if the elements had been correctly isolated and the manner of their possible combinations correctly described – would constitute an explanation of possible political forms, but clearly would not cover societies too small or too decentralized to have a state at all. Would such a theory contradict the 'human universals' thesis?

Similar considerations apply to non-congruence III. It is quite possible that some explanatory mechanisms or principles are applicable both in *some* human societies and *some* non-human ones (say primates, or insects). Does this contradict the 'human universals' thesis?

Once again, this thesis risks becoming tautological or trivial, if it is reduced to the mere assertion that there are *some* (unspecified) human explanatory universals in some fields, covering all mankind, but without excluding the possibility of important *specific* explanations for *some* men only in other fields. What presumably those who uphold the idea of 'universals' mean, that in important fields (politics, kinship, economy, mythology, ritual – either in all, or perhaps more modestly just in some of them) identical principles do operate for all human societies: and if the uniqueness of man is added to universality, that they operate only in human societies. What would be the evidence for or against such a view?

Partly, this will turn out once again to be a matter of definition, in a number of ways. If some organizational principles only apply to, say, societies endowed with agriculture, or to societies above a certain size, then nevertheless pre-agrarian or small societies can be incorporated in the scheme, if the absence of a certain factor or variable (e.g. agriculture, size) is itself included as one possible variant in the range of situations 'generated' by the elements in the theory.

In brief, in as far as theories endeavour to unify, the question about the unity of mankind, at the explanatory level, risks having a trivial answer, an affirmation which simply reflects our theoretical aspiration towards unitary explanation.

Nevertheless, I suspect that those who assert the unity-of-mankind thesis have a non-trivial point in mind, and one which hinges on the distinction between genetic and social explanation: what is asserted is that social forms are so to speak indifferent to the individual human material which is fed into it. Just as any man could have been brought up in any language, so also no social formation depends on the *genetic* specificity of the men composing it. There is a good deal of evidence to support such a supposition: the diversity of human performance appears to depend on socio-cultural factors to an incomparably greater degree than it does on individual genetic equipment. The regions of the world which produced most of the innovations which lie at the base of modern industrial civilization, for instance, were themselves cultural backwaters a fairly small number of generations earlier, and yet it is unlikely that their 'gene pool' changed radically. (If anything, one might suspect that medieval clerical and monastic celibacy may have caused it to degenerate.)

At the same time, the argument requires refinement. Genetic equipment imposes a ceiling on performance, even if socio-cultural factors are crucial within that ceiling; and a community with a higher average ceiling would presumably have a different range of possible performances from one with a lower ceiling. A community artificially recruited, say, from physics professors, would presumably, in the next generation, have a different range of possible performance from a randomly selected one, even if the two new populations were given similar training.

In other words, if some potentialities are genetically limited (or rather, if the limitations are not distributed with absolute evenness), as indeed is plausible, and if communities were recruited so as to accentuate such uneven distribution, we could *then* possibly have a so to speak non-universalistic sociology. This doesn't however appear to be the world we actually live in. Whilst there is no reason to suppose that the genetic ceiling is absolutely even and flat all over humanity, any more than anything else is distributed with total evenness (such an assumption is terribly unplausible), yet the differences in performance by the same and genetically continuous community at different times are *so* much greater than are the differences between individuals which may be attributed to differences in inherent equipment, that for most problems it would seem bad strategy to seek genetic explanations. It seems to me extremely unlikely, moreover, that such genetic unevenness as may exist correlates at all with the historic performance of communities. The two things are probably often related *inversely*. For instance: some gene pools must be richer than others in potential great footballers. But is there the slightest likelihood that the point of high concentration of such talent is *also* the area where football historically emerged? The same argument applies to other cultural achievements. But it would be wrong to treat any interest in genetic preconditions as logically absurd.

Those who exclude it moreover make what could be called the Continuity Assumption, which has at least two aspects: that, although the genetic ceiling can be assumed to vary, and that its distribution need not be even, any more than the land surface of the earth is totally flat, nevertheless, it only varies statistically and the unevennesses are not very extreme. If, for instance, a given social performance requires the presence of some individuals with special talents, i.e. with a high ceiling with respect to some specific kind of performance, then the *numbers* required to ensure that some such individuals are found will not vary very much in different human populations. If a given social performance requires the presence of, say five people of unusual mathematical potential, the population size required so that it should contain five such persons *may* vary in different parts of the world, but probably does not vary very much.

The second aspect of the continuity thesis is this: that although human performance or individual ceilings vary, they vary in degree rather than in kind. The difference between the ability to speak at all and to use language like Shakespeare is great and important, but it is in some sense much less radical than the difference between having and not having the potential of speech at all. Not all men are Shakespeares, but all sane healthy men have the power of speech. The genetic precondition of social forms consists of the former kind of potential rather than the latter.

Neither aspect of the Continuity Thesis has been formulated with any precision; and perhaps it would be in principle impossible to do so. What precisely is, in general, the difference between a difference in degree and in kind? Nevertheless, despite this imprecision there *is* something like a natural interpretation of the Continuity Thesis; and it is also reasonable to suppose that it holds true. In other words, the existence of explanatory schemata which apply to some human societies only, if such schemata exist at all, need not be attributed to the non-universality of some human *element*, but only to the specificity of some forms of social *organization*, which however remain open to all human populations in similar circumstances.

These, as far as I can see, are the ideas or issues which underline the question about 'human universals'. The issue can be advanced, but it can hardly be settled. But to recapitulate:

The problems of relativism and that of the existence of human universals are *not* identical.

The doctrine of 'human universals' is often tacitly conjoined with that of the uniqueness of man: the claim is not only that the essentially human *is* present in all of us, but also that it is *not* present in anything else.

Universality at the phenomenological level is highly questionable or trivial. At the explanatory level, the notion is complex and obscure.

The solution of the problem of relativism does not hinge on the establishment of human universals. If it has a solution, it lies elsewhere.

Relativism is about the existence of One World: and the conceptual unification of the world is, precisely, the work of one particular style of thought, which is not universal amongst men, but is culturally specific.

But this in turn does not actually subvert the Universality Thesis: for although the conceptual unification of the world does have specific socio-historic roots, it is evidently accessible to all men, and is in fact now being diffused generally.

Science needs one world. It does not need one kind of man within it. But one *kind* of man did make the single world. His historical situation may have been unique, his basic constitution was *not*. The single world seems to be gradually adopted by all of them, and appears manifestly accessible to all men.

Tradition and Modernity Revisited

Robin Horton

I INTRODUCTION

In an article published in 1967,[1] I compared and contrasted patterns of thought in Africa and the West, taking Africa as a living exemplar of 'traditionality' and the West as the pioneer of 'modernity'. I began the article by elaborating on Durkheim's neglected insight concerning the continuities between, on the one hand the spiritualistic thought of traditional cultures in Africa and elsewhere, and on the other the mechanistic thought of modern Western cultures. I showed how the former, no less than the latter, gave rise to theoretical systems whose basic *raison d'être* was the extension of the magnificent but none the less limited causal vision of everyday commonsense thinking. I also proposed a technological/economic/sociological explanation for the divergence in theoretical idiom as between Africa and the West. Having made much of continuities between the two streams of thought, I went on to redress the balance by setting out a scheme of contrasts. Here I proposed an amended and developed version of Popper's celebrated 'closed'/'open' dichotomy, with Africa exemplifying the 'closed' and the West exemplifying the 'open'. Finally, invoking once again a technological/economic/sociological determinism, I alluded to a number of factors that seemed to me to have underpinned the transition from 'closed' to 'open' ways of thinking in earlier Europe.

Down through the years, this article has enjoyed a certain notoriety. Some few scholars have agreed enthusiastically with part or all of it.

[1] R. Horton, 'African traditional thought and Western science', *Africa*, 37, 1–2 (1967).

Others, more numerous, have been affronted by its assault on certain hoary orthodoxies in the comparative sociology of ideas, and have given strong critical responses. Yet others have used it as a stick with which to chastise the orthodox, but have then gone on to point to the defects of the stick and to discard it in favour of their own allegedly superior interpretative instruments. Others again have seen it variously as vacuous, naïve, hubristic, Afrocentric and Eurocentric. All in all, the responses to the article have been predominantly unfavourable. But they have continued in surprising profusion down to the present day. So, on the approach of the old thing's fifteenth anniversary, it seems opportune to take an author's second look at it, and to ask what amendments, if any, are necessary.

In what follows, I shall start by reviewing the main lines of criticism, and by trying to sort out the cogent from the misdirected. This done, I shall also review two bodies of recent scholarly work which, though not themselves concerned with my 1967 article, none the less have a bearing on the views expressed in it. One such body deals with change in African world-views, the other with change in Western world-views. Once again, I shall try to extract those aspects of the two bodies of work which suggest a need for reformulation of my 1967 views.

Having thus cleared the ground, I shall propose an amended scheme of continuities and contrasts between African 'traditionality' and Western 'modernity'. This scheme will, I hope, improve on my 1967 effort in two respects. First, in its greater adequacy to the facts. Second, in the greater adequacy of its answers to the two linked major questions which confront all philosophers and historians of science: i.e. 'Just how far can scientific theorizing claim greater cognitive efficiency than its pre-scientific counterparts?' and 'In so far as the claim of cognitive superiority is justified, what is the source of this superiority?'. After presenting my revised scheme, I shall follow up by suggesting how we might account, in technological/economic/sociological terms, for the transition which it implies.

Finally, I shall consider the relevance of the analysis and interpretation presented to some of the broader themes of this symposium. In particular, I shall consider its relevance to the confrontation which I take to be central to the collection – the confrontation between Universalist and Relativist programmes for cross-cultural understanding.

II REVIEW OF CRITICISM

For many scholarly critics of the 1967 article, the entire project is invalidated at the outset by the arbitrariness and/or Eurocentricity of the comparison between African and Western thought-systems.[2] This reaction, I believe, demonstrates above all else the failure of the scholars concerned to think the matter through. None the less, it is clear that lack of an explicit rationale for the comparison has contributed much to the various misunderstandings of the article. So it seems eminently sensible to start this section by providing such a rationale.

At the outset, we have to face the fact that the scholar working on 'traditional' African thought-systems in a contemporary African setting cannot but become involved in broad African/Western comparisons.

In the first place, consider the implications of monographic work on the thought-patterns of a particular African community. Typically, the scholar doing this kind of work is concerned to convey an understanding of such thought-patterns to the world at large. He is therefore compelled to translate these patterns into terms of one or other of the two or three languages that currently enjoy 'world' status. Now there is nothing in any way fixed about such 'world' status. In a few decades, political or demographic upheavals may confer it on languages quite other than those that currently enjoy it. For the moment, however, it is the Western languages of English and French that enjoy this status. Hence their use as translation instruments is unavoidable.

In saying that translation is at the forefront of the intellectual processes involved in the monographic enterprise, moreover, I am talking about something more than a mere rough-and-ready search for dictionary equivalents. I am talking about a search for the appropriate Western conceptual pigeon-holes for African concepts and thought-patterns; about a search in the course of which Western concepts may themselves have to be stretched and bent in order to provide such pigeon-holes.

[2] For responses which criticize the comparison itself as Eurocentric or otherwise ill-conceived, see: S. Tambiah, 'Form and meaning of magical acts', in R. Horton and R. Finnegan, *Modes of Thought* (London, 1973), pp. 224–9; K. Wiredu, 'How not to compare African traditional thought with Western thought', *Philosophy and an African Culture* (Cambridge University Press, Cambridge, 1980).

If this is a correct analysis of the problem, it follows that, in the process of producing an adequate translation, our scholar must inevitably build up for himself a schema of similarities and differences between the African thought-patterns he wishes to expound to the world and the Western thought-patterns in terms of which he is translating. So, given the current prerequisites of expounding the thought-patterns of a particular African community to the world at large, it turns out that the kind of African/Western comparison I attempted in 1967, far from being arbitrary, is quite simply inescapable.

Again, consider the predicament of the scholar doing this kind of monographic work in a present-day African academic setting.

Whether he likes it or not, such a scholar is apt to find himself facing a constant challenge as to the contemporary relevance of his work. Behind this challenge lies a faith in what, for want of a better phrase, we may call 'intellectual modernization'. Now although it is seldom explicitly defined by the academic community, intellectual modernization is seen, above all else, as involving a move *away* from certain aspects of traditional patterns of thought, and *toward* certain aspects of contemporary Western patterns. Such a transition, it is claimed, is justifiable on the grounds of the spectacular increase in efficiency in the explanation, prediction and control of events that it will bring. In the light of this definition and this call, the scholarly student of traditional thought-systems is characteristically branded as someone who wants to hold back the hands of the clock.

This negative image, however, is the product of shallow thinking. Deeper consideration shows that, far from being an obstacle to progress, the scholarly 'traditionalist' has a vital part to play in paving the way for it. How so? Well, to start with, it is clear that the call to intellectual modernization can only be wholeheartedly accepted after thorough critical appraisal. Even if all thinking people involved agree to give priority to the linked ends of explanation, prediction and control (and such consensus is in any case problematic), they must still scrutinize carefully the claim that intellectual modernization can enable African peoples to achieve these ends with greatly improved efficiency. And before they can adjudicate this claim, the character of the transition advocated must be much more carefully charted. But any such charting requires a comparison of the point of departure ('traditionality') with the point of arrival ('modernity'): a comparison for which our 'traditionalist' holds one of the two keys. Once again, then, given an African academic setting, a comparison of the type I attempted in 1967 appears not arbitrary but inescapable. It should now be clear that between myself and my critics, it is they who have been wearing the Euro-tinted spectacles!

So much for the peculiar relevance of a comparison with modern Western thought-patterns to the scholar whose starting-point is that of traditional African thought patterns. There is almost as strong a case to be made for the peculiar relevance of a study of traditional African thought-patterns to the scholar whose primary interest is in the genesis of Western intellectual modernity.

All responsible scholars working in sub-Saharan Africa acknowledge the enormous and fascinating diversity of world-views and thought-patterns nourished by the myriad communities of the continent. One would indeed be lacking in normal human sensitivity if one were not more than a little daunted by this diversity. None the less, scholars through the years *have* searched for the unities underlying this diversity. And I think we now have some idea of what they might be. (As a partial inventory of them, I think my 1967 article still remains useful.) One notable thing about these unities, however, is that, by and large, they do not seem specific to sub-Saharan Africa. Rather, most of the features involved are features which reappear in the earlier cultures of the Mediterranean, the Near East, and Europe. In other words, it begins to look as if the universals of 'African traditional' are in fact universals of 'Old World traditional'. Further, it begins to look as if a study of 'African traditional' can suggest to us quite a lot about the living flesh that once clothed the bare bones presented to us in records, inscriptions and remains of earlier phases of Mediterranean, Near Eastern and European thought.

All this has not been lost on the historians of these neighbouring 'Old World' areas. In varying degrees of co-operation with social anthropologists, they have been looking enthusiastically to Africa to provide them with inspiration as to how the thought-patterns all too often incompletely glimpsed through their records were actually set in a context of ongoing social life. In earlier days, some of the scholars concerned were more than a little incautious, assuming without further question that if a certain thought pattern is found in Africa in a certain social context, and that if the existence of an apparently equivalent thought-pattern in earlier Europe is indicated by the relevant record, then the European equivalent *must* have been set in a similar context. Such rashness threatened at one time to bring the pursuit of African inspiration into total disrepute. Nowadays, as a result, both historians and anthropologists tend to be more cautious. If they find a thought-pattern in Africa set in a certain social context, and an apparently equivalent thought-pattern in earlier Europe, they use the African data on pattern and context as the basis of a hypothesis which, before it can be accepted in the European domain, must be subjected to testing against data related to that domain. Present-day caution notwithstanding, however, it seems that an impressive number of such hunches based on African data are turning up trumps for the historians of these neighbouring non-African areas.[3]

The study of traditional African thought-systems, then, is of peculiar relevance to the historian concerned with the emergence of modern Western thought because it is a fertile source of inspiration for his attempts to build up a picture of that once-living traditionalism from which Western intellectual modernity arose.[4]

---

[3] Perhaps the outstanding example here is that of Goody's work on the effect of the change from oral to written transmission of ideas upon a people's mode of thought. The original inspiration for his general thesis was his fieldwork in North Ghana. However, initially with Ian Watt and later by himself, he explored its applicability to the revolution in thought in sixth-century BC Greece. The verdict of at least some respectable classicists can be summed up by the terse comment of Moses Finley, current doyen of Anglo-American classicists: 'Goody has said what needs to be said.' See: J. Goody, and I. Watt, 'The consequences of literacy', *Comparative Studies in Society and History*, 5, 3 (April 1963); J. Goody, *The Domestication of the Savage Mind* (Cambridge, 1977). For the classisicists' accolade, see M. Finley, *The Use and Abuse of History*, (London, 1975), p. 112.

Another example is that of the work on witchcraft and sorcery pioneered by Evans-Pritchard and carried on by a long line of Africanist scholars. I think it would be fair to say that insights arising from his work and applied to earlier Europe have brought about at least a mini-revolution in our understanding of certain aspects of Western cognitive 'traditionalism'. For the pioneering inspiration, see E. Evans-Pritchard, *Witchcraft, Oracles and Magic among the Azande* (Oxford, 1937). For some idea of the fruitfulness of the interaction between Africanists and Europeanists on this topic, see M. Douglas (ed.), *Witchcraft Accusations and Confessions* (London, 1970). For two of the 'new wave' books on the intellectual history of earlier Europe that have resulted from this interaction, see: A. Macfarlane, *Witchcraft in Tudor and Stuart England* (London, 1970); K. Thomas, *Religion and the Decline of Magic* (London, 1971).

[4] For more on the rationale of applying Africanist insights in the context of earlier Europe, see my 'African thought-patterns: the case for a comparative approach', *Ch'Indaba* (forthcoming).

Finally in this statement of rationale, let me draw the reader's attention to something every good anthropologist knows: namely, that comparison of the world-view in which we ourselves have been reared with *any* world-view less familiar to us has an enormous potential for increasing our grasp of both. First, if we have been brought up within one world-view and later look across to another strongly contrasted with it, we are likely, in our survey of the latter, to be forcibly struck by a number of patterns of thought and belief which have never been remarked upon by their users. This, of course, is because the patterns are strange to us but totally humdrum to the users. Second, if we immerse ourselves long enough and deep enough in this 'alien' world-view, and then look back from it to the world-view in which we were reared, the same thing will apply in reverse. Thought patterns which we would never have remarked on before our 'excursus' now stand out as strange, remarkable, and demanding of explanation.[5]

In this particular case, where the terms of the comparison are the modernizing world-view of the West and the traditional world-views of Africa, we should therefore feel entitled to an increase in our understanding of both. Now if any valid criticism can be made of my earlier shot at this comparison, it is that the increase in understanding was one-sided. Looking across at the world-views of Africa from a Western vantage-point, I believe I was able to highlight certain key patterns that had not been previously remarked upon. However, when it came to looking back at Western intellectual modernity from an African vantage point, I failed to exploit the reverse opportunity. Nothing I said about science would have caused even mild surprise to the professional philosopher or historian of science. Most of it, indeed, must have struck those of that ilk who read it as somewhat out-of-date. This time round, I hope to avoid the one-sidedness. As well as advancing our understanding of the African traditional by looking at it from the vantage-point of Western modernity, I hope to do a little to advance our understanding of modernity by looking at it from the vantage-point of the traditional.

So much for those who have doubted the legitimacy of the comparative exercise itself. Amongst those who concede its legitimacy, however, are a great many who complain of my mistakes in the execution of it. And it is to their criticisms that I now turn.

[5] The classic statement of this point is in C. Lévi-Strauss, *Tristes Tropiques* (Paris, 1955).

Much hot ink has been directed against my thesis of a basic *continuity* of structure and intention as between traditional religious and modern scientific thought. This thesis, indeed, has provoked reactions close to horror from members of two well-established schools. First, from the 'Symbolists', who like to think of all religious life, whether traditional or modern, African or Western, as a species of poetic jollification rather than as a system of theory and practice guided by the aims of explanation, prediction and control.[6] Second, from the Wittgensteinian 'Fideists', who like to think of all religious life as the expression of an autonomous commitment to communion with Spiritual Being, and again as something totally different from thought and action directed by the ends of explanation, prediction and control.[7]

Both 'Symbolist' and 'Fideist' approaches to traditional religious life have already been subject to massive and cogent criticism.[8] And since I have already made my own contribution (certainly massive and I hope cogent) to such criticism,[9] I will not spend long on it here. Two

[6] For symbolist interpretations generally, see: T. Parsons, *The Structure of Social Action* (New York, 1949), 2 vols, pp. 5, 420–5, 431, 721; E. Leach, *Political Systems of Highland Burma* (London, 1954), Introduction; E. Leach, 'Virgin birth', *Proceedings of the Royal Anthropological Institute for 1966* (London, 1967); R. Firth, 'Problem and assumption in an anthropological study of religion', *Journal of the Royal Anthropological Institute*, 89, 2, (1959); J. Beattie, *Other Cultures* (London, 1964), pp. 202–40. For an influential 'symbolist' critique of my ideas, see: J. Beattie, 'Ritual and social change', *Man*, n.s., 1 (1966); 'On understanding ritual', in B. Wilson (ed.), *Rationality* (Oxford, 1970); 'Understanding African traditional religion', *Second Order*, 2, 2 (1973).
[7] For 'fideist' interpretations generally, see: P. Winch, 'Understanding a primitive society', *American Philosophical Quarterly*, 1 (1964); D.Z. Phillips, *Religion without Explanation* (Oxford, 1977). For 'fideist' critiques of my approach, see: P. Winch, 'Savage and modern minds', *Times Higher Education Supplement*, 7 September 1973, p. 13; M. Crick, *Explorations in Language and Meaning* (London, 1976), pp. 157–8.
[8] For critiques of the 'symbolist' approach, see: I. Jarvie and J. Agassi, 'The problem of the rationality of magic', *British Journal of Sociology*, 8, 2 (1967); S. Lukes, 'Some problems about rationality', *European Journal of Sociology*, 8, 2 (1967); J. Peel, 'Understanding alien belief systems', *British Journal of Sociology*, 20 (1969); J. Skorupski, *Symbol and Theory* (Cambridge, 1976). For critiques of the 'fideist' approach, see: I. Jarvie, *Concepts and Society* (London, 1972), ch. 2; H. Mounce, 'Understanding a primitive society', *Philosophy*, 48 (1973); Skorupski, *Symbol and Theory*; J. Skorupski, Review of Phillips, *Religion without Explanation*, *Mind*, 88 (1979).
[9] For my own critiques of these two schools, see the following. On 'symbolists': 'Lévy-Bruhl, Durkheim and the scientific revolution' in Horton and

points, I think, should suffice. First, in denying the paramount importance of explanation, prediction and control as guiding aims of traditional African religious life, both 'Symbolists' and 'Fideists' are committing the cardinal interpretative sin of flouting the actor's point of view. Second, both 'Symbolists' and 'Fideists' have failed to face up to the implications for their position of the historic confrontation between African peoples and twentieth-century missionary Christianity. Now over much of sub-Saharan Africa, large numbers of people have entered the missionary churches. However, very considerable numbers have subsequently come out again, to found and/or support institutions which, though propagating certain key features of the Christian message about God, are in other respects very different in outlook. Fortunately for us, the people concerned in this exodus and regrouping have been most articulate in giving their reasons for it. All over the continent, moreover, they have given much the same reasons. Above all, they have objected to the underplaying of explanation, prediction and control in the missionary credo, and have set up their new institutions with the express purpose of restoring these aims to a central position in religious life. Here, African populations are giving their own unsolicited but beautifully clear answer to 'Symbolists' and 'Fideists' alike. [10]

If relevant evidence and well-aimed argument could have killed, indeed, both 'Symbolism' and 'Fideism' would have fallen in the fields of Africa a decade ago. They survive, not because they have any genuine interpretative value, but because they serve a ideological need: i.e. the need to place traditional religious thought beyond the range of invidious comparison with Western scientific thought in respect of efficiency in the realms of explanation, prediction and control. [11]

'Symbolist'/'Fideist' outrage notwithstanding, I have continued to develop the continuity thesis in post-1967 articles. Thus I have shown that it accounts rather neatly for the apparently paradoxical character

---

Finnegan, *Modes of Thought;* 'Understanding African traditional thought: a reply to Professor Beattie', *Second Order,* 5, 1 (1976). On 'fideists': 'Professor Winch on safari', *European Journal of Sociology,* 17 (1976).

[10] For some of these answers, see Horton, 'Professor Winch on safari', p. 176.

[11] On this, see Horton, 'Lévy-Bruhl, Durkheim and the scientific revolution', pp. 283–300.

of much traditional religous discourse. [12] Again, I have shown that it accounts for stereotypy and other puzzling characteristics of ritual action. [13] Yet again, I am developing a limited comparison to show how it can account for different elaborations of religious ideas in different economic and social settings. [14] By and large, I am optimistic about the future of this approach, if for no better reason than that it is the only one in the field which takes off from the actor's perspective rather than flouting it: I am not saying that one must begin *and* end with the actor's perspective. (I myself go beyond it by asking and trying to answer the question as to why African thinkers have continued to elaborate essentially spiritualistic world-views whilst Western thinkers have been increasingly attracted to mechanistic world-views.) But one must certainly begin with it.

For all the criticism directed at the *continuity* thesis, an equal volume has been directed at my attempt to outline what seemed to me to be the principal *contrasts* between 'tradition' and 'modernity'. Unlike the former, the latter appears to contain much that is well-directed. Since I have made little serious attempt to come to terms with it in previous writings, I make no apology for considering it at length in what follows.

Most readers of the 1967 article have found fault with my use of the Popperian 'closed' versus 'open' contrast as a way of characterizing the difference between traditionalist and modern thinking. Above all, they have found fault with the contrast between static and dynamic thinking allegedly implicit in my use of the Popperian terms. Thus, so far as the individual member of society is concerned, they insist that the tradition-bound thinker is *more* critical and reflective, and *less* conservative, than I make him, and that the modern, scientifically-trained thinker is *less* critical and reflective, and *more* conservative, than I make him. So far as the world-view associated with a society is concerned, they insist that the typical traditionalistic world-view is far more open to change and external influence than I allow, and that the typical modern world-view is rather less open to change than I would like to think. [15]

---

[12] R. Horton, 'Paradox and explanation: a reply to Mr Skorupski', *Philosophy of the Social Sciences*, 3, 3–4 (1973).

[13] Horton, 'Understanding African traditional thought', pp. 20–3.

[14] Horton, 'Social psychologies: African and Western' (in preparation as postscript to projected reissue of Meyer Fortes' classic *Oedipus and Job*).

[15] For a sample of such criticism, see: B. Barnes, 'Paradigms – scientific and

This general line of criticism has been well spiced with examples drawn both from traditionalistic African contexts and from modern Western scientific contexts. Although I could claim that the critics have ignored some of my cautionary qualifications, I think that by and large they have proved their point. The Popperian contrast between 'closed' and 'open', as I applied it in 1967, *did* carry implications of a contrast between static and dynamic thinking, static and dynamic world-views; and, as I now acknowledge, such a contrast *does not* do justice either to the African or to the Western subject-matter.

Most critics have also fastened upon two more particular contrasts from which I tried to derive a multiplicity of others. One of these was the contrast between presence and absence of anxiety about threats to the established body of theory. The other was the contrast between absence and presence of an awareness, on the part of individual thinkers, of alternative theoretical frameworks.

No-one has been much impressed by the 'anxiety thesis'. Some critics have suggested that there is little evidence, either direct or indirect, for the presence of a special anxiety of the kind I postulated for traditional settings.[16] Others have suggested that anxiety about threats to one's own preferred theoretical framework is by no means peculiar to traditional settings, but is equally present at the heart of modernity.[17]

My own inclination is to disagree with the first lot, but to agree with the second. I still believe that the taboo reaction and the rites for annulling the passage of time can be understood, at least in part, as

---

social', *Man*, n.s., 4 (1969); B. Barnes, 'The comparison of belief-systems: anomaly versus falsehood', in Horton and Finnegan, *Modes of Thought;* Beattie, 'Understanding African traditional religion', p. 10; P. Feyerabend, *Against Method* (London, 1975), pp. 296–8; E. Gellner, *Legitimation of Belief* (Cambridge, 1974), pp. 149–67; D. Gjertsen, 'Closed and open belief systems', *Second Order*, 7, 1–2 (1980); Goody, *The Domestication of the Savage Mind*, pp. 42–3; B. Hallen, 'Robin Horton on critical philosophy and traditional thought', *Second Order*, 6, 1 (1977); M. Marwick, 'How real is the charmed circle?', *Africa*, 1 (1973); M. Marwick, 'Witchcraft and the epistemology of science', Presidential Address to Section N of the British Association for the Advancement of Science, Stirling, 1974; Skorupski, *Symbol and Theory*, pp. 189–204.

[16] See for example Peel, 'Understanding alien belief-systems'; Skorupski, *Symbol and Theory*, pp. 189–204.

[17] See for example Feyerabend, *Against Method*, p. 298.

defences against the anxiety-provoking threat of novel experience to
an established theoretical framework. This interpretation accords well
with actors' perceptions of both types of rite as responses to dangerous
(i.e. anxiety-provoking) situations. It relates both types of rite to more
general features of the 'traditional' predicament. And to date, it has no
serious rival. At the same time, it seems evident from a great mass of
historical writing that anxiety about threats to one's preferred theoretical framework *is equally* a motive factor at the heart of modern
intellectual life. If we find taboo and time-annulment rites missing in
the modern setting, this is because here the threats have a rather
different source, and hence require a different type of defence. What I
mean by this last remark will become clearer in the constructive
section of the paper. Meanwhile, let us transfer anxiety about threats
to one's own theoretical framework from the inventory of things
peculiar to traditional settings to that of things common to both
traditional and modern settings.

Many scholars have also lambasted the 'awareness of alternatives'
thesis. A typical line of argument here has been that since, in most of
the traditionalistic societies of Africa, witchcraft, sorcery, gods,
ghosts, etc., provide potential alternative explanations of untoward
events, it can make no sense to say that individual members of these
societies lack an awareness of alternative theoretical possibilities.[18]
Another related line has pointed to the long coexistence, in many of
these societies, of indigenous religion and Islam or Christianity, and
has cited this too as evidence that individuals therein cannot be lacking
in awareness of theoretical alternatives.[19] Some critics have gone even
further than this. Not only have they used arguments of the type just
cited to show that individuals in traditionalistic societies have a well-
developed awareness of alternatives. They have used a Kuhnian
presentation of science to show that it is precisely individuals at the
heart of intellectual modernity who lack a developed awareness of
alternatives.[20]

[18] On this, see: Beattie, 'Understanding African traditional religion', p. 10;
Gellner, *Legitimation of Belief*, p. 156; R. Frankenberg and J. Leeson, 'Choice
of healer in Lusaka' in J. Loudon (ed.), *Social Anthropology and Medicine*
(London, 1976), pp. 226–7.
[19] See Beattie, 'Understanding African traditional religion', p. 10; Goody,
The Domestication of the Savage Mind, p. 42.
[20] See Barnes, 'Paradigms – scientific and social'; Gjertsen, 'Closed and open
belief systems'.

Like the more general criticism of the 'closed' versus 'open' contrast, this line has been well spiced with text and verse drawn from both traditionalistic and modern contexts. None the less, it seems to me far less convincing.

In the first place, the arguments drawing on evidence from traditionalistic contexts do not seem to me to prove what they set out to prove. Take for instance the argument from the fact that most traditionalistic cosmologies allow for the possibility that any one of a number of different types of spiritual agency may be involved in the causation of a given untoward event. Now surely what we have here is not a multiplicity of alternative theoretical frameworks, but a multiplicity of agencies postulated *within* a single theoretical framework. To cite this as a counter-example therefore makes no more sense than would citing a Western medical man's awareness of the potential involvement of any one of a number of different types of bacterial agent in a given illness as evidence that he is poised between alternative theoretical frameworks. Again, take the argument based on the coexistence of indigenous religion with Islam or Christianity. As I have shown elsewhere, both Islam and Christianity allow for a multiplicity of lesser spiritual agencies operating under the aegis of the supreme being, whilst most if not all indigenous cosmologies allow for the same combination. Hence the conflict between the traditional religions and the so-called 'world religions' is not so much a conflict between radically different world-views as a conflict over what to worship and what to eschew within a single pantheon.[21] Indeed, I would say that it is not the missionaries of the 'world religions' who threaten to bring a vivid awareness of alternative theoretical frameworks into the minds of erstwhile traditionalistic thinkers, but rather the bearers of modern Western mechanistic materialism. It is when the latter becomes more influential in Africa than it is at present that we shall see the sparks fly! In short, it would seem that, on the basis of evidence so far cited, the critics have failed to prove their case as regards awareness of alternative theoretical frameworks amongst thinkers in the more traditionalistic sectors of African society.

So much for the arguments drawing on evidence from traditionalistic contexts. The arguments drawing on evidence from modern science seem little better founded. Since I shall be going into more

---

[21] For more on this, see: Horton, 'African conversion', *Africa*, 41, 2 (1971); Horton, 'On the rationality of conversion', *Africa*, 45, 4 (1975).

detail about this later on, let me not waste too much space at this point. Suffice it here to say that more recent scholarship, playing Kuhn at his own game of backing characterization of scientific thought and activity with detailed historical evidence, has shown that his insistence on one-at-a-time dominance of a succession of uncontested theoretical schemes is a gross distortion of the record.[22] If anything, the latter endorses my own contention that individual awareness of alternative theoretical frameworks is a typical feature of scientific milieux.

Perhaps a more cogent criticism of the 'awareness of alternatives' thesis than any of the foregoing is one put forward by Ernest Gellner.[23] Gellner suggests that there is a 'valuable intuition' behind my contrast, but that its value is obscured by an excessively individualist perspective. Though he himself does not elaborate much on this comment, he has said enough to point to the real trouble. It is not that the contrast is invalid. Rather, in concentrating on the individual rather than on individuals-in-a-community, it is incomplete. What we are faced with is not just absence versus presence of individual awareness of alternatives, but also, as its corollary, absence versus presence of a multiplicity of competing theoretical frameworks sponsored by rival 'schools'. Of this, much more anon.

A final line of criticism concerns the alleged lack of a technological, economic or sociological explanatory framework as underpinning for my analysis of continuities and contrasts in thought-patterns.[24]

This line I find rather disheartening. In the first place, my 1967 article contained a technological/economic/sociological explanation for the prevalence of a spiritualistic theoretical idiom in Africa as against that of a mechanistic idiom in the West.[25] Secondly, it suggested a number of technological, economic and social factors behind

---

[22] On this, see: Feyerabend, *Against Method*; I. Lakatos, 'Falsification and the methodology of scientific research programmes', in J. Worrall and G. Currie (eds), *Imre Lakatos: Philosophical Papers*, vol. I (Cambridge, 1978); J. Laudan, *Progress and its Problems* (Berkeley, 1977).

[23] Gellner, E. *Legitimation of Belief*, pp. 157–8.

[24] See for instance: M. Rudwick, *The History of the Natural Sciences as Cultural History* (Inaugural Lecture, Free University of Amsterdam) (Amsterdam, 1975), pp. 30–1; Y. Elkana, 'The distinctiveness and universality of science: reflections on the work of Professor Robin Horton', *Minerva*, 15, 2 (1977); *The Domestication of the Savage Mind*, pp. 36–51, 149; G. Macdonald and P. Pettit, *Semantics and Social Science* (London, 1981), p. 53.

[25] Horton, 'African traditional thought and Western science', pp. 64–5.

the transition from a 'closed' to an 'open' style of theoretical thought.[26] However naïve or inept these explanation-sketches may appear to subsequent scholars, they are incontrovertible evidence of my guiding intellectual passion at that time, which was precisely the quest for an explanatory framework which would deal 'symmetrically' (to use the now fashionable term) with the 'traditional' and the 'modern', the 'pre-scientific' and the 'scientific'.

If the above be granted, then why this aspect of the critical reaction? Well, part of it seems simply enough explained. Thus most of the critics, judging by their citations, read, not the original article, but the abridged version of it reprinted in 1970.[27] During the production of this version, foolishly as it seems in retrospect, I agreed to the excision of that very section in which suggestions about the technological, economic and social factors underpinning the transition from 'closed' to 'open' thinking were contained. Now it seems to me that the reader of an abridged version prepared with the author's co-operation can reasonably assume that the abridgements were guided by the author's assessment of what was important and what unimportant in the original. So the failure to go back to the original and to register its contents is perfectly understandable. None the less, it seems worth-while drawing the critics' attention to what those contents actually were. More puzzling is the failure to spot the technological/economic/sociological explanation for the contrast between the spiritualistic and the mechanistic idioms in theory, an explanation which *was* included in the 1970 abridged version.[28] The one suggestion I can make here is that, having been identified by the 'Symbolists' as a 'Neo-Tylorian Intellectualist' (an identification which must seem incongruous to anyone who has ever read Tylor!), I have become the victim of a well-entrenched dogma to the effect that 'Intellectualist' and 'Sociological' explanations are mutually incompatible, coupled with a failure to recognize anything on the printed page that does not square with the dogma. I hope those who carry on to read the latter part of this article will see what a load of nonsense this alleged incompatibility is.

---

[26] Ibid., pp. 179–86. Goody's criticisms, in particular, read very oddly against the background of this section of the paper. For not only do I take the change from oral to written transmission of ideas as one of several factors behind the transition from 'closed' to 'open', I explicitly follow his lead in discussing *how* this change may affect modes of thought.

[27] In Wilson, *Rationality*.

[28] Ibid., p. 147.

All in all, quite a lot of the 1967 article seems to have survived the critical assault. The basic comparative excercise itself stands vindicated. The continuity thesis is virtually undamaged. The scheme of contrasts is shown as standing in need of extensive amendment rather than of complete replacement. And the explanatory suggestions, having had their existence denied, still await the critics' jaws.

III SOME RECENT RESEARCH RESULTS AND THEIR IMPLICATIONS FOR THE PROJECT

Some of the most fruitful inspiration for improvement on my 1967 effort has come, not only from the numerous critical ripostes, but from recent work in a number of fields which either makes no allusion to my ideas or is at most peripherally concerned with them. A brief review of such work would seem a sensible prelude to the more constructive part of this essay.

The first item I want to consider under this heading bears on the thesis of a basic continuity between traditional religious and modern scientific thinking. This thesis, as I pointed out in the last section, has stood up well enough to the barrage of criticisms directed at it. None the less, certain recent work in the philosophy of science has brought home to me the need to amend one aspect of it.

Here, I refer to the challenge to the distinction between 'observational' or 'everyday' language on the one hand, and 'theoretical' language on the other. Mary Hesse, for one,[29] has argued convincingly that 'everyday' concepts like 'earth', 'sky', 'man', 'tree', 'fish' are as indissolubly linked to causal laws as are 'theoretical' concepts like 'proton', 'atom', 'wave' and 'electric current', and that in this respect they are neither more nor less 'theoretical' than the latter. Hence, in so far as established usage implies that the 'observational' or 'everyday' level is 'non-theoretical', it sets up a false antithesis.

Now both in my 1967 article and in subsequent writing, I have taken the complementary coexistence of 'everyday' and 'theoretical' languages as one of the most important continuities between African traditionalism and Western modernity.In particular, I have tried to show in detail how the more puzzling features both of African spiritu-

---

[29] M. Hesse, *The Structure of Scientific Inference* (London, 1974), ch. 1.

alistic theory and of Western mechanistic theory arise from the peculiar relationship between these two types of language.[30] If Hesse and others are correct, however, this aspect of my exposition of continuities is built on a false antithesis. In the circumstances, either rejection or reformulation seems called for.

Of the two, my preference is for reformulation. Timely and apt as Hesse's challenge may be, it could lead the over-enthusiastic to throw out the baby with the bathwater. True, the established usage leads us to misconstrue the character of the difference between the two levels of language. But there is a danger that the rebels against it, chanting the slogan 'everything is theory', may blind us to the fact that there *is* a difference, albeit one that has not yet been properly characterized. The need, then, is for a fresh characterization of the two-levels distinction that avoids the false implications of established usage but none the less does justice to the difference that undoubtedly is there. I shall attempt such a characterization in the later and more constructive part of this essay.

The second item for consideration bears on the question of change in the thought-patterns of 'traditionalistic' African communities. As we saw earlier, the critics have rightly rejected the implication of changelessness which attends the application of the Popperian term 'closed' to such thought-patterns. However, it is to a body of monographic studies of change in African religious thought conducted over the last thirty years that we must turn in order to form a judgement, not only as to the *extent* of change in such contexts, but also as to its *mode*.

The studies in question can be divided for convenience into two sets: first, those concerned with the indigenous (i.e. pre-Islamic, pre-Christian) religious traditions; second, those concerned with so-called conversion to Islam and Christianity.

Social anthropologists, who have long held a virtual monopoly of intensive studies of indigenous African religions, have often been castigated by members of other disciplines, first for presenting entirely synchronic pictures of African religions, and worse for implying that such pictures have a sort of timeless validity. It is true that some anthropologists (notably members of the Griaule school in France) have fallen so deeply in love with the systems of thought they have

[30] For post-1967 writing on this, see especially my 'Paradox and explanation'.

encountered that they have been well content simply to map them as they stood at the time of encounter. On the other hand, many more (particularly members or followers of Evans-Pritchard's Oxford School) have genuinely strained to put historical depth into their accounts. If the results are scanty and the historical depth seldom exceeds fifty to a hundred years, this is above all due to the intractability of the sources, of which oral tradition is the most prominent. As we shall have cause to recall several times before this essay is through, oral tradition, over three or four generations, preserves a fair recollection of religious innovations and their authorship; but, as more and more generations slip by, it tends to relegate such innovations and their authors to a timeless, eponymously-peopled 'time of the beginnings'.[31] Even so, more recent monographic work carried out within the limits set by this constraint has given us a picture of the traditional world-views very different from anything available fifty years ago.[32]

None of these studies, it is true, has seriously called in question the importance to the peoples they deal with of a 'traditionalistic' mode of legitimation of belief – a mode, that is, which treats a belief as valid when it can be shown to be part of the legacy of the ancients. Nor, I think, would their authors deny that this type of legitimation is a powerful factor favouring cognitive conservatism. At the same time, however, none of these studies allows us to see 'traditionalistic' legitimation as the overwhelming brake on cognitive change that earlier observers judged it to be. On the contrary, despite the short

[31] On this, see: Goody and Watt, 'The consequences of literacy'; Goody, *The Domestication of the Savage Mind*, pp. 26–9; G.I. Jones, 'Time and oral tradition', *Journal of African History*, 6, 2 (1965).

[32] From this point of view, the classic monographs still remain those of the Oxford School, notably: E. Evans-Pritchard, *Nuer Religion* (Oxford, 1956); G. Lienhardt, *Divinity and Experience: The Religion of the Dinka* (Oxford, 1961); J. Middleton, *Lugbara Religion*, (Oxford, 1960); J. Buxton, *Religion and Healing in Mandari* (Oxford, 1973). As we go through this series, we find a steadily-increasing attention to ideational change. A seminal recent work from outside the Oxford School is M.L. Swantz, *Ritual and Symbol in Transitional Zaramo Society* (Uppsala, 1970). For my own small contributions on this topic, see: 'Types of spirit possession in Kalabari religion' in J. Beattie and J. Middleton, (eds.), *Spiritual Mediumship and Society in Africa* (London, 1969); 'On the rationality of conversion', pt. I, *Africa*, 45, 3 (1975). Ironically, these contributions can be and have been cited as evidence against my 1967 thesis of traditional 'closure'!

time-spans within which their authors have been forced to work, they have painted a striking picture of adaptability and responsiveness to novel experience.

For those who want to get an index of the degree of ideational change over longer periods, indirect but none the less illuminating clues can be obtained through co-operation with the linguists. Thus linguistic evidence indicates pretty clearly that whole clusters of present-day sub-Saharan societies have come into being through the expansion, fission and dispersal of single ancestral groups. This is almost certainly true, for instance, of the Bantu- and Mande-speaking peoples. In each of such clusters at the present day, we find a spectacular variety of religious belief-systems. In each member of a given cluster, moreover, we find two things. On the one hand, a conviction that the main pillars of the belief-system have been handed down from the ancients. On the other, a belief-system *in fact* elaborated in such a way as to give a subtle and sophisticated explanatory account of the particular social and environmental situation in which it flourishes *at the present day*. Given the evidence as to origins, it would seem that, convictions as to antiquity of belief notwithstanding, the spectacular religious variety shown by each cluster can only be interpreted as the result of equally spectacular divergences from an original unity – diverences arising from adaptive change over the centuries to widely diverging social and environmental circumstances. Once again, then, the picture is of a conservatism which none the less permits a high degree of adaptability and responsiveness to change.

So much for the general picture of a balance between conservatism and adaptability as it emerges from these newer monographs. Before moving on, let me draw attention to two particular sets of observations that seem to point to a way in which we may shortly fill out the picture yet further. One such set is the fruit of work in Yorubaland, the other that of work in Kalabari.

The Yoruba study I have in mind is that recently reported by Chappell, on ideas about twin-birth in Yorubaland.[33] Chappel shows fairly conclusively that, before the mid-eighteenth century, Yoruba, like many African peoples, regarded twins as a challenge to the established distinction between men and animals, and hence as an abomination to be countered with an eliminative taboo reaction.

[33] T. Chappel, 'The Yoruba cult of twins in historical perspective', *Africa*, 44, 3 (1974).

Later, however, various pressures, including, one may suspect, an abnormally high twinning rate followed by a concern for population maintenance during the internecine wars of the nineteenth century, triggered off a series of attempts to devise an explanation of the phenomenon within the general framework of existing religious theory. As a result, twins came to be seen as a means whereby Eshu, the traditionally revered trickster god, gave a sign of his interest to families whom he wished to serve him. And as the explanation became established, so the taboo reaction weakened and finally disappeared.

A parallel example, so far unpublished, comes from my own experience among Kalabari of the Eastern Niger Delta. Kalabari say that, when a fisherman first reported the appearance of white men at the mouth of their estuary, the initial response was one of horror, and was followed by massive purification of the community. Their account, in short, describes a typical taboo reaction. At the same time, they have a perfectly good explanation for the symbiotic relationship between themselves and white people which developed during the centuries after the latter's initial appearance; an explanation which postulates that the national goddesses of Kalabari and of the whites are in fact sisters. Furthermore, whatever may have been the initial reaction to the appearance of white people, they have not, it seems, been taboo objects during the past century or two. If (as I think we reasonably may) we take the story of the first appearance as having a core of historical truth, then we may take this as another instance where the initial response to novel experience took the thoroughly conservative form of a taboo reaction, but where this initial response was followed by explanatory innovation and disappearance of the taboo reaction.

Though we can hardly draw firm conclusions on the basis of these two instances, they do provoke a tentative suggestion. This is that the taboo reaction, that classic 'traditionalistic' defence against the threat of novel experience, is not so much an absolute support of the *status quo*, as a holding device that allows the theoretical system to adjust in its own good time. So the very reaction that once seemed to be purely and simply a bulwark of cognitive conservatism now looks as though it might have an additional function as part of the mechanism of adaptive innovation!

Let us turn now from studies of the indigenous religious traditions to studies of so-called 'conversion'. On first reflection, the reader may find it strange that studies of 'conversion' should be considered relevant to gaining a further understanding of the traditional religious systems. But I think he will get the point soon enough.

Earlier writing on 'conversion' to Islam and Christianity in Africa tended to treat it as an all-or-nothing jump from error to enlightenment, and as a more or less inevitable consequence of exposure to the 'true message' carried by God's appointed bearers. Such writing, however, failed dismally to make sense of the most prominent features of the sub-Saharan response to the so-called 'world religions'. Notably, it failed to provide any kind of explanation as to why, despite its enthusiastic acceptance in some areas, the 'message' was flatly rejected in others. Again, it had nothing illuminating to say about the constantly recurring situation in which what looked like simple acceptance contained in reality such a large element of selection and remoulding that the results were no longer identifiable as 'Islam' or 'Christianity'.

In recent years, scholars drawn from a variety of disciplines have come to see that the earlier approach has created an impasse. And in their attempts to find a way out of this impasse, they have shown a degree of intellectual convergence which is remarkable given the diversity of their disciplinary origins and personal religious commitments. Above all, there is now a very general agreement that the phenomena of 'conversion' can only be understood if we put the initial emphasis, not on the incoming religious messages, but rather on the indigenous religious frameworks and on the challenges they face from massive flows of novel experience.[34] Advocates of the new approach accept, of course, that the ideational changes subsumed under the label 'conversion' have involved extensive borrowing, from Islam, from Christianity, and, sometimes, from both at once. At the same time, they see such borrowing as largely directed, (a) by the structure and content of the existing cosmology, and (b) by the challenge to the explanatory capacity of this cosmology offered by novel events in the local social and natural environment.

---

[34] A few of the early items in what is now a growing tide of writing along these lines are: J. Peel, *Aladura: a Religious Movement among the Yoruba* (London, 1968); J. Fernandez, 'Fang Representations under acculturation', in P. Curtin (ed.), *Africa and the West* (Madison, 1972); W. McGaffey, 'The West in Congolese experience', in ibid.; J. Janzen 'The tradition of renewal in Kongo religion', in N. Booth (ed.), *African Religions* (New York, 1977); R. Horton, 'A hundred years of change in Kalabari religion', in J. Middleton (ed.), *Black Africa* (London, 1970); R. Horton, 'On the rationality of conversion'; H. Bucher, *Spirits and Power* (Cape Town, 1980).

This newer approach accounts for just those aspects of 'conversion' that the earlier writers found so puzzling. Thus it accounts for the way in which the messages of the world religions are accepted in some circumstances and rejected in others. Again, it accounts for the high degree of selection and remoulding which so often brings despair to the hearts of the proselytes of these religions. At the same time, this approach reveals 'conversion' as a further actualization of the traditional cosmologies' vast potential for creative elaboration in response to the challenge of new experience.

All in all, then, the picture emerging from the work just reviewed is one of a balance between opposing tendencies. On the one hand, there is the 'traditionalistic' view of belief, pressing toward cognitive conservatism. On the other, there is the desire for an adequate response to new experiential challenges, pressing toward cognitive innovation. Such innovation involves both purely endogenous creativity, and development of the existing belief-system through borrowing, reworking and integration of originally alien ideas. 'Traditionalistic', then, the thinking of these societies may be, but 'closed' it obviously is not.

So much for the reality of ideational change in these cultures. What can we say about the *mode* of change?

In general, the mode of change characteristic of the thought of a given 'traditionalistic' community would seem to be one in which a single theoretical framework is subject to a more or less continuous series of innovations in response to the flow of novel experience. However loosely articulated and whatever its inconsistencies, this framework none the less retains an enduring unity through change. In talking like this, of course, we must avoid the extreme which Paulin Hountondji so scornfully labels 'the myth of primitive unanimity'.[35] Every thinking individual in a 'traditionalistic' community does his own little bit of reworking of the world-view handed down to him, in the course of applying it to everyday life in the light of his own interests. So every thinking individual has his own idiosyncratic version of such a world-view. Again, particular categories and sections within the community engage in similar reworking, and develop similar categorial and sectional versions. However, although the different interests and viewpoints of different individuals, categories and

[35] On this, see: P. Hountondji, *Sur la 'Philosophie Africaine'*, (Paris, 1976), chs 3, 8.

sections within the community do give rise to markedly different versions of the overall world-view, the disparity between these versions seldom becomes so great as to lead to the formation of a plurality of competing theoretical frameworks.

Thus it is true that, within a given community, we often find differences of opinion between interested parties as to the relative power and importance of the various categories of spiritual agency postulated by its cosmology. In Kalabari, for example, the 'wives' (possession priestesses) of the water-spirits tend to extol the powers of the water beings relative to those of other types of spirit; whilst specialists in clairvoyance tend to extol the powers of ancestral and medicine spirits relative to those of water-spirits. Again, in eastern Yorubaland, priests of the *orisa* (nature spirits) tend to extol the powers of their spiritual masters and mistresses *vis-à-vis* those of medicine spirits; whilst herbal healers tend to extol the powers of medicine spirits *vis-à-vis* those of the *orisa*. [36] Such differences, however, are differences between parties accepting the same inventory of categories of spiritual force, and the same ideas about how forces in the various categories work. They are not differences between parties adhering to rival and competing frameworks.

Not only do the bearers and developers of a particular framework successfully keep their differences within its confines. They actively resist attempts to create a confrontation between that framework and any other. Thus one of the more remarkable findings of recent monographic studies is that, even where the agents of trans-Saharan world-views, and in particular the agents of Christianity, have tried to confront the bearers of the indigenous world-views with what *they* see as competing alternatives, the local thinkers have nearly always succeeded in taking over some of the key concepts of these supposed alternatives, reworking them for their own purposes, integrating them into their own frameworks, and blissfully ignoring the attempts at confrontation. [37]

To sum up on 'traditionalistic' thinking as it emerges from recent monographic studies in Africa, let me reiterate two points. First,

[36] For the Kalabari example, see R. Horton, 'Kalabari diviners and oracles', *Odu*, n.s., 1, 1 (1964), pp. 12–13. For the Yoruba example, see Hallen, 'Robin Horton on critical philosophy', pp. 84–6.
[37] This aspect of modern ideational change emerges very clearly from the writings on 'conversion' cited in note 32.

despite its conservatism, such thinking has an essentially 'open' character. Second, it tends to produce and sustain a single over-arching theoretical framework rather than a multiplicity of such frameworks.

Finally in this review of relevant findings from recent research, let me turn to work that bears on the characterization of intellectual 'modernity' generally and of scientific thinking in particular.

The last fifteen years have produced a spate of work both in historically-informed philosophy of science and in philosophically-informed history of science. And for an outsider to these disciplines, the problem has been one of selection. None the less, I have found two bodies of work particularly stimulating in relation to the preoccupations of this essay.

The first of these consists of works concerned with the development and vicissitudes of the idea of progress in both early and later modern Europe. Here I think of Toulmin's *Discovery of Time;* Plumb's *Death of the Past;* Medawar's essay 'On the effecting of all things possible'; Sklair's *Sociology of Progress;* and above all Webster's *The Great Instauration.*[38] If these works convey any one message relevant to the present project, it is that the idea of cognitive progress, far from being something derived by simple induction from the actual course of early scientific achievement, was something in the air *before* modern science took off; something which was in fact a powerful motive force in this take-off.

The second body of work is concerned with the central role of inter-theoretic competition in the growth of knowledge. Here, let me start by reminding readers of Mill's *Essay on Liberty,* which is the precursor and inspirer of much of the more recent writing on this topic.[39] As regards the latter itself, I think particularly of Feyerabend's *Against Method;* of Lakatos' *Methodology of Scientific Research Programmes;* and of Laudan's *Progress and its Problems.*[40] These are some of the authors I mentioned earlier as playing Kuhn at

---

[38] S. Toulmin and J. Goodfield, *The Discovery of Time* (London, 1965); J. Plumb, *The Death of the Past* (London, 1969); P. Medawar, 'On the effecting of all things possible' in his *The Hope of Progress* (London, 1972); L. Sklair, *The Sociology of Progress* (London, 1970), chs 1–6; C. Webster, *The Great Instauration* (London, 1975).

[39] J.S. Mill, *On Liberty,* first published 1859.

[40] Feyerabend, *Against Method;* Lakatos, 'Falsification and methodology'; Laudan, *Progress and its Problems.*

his own game of backing characterization of science with detailed historical case-studies, and as demonstrating that his insistence on the one-at-a-time dominance of a succession of uncontested theoretical frameworks or 'paradigms' was not supported by the historical data.

In place of Kuhn's vision, these writers have proposed one in which the growth of knowledge depends precisely on healthy competition between supporters of rival theoretical frameworks. They back up their own vision, moreover, with a series of compelling examples. Thus they show how, from its beginnings, Copernican-Galilean astronomy developed in competition with a Ptolemaic rival. Again, they show how, both during the lifetime of its founder and for long after his death, Newtonian dynamics grew and flourished in intense competition with Hobbesian, Cartesian and other bodies of theory. Yet again, they show how the Huyghenian wave theory of light appeared and developed in competition with Newtonian particle theory. Perhaps the most telling point in this context is made by Lakatos,[41] who reminds us that the posthumous development of Newtonian dynamics was at its most sluggish in England, which was precisely where it enjoyed unchallenged dominance, and at its most vigorous on the Continent, where it faced intense Cartesian competition.

We can, I think, carry the story nearer to our own times with two further examples. The first is that of Darwinian evolutionary theory. Darwin originally developed his theory in the face of intense resistance from the supporters of a variety of rival doctrines. And the development of neo-Darwinian orthodoxy owes much more than it cares to admit to the way in which respected supporters of these rival doctrines have continued, through their hostile criticism and competition, to keep its leading thinkers 'on their toes'.[42] The second example is that of Quantum Theory in physics. Once again, the originators of this theory developed it in the teeth of resistance from supporters of competing doctrines. And their successors have been kept on their toes by similar resistance down to the present day.[43]

---

[41] Lakatos, 'Falsification and methodology', p. 219.
[42] For a sample of this criticism, see some of the biologists' contributions to A. Koestler and J. Smythies, *Beyond Reductionism* (London, 1972). See also R. Sheldrake, *A New Science of Life* (London, 1981).
[43] The continuity of respectable opposition to the Quantum Theory is well shown by the fact that the preface to David Bohm's iconoclastic *Causality and Chance in Modern Physics* (London, 1957) was written by that great early opponent of the orthodoxy, Prince Louis de Broglie.

So much for inter-theoretic competition as a necessary if not sufficient condition for the flourishing of science. But just how, according to our authors, does it work its creative magic?

The post-Kuhnian scholars I have mentioned are not always as clear as they might be on this question. Two crucial points, however, emerge from their writing. The first, which is implicit in Feyerabend and Lakatos, and more or less explicit in Laudan, is that some if not all judgements of theoretical merit depend on criteria, such as economy, coverage, and predictive power, which are relative rather than absolute in character. Hence a context of inter-theoretic competition is necessary if they are to be brought to bear effectively. The second, which emerges most clearly in Feyerabend and Lakatos, is that supporters of a body of theory in competition with a rival constantly search out and/or devise new configurations of experience, in the hope that the rival will be unable to cope with them whilst their own theory will digest them with ease. Hence competition generates new experience, and new experience provides stimulus to new theorizing.

In summing up the broad implications of this recent work in the history and philosophy of science, let me emphasize two things. First, the fundamental importance of a faith in cognitive progress as a motive force in the scientific enterprise. Second, the equal importance of inter-theoretic competition.

The critical response reviewed earlier and the work in various fields just considered can be seen as complementary in relation to my 1967 essay. From the critical response, one learns more about what was wrong with it, and less about what, if anything, would put it right. From the recent work considered, one learns again a certain amount about what was wrong with it, but more about what would put it right. Taken together, however, the two would seem to provide a fairly consistent set of indications for revision. Let me end this section by trying to summarize these indications.

First, the basic enterprise, of African-Western comparison, is potentially fruitful in a number of ways.

Second, subject to a little reformulation, the thesis of important continuities between traditional religious and modern scientific thinking is fundamentally sound.

Third, the 'closed'/'open' dichotomy is ripe for the scrap heap.

Fourth, more prominence must be given to the contrast between faith in tradition and faith in progress. This now seems to me to be basic and not merely subsidiary.

Fifth, the contrast between presence and absence of anxiety about threats to one's established theoretical framework must go. Such anxiety should be seen, not as peculiar to traditional settings, but rather as a human universal manifesting itself in different ways in traditional and in modern settings.

Sixth, the contrast between absence and presence of an awareness of theoretical alternatives should be replaced by a contrast which emphasizes lack of inter-theoretic competition in the traditional setting as against prominence of such competition in the modern setting. Here, I am not so much abandoning my earlier position as following Gellner's advice to reformulate the basic intuition behind it in a less solipsistic and more sociological manner. Thus in talking now of absence versus presence of inter-theoretic competition, I am not denying the significance for the individual thinker of the factor of awareness of theoretical alternatives. Rather, I am drawing attention to the fact that, where they are present, these alternatives are not just passively floating in the thinker's mind, but are being aggressively projected into it by other thinkers who wish to obliterate his own preferred theory.

Seventh, elements of a technological/economic/sociological interpretation should be spelt out in letters large enough for the most myopic 'anti-intellectualist' to read.

IV TRADITION AND MODERNITY: A REFORMULATION

Continuities

Since my original continuity thesis has been further elaborated in a number of articles since 1967,[44] and since it seems to need relatively little amendment, I shall try here to keep discussion of it short. I cannot avoid it altogether, however, because it is in terms of the cognitive 'common core' shared by African traditionalism and Western modernity that I hope to elucidate the contrasts between them.

---

[44] See for instance Horton, 'Paradox and explanation'; 'Understanding African traditional thought'; 'Professor Winch on safari'; 'Material-object Language and theoretical language: towards a Strawsonian sociology of thought' in S.C. Brown (ed.), *Philosophical Disputes in the Social Sciences* (Brighton, 1979).

The most important element of continuity between African traditionalism and Western modernity is the presence of two distinct yet
intimately complementary levels of thought and discourse: the two
levels which, up till recently, I have been content to refer to, on the one
hand as 'commonsense' or 'everyday' and on the other hand as 'theoretical'. For the reasons given earlier, I now accept that this orthodox
formulation of the relation between the two levels implies an antithesis
which is in fact false. At the same time, I insist that there *are* two
distinct levels of thought and discourse, and that we need a terminology which does justice to their existence and their relationship. With
these considerations in mind, I propose that, for 'everyday discourse'
and 'theoretical discourse', we substitute 'primary theory' and 'secondary theory'. I hope that the aptness of this terminology will become
apparent in what follows.

Primary theory really does not differ very much from community to
community or from culture to culture. A particular version of it may
be greatly developed in its coverage of one area of experience, and
rather undeveloped in its coverage of another. The next version may
be undeveloped in its coverage of the first area, but greatly developed
in its coverage of the second. These differences notwithstanding,
however, the overall framework remains the same. In this respect, it
provides the cross-cultural voyager with his intellectual bridgehead.

Primary theory gives the world a foreground filled with middle-
sized (say between a hundred times as large and a hundred times as
small as human beings), enduring, solid objects. These objects are
interrelated, indeed interdefined, in terms of a 'push-pull' conception
of causality, in which spatial and temporal contiguity are seen as
crucial to the transmission of change. They are related spatially in
terms of five dichotomies: 'left'/'right'; 'above'/'below'; 'in-front-of'/
'behind'; 'inside'/'outside'; 'contiguous'/'separate'. And temporally
in terms of one trichotomy: 'before'/'at the same time'/'after'. Finally,
primary theory makes two major distinctions amongst its objects:
first, that between human beings and other objects; and second,
among human beings, that between self and others.

In the case of secondary theory, differences of emphasis and degree
give place to startling differences in kind as between community and
community, culture and culture. For example, the Western
anthropologist brought up with a purely mechanistic view of the world
may find the spiritualistic world-view of an African community alien
in the extreme. And Nigerian university students frequently find the

modern Western mechanistic world-view equally alarming.[45] The diversity of world-pictures presented by secondary-theoretical discourse, indeed, is such that it almost defies any general characterization.

Amongst the few general remarks one can make about the content of secondary theory are the following. For a start, whilst the entities and processes of primary theory are thought of as directly 'given' to the human observer, those of secondary theory are thought of as somehow 'hidden'. This idea of the 'hiddenness' of the entities and processes of secondary theory is as central to African thought about gods and spirits as it is to Western thought about particles, currents and waves. Again, when contemplated against the background furnished by primary theory, the entities and processes postulated by secondary theory present a peculiar mixture of familiarity and strangeness. Characteristically, they share some properties with their primary-theory counterparts, lack some which the latter possess, and have many others which the latter do not possess. Once more, this blend of the familiar and the strange is as characteristic of the gods and spiritual forces of African world-views as it is of the impersonal entities of Western world-views.

From the above remarks, it should be clear that it is difficult to talk generally about the content of secondary theory except by making comparisons with that of primary theory. And this suggests the need for a general characterization of the relationship between the two levels of theory. Here, I think, two main points stand out.

The first point relates to causal vision. As the 'Ordinary Language' philosophers have never ceased to stress, primary theory is a marvellous instrument for coping with the world. But it is an instrument associated with a limited, 'push-pull' causal vision, and as such leaves man with a wide range of events and contingencies for which he cannot account and which he therefore has no prospect of predicting or bringing under control. Now if there is any single characteristic which enables us to make a clear functional distinction between primary theory and its secondary counterpart, it is the latter's vastly enlarged causal vision. Hence it seems plausible to suggest that it is the desire to transcend the limited causal vision of primary theory that has sustained secondary theory down the ages in societies both African and Western.

[45] Nigerian students in my classes are always incredulous when I tell them that the majority of my Western friends and acquaintances live in the light of entirely non-spiritualistic views of the world.

How does secondary theory help its users to achieve this aim? Principally by the postulation of a 'hidden' or 'underlying' realm of entities and processes of which the events of everyday experience, as described in primary-theory terms, are seen as surface manifestations. Once the causal regularities governing this hidden realm have been stated, their implications for the world as described in primary-theoretical terms are spelled out by a process akin to translation, guided by a 'dictionary' which correlates aspects of the 'hidden' world with aspects of the 'given'. As a result, many types of event which were previously inexplicable, unpredictable and uncontrollable lose this disturbing status.[46]

The second point is that, successful as it has been in transcending the limitations of primary theory, secondary theory remains, in at least four major ways, indebted to and/or dependent upon its primary counterpart.

To begin with, development of ideas as to the character of the 'hidden' realm is based on the drawing of analogies with familiar everyday experiences as described in primary-theory terms. Thus in the building of secondary theory in traditionalistic African contexts, ideas of gods and spirits are developed on the basis of analogies drawn from experiences of human action and interaction. And in modern Western theory-building, ideas concerning atoms, molecules, elementary particles, electric currents, waves and rays are developed on the basis of analogies drawn from experiences of moving and colliding balls, water-currents, water-waves, and so on. Subsequently, of course, the ideas about entities and processes so built up are subjected to further development by way of response to fresh explanatory challenges. This kind of development may involve: either the modification of features drawn from the original analogy; or the building in of features drawn from new analogies unrelated to the first one; or a mixture of both. The results, not surprisingly include such 'bizarre' entities as gods who combine human and animal attributes, and particles that are also wave-packets. Hence the characteristic impression which secondary theory creates, of an amalgam of the familiar and the strange. In some cases, the process goes to extremes in which some of the newly built-in attributes are to all intents and purposes incompatible with some of those derived from the original

---

[46] For examples drawn from African as well as from Western cultures, see my 'African traditional thought and Western science', pp. 53–8.

analogy. Thus we have gods who are thought of as enjoying both definite location and omnipresence; particles that move from point A to point B without traversing any intermediate positions, or can be located in two places at a given time. Here, clearly, the resources of primary-theoretical discourse are being strained almost to breaking-point. [47]

Again, ideas of causality in secondary theory both African and Western have retained to a remarkable extent the age-old primary-theory emphasis on 'push-pull' or contact action. Thus in African religious theory, the emphasis on the omnipresence of spiritual force is nothing more or less than a way whereby, whilst respecting the principle of contact action, a spirit can be thought of as acting at any place. [48] And in Western secular theory, many of the modern developments of physical ideas can be seen as attempts to escape from the unwelcome hints of action-at-distance implicit in the Newtonian world-picture. [49]

Yet again, ideas about the relationship between the-world-as-described-by-primary-theory and the-world-as-described-by-secondary-theory have consistently been framed in terms which are primary-theoretical in origin. Thus the two 'worlds' have been variously characterized: as identical; as standing in a causal relationship to one another; as standing in the relationship of illusion to reality, and, lastly but perhaps most commonly, as standing in the relationship of the manifest to the hidden. Each of these characterizations proves inadequate when pursued to any length, leading its users into a bog of contradiction and paradox. In the attempt to overcome the inadequacies of the various individual characterizations, thinkers often oscillate between two or more of them. But since the individual characterizations are themselves mutually incompatible, such oscillation creates a further round of contradictions. Once again, then, it seems that we have a stretching of the resources of primary-theoretical discourse almost to breaking-point. [50]

---

[47] For more on this, see ibid., pp. 66–9; and my 'Paradox and explanation', pp. 250–3, 292–6.

[48] I am indebted for this idea to John Skorupski. See his 'Science and traditional religious thought', *Philosophy of Social Science*, 3 (1973), p. 214.

[49] On this, see: M. Born, *Natural Philosophy of Cause and Chance* (Oxford, 1951), pp. 8–9, 16–17, 25–30; *Physics in my Generation* (London, 1965), pp. 21–2, 96–8.

[50] For more on this, see my 'Paradox and explanation', pp. 233–50, 290–2.

Lastly, it would seem that explanations couched in terms of secondary theory are only complete when their implications for the world *as described by primary theory* have been set out.

Even from these highly condensed remarks, it should be obvious that we are faced here with a most curious situation. For whilst on the one hand the whole *raison d'être* of secondary theory is its success in transcending the limited causal vision of its primary counterpart, it seems on the other hand shackled to, dependent upon, and sometimes even hamstrung by, the resources of this counterpart. If what we have here is merely two bodies of theory, one with a more restricted causal vision and one with a wider, why does the latter, far from replacing the former, remain enslaved to it?

A search for the solution to this puzzle takes us into some of the mistier realms of prehistory, biology and psycho-linguistics, and involves a collation of findings which are as yet only tentative. Nonetheless, the outlines of a possible answer can, I think, be discerned.

Let us start by taking another look at primary theory. Now, there is a sense in which such theory must 'correspond' to at least certain aspects of the reality which it purports to represent. If it did not so 'correspond', its users down the ages could scarcely have survived. At the same time, its structure has a fairly obvious functional relationship to specific human aims and to the specific human equipment available for achieving them. In particular, it is well tailored to the specific kind of hand–eye co-ordination characteristic of the human species and to the associated manual technology which has formed the main support of everyday life from the birth of the species down to the present day. Think here of the 'manageable' dimensions and the enduring character of the foreground objects; also of the causal attributes in terms of which they are defined, so many of which are functional in the context of manual technology. Further, it is well tailored to the fact that this manual technology depends to an important extent on a type of social co-operation mediated by verbal communication. Here, think again of the dimensions of the objects, of their enduring character, and of the system of concepts for locating them in space; all of these in relation to the prerequisites of conveying reference to aspects of reality between human speaker and human listener.[51]

[51] In thus setting primary theory in its technological, economic and social context, I am heavily indebted to: S. Hampshire, *Thought and Action* (Lon-

This striking 'fit' between primary theory and a co-operative manual technology suggests a great antiquity for the former. Thus, if we are to believe the prehistorians, co-operative manual technology is something which can be traced back to the birth of the human species. Moreover, primary theory seems to be, not just a happy adjunct to an economic and social set-up which could have been in operation for hundreds of thousands of years before its invention, but a *sine qua non* of anything more than the most rudimentary development of such a set-up.[52] Primary theory, then, must date back at least to the very early days of a co-operative manual technology.

Having thus dated primary theory back to the dawn of human history, we find ourselves face-to-face with a further interesting possibility: the possibility that an element of innate predisposition lies behind its obstinate entrenchment at the base of human intellectual life. Thus, if we are to believe the prehistorians once more, we are talking about an era in which active evolution of the human brain under the pressures of natural selection was still in progress. Now for early human groups, the survival value of the cultural complex comprising co-operative manual technology and a language structured in terms of primary theory must have been immense. And the survival value of all those genetic traits making for the type of cerebral organization capable of supporting such a complex must have been correspondingly great. So, given the working of natural selection on such traits over hundreds of thousands of years, the human species may well have come to have a central nervous system innately fitted, not just for co-operative manual technology, but for the primary-theoretical

---

don, 1959), esp. ch. 1; P. Strawson, *Individuals* (London, 1959), esp. chs 1 and 3. These two books deserve to be far better known than they are to English-speaking 'sociologists of knowledge'. To the great detriment of their subject, the latter show an excessive fondness for the Teutonic mists, and an unwarranted contempt for the clearer air of home.

[52] Hominid palaeontologists have pointed to two features of pre-*homo sapiens* hominid life for which at least a simple system of linguistic communication on primary-theory lines seems likely to have been a prerequisite. The first is the rather exact repetition of tool forms, which is hard to conceive of as having been executed in the absence of some sort of verbal instruction. The second is the hunting and killing of large and dangerous animals, which again is hard to conceive of as a possibility in the absence of co-operation directed by a verbally preconcerted plan. On this, see J. Monod, *Chance and Necessity* (London, 1972), pp. 125–7.

thought and discourse which is essential to it.[53]

If this version of human emergence is correct, there should be telltale present-day clues, both in the realm of cerebral structure and function, and in that of behavioural development. In fact, such clues do seem to have been coming to light in recent years. Thus, after a long period of flirtation with a *tabula rasa* model of higher brain centres, human biologists seem inclined by more recent evidence to think that the brain has elements of genetically-programmed structure and physiology particularly fitted to seeing, thinking and talking in primary-theoretical terms.[54] Again, the psycho-linguists, contemplating the extraordinary facility with which children learn primary-theoretical discourse under a minimum of deliberate instruction, have felt compelled to invoke an element of genetic programming to account for this phenomenon.[55]

All this, of course, does not mean that we can ignore any other factor in intellectual and linguistic development. Thus we have to face the fact that a child does not come to produce primary-theoretical discourse unless he is exposed to his elders' use of such discourse; and the fact that, when he does come to produce primary-theoretical discourse, it is couched in the language of the community in which he has been brought up. And these facts, it would seem, can only be accounted for in terms of a large element of learning. However, the recent findings in human biology and psycho-linguistics would seem

[53] For an excellent exposition and defence of the thesis of a long period of overlap and two-way interaction between cultural and biological evolution, by one of the few social anthropologists willing to come to terms with the findings of human biology and palaeontology, see C. Geertz, 'The growth of culture and the evolution of mind' in his *The Interpretation of Cultures* (London, 1975). For biologists' expositions see: S. Washburn, 'Speculations on the inter-relations of tools and biological evolution' in J. Spuhler (ed.), *The Evolution of Man's Capacity for Culture* (Detroit, 1959); Monod, *Chance and Necessity*, pp. 120–30.

[54] For relevant findings from recent research into the structure and physiology of primate and human central nervous systems, see: E. Lenneberg, *Biological Foundations of Language* (New York, 1967); N. Geschwind, 'The development of the brain and the evolution of language' in his *Selected Papers on Language and the Brain* (Dordrecht, 1974); C. Laughlin and E. d'Aquili, *Biogenetic Structuralism* (New York, 1974); G. Stent, *Paradoxes of Progress* (San Francisco, 1978), chs 2, 8, 10.

[55] For the classic arguments here, see: N. Chomsky, Review of B. Skinner, *Verbal Behaviour, Language*, 35 (Jan-Mar 1959); *Language and Mind* (New York, 1968); Lenneberg, *Biological Foundations of Language*.

to rule out for good the old empiricist emphasis on a *tabula rasa* brain and a development of intellectual and linguistic skills that depends entirely on learning. Present-day debate, indeed, centres, not on innate disposition versus learning, but on the question of just how these two factors are combined.[56]

Whatever the exact manner in which innate predisposition and learning are combined, it seems clear that, in each new generation, the foundations of primary-theoretical thinking are laid afresh in the pre-verbal phase of infancy, and that non-verbal schemata prefiguring the principal primary-theory concepts arise during the infant's active exploration of his surroundings. If this is indeed so, it follows that, by the time he is ready to start trying to talk, the infant has already begun to see and think about the world in a manner which is consistent with the emphases of primary-theoretical discourse. Again, if the infant's world is already so structured by the time he starts making his first efforts to talk, it seems likely that his linguistic socialization can get under way only through his exposure to that aspect of discourse that latches on to the existing structures: i.e. primary-theoretical discourse.[57]

And what of secondary theory? Well, although we shall never have even the roughest idea of the *time* of its first emergence, it seems likely that the *cause* of such emergence was the sheer efficiency of primary theory in explaining, predicting and controlling the course of events in so many areas of human experience. This efficiency in so many areas would have served to highlight its incompetence in a few. And since these few included some of great significance to human welfare, the

---

[56] For a general commentary on the fruitlessness and pigheadedness of the older debate between extremists on both sides, see M. Midgely, *Beast and Man* (Hassocks, 1979). For more detailed accounts dealing with the intricate relationship between development guided by innate predisposition and behavioural change resulting from learning, see: K. Lorentz, *Evolution and the Modification of Behaviour* (London, 1966); T. Bower, *Human Development* (San Francisco, 1979).

[57] On this, see my 'Paradox and explanation', pp. 303–4. For a more elaborate treatment, see J. Ziman, *Reliable Knowledge* (Cambridge, 1978), pp. 111–23. Ziman seems to shy away from acknowledging any element of innate predisposition in the formation of infant cognitive schemata. None the less, he surely has to concede that, from birth onward, the infant responds to his environment in a manner which is quite distinct from that of any other animal species. And this can only be because of some element of genetically-based programming.

highlighting would have brought in its train anxiety and further intellectual effort aimed at rectifying the situation. Such effort, however, would have had to use the resources already available: i.e. those of primary theory. Existing ideas of 'hidden' agency (e.g. enemy throwing spear from cover) would have provided the prototypes for ideas concerning the more radical 'hiddenness' of the entities and processes postulated by nascent secondary theory. Other existing concepts, subjected to analogical extension, would have been used to fill in the details of such theory.

So much for conjectural history. In each new generation, the secondary status of secondary theory is reinforced by the processes of pre-verbal exploration and early linguistic socialization I have already outlined. These leave secondary-theoretical discourse in the position of a Johnny-Come-Lately in every individual life. The very learning of it by the individual can only be through analogical elucidation in terms of primary-theoretical ideas.

In short, then, if the picture I have presented is anywhere near correct, the two types of theory are respectively primary and secondary not only in an historical but also in a developmental sense. Hence the inevitable dependence of the latter on the former in all ongoing intellectual activity.

At this point, we can truly appreciate both the aptness and the irony of Russell's famous characterization of 'Ordinary Language' as 'Stone Age Metaphysics'. With this striking phrase, he was one of the first to draw attention to the fact that 'Ordinary Language', far from being a 'Neutral Observation Language', embodied a theory like any other, and an ancient and in many respects outmoded one at that, tailored as it was to age-old and rather limited human capabilities and interests. Russell, however, used the characterization as a means of denigrating 'Ordinary Language' and of pouring ridicule on those philosophers who devoted their lives to studying it. What he failed to consider was the possibility that, through the operation of evolutionary processes at the dawn of human history, 'Stone Age Metaphysics' had left an indelible imprint on the human brain. If indeed it has left such an imprint, then, like it or not, we are stuck with it. [58]

---

[58] It seems to me that, had the 'Ordinary Language' philosophers cared to devote more thought to the relation between ordinary language and scientific language, they might well have replied to Russell along the lines adumbrated here.

So far in this survey of continuities between African and Western thought, I have made little of the fact that impresses most people, whether laymen or anthropologists, more than any other. Here I refer to the fact that the 'hidden world' presented by secondary theory in the typical African community is, and probably has been since very early ·times, a world of personal forces; whereas the 'hidden world' presented by Western secondary theory has, in recent centuries, become more and more a world of impersonal entities and processes. For a person who lives with one type of 'hidden' world, it is sometimes difficult even to imagine what it would be like to live with the other type.[59] Clearly, then, unless the approach in terms of continuities can also do justice to this momentous difference, it is not going to impress anyone. Fortunately the approach can cope quite adequately, as I shall now show.

Here, let me start from the observation that the builder of secondary theory is concerned above all to show order, regularity and predictability where primary theory has failed to show them. In search of his key analogies, therefore, he tends to look to those areas of everyday experience maximally associated with these qualities.

Now in the African setting, we are faced with societies possessed of fairly clear-cut patterns of social organization; societies changing, it is true, but changing for the most part at an easy pace which allows those who are members at any given time a good deal of certainty in their expectations as to the responses of those around them. At the same time, these societies have a fairly simple manual technology and a relatively low degree of control over the vicissitudes of non-human nature. In the consciousness of the member of such a society, it is human action and interaction that is maximally associated with order, regularity and predictability: hence it is from this area of experience that the key analogies are mostly drawn, with largely personalized theoretical schemes as a result.

The remarks made above about African societies are also applicable to Western societies up till about AD1200. From that time on, however, there was a steady acceleration of social change coupled with a steady increase in technological development and environmental control. Many historians, indeed, would probably agree that the tech-

[59] Perhaps it is because of my circle of near and dear has always included adherents of both types of 'hidden' world that the similarities between the two types have come to impress me more than the differences.

nological advances were a major factor in the destabilization of society. Be this as it may, the result was that order, regularity and predictability came to be associated less and less with the realm of human action and interaction, more and more with that of non-living phenomena, both artificial and natural. Hence the search for key analogies, though it started with the former, shifted gradually but inexorably to the latter. As a result, secondary theory become more and more impersonal and mechanistic in its content.[60]

To sum up, it would seem that even those differences in the content of secondary theory, which make most people feel that the religious world-views of Africa and the impersonal world-views of the modern West are poles apart, turn out to be readily explicable in terms of the continuity thesis. In the light of this thesis, indeed, such differences come to seem relatively superficial. The really deep differences between traditionalism and modernity lie elsewhere. It is to them that we must now turn.

Contrasts

Let me start this section by blocking out two contrasts which I take to be basic. First, that between a 'traditionalistic' and a 'progressivist' concept of knowledge. Second, that between a 'consensual' and a 'competitive' mode of elaborating secondary theory.

By a 'traditionalistic' concept of knowledge, I mean one which sees the main lineaments of the community's accepted body of theory as having been handed down from the ancients. By a 'progressivistic' concept of knowledge, I mean one which sees the body of theory as something in the process of gradual but steady improvement; one which sees the ancients as having had a minimum of acceptable theory, the thinkers of today as having a rather better theoretical achievement, and the thinkers of tomorrow as likely to have an achievement much

---

[60] This general characterization of technological/economic/social trends in Western society from c.AD 1200 to the present day sums up the diagnoses, on the one hand, of a distinguished line of historical sociologists running from Karl Marx to Peter Berger, and on the other hand of such shrewd general commentators on Western society as Donald Schon and Alvin Toffler. See: K. Marx and F. Engels, *The Manifesto of the Communist Party* (London, 1847), Section XVIII, 2; P. Berger, B. Berger, and H. Kellner, *The Homeless Mind* (London, 1973), esp. chs 3, 4, 8; A. Toffler, *Future Shock* (London, 1970); D. Schon, *Beyond the Stable State* (London, 1971).

greater than anything we can conceive of today.[61]

By a 'consensual' mode of theorizing, I mean a situation in which all members of a community, differences over matters of detail notwithstanding, share a single over-arching framework of secondary-theoretical assumptions, and carry out intellectual innovation within that framework. By a competitive mode of theorizing, I mean a situation involving competition between rival 'schools' of thinkers promoting mutually-incompatible frameworks of secondary-theoretical assumptions.[62]

Having sketched these contrasts, I define cognitive 'traditionalism' in terms of a 'traditionalistic' concept of knowledge closely coupled with a 'consensual' mode of theorizing, and cognitive 'modernism' in terms of a 'progressivistic' concept of knowledge closely coupled with a 'competitive' mode of theorizing.

Why emphasize these particular contrasts? Quite simply because they are pivotal. Thus on the one hand, they underpin most if not all of the other cognitive contrasts which we normally associate with the labels 'traditionalism' and 'modernism'. And on the other hand, they themselves are more or less directly underpinned by contrasts in the realms of technology, economy and social organization.

In what follows, I shall start by presenting, first 'traditionalism', then 'modernism', as syndromes underpinned by the two pairs of key factors mentioned above. I shall then try to place the two syndromes in their broader technological, economic and social contexts.

If we are to gain a proper understanding of cognitive 'traditionalism', a little more needs to be said at the outset about the 'traditionalistic' concept of knowledge.

Considered superficially, the concept is a descriptive one. Thus it tells us the source of our main pillars of knowledge (the ancients), and the means whereby they reached us (person-to-person transmission down the ages). However, it also contains within itself a criterion for legitimating any item of belief. (The item has been passed down from the ancients, therefore it must be valid.)

[61] In emphasizing the key importance of people's own concept of the sources and nature of knowledge, I follow Yehuda Elkana. See for example his *The Problem of Knowledge in Historical Perspective* (Athens, 1973).
[62] Note that it is secondary theory that is involved in this competition. Primary theoretical activity remains consensual, which is what we should expect given what I have said about its foundations.

This manner of legitimating belief, moreover, presumes rather than excludes legitimation in terms of efficacy in relation to the aims of explanation, prediction and control. Thus an item of belief is legitimated, *not just* because it is certified as having come down to us from the ancients; but *ultimately* because the beliefs of the ancients, in general, are thought to have proved their worth down the ages as instruments of explanation, prediction and control. To put it in a nutshell, beliefs are accepted, not just because they are seen as age-old, but because they are seen as time-tested.

Thus defined, the 'traditionalistic' concept of knowledge does have some braking effect on intellectual innovation. For a start, the idea that the main lines of worthwhile knowledge were revealed once and for all to the ancients is in itself a profound discouragement, both to anyone carrying the rudiments of a new vision of the world, and to any wider audience to whom he may expose these rudiments. Again, the idea that these main lines of knowledge have served the community well from the time of the ancients down to the present day does much to take the edge off a current run of predictive failures. For where a body of theory is seen as having such a long run of predictive success behind it, any current run of failures must seem of relatively minor consequence. In these circumstances, certainly, such a run can hardly encourage ideas of replacing current theory with something totally new.

Having acknowledged the undoubted conservative influence of the 'traditionalistic' concept of knowledge, we must also note that this influence is far from putting a complete stop to change. As we have seen, 'traditionalistic' legitimation of belief itself implicitly acknowledges efficacy in relation to explanation, prediction and control as the ultimate criterion of cognitive validity. And where this criterion reigns supreme, it must exercise a residual pressure for change. Thus whenever new events occur which cannot be explained, predicted or controlled by means of the existing body of theory, the latter is shown up as wanting, and pressure created toward whatever innovation is necessary to remedy the defect. Nor do the results necessarily offend against 'traditionalistic' sentiments; for those main lines of the body of theory which are thought to have been passed down from the ancients are broad enough to permit quite a lot of detailed change. Successive doses of such detailed change down the centuries can, and do, of course, eventually amount to a change in the main outlines of the body of theory. But this is a process of which, for reasons which we shall enlarge on later, members of the community at a particular time remain unaware.

So much for the 'traditionalistic' concept of knowledge. The 'consensual' mode of theorizing makes an equally important contribution to the general character of the 'traditional' syndrome.

In the first place, where this mode of theorizing predominates, anxiety-provoking challenge to the theoretical *status quo* comes not from rival theory (which is by definition absent) but from the flow of experience. Hence the prominence in such settings of the taboo reaction, which is an attempt to hold at arm's length and where possible eliminate recalcitrant experience; and of the time-annulment rite, which is an attempt to set at nought the very process which brings about the accumulation of such experience. Striking though these defensive reactions are, however, we should remember that they are only one side of the response to novel experience, and that another more positive side is provided by theoretical innovation. Perhaps, as I suggested earlier, we should view them, not as attempts to ward off novelty in any absolute and final way, but as attempts to buy time for the intellectual innovators.

Secondly, where the consensual mode prevails, there is little to promote the sort of continuous critical monitoring of the theoretical framework which we associate with cognitive 'modernism'.

For a start, the Old Adam, observed either at the heart of African traditionalism or at the spearhead of Western modernity, is anything but spontaneously self-critical. So far as possible, he hangs on to his established framework come what may. If he starts to criticize it himself, this is usually only by way of anticipating the critical assaults of other thinkers committed to rival frameworks. In the consensual setting, such others are by definition absent.

Again, most of the criteria so far devised for the critical assessment of efficacy in relation to the goals of explanation, prediction and control – e.g. simplicity, scope, degree of dependence on *ad hoc* assumptions, predictive power – are essentially relative rather than absolute in character. They are designed to tell us which of a pair of theoretical frameworks is, cognitively speaking, the 'better'. They are not designed to tell us whether a single framework, considered in isolation, is 'good' or 'bad'. In a setting where a single over-arching framework is what we have, there is nothing to stimulate their formulation, and nothing to apply them to, even were they by some miracle to be formulated.

Thirdly, there is nothing in the 'consensual' setting to break the 'natural' link between secondary theory and practical life. I use the word 'natural' here because, as I suggested earlier, secondary theory very probably originated as a response to the demands of practical life; and because, in more recent times, the *ultimate* sustainer of secondary theorizing in cultures both African and Western does seem to have been the belief of the community at large in the actual or potential relevance of such theorizing to practical life. If the link is a natural one, it follows that it requires rather special circumstances to break it; and in this setting such circumstances do not arise. As a result, secondary theory is closely geared to such concerns as war and peace, social harmony, health, adequate food supplies and so on. And the specialist custodians, elaborators and innovators of this theory are the very men who are engaged in applying it to such concerns. This is not to say that their thought does not sometimes soar above everyday matters. None the less, it returns to them again and again as does a ground-feeding bird to earth.

One consequence of this link between theory and practice would seem to be a concern with systematization and consistency somewhat slighter than that which prevails among 'modernized' intellectuals. Now I don't want to put as much emphasis on this business of consistency as do some scholars obsessed with their own idiosyncratic reading of Evans-Pritchard on the Azande. On the one hand, 'traditionalistic' thinkers find inconsistency as repugnant as do 'modernists' when it is thrust under their noses.[63] On the other hand, as I pointed out earlier, all thinkers engaged in elaborating secondary theory stretch the resources of primary theory in a way which leads them constantly toward inconsistency and contradiction. And the results of this show up, not just in African religious theory, but also at the heart of such Western theoretical enterprises as Quantum Theory. However, where secondary theory is also predominantly applied theory, it tends to be developed and mobilized piecemeal, as particular kinds of practical exigency arise. In the absence of any pressure for constant cross-reference between one piece and another, there is a tendency toward loose articulation and what seems to the unsympathetic 'modernist' an undue tolerance of contradictions.

---

[63] It seems that this is as true of the Azande as it is of other 'traditionalists'. For their attempts to escape from a central inconsistency of their theory when this is thrust under their noses, see E. Evans-Pritchard, *Witchcraft, Oracles and Magic*, p. 25.

Another consequence of the theory-practice link is a limitation in the sheer scope of secondary theory. For whilst the link remains unbroken, the theorist's attention remains centred on the somewhat restricted circle of experience that has current practical significance[64] to himself and to his community. Though he may sometimes venture briefly beyond the perimeter of the circle, there is nothing in his setting to force him into sustained exploration of the vast territories outside.

Let me now try to sum up the characteristics of the 'traditionalistic' syndrome. To start with, there is an overall conservatism which none the less allows for gradual adaptive change. Then there is a well-developed set of defences against new and/or recalcitrant experience, which however seems designed less to block off such experience for good than to give breathing space for its assimilation. Again, although there is a determined pursuit of the goals of explanation, prediction and control, there is little if any explicit critical monitoring of secondary theory in terms of general criteria of empirical adequacy or consistency. Finally, there is a limitation of scope which stems from the fact that the coverage of secondary theory is centred on experience that is of current practical significance.

If this seems a rather negative characterization of cognitive 'traditionalism', let me not give the reader the impression that I ignore or despise its fruits. On the contrary, I maintain that, although these fruits may be limited in the domain of non-human phenomena, they are much more impressive than most Western scholars have so far acknowledged in the domain of human affairs.[65] But of this, more anon.

Let us now turn to a brief sketch of cognitive 'modernism'. Here, we are on more difficult ground; for the two underlying factors, a 'progressivistic' concept of knowledge and a 'competitive' mode of theorising, generate, not one set of consequences, but a whole spectrum of

---

[64] I stress *current* significance because it seems to me that, in such settings, as new problems and new theoretical developments aimed at resolving them come to the fore, bygone problems and the relevant theoretical developments fade out of collective awareness.

[65] I have said a little about this more positive aspect of cognitive 'traditionalism' in my 'African traditional thought and western science', pp. 55–8. I intend to expand on it considerably in 'Social psychologies: African and Western' (forthcoming).

sets. Given limitations of space, perhaps the only solution is to convey
the range of the spectrum by brief descriptions of its two poles. In
order not to run ahead of the argument, let me give these poles the
characterless labels A and B.

Pole A

The 'progressivist' concept of knowledge has some profound consequences for human intellectual activity. The idea that very little of
enduring worth has been handed down to us by the ancients, that even
the theoretical contributions of today's older generation are likely to
turn out flawed, and that the future will bring a much larger revelation
of theoretical truth than any available to us at the present day, is clearly
a liberating one so far as individual intellectual innovation is concerned. For a start, whilst the 'traditionalist' concept enjoined a broad
adherence to the theoretical *status quo*, the 'progressivist' concept
enjoins attempts either to modify it drastically or to overthrow it.
Again, where the 'traditionalist' concept encouraged the thinker to
make light of a run of predictive failure in accepted secondary theory,
the 'progressivist' concept encourages a less forgiving attitude.

Profound though its effect may be, however, the 'progressivist'
concept of knowledge is not the sole key to the understanding of
intellectual modernity. Just as important, if not more so, is the
'competitive' mode of theorizing. Indeed, one can say without exaggeration that, once consensus gives way to competition, an entirely
new situation arises.

To start with, the principal challenge to existing secondary theory
comes, not primarily from novel experience, but from rival theory;
and the principal source of anxiety is no longer recalcitrant fact but
aggressive intellectual competitor.

As in the 'consensual' setting, such anxiety evokes a defensive
response designed to eliminate the threat that triggered it. But as the
character of the threat is now different, so too is that of the defensive
response. In place of taboo reaction and time-annulment rite, we now
have the campaign of denigration against the rival school of theorists,
and the attempt to suggest a degree of silliness that renders their
product unworthy of serious consideration.[66]

---

[66] I have a horrid suspicion that, given the right conditions, supposedly
reputable scientists could lend support to total elimination of members of a

Again, as in the 'consensual' setting, the purely negative response is combined with a more constructive one. But again, as the challenge is now different, so too is the response. This time round, each school of theorists attempts to show the superiority of its product by invoking criteria of cognitive adequacy common to all parties.

One criterion which features prominently in these inter-school disputes is that of consistency or freedom from contradiction. Each party devotes a great deal of time and energy, not just to pointing out the inconsistencies of the theory promoted by its rivals, but also to scanning for and eliminating inconsistencies in its own theory in anticipation of counterattacks by those rivals. The result is a considerable increase, on all sides, in the systematization of theory.

Other criteria prominent in these battles include simplicity, scope, explanatory power and predictive power. As we saw earlier, such criteria are essentially relative. In the 'consensual' setting, therefore, they can hardly be formulated, let alone brought into operation. Once inter-theoretic competition is established, however, they can be developed and used to make invidious comparisons between bodies of theory. Here again, each party uses such criteria, not just to expose the inadequacies of the theory promoted by its rivals, but also to spotlight and stimulate development work on those aspects of its own favoured theory which require strengthening if counterattacks are to be successfully repelled.

Most if not all of the criteria in this second group are concerned, not so much with the internal characteristics of theory, as with its ability to cope with experience. Not surprisingly, then, the offensive use of such criteria often involves the searching out or devising of new configurations of experience with the aim of showing up the explanatory-cum-predictive incompetence of rival theory whilst highlighting the corresponding competence of one's own product. Hence a tremendous emphasis on observation and experiment. From one point of view, this could be seen simply as an expansion of something that was there already in the consensual setting. The situation, however, is not quite so simple as that. For whereas in the 'consensual' setting it is practically significant experience which serves as the challenge and stimulus to theoretical innovation, in the 'competitive' setting it is

---

rival school. The case of Lysenko and the Russian Darwinists comes to mind here.

inter-theoretic competition that stimulates the quest for new experience through observation and experiment. In a sense, then, the relation between theory and experience is reversed as we pass from 'consensual' to the 'competitive' setting.[67]

We can, of course, qualify the contrasts made above by pointing out that, whatever the *ultimate* stimulus to theoretical innovation in the 'competitive' setting, the *proximate* stimulus still remains experience. But if we look at the matter in this way, we are forced to attend to yet another striking contrast. Thus in the 'competitive' setting, the leading part in stimulating theoretical innovation is played, not by practically-significant experiences and problems, but by configurations of experience selected or devised specifically for purposes of inter-school warfare. As a result, we get a progressive divorce of secondary theory from practical life. Such a divorce has been a major feature of the development of Western 'modernism'. From the beginning of the seventeenth century to the middle of the nineteenth, the great flowering of secondary theory owed little to practically-significant experience and had virtually no impact on practical life.[68] As for the spectacular increase in such impact from the middle of the nineteenth century to the present day, this has been due almost entirely to the growth of an army of specialist intermediaries between unrepentantly unpractical theorists and unrepentantly non-theoretical practical men.

Perhaps the most striking thing about all this is the relation which it creates between expansion of the range of experience and expansion of the empirical coverage of theory. Thus inter-theoretic competition generates a constantly expanding range of experience. In turn, the constantly expanding range of experience faces each school of theorists involved in the competition with a standing ultimatum: 'Either match each new access of experience with an appropriate extension of theoretical coverage; or see your theory drop out of the competition.' The result is a kind of dynamic and direction which is absent from cognitive 'traditionalism'.

[67] The way in which inter-theoretic competition generates a continuous flow of new experience is well brought out by Lakatos in his discussion of so-called 'crucial experiments'. See his 'Falsification and methodology', esp. pp. 68–86.
[68] On this, see S. Toulmin, and J. Goodfield, *The Architecture of Matter* (London, 1962), p. 38–40.

As to the actual area of human intellectual enterprise to which this description is meant to apply, it is broadly that of secondary-theoretical thinking about non-human nature in Europe and North America over the last three hundred years.

Pole B

Like its Pole A counterpart, the Pole B outcome is one in which the 'progressivist' concept of knowledge encourages theoretical innovation and proliferation. In this respect, indeed, the latter concedes nothing to the former.

Again like its Pole A counterpart, the Pole B outcome is one in which the 'competitive' setting ensures that rival theory rather than practically significant experience provides the ultimate challenge to any given body of theory and the ultimate source of anxiety for the theorist. Here, however, there are some significant differences in the manner of response to the challenge and to the anxiety.

In the first place, the negative aspect of the response is far more pronounced. Participants in inter-school rivalry sometimes give one the impression that, if they could get away with it, they would stick at nothing to eliminate members of other schools from the arena.

Secondly, whilst there are elements of the more positive response described for the Pole A outcome, they are overshadowed by other, very different phenomena. Thus it is true that criteria of cognitive adequacy such as consistency, simplicity, scope, explanatory power, predictive power and so on are brandished in inter-school battles. Again, lip-service at least is paid to the strategy of searching for experience which will show up the incompetence of rival theory and the competence of one's own theory in the light of these criteria. Such elements, however, are above all a façade for polemical exchanges of another kind, governed by considerations quite distinct from those of strictly cognitive adequacy. At stake here are the moral, aesthetic or emotional acceptability of particular theoretical schemes. This is an area in which there is very little in the way of agreed criteria of 'better' and 'worse'; and as a result, inter-school argument tends to take on a no-holds-barred 'smear and sneer' quality.

Here, then, for all the innovation, the proliferation and the competition, there is none of the steady expansion of the circle of experience and the empirical coverage of theory which we found to be the hallmark of the Pole A outcome.

Very few people except some of the more humourless of those involved will be in any doubt as to the area of human activity which this description is intended to apply to. It is of course that of the so-called social sciences as pursued in Europe and North America over the last hundred years.

The two outcomes just sketched are, as I pointed out earlier, the poles of a spectrum; hence there is a virtual continuum between them. The nearer we are to the domain of non-living phenomena, the more the course of inter-school warfare is dominated by shared criteria of efficacy in relation to explanation, prediction and control, and by aggressive use of newly-discovered or devised configurations of experience to criticize rival theory and boost one's own in the light of such criteria. The nearer we get to the domain of human social life, the more such warfare is dominated by rival visions of what is morally, aesthetically, or emotionally acceptable, with little in the way of shared criteria of 'better' or 'worse' to encourage any element of genuine reasoning.

The key factor here seems to be the strength of all parties' commitment to the goals of explanation, prediction and control relative to that of their commitment to other values. The greater the relative strength of this commitment, the more the outcome approximates to that described for Pole A. The smaller its relative strength, the more the outcome approximates to that described for Pole B.

I think we have now arrived at the point at which we can appraise the claims of intellectual 'modernism' to some sort of cognitive superiority over 'traditionalism'.

As long as we stay near Pole A, such claims seem very plausible. First, the 'progressivist' concept of knowledge encourages a willingness to try radically new theoretical ideas which has no counterpart in traditional settings. Secondly, inter-theoretic competition brings with it a continuous critical monitoring of theory, in respect both of consistency and of empirical adequacy. Such monitoring, which is surely important in eliminating cognitive defects, also has no real counterpart in traditional settings. Thirdly and most significantly, inter-theoretic competition leads to a more or less continuous expansion in the range of experience; and this in turn leads to a more or less continuous expansion in the empirical coverage of theory. The practical orientation of theory in traditional settings encourages no comparable expansion in the range of experience, and therefore provides no comparable stimulus to expansion of empirical coverage.[69]

The nearer we stray to Pole B, the less plausible the claims to cognitive superiority. The willingness to try radically new theoretical ideas is still there. But competition, however fierce, now produces little or no serious critical monitoring in respect of consistency or empirical adequacy. Nor does it produce that steady expansion in range of experience and degree of empirical coverage which is perhaps the strongest ground for any 'modernist' claims to cognitive superiority.[70]

On the question of cognitive superiority, then, our answer must be: it depends on the domain in which the theorizing is being carried out. 'Yes' in the domain of non-living things. 'No' in the domain of human social life. 'Perhaps' in the middle.

This, of course, is an answer proposed by a 'modernist'. In principle, however, it is one which the 'traditionalist' himself might be brought to accept; for it appeals to criteria of efficacy in relation to goals which have a high priority in his own approach to the world: explanation, prediction and control.

Having given descriptive sketches of the two syndromes, let me complete my task with some brief suggestions as to their broader human and environmental contexts.

Here, I am going to make two assumptions. First, that much of what I have said about the 'traditionalistic' syndrome in Africa is applicable to the thought of earlier Europe. Second, that much of what I am about to say as to the technological, economic and social background of this syndrome is also applicable in the case of earlier Europe. The reader

[69] Some readers may feel surprised that, having noted how inter-theoretic competition breaks the link between secondary theory and practical life, I do not go on to say something about the cognitive fruits of the resulting 'detachment'. The reason is that I think the supposed 'detachment' is largely spurious. Members of competing schools are often passionately committed to their respective bodies of theory, and strongly antipathetic to the theories and persons of their opponents. It is not that 'detachment' gives theorists 'clearer' sight; but rather that the ever-expanding horizon of experience stimulates them to ceaseless cognitive effort.

[70] One may well see cognitive 'modernism' as a sort of Pandora's Box. For not only does it contain possibilities of cognitive progress which have hitherto been beyond the traditionalist's grasp. It also contains an array of intellectual diseases which have no parallel in traditionalistic theorizing.

will have to judge the validity of these assumptions for himself.[71] Meanwhile, it follows that the explanatory suggestions I am about to make concern, not only the differences between African 'traditionalism' and Western 'modernism', but also the transition from Western 'traditionalism' to Western 'modernism'.

At the outset, note that, in both of our two pairs of key underlying factors, each member of the pair supports the other.

Consider the two factors underlying the 'traditionalistic' syndrome. On the one hand, the 'traditionalistic' concept of knowledge receives crucial support from the 'consensual' mode of theorizing. Since 'tradition' can be taken as a guide to present-day affairs only when it speaks with a reasonably unanimous voice, the 'traditionalist' concept of knowledge will wax strong only where there is a broad theoretical consensus available for handing down. As soon as 'tradition' starts to transmit two or more clearly competing bodies of secondary theory, it must lose its influence as a guide to the present. On the other hand, the 'consensual' mode of theorizing also gets support from the 'traditionalistic' concept of knowledge. The latter, as we have seen, discourages the elaboration of radically new theoretical schemes which would convert the 'consensual' setting into a 'competitive' one.

Consider also the two factors underlying the 'modernistic' syndrome. On the one hand, the 'progressivist' concept of knowledge receives support from a well-established 'competitive' situation. For at least in the domain of non-living things, the steady increase in empirical coverage of theory which results from such a situation has a clearly progressive character. On the other hand, the 'competitive' situation is supported by the progressivist concept. For by encouraging the elaboration of radically new theoretical schemes, the latter ensures the theoretical proliferation which sustains competition.

From the above, it follows that any external influence which tends to strengthen or weaken one member of a pair of underlying factors will, albeit indirectly, have a corresponding effect on the other member.

With this preliminary clarification, let us get down to some specific suggestions as to what the relevant external influence may be.

Two variables would seem to be particularly relevant to the strengthening or weakening of the 'traditionalistic' concept of know-

---

[71] But see references to work supporting this contention in note 3.

ledge: mode of transmission of ideas and pace of social and environmental change.

As regards mode of transmission, it would seem that the oral mode favours the 'traditionalistic' concept of knowledge, whilst the written mode tends to weaken its hold.[72]

In considering oral transmission, we must stress that its most distinctive effects depend on the use of the human memory as a storage device. On the one hand, memory tends to remould the past in the image of the present, and hence to minimize the amount of change that has taken place down the ages. On the other hand, memory tends, over the generations, to ascribe all innovations, whether socio-cultural or intellectual, to an initial 'time of the beginnings'. Oral transmission, therefore, encourages a view of the past which sees the main outlines of one's society as having been shaped long ago and as having undergone little essential change since then. Again, it tends to produce a conviction that the main outlines of the body of theory which guides present-day life were laid down equally long ago and have served well ever since. Here, clearly, we have one foundation of the 'traditionalistic' concept of knowledge and the 'traditionalistic' legitimation of belief. For, as Ernest Gellner remarked some years ago in a passage which deserves more recognition than it has had, if all available information leads one to believe that present-day society and its environment are not essentially different from earlier society and its environment, then it is good inductive policy to use a supposedly age-old, time-tested body of secondary theory to cope with present-day exigencies.[73]

When written transmission comes in alongside oral, it profoundly shakes the view of the past encouraged by the latter. Thus, on the one hand it highlights the difference between the present state of society and various earlier states. And on the other hand, it reveals that a body of secondary theory taught by the accredited socializing agents as age-old and time-tested is nothing of the sort. Now once the difference between the present and earlier states of society and environment is thus emphasized, use of allegedly age-old theory no longer looks like good inductive policy. And in any case, no body of theory with such claims to antiquity is now in sight. In this way, then, written transmission weakens the hold of the 'traditionalistic' concept of know-

---

[72] In what follows, I am indebted (as in 1967!) to Goody and Watt, 'The consequences of literacy'.

[73] E. Gellner, *Thought and Change* (London, 1964), pp. 64–8.

ledge and hence of the 'traditionalistic' legitimation of belief.

Pace of change would seem to have much the same relation to the 'traditionalistic' concept of knowledge as does mode of transmission of ideas. All societies, of course, are involved in more or less continuous change. None the less, change is sometimes slow and gentle; sometimes rapid and all-disturbing. And whether it is one or the other would seem to have appreciable effects on the concept of knowledge.

In periods of slow and gentle change, the idea of a fundamental continuity between social present and social past is easily sustained, particularly where oral tradition prevails. Such periods, accordingly, favour the use of allegedly age-old and time-tested secondary theory, and hence the 'traditionalistic' concept of knowledge.

In periods of prolonged and drastic social upheaval, however, the conviction of fundamental continuity between past and present is shattered, oral transmission or no oral transmission. During such a period, the thinking man is painfully aware that he faces a totally new situation. Confronted with allegedly age-old and time-tested theory, he can only see it, as a gigantic irrelevance. In such circumstances the hold of the 'traditionalistic' concept of knowledge is greatly weakened.[74]

So much for the ways in which switch from oral to written transmission of theory and an acceleration in the pace of social change may, singly or jointly, weaken the 'traditionalistic' concept of knowledge. How far, if at all, do these factors contribute to the emergence of its 'progressivistic' counterpart?

This is a difficult question to answer. To start with, it is clear that deprivation of the guidance of 'tradition' leaves the thinking man in a terrifying vacuum. What is not clear is whether or not there is any inevitability about the filling of this vacuum with a 'progressivstic' concept of knowledge. After all, a community and its thinkers, faced with such a vacuum, may just fall into despair and cognitive inaction. There is some evidence that this is what happened to some of the Greek centres of thought in the century or two before the birth of Christ. And it seems to have been the reaction of some thinkers in sixteenth-century Europe.[75] None the less, historical and comparative studies

---

[74] Ibid., pp. 64–73.
[75] For sixteenth-century negativism, see: M. Montaigne, *Essays*, Great Books no. 25 (Chicago, 1952); Toulmin and Goodfield, *The Discovery of Time*, pp. 77–8.

would seem to teach us that despair generates amongst those it afflicts a fairly desperate search for means of escape. Such studies would also seem to teach us that one very characteristic means of escape from current despair is the development of a faith in 'jam tomorrrow'. Perhaps, then, we may see the 'progressivist' concept of knowledge as a means of escape through faith in cognitive 'jam tomorrow'!

If this sounds a little crude, I think it has to be admitted that it fits the historical evidence for Europe rather well. True, as I have pointed out, the 'progressivistic' concept gets inductive support from the fruits of well-established competitive theorizing in the 'hard sciences'. However, in the actual course of European history, this concept was first developed at the start of that great flowering of competitive theorizing which we call the Scientific Revolution, and not at its heyday. As one of the first prophets of cognitive progress, Bacon was an inspirer of the revolution, not a summarizer of its achievements.[76] One could perhaps argue that the 'progressivistic' concept was an inductive extrapolation from progress in technology, which had been considerable since about AD1000, and which had borne practical fruit in a number of fields.[77] This achievement, however, was the result of applying, either genuinely age-old secondary theory (e.g. Ptolemaic astronomy), or even older primary theory. And it had coexisted for some time with an essentially 'traditionalistic' concept of knowledge. Considered purely as a piece of induction, then, the 'progressivist' concept would have been an over-extrapolation, and a belated one at that. So even if we do take this possibility into account, we still need some additional factor to complete our explanation. One factor which has been mooted frequently in recent historical writings is the Judaeo-Christian religious heritage; the suggestion being that the millenial overtones of this heritage provided the seeds from which a full blown 'progressivist' faith developed.[78] Whilst accepting the probable importance of this factor, however, we should also note that the millenial aspect of Judaeo-Christian ideas has tended to lie dormant for long periods, and to emerge to prominence only when and where widespread anxiety and despair are the order of the day. Once again, then, we are back with the idea of the 'progressivist' concept as

---

[76] On Bacon's position in relation to the revolution, see Webster, *The Great Instauration*.

[77] On technological progress in medieval Europe, see L. White, *Mediaeval Technology and Change* (London, 1962).

[78] On this, see again Webster, *The Great Instauration*.

drawing its strength from the solace it provides to thinkers deprived of the comforting support of 'tradition'.

Let us turn now to variables more particularly relevant to the prevalence of a 'consensual' or a 'competitive' mode of theorizing.

Here too, mode of transmission of ideas seems important. By minimizing differences between past and present secondary theory, and by pushing back credit for theoretical innovation into a remote 'time of the beginnings', oral transmission lessens the possibility of contention arising between supporters of an earlier body of secondary theory and supporters of the present-day body of theory. In this way, it helps to support a 'consensual' mode of theorizing. On the other hand, by highlighting differences between present and past secondary theory, written transmission encourages a theoretical pluralism which could become the basis for inter-theoretic competition. This of course is one of the things that happened at the beginning of the European Scientific Revolution – as witness the battle between 'Ancients' and 'Moderns'.[79]

Another variable which would seem to be of key importance in this context is degree of homogeneity in cultural background and in range of everyday experience. Since the drawing of analogies based on culturally-conditioned perceptions of everyday experience is the key to the building of secondary theory, it follows that a high degree of cultural and experiential homogeneity is likely to encourage a high degree of homogeneity in the realm of secondary theory, and so to promote the 'consensual' mode of theorizing, whilst a low degree of cultural and experiential homogeneity is likely to make for a correspondingly low degree of homogeneity in the realm of secondary theory, and so to facilitate 'competitive' theorizing.

What further factors affect the degree of cultural and experiential homogeneity? This, obviously, is a question one could spend a lifetime trying to answer. Here, I can offer only a few tentative thoughts.

On the one hand, if all sections of a community have lived and moved together over a long period, and have faced common challenges over that period, this will have encouraged homogeneity. Again, where the economy is such as to encourage a rather low degree of occupational specialization, occupationally-specific sub-cultures and occupationally-specific ranges of experience will have little chance to develop, and the tendency once more will be to homogeneity. The

[79] R. Jones, *Ancients and Moderns* (St. Louis, 1936).

agriculturally-based societies of pre-colonial Africa and early medieval Europe probably came nearer to exemplifying these conditions. And this, I would suggest, is one reason for the prevalence in them of a 'consensual' mode of theorizing.

On the other hand, consider the case of the kind of 'melting pot' or 'frontier' community where, usually through the exigencies of commerce, groups having very different historical and cultural origins find themselves bound together into a single social unit. Here, the plurality of disparate world-views gives strong encouragement to the 'competitive' mode of theorizing. This is a situation that seems to have played a recurrent part in the development of Western cognitive 'modernism'. Think of the 'frontier' communities of sixth-century BC Greece; of the Judaic/Christian/Islamic communities of southern Spain toward the end of the Middle Ages; and of the commercial cities of the Netherlands at the beginning of the era of Scientific Revolution.[80] Again, where the economy is such as to encourage a high degree of occupational specialization, occupationally-specific sub-cultures and ranges of experience will develop, and thus provide another source of heterogeneity. Such occupational specialization is typical of a commercial-cum-industrial economy, and has often developed most precociously in the type of community alluded to above, thus giving additional encouragement to the development of theoretical pluralism and competition.

Finally in this consideration of influences relevant to the mode of theoretical activity, let me focus on one highly specific change which seems to me to have played a key part in the development of 'competitive' theorizing in the modern West. Here I refer once more to the growth of the commercial and industrial sectors of the economy, and to the way in which this growth produced, on the one hand, a period of prolonged change which meant a marked decline in the stability and predictability of all social relationships, and on the other hand a tremendous development in control of the non-human environment through technology. Earlier on, I suggested that it was this set of changes that led to a gradual but steady shift from a spiritualistic to a

---

[80] For the importance to late medieval thought of communities around the Western Mediterranean in which Jewish, Christian and Islamic cultural traditions were juxtaposed, see F. Heer, *The Mediaeval World* (London, 1961). For the importance to the thought of the nascent scientific revolution of the commercial cities of the Netherlands. See R. Mandrou, *From Humanism to Science* (London, 1973), esp. 224–7.

mechanistic idiom in secondary theory. And it is this shift to which I wish to draw attention here. Now as I said earlier, I do not follow the various neo-Marxist and neo-Weberian scholars in taking 'dis-enchantment' as the key to intellectual modernization. The exchange of a personal for an impersonal idiom in theory seems to me a relatively superficial transformation, and one which, in itself, cannot account for the profound changes involved in such modernization. [81] What I do want to stress is the fact of a long period of transition during which, although some thinkers had gone over to the impersonal idiom, others remained attached to the personal idiom. The resulting coexistence of two dramatically contrasted types of secondary theory, both supported with equal fanaticism, gave what was perhaps the biggest boost of all to the 'competitive' mode of theorizing.

What I have done in this section obviously does not begin to amount to a proper sociological or historical analysis. None the less, it does provide a number of specific suggestions as to how the principal contrasts between cognitive 'traditionalism' and cognitive 'modern-ism' can be set in a broader framework of technological, economic and social variables. In this way, it provides at least a starting-point for the sociologists and the historians.

V CONCLUDING REMARKS

In this essay, I have tried to present a programme for the cross-cultural study of human thought-systems. Although I have applied it here to the thought-systems associated respectively with the peoples of sub-Saharan Africa and with those of Western Europe, I should like to think that, with some modifications and elaborations, it might turn out to be universally applicable.

Basic to this programme is the assumption of a strong core of human cognitive rationality common to the cultures of all places on earth and all times since the dawn of properly human social life. Central to this 'common core' of rationality is the use of theory in the explanation, prediction and control of events. Central too is the use of analogical, deductive and inductive inference in the development and application of theory.

I distinguish two types of theory: primary and secondary. Secon-

[81] As to why it has to be a 'world' language, see pp. 203 *et seq.* above.

dary theory strives endlessly, and often with considerable success, to transcend the limitations of its primary counterpart; but it is brought back to earth, just as endlessly, by its dependence on the latter's resources. This curious relationship is the source of most if not all of the apparently paradoxical features of secondary theory. I have argued that it can be understood on the supposition that primary theory, though neither more nor less theoretical than secondary theory, is none the less historically and developmentally prior to it.

How do we get from the 'common core' of rationality to the dramatic differences which we observe between, for example, the styles and patterns of thought in sub-Saharan Africa and the styles and patterns in the recent West? Or indeed, from the 'common core' to the almost equally dramatic differences between twelfth-century and twentieth-century Western styles and patterns? Very briefly, the answer is that, in different technological, economic and social settings, the 'logic of the situation' dictates the use of different intellectual means to achieve the same ends. In this programme, then, the typical explanation of differences involves specification (*a*) of the 'common core', and (*b*) of the different settings within which it operates.

The programme outlined in this essay exposes a number of hoary misconceptions in the field of cross-cultural studies.

First, it gives the lie to the idea of a deep-seated antithesis between an 'intellectualist' and a 'sociological' scheme of explanation. For in its own scheme, the 'intellectualist' and 'sociological' elements are both complementary and mutually indispensible.

Second, it gives the lie to the idea that if one asserts that the goals of explanation, prediction and control are of more or less equal importance in all cultures, but also asserts that the yield from pursuing these goals is greater in modern Western scientific culture than in others, one is asserting the superior rationality of Westerners. It does this by showing that what has led to the high cognitive yields of modern Western science is nothing more than *the universal rationality* operating in a particular technological, economic and social setting. This conclusion, I venture to think, could have momentous implications for cross-cultural studies generally.

For most people seriously involved in cross-cultural studies, the evident success of the 'hard' sciences in the modern West is an embarrassment. Because on their assumptions such success suggests a superior rationality in the pioneers of these sciences, if not also in their most prominent followers, it offends against a strong egalitarian commitment. As I said earlier, most of the more recent programmes for cross-cultural understanding have been attempts to evade this offensive implication by insisting that much of what looks like theoretical thought in non-Western cultures is in reality thought of an entirely different genre, with goals quite distinct from those of explanation, prediction and control. As such, it cannot be subjected to invidious comparison with Western scientific thought in respect of cognitive yield. Because they flout the actor's point of view, all of these programmes run aground sooner or later on the hard facts. But because of the horror inspired by what seems to be the anti-egalitarian alternative, otherwise reputable scholars cling on to them.

I believe that the explanatory scheme outlined in this essay is one that can bring an end to this unwholesome state of affairs. For, by accounting for the cognitive success of the 'hard' sciences in terms, not of a superior rationality, but of the universal rationality operating in a particular setting, it enables the egalitarian scholar to cast away his fear of invidious comparisons and look at non-Western theory with the eye of its user.

Third, my scheme (here following Gellner) undermines the still fashionable Weberian antithesis between 'traditional' and 'rational' legitimation of belief. Thus on the one hand, it shows that 'traditional' legitimation, given the settings in which it flourishes, is impeccably 'rational'. And on the other hand, it shows that Weber's beloved culture of 'rational' legitimation, in so far as it is sustained by a 'progressivist' concept of knowledge, is grounded in an idea whose origins, at least, emit a strong whiff of 'irrationality'. Clearly the relations between rationality and cognitive yield are more complex than we had thought!

To close this essay, let me try to place the explanatory scheme outlined in it in the context of the confrontation which the present symposium is designed to highlight: the confrontation between Universalist and Relativist programmes for cross-cultural understanding. If we follow the implicit definitions shared by editors and fellow-contributors, my scheme falls fairly and squarely into the Universalist category, and is opposed to all efforts that fall into the Relativist category. In the last few paragraphs, let me have a quick shot at demonstrating the superiority of this particular form of Universalism to Relativist alternatives.

To start with, note that Relativist enthusiasm flourishes on the alleged deficiencies of the sort of Universalism propounded in this essay. In particular, it flourishes on the alleged inability of this sort of scheme to account for the dramatic differences in thought-patterns that confront the cross-cultural enquirer at every turn; and on its allegedly invidious comparisons in respect of rationality.

Both of these alleged deficiencies, it seems to me, exist only in the minds of Relativists. Thus it should be clear from the present essay that the kind of Universalism I have been pursuing in it has a large and exciting potential for the explanation of all manner of cross-cultural differences in thought-patterns. Again, it should be clear that this kind of Universalism makes no invidious comparisons in respect of rationality. In short, Relativist enthusiasm flourishes on the basis of purely imaginary deficiencies in Universalism. On this ground alone, it is suspect.

Again, for all the talk about the desirability of their kind of programme, Relativists have not yet presented even the outline of a descriptive and explanatory scheme of their own. Nor is this a coincidence; for the basic premises of Relativism make the attempt to pursue it self-defeating.

In the first place, any programme of cross-cultural understanding must start by translating all of the idea-sets under consideration into terms of a single 'world' language.[81] It is only when this has been done that a schema of similarities and differences can emerge to constitute an explanandum. But without the kind of area of comparable concepts, intentions, rules of inference and so on which primary theory *ex hypothesi* provides, there can be no 'bridge' for the crossing from one language to another, and translation cannot get under way. In so far as thoroughgoing Relativism denies such an area of comparability, it precludes the possibility of translation and is therefore, literally, a non-starter.[82]

Secondly, even if a Relativist programme managed by some logical miracle to circumvent this obstacle, and to produce a schema of irreducible differences between thought-systems, there would still be something profoundly unsatisfactory about any explanation of these differences which it proffered. For any such explanation would be (*a*) acceptable in the light of canons of inference peculiar to the scholar's own culture, and (*b*) couched in the language of that culture.

[82] This point is well made in M. Hollis, 'The limits of irrationality' and 'Reason and ritual', in Wilson, *Rationality*.

Hence, on Relativist assumptions, it would be in principle both unacceptable and unintelligible to members of any other culture. For a programme whose specific object is cross-cultural understanding, this would seem to be rather a large defect.

By comparison with the prospect for Relativism sketched above, the prospect for the kind of Universalist programme outlined in the body of this essay seems bright indeed.

First of all, there is no obviously self-defeating element in the programme. The assumption of a 'common core' of rationality, based on the universality of primary theory and of the goals of explanation, prediction and control, gives the go-ahead to the would-be translator. The same assumption ensures that, once a schema of similarities and differences has been unearthed by the translator, any explanation of its contents will be at least potentially acceptable, not to say intelligible, to members of a culture other than that of the scholar propounding it.

Again, and this is just as important, the programme is not just emptily self-fulfilling.[82] True, the idea of a 'common core' of rationality is a presupposition of anyone embarking on the translation phase of a programme of cross-cultural understanding. Nonetheless, so long as we can conceive of the possibility of defeat for the translation enterprise (and surely we *can* do this), the presupposition remains one that experience could prove misguided.

Not only, then, has Relativism so far failed to deliver whilst the kind of Universalism sketched in this essay has already shown at least promise. Relativism is bound to fail whilst Universalism may, one day, succeed.

[83] It is here, I think, that I have a disagreement with Hollis. See his 'The epistemological unity of mankind' and my 'A reply to Martin Hollis' both in S. Brown (ed.), *Philosophical Issues in the Social Sciences* (London, 1979).

Relativism in its Place

Steven Lukes

In this concluding chapter I shall examine five distinct but related issues that arise in the interpretation and explanation of beliefs. I shall first consider what assumptions must be made in order that beliefs and belief systems may be identified; and second, what status such assumptions have. Third, I shall consider what strategies for inter- preting beliefs are available and how selection among them may be made. Fourth, I shall turn to the explanation of beliefs and, in the light of the foregoing, ask whether the truth or rationality of the beliefs that have been identified and interpreted makes any difference to how they are to be explained, and if so what difference. And finally, I shall ask what, in the light of all this, survives in the case for relativism, with reference to features distinctive of the social as against the natural sciences. Like the other contributors to this volume, I shall use as examples alien beliefs of tribal and traditional societies, and pre- modern scientific theories, since these illustrate with especial clarity general points about trans-cultural and trans-theoretical understand- ing and in some cases about mutual understanding in general.

I am grateful to Robert Alford, Jonathan Barnes, Donald Davidson, Jon Elster, Martin Hollis, John Hyman, Gustav Jahoda, Bill Newton-Smith and Peter Rivière for discussing the various themes of this chapter with me as I wrote it. It arises, as does this volume, from an Oxford seminar in Balliol College, running over several years, conducted by Bill Newton-Smith, Charles Taylor and myself, in which most of the contributors, and during his year with us Clifford Geertz, participated.

I ASSUMPTIONS OF INTERPRETATION: CHARITY OR HUMANITY?

I start from the position, argued for elsewhere,[1] that in the very identification of beliefs and *a fortiori* of belief systems we must presuppose commonly shared standards of truth and of inference, and that we must further presuppose a commonly shared core of beliefs whose content or meaning is fixed by application of the standards. Neither the evidence of cross-cultural variation in schemes of classification, nor that of radically divergent theoretical schemes or styles of reasoning, nor arguments for the possible applicability of alternative logics undermine this position, which must, indeed, be accepted before the problem of relativism can be set up in the first place.[2] The common standards are required to fix the meaning of beliefs, common and uncommon; and only from the bridgehead of common beliefs can the uncommon be discerned. But what occupies the bridgehead and on what principle is it constructed?

One approach to answering these questions is to appeal to the so-called Principle of Charity. According to this, one should be maximally charitable in assigning truth conditions across the indicative sentences of the language which are held true by those being interpreted. As Davidson has put it,

> the basic strategy must be to assume that by and large a speaker we do not yet understand is consistent and correct in his beliefs – according to our own standards, of course. Following this strategy makes it possible to pair up sentences the speaker utters with sentences of our own that we hold true under like circumstances. When this is done systematically, the result is a method of translation. Once the project is under way, it is possible, and indeed necessary, to allow some slack for error or differences of

[1] S. Lukes, 'Some problems about rationality' and Martin Hollis, 'The limits of irrationality' and 'Reason and ritual' all in Bryan R. Wilson (ed.), *Rationality* (Blackwell, Oxford, 1970), S. Lukes, 'On the social determination of truth' in R. Horton and R. Finnegan (eds), *Modes of Thought: Essays on Thinking in Western and Non-Western Societies* (Faber, London, 1973), and the essays by Hollis and Newton-Smith in this volume.
[2] See Bernard Williams, 'The truth in relativism', *Proceedings of the Aristotelian Society*, n.s., 75 (1974–5), pp. 215–28, reprinted in his *Moral Luck: Philosophical Papers 1973–1980* (Cambridge University Press, Cambridge, 1981).

opinion. But we cannot make sense of error until we have established a base of agreement.[3]

As he says elsewhere, 'the only possibility at the start is to assume general agreement on beliefs': the method of charity has as its purpose 'to make meaningful disagreement possible, and this depends entirely on a foundation – *some* foundation – in agreement'. Such charity is 'forced on us; whether we like it or not, if we want to understand others, we must count them right in most matters'.[4] In short, we can

> take it as given that *most* beliefs are correct. The reason for this is that a belief is identified by its location in a pattern of beliefs; it is this pattern that determines the subject-matter of the belief, what the belief is about. Before some object in, or aspect of, the world can become part of the subject-matter of a belief (true or false) there must be endless true beliefs about the subject-matter.[5]

As I understand it, this is an entirely general and convincing argument for the inseparability of meaning and truth. But conceived of as a *method* of translation, it faces some very serious difficulties, among them: how are the true beliefs to be individuated, and counted, let alone maximized? And are not some more relevant than others? More seriously, for our present purpose, which beliefs and which domains of belief are to be counted as true? As so far stated, the Principle of Charity gives us no guidance as to *where* agreements are to be assumed before disagreements can show up: it speaks only of assuming 'general agreement', 'by and large', as covering 'most matters', and so on. But in fact Davidson does give some clue as to how to advance on this front, by suggesting that the assigning of truth conditions that actually obtain to speakers' sentences held true should be done 'as far as possible, subject to constraints of simplicity, hunches about the effects of social conditioning, and of course our common sense, or scientific, knowledge of explicable error'.[6]

[3] D. Davidson, 'Psychology as philosophy' (1974), reprinted in his *Essays on Actions and Events* (Clarendon Press, Oxford, 1980), pp. 238–9.
[4] D. Davidson, 'On the very idea of a conceptual scheme', *Proceedings and Addresses of the American Philosophical Association*, 47 (1973–4), p. 19.
[5] D. Davidson, 'Thought and talk' in S. Guttenplan (ed.), *Mind and Language* (Clarendon Press, Oxford, 1975), p. 20.
[6] Davidson, 'On the very idea of a conceptual scheme', p. 19. See also his 'Belief and the basis of meaning', *Synthese*, 27 (1974), pp. 309–23, esp. p. 321;

Steven Lukes

This qualification is based on the idea that in deciding which beliefs are true and which false we should consider how the beliefs we are seeking to identify could come to have been held and, in particular, the situations and histories of the agents involved. The trouble with unqualified charity is that it bases the necessary agreement on too many truths. Some truths we hold to may be ones they could not intelligibly have acquired, and it may be far easier to explain their disagreeing than their agreeing with us. As Richard Grandy has put it, in such cases, it may be better to attribute to them an explicable falsehood than a mysterious truth.[7] Instead of the Principle of Charity, Grandy proposes the Principle of Humanity as a pragmatic constraint on translation. This is 'the condition that the imputed pattern of relations among beliefs, desires and the world be as similar to our own as possible'.[8] Whether the beliefs are true or false, their being held must be intelligible. On this principle, what must be presupposed before translation can begin involves both rationality and explicability. Judgements as to rationality will affect our judgements as to explicability. If they are true and rationally held, then they will be explicable; if they are false, their being held must be explicable, but a different kind of explanation may be needed depending on whether they are rationally or irrationally held (on this see section IV below).

The Principle of Charity counselled 'Count them right in most matters'. The Principle of Humanity counsels 'Count them, intelligible or perhaps count them right unless we can't explain their being right or can better explain their being wrong'. In other words, it prescribes the minimizing of unintelligibility – that is, of unintelligible agreement and disagreement. It has the singular virtue of being the principle we do in practice apply in the interpretation and translation of beliefs. Of course, it relies upon a notion of 'intelligibility', an account of what counts as the explanation of beliefs being held. Grandy suggests that 'we must have some model of the agent that we

---

David Lewis's critical comments in his 'Radical interpretation', *ibid.*, pp. 331–4; and Davidson's reply, *ibid.*, pp. 345–9, in which he writes: 'Surely we can do better by allowing for explicable error. I completely agree. The improved principle of charity, in so far as it says there are cases where you make exceptions right from the beginnning, is what I espouse' (p. 346).
[7] R. Grandy, 'Reference, meaning and belief', *Journal of Philosophy*, 70 (1973), p. 445.
[8] Ibid., p. 443.

use to assist us in making a prediction' and that we use ourselves in order to arrive at it: 'we consider what we should do if we had the relevant beliefs and desires'. Whether 'our simulation of the other person is successful will depend heavily on the similarity of his belief-and-desire network to our own . . . If a translation tells us that the other person's beliefs and desires are connected in a way that is too bizarre for us to make sense of, then the translation is useless for our purposes.[9] The necessary model of the agent appears to require at least that those whose beliefs are to be identified are in general behaviourally rational in their actions and that they are, in general, sensitive to deductive argument and inductive evidence (though the degree to which these propensities are developed will depend on situation and opportunities). It will also involve the assumption that they have at least two fundamental cognitive interests: in explaining, predicting and controlling their environment, and in achieving mutual understanding.[10] Given at least all of this as conditions of intelligibility, along with the Principle of Humanity, it will immediately become obvious why practical everyday beliefs, comprising what Horton calls 'primary theory', will, in general, be prime candidates for the bridgehead. Truths of this kind cannot in general be assumed not to be common, since that would be strictly unintelligible. As Grandy remarks,

> If a translation plus our observations seem to indicate that a speaker denies the truth of a sentence in circumstances where the truth of the translation would be obvious to us, then, unless we have some explanation of this fact on our model, this counts heavily against the translation.[11]

On the other hand, scientific or magical or religious beliefs of secondary theory are highly unlikely candidates, though the explanation of how they come to be held will involve relating them to beliefs of the

---

[9] Ibid. Compare Lewis's 'fundamental principles of our general theory of persons' which he proposes as constraints on radical translation ('Radical interpretation', cited in n. 6). The first of these, Lewis's 'impreeved Principle of Charity', is very close to Grandy's Principle of Humanity. See also G. Macdonald and P. Pettit, *Semantics and Social Science* (Routledge & Kegan Paul, London, 1981), ch. 1.

[10] See J. Habermas, *Knowledge and Human Interests* (Heinemann, London, 1972).

[11] Grandy, 'Reference, meaning and belief', p. 443.

first kind in various complex and intricate ways, as Horton shows. [12]

To all of this the relativist may well counter that there is no common core of beliefs or standards to fix their meaning and relations to one another that are not relative to language or culture or theoretical paradigm, and thus neither a bridgehead nor any need for one. So Barnes and Bloor forthrightly assert that 'there is no bridgehead', what counts as 'evidencing reasons' is 'contingent' and 'socially variable' and 'although we may well share the same unverbalized environment, there are any number of equally reasonable ways of speaking of it'. [13] In short, a thoroughgoing relativism of truth and of reason is applied to the practical beliefs of primary theory no less than to all other beliefs. But if the argument for the Principle of Humanity and the bridgehead is valid, then such relativism is not merely incoherent, it is self-subverting. For without such a common core, the entire enterprise of interpretation and translation cannot get started: the meaning of beliefs cannot be identified and so questions about the relativity or otherwise of their truth values or rationality cannot even be raised.

In fact, the considerations advanced by Barnes and Bloor – that classifications are 'socially sustained' and patterns of knowledge 'institutionalized', that language learning involves the acquisition from the culture of specific conventions, that concepts seen as arrays of judgements of sameness may not coincide across cultures, and that the 'facts' are 'theory-laden' and have different imports to different scientists depending on their theoretical frameworks – all of this argues at best for conceptual and perhaps perceptual relativism. Neither the social aspects of language learning and use, nor the evidence of non-coincidence across cultures of conceptual or classificatory boundaries, nor the theory-ladenness of the facts entail that sentences cannot be translated (albeit at the cost of elaborate circumlocutions) or that beliefs cannot be common across languages and cultures, whether before or after such translation. The empirical variations of concepts, even basic concepts, or 'categories', according to technical or social context, can moreover be given a non-relativist explanation. [14] And

[12] This volume, pp. 229–32.
[13] This volume, pp. 38, 28, 40.
[14] See, for instance, the work of Jerome Bruner, and Piaget and his followers. (For the implications of the latter, see C. Hallpike, *The Foundations of Primitive Thought* (Clarendon, Oxford, 1979).) Consider the following example: 'With the information now at hand we would suggest that classifying

perceptual relativism, provided it is not given an 'idealist' formulation, is simply the (doubtless fertile) hypothesis that how we recognize and interpret what we see will be relative to (divergent) languages or conceptual or theoretical frameworks.

In fact, the evidence for such conceptual and perceptual relativism – let alone relativism of stronger beer – at the level of basic observation and practical beliefs, or primary theory, is by no means compelling. Consider first the so-called Sapir–Whorf hypothesis. Some forty years ago Whorf suggested that

> We dissect nature along lines laid down by our native languages. The categories and types that we isolate from the world of phenomena we do not find there because they stare every observer in the face; on the contrary, the world is presented in a kaleidoscopic flux of impressions which has to be organized by our minds – and this means largely by the linguistic system in our minds.[15]

To render this hypothesis testable and then test it is not easy, but a series of attempts have been made.[16] The upshot of such language-cognition research, more especially since Berlin and Kay's now classic study of the relation of basic colour terms in different languages and perception,[17] is not favourable to the Sapir–Whorf hypothesis. It has been observed that 'the fascinating irony of this research is that it

---

operations do seem to change with exposure to Western or modern living experiences. Taxonomic class membership seems to play a more dominating role as the basis for grouping items when people move from isolated village life to towns more affected by commerce and the exchange of people and things. Attendance at a Western-type school accentuates this switchover to taxonomic grouping principles', etc., in M. Cole and S. Scribner, *Culture and Thought: A Psychological Introduction* (Wiley, New York, 1974), p. 122.

[15] B.L. Whorf, *Language, Thought and Reality* (MIT Press, Boston, and Wiley, New York, 1954), p. 213.

[16] See Cole and Scribner, *Culture and Thought*, ch. 3, and Eleanor Rosch Heider, 'Linguistic relativity' in A. Silverstein (ed.), *Human Communication: Theoretical Perspectives* (Laurence Erlbaum Associates, Hillside, N.J., 1974).

[17] B. Berlin and P. Kay, *Basic Color Terms* (University of California Press, Berkeley, 1969). Berlin and Kay concluded that there are eleven universally salient 'focal' colours 'from which the eleven or fewer basic color terms of any given language are always drawn' (ibid., p. 2). For surveys of this research, see Rosch Heider, 'Linguistic relativity', and M.H. Bernstein, 'The influence of visual perception on culture', *American Anthropologist*, 77 (1975), pp. 774–98,

began in a spirit of strong relativism and linguistic determinism and has now come to a position of cultural universalism and linguistic insignificance'.[18] It suggests rather that basic colour terminology appears to be universal, and that the colour space is 'naturally organized' into focal colours and that perceptually salient focal colours appear to form natural prototypes for the development of colour terms. In this domain at least, the human perceptual system appears to determine linguistic categories rather than the reverse. Furthermore, similar evidence exists with respect to geometric forms and facial expressions of emotion: both of these domains appear to be structured into 'natural categories' invariant across languages and cultures.[19] And even categories that are plainly culturally relative appear to obey culture-neutral psychological laws for the perception and segmentation of experience.

Or consider Lévy-Bruhl's idea that primitives live and act in a pre-logical and mystical world. As he wrote,

> the reality in which primitives move is itself mystical. There is not a being, not an object, not a natural phenomenon that appears in their collective representations in the way that it appears to us. Almost all that we see therein ecapes them, or is a matter of indifference to them. On the other hand, they see many things of which we are unaware.[20]

As long ago as 1934, Evans-Pritchard exposed the fallacy in this:

> Most specialists who are also fieldworkers are agreed that primitive peoples are predominantly interested in practical economic

---

and S. Tornay (ed.), *Voir et nommer les couleurs* (Laboratoire d'ethnologie et de sociologie comparative, Nanterre, 1978). For a relativist view, see M. Sahlins, 'Colors and Cultures', *Semiotics*, 16 (1976), pp. 1–22. And for a useful general survey, see H. Gipper, *Gibt es ein Sprachliches Relativitätsprinzip? Untersuchungen zur Sapir-Whorf Hypothese* (Conditio humana, S. Fischer Verlag, Frankfurt, 1972).

[18] R.W. Brown, 'In Memorial tribute to E. Lennenberg', *Cognition*, 4 (1976), p. 152.

[19] For references, see Rosch Heider, 'Linguistic relativity'. See also Manfred Clynes, *Sentics: The Touch of Emotions* (Doubleday, N.Y., and Souvenir Press, London, 1977), especially pp. 44–51.

[20] L. Lévy-Bruhl, *Les Fonctions mentales dans les sociétés inférieures* (Alcan, Paris, 1910), pp. 30–1. Of course, Lévy-Bruhl's position changed: see especially his *Carnets*, translated by P. Rivière as *The Notebooks of Lévy-Bruhl* (Blackwell, Oxford, 1975)

pursuits: gardening, hunting, fishing, care of cattle, and the manufacture of weapons, utensils and ornaments, and in their social contacts; the life of household, family and kin, relations with friends and neighbours, with superiors and inferiors, dances and feasts, legal disputes, feuds and warfare. Behaviour of a mystical type in the main is restricted to certain situations in social life. [21]

For example, he wrote:

I have often noticed Azande lean their spears up against, or hang baskets on, the shrines they build for the spirits of their ancestors in the centre of their homesteads, and as far as it is possible to judge from their behaviour, they have no other interest in the shrine than as a convenient post or peg. At religious ceremonies their attitude is very different. Among the Ingassana of the Tabi Hills God is the sun and on occasions they pray to it but, as far as I could judge, in ordinary situations they looked upon the sun very much as I did as a convenient means of telling the time, as the cause of intense heat at midday, and so on. If one were not present at some religious ceremony on a special occasion, one would remain ignorant that the sun is God. Mystical thought is a function of particular situations. [22]

Yet although Lévy-Bruhl at times accepted that this was true of primitive peoples, he did so, as Evans-Pritchard noticed,

only as a minor concession, and without prejudice to his position. Yet it is self-evident that, far from being such children of fancy as he makes them out to be, they have less chance to be than we, for they live closer to the harsh realities of nature, which permit survival only to those who are guided in their pursuits by observation, experiment and reason. [23]

[21] E. E. Evans-Pritchard, 'Lévy-Bruhl's theory of primitive mentality', *Bulletin of the Faculty of Arts* (Faud I University, now Egyptian University, Cairo), II, 1 (1934), extract deposited in Tylor Library, Institute of Social Anthropology, Oxford, p. 9.

[22] Ibid., p. 27.

[23] E.E. Evans-Pritchard, *A History of Anthropological Thought*, edited by A. Singer (Faber, London, 1981), p. 128. Compare this comment by an African philosopher: '. . . no society would survive for any length of time without basing a large part of its daily activities on beliefs derived from the evidence. You cannot farm without some rationally based knowledge of soils, seeds and climate; and no society can achieve any reasonable degree of harmony in human relations without the basic ability to assess claims and allegations by

The impression which continues to survive that the contrary is true is due partly to the fact that 'Europeans are inclined to record the peculiar in savage cultures rather than the commonplace'[24] and partly to anthropologists' professional preoccupation with collective representations, with myth, symbolism and ritual, as against the practicalities of living, and the beliefs associated with these. As Maurice Bloch has observed, they have tended to contrast 'their' ritual communication view of the world with 'our' everyday practical one.[25] None the less, there is a mass of material in anthropologists' writings bearing out the truth of Evans-Pritchard's remarks, from descriptions of house-building, fishing and navigation and trade and exchange to analyses of legal reasoning.[26] And as for Lévy-Bruhl's thesis about prelogicality among primitive peoples, Cole and Scribner cautiously observe that 'the most firmly based, and perhaps the most important, conclusion we can reach at the present time is that thus far there is no evidence for different *kinds* of reasoning processes such as the old classic theories alleged – we have no evidence for a 'primitive logic'.[27]

Or consider finally Kuhn's claim that after a revolution the scientist 'works in a different world'[28] – a proposition he intended, in some obscure sense, not to be taken metaphorically. On this issue I think that Hacking has conclusively refuted the case for a strong in-

---

the method of objective investigation. The truth, then, is that rational knowledge is not the preserve of the modern "West" nor is superstition a peculiarity of the African': K. Wiredu, 'How not to compare African traditional thought with Western thought' in his *Philosophy and an African Culture* (Cambridge University Press, Cambridge, 1980), pp. 42–3. Compare also Wittgenstein's remark: 'The same savage who, apparently in order to kill his enemy, strikes his knife through a picture of him, really does build his hut of wood and cuts his arrow with skill and not in effigy': L. Wittgenstein, *Remarks on Frazer's 'Golden Bough'*, ed. R. Rhees (Brynmill, Notts., and Humanities Press, Atlantic Highlands, N.J., 1979) p. 4e.

[24] Evans-Pritchard, 'Lévy-Bruhl's theory of primitive mentality', p. 8.

[25] M. Bloch, 'The past and the present in the present', *Man*, n.s., 12 (1977), pp. 278–92.

[26] Cited in G. Jahoda, *Psychology and Anthropology* (Academic Press, London, forthcoming), ch. 9, which consists of a very interesting discussion of these themes. See in particular the writings of Audrey Richards, Raymond Firth, S.F. Nadel, Max Gluckman and, most recently, E. Hutchins, *Culture and Inference: A Trobriand Case Study* (Harvard University Press, Cambridge, Mass., 1980).

[27] Cole and Scribner, *Culture and Thought*, p. 170.

commensurability with regard to what one might call 'thin' descriptions of observations located at the level of Horton's primary theory – statements, as Hacking says, that 'may be made in any language, and which require no style of reasoning', such as Herschel's observation that his skin was warmed when using filters of certain colours.[29] Wittgenstein's duck-rabbit can be neutrally described as a set of lines drawn in a certain manner – indeed it could not but be so described. Feyerabend may insist that profound scientific changes may cause us to 'concede that our epistemic activities may have a decisive influence even upon the most solid piece of cosmological furniture – they may make gods disappear and replace them by heaps of atoms in empty space'.[30] But not all the world's furniture is movable, and both gods and atoms are anchored in theory-neutral, if not theory-free, observations of a boring, mundane sort. And Lakatos may proclaim the need to abandon the theory-observation distinction, yet, as Hacking has observed,

> *of course* there is a rough and ready distinction between theory and observation, and *of course* we often look and see what is true. *Of course*, some theories are just false and, after diligent attempts at patching, have to be abandoned.[31]

What I have suggested in this first section is that the identification of beliefs requires a bridgehead of common standards and common beliefs, that it is constructed on the Principle of Humanity and populated by double-agents, and so contains at least a common body of beliefs informing everyday practical activities and observations. I have further argued that relativists' objections not only fail to dislodge the bridgehead but that they cannot even claim evidential support for less ambitious theses that purport to relativize the low-level concepts and percepts of everyday observation and practice to language, culture or scientific paradigm.

[28] T. Kuhn, *The Structure of Scientific Revolutions* (University of Chicago Press, Chicago, 1964), p. 120.
[29] Ian Hacking, this volume, pp. 62–3.
[30] P. Feyerabend, *Science in a Free Society* (New Left Books, London, 1978), p. 70.
[31] Review of I. Lakatos, 'Imre Lakatos's Philosophy of Science', reviewing Lakatos's *Philosophical Papers*, *British Journal for the Philosophy of Science*, 30 (1979), p. 401.

II THE STATUS OF THE ASSUMPTIONS: A PRIORI OR EMPIRICAL?

One issue that has divided non-relativists in relation to this topic concerns the status of the assumptions I have just claimed to be essential to the identification of beliefs. Are they, as Hollis thinks, epistemological and *a priori* or, as Newton-Smith and Horton suggest, do they amount to an empirical hypothesis?[32] Is the bridgehead fixed or floating?

In the light of the foregoing, it seems to me that, in one sense, the answer to this question is clear and simple, and implicit in Davidson's statement already quoted that making meaningful disagreement possible depends 'entirely on a foundation – *some* foundation – in agreement'. This is an *a priori* truth: no conceivable state of affairs could show it to be false. In this sense Hollis is right to say that 'any fieldwork is bound to confirm the epistemological unity of mankind'.[33] But *what* that foundation is, what must be presupposed for the interpretation of beliefs and belief systems to proceed is in a sense an empirical matter, or at least revisable in the light of experience,[34] in two ways. First, as Horton has argued, such presuppositions may prove misguided in the sense that the translation enterprise could be defeated. We may have no access to what we are seeking to interpret; or, more radically, there may be no access possible for us. After all,

> one day, an anthropologist may go into the 'field', only to find himself thwarted by the fact that the vocal noises made by the particular group of human beings he has chosen to get involved with simply do not jell into a translatable language. In such a situation, though the necessary preconditions of his art remain unchanged, hard fact will drive him home . . . That such an eventuality has not yet arisen in the history of social anthropology seems to me to constitute rather strong empirical con-

---

[32] For a debate between Hollis and Horton largely on this point, see their contributions to S.C. Brown (ed.), *Philosophical Disputes in the Social Sciences* (Harvester, Brighton, and Humanities Press, Atlantic Highlands, N.J., 1979). See also the chapters by Hollis, Newton-Smith and Horton in this volume.

[33] M. Hollis, 'The epistemological unity of mankind' in Brown, *Philosophical Disputes*, p. 230.

[34] A point specifically denied by Hollis, when he claims that this 'too is an epistemological question, illuminated perhaps but not settled by experience': ibid., p. 231.

firmation of the Strawsonian thesis (of a 'massive central core of human thinking that has no history').[35]

But second, one may always turn out to be wrong in particular cases in assuming (in accordance with the Principle of Humanity) that imputing to our translatees some obvious truth is going to be more successful in making sense of their verbal or non-verbal behaviour than imputing some less obvious belief, whether true or false. What we assume to be in the common core will be subject to endless correction by the consequences of making such assumptions: evidence for any given assumption comes from whether the translations that result make better sense of what they say and do than translations flowing from alternative assumptions.

Notice, however, that background assumptions about what is intelligible, what counts as explanatory, enter into both the initial identification of beliefs (according to the Principle of Humanity) and this process of testing. At both points what we take to be intelligible will affect our interpretation, and this will involve both a view of explanation and an explanatory theory. Compare, say, Durkheim, Freud and Lévi-Strauss on totemism; or different interpretations of magic or traditional medicine. What we take those we are interpreting to believe will depend in part on what we believe to be plausible; and whether this in turn makes sense of their practice and beliefs will also depend on our view of what counts as an explanation and of what is explanatory.

At this point the relativist may return with a further thesis: relativism of explanation. He may say, with Mary Hesse, that where explanation stops is 'where, temporarily perhaps, it is not questioned by the relevant local consensus'.[36] Or he may, like Barnes and Bloor, propose a more radical view according to which the criteria of explanatory success are as relative as those of truth and reason. To such positions there are, I suggest, three replies.

First, the interpreter's 'translation manual', to use Quine's phrase, should be relatively more successful at predicting the words and actions of those being interpreted (e.g. how they will react to a given situation or respond to given communications, or what they will do, given that

[35] R. Horton, 'Reply to Martin Hollis' in Brown, *Philosophical Disputes*, pp. 236–7.
[36] M. Hesse, *Revolutions and Reconstructions in the Philosophy of Science* (Harvester, Brighton, 1980), p. 45.

they hold certain beliefs). In real-life cases, *contra* Quine (and David-son) two such manuals are never going to be equally successful. Of course, there is some real and potentially troubling indeterminacy as to *what* they predict, in particular words or deeds, especially when these appear to be at variance with one another. So, for instance, if in West Africa what is regularly said is 'We insult' but the response is laughter, do we fix on what is said or what is done?[37] But despite such difficulties, the test of predictive success is a significant constraint upon relativism of explanation, since translations which fail by this test will be non-starters.

Second, as I have already indicated, the rudimentary model of the agent implicit in the Principle of Humanity, embodying assumptions about rationality and cognitive interests, sets narrow limits to which translations will prove acceptable. Here too however there is room for dispute. What counts as a reason or as a good reason for belief may be seen as more or less narrowly defined. As noted in the Introduction to this volume, this is a point on which the editors continue to disagree. I unlike Hollis am prepared to admit a degree of contextual variation in this regard;[38] on the other hand, plainly, not *any* consideration can count as a reason for belief, or indeed as a good reason. I suspect that this may also be one of the matters at issue between Newton-Smith and Hacking. (Actually, the matter is more complex still. Davidson has written, 'When we turn to the task of interpreting the pattern [of verbal behaviour], we notice the need to find it in accord, within limits, with standards of rationality.'[39] So two questions arise: how slack are the standards? And how wide are the limits of deviation?).

Third, the Principle of Humanity requires that the beliefs imputed should be intelligibly held, and the relativists' objection is that this

[37] This example is cited in G. Macdonald and P. Pettit, *Semantics and Social Science* (Routledge & Kegan Paul, London, 1981), pp. 36–7.

[38] See my 'Some problems about rationality'.

[39] D. Davidson, *Essays on Actions and Events*, p. 239. He further remarks that 'there is no way psychology can avoid consideration of the nature of rationality, of coherence and consistency . . . [it] cannot be divorced from such questions as what constitutes a good argument, a valid inference, a rational plan, or a good reason for acting' (p. 241). One difference between Martin Hollis and myself is that I believe that such questions cannot be settled without reference to sociology and anthropology: it is not that the answers are simply relative, but rather that the right answers require detailed reference to context.

requirement can be met in different, even radically different and incompatible, ways, depending on different construals of 'intelligibility'. But this is hardly convincing. After all any attempt to provide an explanation of the holding of some bizarre and apparently irrational belief or set of beliefs has to be set *forth* and set *against* other such attempts and the criteria against which they are finally judged are not all themselves internal to each explanatory scheme. Such criteria include simplicity, comprehensiveness, and, as I have argued, predictiveness, but also plausibility in the face of all available evidence. Consider Evans-Prichard's explanation of how the Nuer's statement that 'twins are birds' 'appears quite sensible and even true to one who presents the idea to himself in the Nuer language and within their system of religious thought'.[40] Or Christopher Crocker's account of why the Bororo suppose that they are red macaws.[41] Or, more bizarre and apparently nearer to the limits of the unintelligible, some of the (verbal and non-verbal) behaviour of the Ik (e.g. 'men would watch a child with eager anticipation as it crawled towards the fire, then burst into gay and happy laughter as it plunged a skinny hand into the coals') and the attempts by Turnbull to render it comprehensible.[42] In short, implicit theories of translation, like other explanatory theories, are parties to a game that can be, and constantly is, won and lost.

III STRATEGIES OF INTERPRETATION: INTELLECTUALIST AND SYMBOLIST

The attentive reader will have noticed that I have not so far raised the question of how 'belief' is to be construed, or distinguished between the different ways in which people may hold their 'beliefs': I have spoken so far as though concerned only with the acceptance and rejection of the truths or falsehoods expressed by indicative sentences. But there is of course a wide-ranging and long-standing dispute within social anthropology which centres on just these issues, concerning

[40] E.E. Evans-Pritchard, *Nuer Religion* (Clarendon Press, Oxford, 1956), p. 131ff.
[41] J. C. Crocker, 'My brother the parrot' in J.D. Sapir and J.C. Crocker (eds), *The Social Uses of Metaphor: Essays in the Anthropology of Rhetoric* (University of Pennsylvania Press, Philadelphia, 1977), cited in Sperber, this volume pp. 152–3.
[42] C. Turnbull, *The Mountain People* (Picador, London, 1974), pp. 93–4.

what one might call the 'pragmatics' of belief (assuming, for the sake of argument, that one can separate such questions from identifying the meaning of what is believed): what are people to be taken to be *doing* when they appear to be holding a given belief or set of beliefs? Are they engaged in explanation, or something else, and if so, what else? Horton has usefully classified the main divisions on this topic into the intellectualist, the symbolist and the fideist.[43] Of course, such classification is not exhaustive, and there are clearly various significantly different versions of each view, not to mention considerable disputes about what each is claiming. And, it should perhaps be noted, these divisions are quite distinct from those between relativists and non-relativists. In particular, intellectualists are likely to be non-relativists, but they may not be (though if they are not, and their relativism is in earnest, then, as argued above and below, their position is incoherent). And symbolists are quite likely to be relativists, but they may not be (indeed their motivation is sometimes to withdraw certain domains of thought and practice from the applicability of what they see as non-relative cognitive criteria).

Intellectualists hold that apparently irrational beliefs, including magical and religious beliefs, should be seen as attempted explanations. On the Frazerian version, the attempts broadly failed; they were 'simply hypotheses justifiable as such at the time when they were propounded, but which a fuller experience has proved to be inadequate'. On the other hand, 'in reviewing the opinions and practices of ruder ages we should do well to look with leniency upon their errors as inevitable slips made in the search for truth, and to give them the benefit of that indulgence which we ourselves may one day stand in need of'.[44] On the neo-intellectualist version, of which Horton gives the most elaborate contemporary expression, 'their' attempts also often fail, as compared with 'ours', but in some cases they succeed where we fail (as in traditional African diagnoses of psychosomatic diseases). But on this version, the focus is not on failure and success merely, but rather on the specificities of context (whether technical, economic, cultural or psychological) and the commonalities of cognitive rationality. A common interest in explanation, prediction and control and common ways of reasoning are seen to be at work in more

---

[43] This volume, pp. 208–10.
[44] Sir James Frazer, *The Golden Bough. A Study in Magic and Religion* (abridged edition, Macmillan, London, 1922), p. 264.

or less radically different environments, facing different ranges of evidence, with different possibilities of investigation, comparison and retention, and yielding explanatory schemes of different kinds. Judgements as to rationality ('What do they have good or sufficient reasons to believe?') will be distinct from questions as to truth, though neither will be relative; the former will, however, be contextual, that is, they will turn on questions such as: what else do they know? what can they find out? how much information can they store, and in what ways can they put it to use? etc.

Consider the case of eighteenth-century embryology. The 'preformationists' believed that a perfect miniature homunculus inhabited the human egg and that embryological development involved nothing more than its increase in size. According to textbook histories of science, this is obviously an absurd doctrine, since it implies that Eve's ovum must have contained a homunculus, and this a tinier one and so on into the inconceivable. By contrast, the textbook 'heroes', the 'epigeneticists' argued that the complexity of adult form developed gradually in the embryo. But it can plausibly be maintained that, in the eighteenth century context, it was they who were unreasonable, since on their view the fertilized egg was formless, and they had no account to offer of what force could create a design on such formless matter. By contrast the preformationists' view appears in context far more reasonable, given that the contemporary view was that the world had only existed for a few thousand years, and that they had no cell theory to set a lower boundary to organic size. Indeed, the corpuscular theory of light positively encouraged the idea of such minuscule entities. Observation argued neither way, and if anything it could be said the preformationists 'represented the best of Newtonian science', looking behind appearances, interpreting raw sensation, etc. Their theory was 'reasonable in its time and enlightening in our own'.[45] Or consider the context of so-called 'primitive thought' – a small face-to-face community, whose experience tends to be relatively homogeneous, without schooling or literacy, with an unchanging primitive technology offering 'a very narrow range of problem-solving compared with ours' and which is 'integrated with the rest of social relations, so that it is very hard to think of a technological problem *purely* as its problem': in such

[45] S.J. Gould, 'On heroes and fools in science' in his *Ever Since Darwin: Reflections on Natural History* (Burnett Books and André Deutsch, London, 1978), pp. 201–6.

a society Hallpike has argued, 'the cognitive development of its members will be correspondingly retarded and stabilized at a level below that of formal thought'.[46] Whether this (Piagetian) conclusion be accepted or not, it is clear that psychological capacity too should be taken into account when assessing what agents in context have reasons, good reasons or sufficient reasons to believe.

Now, where the intellectualist treats apparently irrational beliefs as either mistaken or rational in context, the symbolist approach is to interpret them as 'symbolizing' meanings or referents in a non-cognitive mode, and thus not subject to rational evaluation as to their truth, plausibility, consistency, etc. Various attempts to account for what such 'symbolizing' involves are on offer (into which we cannot enter here)[47] as are alternative solutions to some of the deep hermeneutic problems inherent in this approach. Symbolizing is, presumably, not the same as expressing or communicating, though in principle it involves both. At the least, it seems to involve the alerting and focusing of attention, through poorly understood mechanisms, involving metaphor or analogy.[48] Some have identified it, negatively, as contrasting with causal thinking and not instrumentally rational, and Goody has even suggested that the symbolic should be defined in opposition to the instrumentally rational as constituting 'a residual category to which "meaning" is assigned'.[49] As Huizinga wrote, 'Instead of looking for the relation between two things by following the hidden detours of their causal connections, thought makes a leap and discovers their relation in a connexion of signification or finality'.[50] Some have identified it, positively, with ritual contexts, such as Turner and Firth. Some, like Beattie, hold both negative and positive views, arguing that 'the chief difference between what we call practical

[46] C. Hallpike, *The Foundations of Primitive Thought*, pp. 101, 133, 31. For a very telling critique of Hallpike, see Jahoda, *Psychology and Anthropology*.

[47] See Dan Sperber, *Rethinking Symbolism* (Cambridge University Press, Cambridge, 1975).

[48] See G. Lewis, *Day of Shining Red: An Essay on Understanding Ritual* (Cambridge University Press, 1980), ch. 2 and my 'Political ritual and social integration' in *Essays in Social Theory* (Macmillan, London, and Columbia University Press, New York, 1977).

[49] J. Goody, 'Religion and ritual: the definitional problem', *British Journal of Sociology*, 12 (1961), p. 156.

[50] J.H. Huizinga, *The Waning of the Middle Ages* (Penguin, Harmondsworth, 1955), p. 204.

common sense techniques for doing things, and ritual or "magico-religious" ways of doing them lies basically in the presence or absence of an institutionalized symbolic element in what is done'.[51] Some, like Leach, see it as linked to the aesthetic and communicative aspect of all behaviour.[52] But all concerned with beliefs of this kind must face some deep hermeneutic issues. The 'meaning' of what those interpreted believe is not simply whatever they say it is but nor is the interpreter free to assign any meaning his interests or theories might dictate. To what extent and in what ways must his account be constrained by actors' accounts or perhaps those available to actors in general in a community? Is interpreting such beliefs like 'decoding' them, especially in cases where the whole point of the symbolism appears to be mystery rather than clarity? In such cases is there any reason to suppose there to be a determinate solution to the decoding problem? And symbols may have multiple referents, and referents multiple symbols, and the referents of symbols may themselves be symbolic. Recall Huizinga's account of symbolism in the late Middle Ages:

> Symbolist thought permits of an infinity of relations between things. Each thing may denote a number of distinct ideas by its different special qualities, and a quality may also have several symbolic meanings. The highest conceptions have symbols by the thousand. Nothing is too humble to represent and to glorify the sublime. The walnut signifies Christ: the sweet kernel is his divine nature, the green and pulpy outer peel is His humanity; the wooden shell between is the cross. Thus all things raise the thoughts to the eternal . . . [53]

What one might call a 'cognitive' approach, as advocated by Sperber,[54] propounds an account of 'beliefs', such as those of magic and religion, that treats them as cognitive but still not properly subject to rational assessment. On this view they represent ways of dealing with information that exceeds our conceptual capacities, though the point of expressing and communicating them may well be the very exploration of their multiple meanings.

What Horton calls the 'fideist' approach might plausibly be seen as a

---

[51] J.H. Beattie, 'Ritual and Social Change', *Man*, n.s., I (1966), p. 202.
[52] E. Leach, 'Ritual' in *International Encyclopedia of the Social Sciences* (Macmillan and Free Press, New York, 1968), vol. 13, p. 526.
[53] Huizinga, *The Waning of the Middle Ages*, p. 207.
[54] See Sperber, *Rethinking Symbolism* and his chapter in this volume.

further version of the symbolist approach which appeals to an understanding – assumed to be commonly shared by interpreters and interpretees – of religion and religious experience. It contrasts with the intellectualist approach in systematically refusing to regard beliefs it interprets as magical and, especially, religious as amenable to assessment by cognitive criteria. Hence Winch's critique of Evans-Pritchard on the Azande and Wittgenstein's of Frazer's *The Golden Bough*.

Wittgenstein began from a critique of Frazer on just such grounds:

> Frazer's account of the magical and religious notions of men is unsatisfactory: it makes these notions appear as *mistakes*. Was Augustine mistaken, then, when he called on God on every page of the *Confessions?* Well – one might say – if he was not mistaken, then the Buddhist holy-man, or some other, whose religion expresses quite different notions, surely was. But *none* of them was mistaken except where he was putting forward a theory.[55]

In the case of 'the religious practices of the people', what we have is '*not* an error':

> Put [Frazer's] account of the King of the Wood at Nemi together with the phrase 'the majesty of death', and you see that they are one. The life of the priest-king shows what is meant by that phrase. If someone is gripped by the majesty of death, then through such a life he can give expression to it. – Of course, this is not an explanation: it puts one symbol in place of another . . . A religious symbol does not rest on any *opinion*. And error belongs only with opinion.[56]

So, for example, when a mother adopts a child by simulating birth, pulling him from beneath her clothes, 'it is crazy to think there is an *error* in this and that she believes she has borne the child'. One might, Wittgenstein says,

> begin a book on anthropology in this way: Where we watch the life and behaviour of men all over the earth we see that apart from what we might call animal activities, taking food &c.,&c., men also carry out actions that bear a peculiar character and might be called ritualistic. But then it is nonsense if we go on to say that the characteristic feature of *these* activities is that they spring from wrong ideas about the physics of things. (This is what Frazer does when he says magic is really false physics, or, as the

[55] Wittgenstein, *Remarks on Frazer's 'Golden Bough'*, p. 1e.
[56] Ibid., pp. 2e, 3e.

case may be, false medicine, technology, etc.) What makes the character of ritual action is not any view or opinion, either right or wrong, although an opinion – a belief – itself can be ritualistic, or belong to a rite. [57]

What then is the peculiar character of ritual belief and practice? Wittgenstein criticizes Frazer's explanations of primitive observances as 'much cruder than the sense of the observances themselves'. [58] But what sense does Wittgenstein see in them and how does he grasp it? The answer appears to be: he claims to recognize and render 'perspicuous' forms of thought and experience with which we are already familiar – and for which we already have the appropriate language ('ghost', 'shade', 'soul', 'spirit', etc.). So, for example, the Beltane fire festival is given 'depth' by 'its connection with the burning of a man'. It shares features with other such rites which connect 'with our own feelings and thoughts'. What 'gives us a sinister impression is the inner nature of the practice as performed in recent times, and the facts of human sacrifice as we know them only indicate the direction in which we ought to see it'. The 'deep and sinister aspect is not obvious just from learning the history of the external action, but *we* impute it from an experience in ourselves'. [59]

But who are 'we'? Wittgenstein criticizes Frazer as 'much more savage than most of his savages, for these savages will not be so far from any understanding of spiritual matters as an Englishman of the twentieth century'. [60] But is his own understanding (what '*we* impute') any less local? Is a Viennese of the twentieth century, albeit one located in Cambridge, better placed to achieve such understanding, and even if he is why assume it is nearer to 'the sense of the observances themselves'? Whatever the answer to this, the 'fideist' version of the symbolist strategy of interpretation embodies the assumption of a shared (if not by twentieth-century Englishmen), recognizable and distinct form of experience to which symbolism and ritual give expression.

How can a choice be made between strategies of interpretation? In

[57] Ibid., pp. 4e, 7e.
[58] Ibid., p. 8e.
[59] Ibid., pp. 9e, 14e, 16e. See F. Cioffi, 'Wittgenstein and the fire-festivals', in I. Block (ed.), *Perspectives on the Philosophy of Wittgenstein* (Blackwell, Oxford, 1981).
[60] Wittgenstein, *Remarks on Frazer's 'Golden Bough'*, p. 8e.

the first place, it is clearly a mistake, as Taylor's essay shows, to suppose that they must be mutually exclusive. In pre-scientific cultures, the very distinction between explaining, predicting and controlling the world, and whatever understanding it symbolically involves is in many areas of life not made. So, for example, Fortes describes the Dobuans as not distinguishing the magical from the technical, and Barth noticed that the Baseri nomads of South Persia, when they migrate each spring, are both adapting to a harsh environment and engaging in their society's central rite.[61] And among the Kpelle,

> Rice growing is not an analysed, isolated technical activity in the Kpelle way of life. What Western cultures would compartementalise into technical science, the Kpelle culture weaves into the whole fabric of existence. The relevant question is not 'How do you grow rice?' but 'How do you live?'[62]

But, more deeply, how is the appropriate interpretation to be discovered? Here I wish to claim that it is, indeed, *discovered*, by confronting, and eliciting, crucial evidence. The trouble with the advocates of contending strategies is that they so often justify them on general grounds, in advance of evidence that tells one way or another in particular cases. Thus Horton may complain that the symbolist approach neglects 'the actor's point of view'[63] (in a sense, of course, it must do so) and Leach may engage in ritual slaying of Frazer, Tylor and the 'neo-Tylorians': yet the only test lies in working through the data and as I argued in the case of identification and translation, this, though it may often be ambiguous and difficult of access, will generally be capable of deciding the issue. Strategies are not simply self-verifying.

Consider the classical controversy, in which Frazer himself played an early and central role, about parthenogenesis: are certain primitive peoples, notably Australian aboriginals and Trobrianders, 'ignorant' of physiological paternity? This controversy was replayed most instructively by Spiro and Leach in the 1960s,[64] and their debate has

---

[61] Cited in Lewis, *Day of Shining Red*, pp. 9 and 15.

[62] J. Gay and M. Cole, *The New Mathematics and an Old Culture* (Holt, Reinhart & Winston, New York, 1967), p. 21.

[63] This volume, p. 209.

[64] M. E. Spiro, 'Religion: problems of definition and explanation' in M. Banton (ed.), *Anthropological Approaches to the Study of Religion* (Tavistock,

recently been subjected to a useful analysis by Stephen Turner[65] on which I here seek to build.

First consider a piece of exemplary primary evidence. In 1903, W.E. Roth reported on the beliefs of the Tully River Blacks on this subject as follows:

> A woman begets children because (a) she has been sitting over the fire on which she has roasted a particular species of black bream, which must have been given to her by the prospective father, (b) she has purposely gone a-hunting and caught a certain kind of bullfrog, (c) some men may have told her to be in an interesting condition, or (d) she may dream of having the child put inside her.
>
> By whichever of the above methods the child is conceived, whenever it eventually appears, the recognised husband accepts it as his own without demur.[66]

Let us follow the disputants in not doubting the essentials of this report, which though involving interpretation and translation, and thus theories in the manner already indicated, is neutral between their contending interpretive strategies.

Spiro, following Roth himself and Frazer, insists that 'the aborigines are indeed ignorant of physiologial paternity, and that the four statements quoted in Roth are in fact proffered explanations for conception'.[67] Leach firmly insists rather that their belief is a 'kind of religious fiction', a 'myth' that 'establishes categories and affirms relationships'; a 'species of religious dogma . . . Christians who say that they "believe" in the doctrine of the Virgin Birth or in the closely-related doctrine of the Immaculate Conception are not ordinarily arguing from a position of ignorance; on the contrary, these are doctrines which are compatible with extreme philosphical sophisti-

---

London, 1966), E. Leach, 'Virgin birth', *Proceedings of the Royal Anthropological Institute for 1966* (London, 1967), and M.E. Spiro, 'Virgin birth, parthenogenesis and physiological paternity: an essay in cultural interpretation', *Man*, n.s., 3 (1968) pp. 242–61. Leach's essay was reprinted in his *Genesis as Myth and Other Essays* (Cape, London, 1969).

[65] S. Turner, *Sociological Explanation as Translation* (Cambridge University Press, Cambridge, 1980), pp. 46–63. Unfortunately Turner's discussion is marred by his failure to take Spiro's second article into account.

[66] W.E. Roth, 'Superstition, magic and medicine', *North Queensland Ethnographical Bulletin*, 5 (1903), p. 22.

[67] Spiro, 'Religion: problems of definition', p. 112.

cation. This type of explanation is to be preferred to the other.'[68] For Leach it is not 'a legitimate inference to assert that these Australian aborigines were ignorant of the connection between copulation and pregnancy'; instead,

> The modern interpretation of the rituals described would be that, in this society, the relationship between the woman's child and the clansmen of the woman's husband stems from the public recognition of the bonds of marriage, rather than from the facts of cohabitation, which is a very normal state of affairs.

Indeed,

> If we put the so-called primitive beliefs alongside the sophistic-ated ones and treat the whole lot with equal philosophical respect we shall see that they constitute a set of variations around a common structural theme, the metaphysical topography of the relationship between gods and men.[69]

By contrast, Spiro maintains that

> Since the Australian conception belief states that conception is caused by the entry of a spirit child into the mother, and since – in the absence of any evidence which indicates the contrary – it is gratuitous to assume that this cultural belief does not mean what it says, it would seem not unreasonable to assume that it en-unciates a theory of conception. Since, moreover, it is a non-procreative theory, and since – in the absence of any evidence which indicates the contrary – it is gratuitous to assume that the natives do not believe what it says, it would seem not injudicious to assume that the belief implies that the natives are ignorant of physiological paternity.[70]

He not only disputes Leach's account on evidential and logical grounds; but also offers alternative explanations of how the beliefs, as he interprets them, come to be held.

Now one useful way to see this dispute about conceptions of concep-tion is as a contest between strategies of interpretation. According to Spiro, evidence such as the beliefs reported by Roth are interpreted as meaning what persons unaware of certain causal relationships would mean if they said that the causes of pregnancy were dreams, catching

[68] Leach, 'Virgin birth', pp. 42, 45, 46.
[69] Ibid., p. 39.
[70] Spiro, 'Virgin birth . . .', p. 255.

frogs etc. According to Leach, they are interpreted as meaning what a devout Catholic means when speaking of the Virgin Birth (perhaps he should have rather said a devout but sophisticated Anglican?), and by 'cause' they mean what such a Catholic would mean if he pointed to 'signs' of this divine act, such as the Annunciation. Turner suggests that both of these strategies can be seen as alternative and contending versions of what he calls the 'same practices hypothesis', which has the general form: '*Where we (or another group) would follow such and such a rule or practice, or act in such and such a way given some reason, they (or some other group) would do the same.*'[71]

Applying such a hypothesis in any given case – as Leach and Spiro respectively do – will in the first place always generate puzzles, above all where the hypothesis appears to break down, for which explanation is required (how *can* they be ignorant of this? why symbolize *this* in *that* way – or indeed at all?); and if no adequate explanation is forthcoming, to save the hypothesis, abandonment of that interpretation, or choice of practice, is called for. The disputants will seek to support their respective interpretations, partly by appealing to evidence and seeking to discredit the evidential basis of alternative interpretations, partly by arguing *for* the analogy in practices assumed, and *against* that assumed by their rival(s).

Taking these last points first, Spiro and Leach both claim that the ethnographic evidence supports their respective interpretations. But they disagree interestingly as to what evidence is *relevant*. So, for example, Spiro asks whether Leach's interpretation is

> the interpretation which the aborigines place on their beliefs? There is certainly no evidence for this assumption. Perhaps, then, this is the meaning which they intended to convey, even though they did not do so explicitly? But even if we were to grant that, for some strange reason, aborigines prefer to express structural relationships by means of biological symbolism, how do we *know* that this was their intention? Perhaps, then, the symbolism is unconscious, and the structural meaning which Leach claims for these beliefs, although intentional, is latent? . . . Again, however, we are hung up on the problem of evidence.[72]

To which Leach replies that for statements of dogma, evidence as actors' intentions is irrelevant:

---

71 Turner, *Sociological Explanation*, p. 56.
72 Spiro, 'Religion: problems of definition', pp. 111–12.

Instead of looking for patterns in the way people behave Spiro would adopt the naive procedure of asking the actor why he behaves as he does . . . [English marriage rituals] are . . . structured in an extremely clear and well-defined way, but not one bride in a thousand has even an inkling of the total pattern.[73]

Or again Leach argues against Spiro from the Tully River Blacks' knowledge of the causes of pregnancy in animals to their obviously knowing it in humans. But in response, Spiro cites Roth himself, who wrote:

Although sexual connection as a cause of conception is not recognised among the Tully River Blacks as far as they themselves are concerned, it is admitted as true for all animals; – indeed this idea confirms them in their belief of superiority over the brute creation.[74]

In arguing for his intellectualist 'ignorance' interpretation, Spiro maintains that, in the absence of counter-evidence, the natives both mean and believe what they say. Thus, for example, the reported belief that 'a woman begets children because she may dream of a child put inside her' is about conception not patrilateral filiation. In holding such beliefs, the aboriginals are, in their context, quite *rational*. There are many reasons for limitation in their knowledge in this sphere, and

for the aborigines to believe in their spirit-children theory of conception is entirely rational: it explains all the facts, it accounts for all the anomalies rendered inexplicable by a procreation theory . . . it is contradicted by no available knowledge, and it leads to valid deductive and inductive conclusions. To be sure this conception theory is false; but to hold a false belief is not in itself irrational . . .[75]

Leach argues *against* the 'ignorance' interpretation, first, because it is 'improbable on common-sense grounds', given what else they know, their familiarity with animal husbandry and their cultural contacts; and, second, on the grounds that if the ethnographer believed what he was told it was because such belief corresponded to his own private fantasy of the natural ignorance of childish savages'.[76]

[73] Leach, 'Virgin birth', p. 47.
[74] Roth, 'Superstition, magic and medicine', p. 22, cited in Spiro, 'Virgin birth . . .', p. 242.
[75] Spiro, 'Virgin birth . . .', p. 245.
[76] Leach, 'Virgin birth', p. 41.

In reply to which Spiro points to the evidence of what they *say* (that women are entered by spirit children and that sexual intercourse is irrelevant to pregnancy) and denies any imputation of childishness to the savage, citing among others Ashley Montague, the classical exponent of the ignorance interpretation:

> The mind of the Australian is no more pre-logical than that of the modern educated man or woman. Essentially, the mind of the savage functions in exactly the same way as our own does, the differences perceptible in the effects of that functioning are due only to the differences in the premises upon which that functioning is based, premises which represent the logical instruments of the native's thought, and have their origin in categories and forms of judgement which are to some extent different though quite as rigorously organised as our own.[77]

In arguing for his symbolist 'religious dogma' interpretation, Leach maintains that it makes far better sense of what they say and above all *do:* it treats the natives, not as cognitive idiots, but rather as religious believers applying 'principles of faith' to which 'canons of rationality are irrelevant'. The aboriginals and Trobrianders are like good Catholics who say 'we know that virgins do not conceive: but we also know that the Holy Mother of God was and ever shall be an immaculate Virgin'. Frazer's childish savage, he says, should be finally abandoned and replaced by 'a slightly muddle-headed theologian'.[78]

But Spiro argues *against* this 'dogma' interpretation by claiming there to be a crucial fallacy in the analogy between Australian parthenogenesis and Christian Virgin Birth. For the former concerns ordinary births and the latter is a 'miracle'. In the former case, non-virgins conceive, but not because of intercourse with a genitor; in the latter case, a Virgin (paradoxically) conceives because fertilized by a (spiritual) genitor. Virgin Birth, unlike parthenogensis, is abnormal and miraculous, and actually requires knowledge of physiological paternity:

> Only on the assumption that normal conceptions are non-virginal can the dogma claim that the virginal conception of Jesus is a miracle (which is why His birth is not just another virgin birth, but *the* Virgin Birth). And it is precisely because it is a miracle that the Virgin Birth is a dogma of the church, ie., an

[77] Cited in Spiro, 'Virgin birth . . .', pp. 245–6.
[78] Leach, 'Virgin birth', pp. 43, 44, 45.

article of faith. For, like all miracles, the Virgin Birth is not
normal but abnormal, not ordinary but extraordinary, nor
rational but irrational – in a word (as Tertullian put it) absurd.
And to believe in the absurd requires a leap into faith: *credo quia
absurdum est.*[79]

Furthermore, Spiro argues, Leach's claim that in the Christian case
the basic message is sociological, establishing categories and affirming
relationships, also fails, thereby showing a further breakdown in the
supposed analogy between the primitive and the Christian cases: if
'the dogma of the Virgin Birth claims that God is Jesus's genitor, it is
not to announce that Joseph is His pater, but to proclaim that He is
Saviour'.[80]

Both the intellectualist (ignorance) and the symbolist (dogma) interpretations have to cope with distinctive explanatory problems arising
from puzzles raised by their respective applications of the 'same
practices hypothesis'. Thus Spiro has to answer the question: Why do
Roth's informants hold to their (mistaken) explanatory beliefs? In
response to this Spiro in fact suggests two alternative possibilities. The
first, which has the virtue of simplicity, comes from Malinowski: 'for a
variety of perfectly rational reasons (both logical and empirical) . . .
knowledge of the causal relationship between sexual intercourse and
conception is absent from their cultural inventory of biological
knowledge'.[81] In short, they just don't know. This might seem
unproblematic; after all, they get many other things wrong, as indeed
do we. But, Spiro admits, this does raise 'a serious ethnographical
problem':

> Since most peoples seem not to be ignorant of physiological
> paternity, it is somewhat difficult to understand why the Austra-
> lians, too, have not discovered the causal link between sexual
> intercourse and conception.

And so he proposes a second possible explanation, broadly Freudian
in character, following Ernest Jones: that the natives' procreative
ignorance is based 'not on the absence of biological knowledge, but on
its rejection' and is motived by 'the wish to deny physiological paternity'. On this view, 'the spirit-child belief enunciates a non-procreative

---

[79] Spiro, 'Virgin birth . . .', pp. 249–50.
[80] Ibid., p. 252.
[81] Ibid., p. 255.

theory of conception, not in *default*, but *in lieu*, of a procreative explanation'.[82] On the first explanation, you have the natives' explanatory attempt misfiring; on the second, a cultural solution to their oedipal conflict.

Conversely, Leach has to anwer the question: why do Roth's informants express 'their social situation and . . . social condition' through the symbolism of black bream, bullfrogs, spirit-children, and so on? And he answers this by considering 'the whole range of materials relating to what *we* consider to be supernatural births' and offering a broadly 'structuralist' analysis, relating the structure of myths (specifically those concerning supernatural births) and social systems. The proposed explanation involves tracing different patterns in the elements of the myths and correlating them with different patterns in caste, class and kinship systems, in Catholic and Protestant colonial societies, in India, and in the Australian and Trobriand cases. And he further argues that 'the themes of decent filiation and of sexual and/or marital alliance between gods and humans necessarily have basic relevance for the symbolisation of time and for our topographical apprehension of the other world'. But, as Spiro asks, why use the apparent denial of physiological paternity (in which in any case they allegedly disbelieve) as the means of such symbolism? To which he answers that, in the representation of the relationship between 'the here-now and the other'.

> there must also be continuity and mediation. Cross-cutting the idea that impotent men are the descendants of potent gods we have the incestuous dogma that gods and man may establish sexual connection. Dogmas of virgin birth and of the irrelevance of human male sexuality appear as by-products of such a theology; . . . this is where they fit in, and this is the case in primitive as well as in sophisticated societies.[83]

How then to choose between these contending interpretive strategies? Is this a dramatic case of the underdetermination of theories by (all possible) data? Plainly, they are both equally compatible with much, perhaps most, of the available evidence (though their respective adherents may vehemently deny this of the other). But not with all the evidence, or not plausibly so. What about the Australians' and the Trobrianders' birth-control practices? Do they avoid sex

[82] Ibid., p. 256.
[83] Leach, 'Virgin birth', p. 43, 45, 46.

or the heralds of conception? How do they account for illegitimate births? Do 'they', in any case, agree? Do women have the same beliefs as men, or do they, as Hocart suggests, conceal the facts of life from their menfolk?[84] Cannot test-questions be devised to discover whether sex is a *necessary* condition of conception? There are of course further tricky interpretive issues here. 'Ignorance' after all, is relative and, as Spiro himself suggests, can take different forms and operate at different levels of consciousness, though these questions too can surely be investigated. Of course, the *relevance* of attributing ignorance is a further issue. To do so seems to imply the correlative claim that they do not know what they could in some sense have discovered. But what if *they* are indifferent or agnostic – perhaps because they foreswear or even actively reject an explanatory approach to this issue? But surely this too can be investigated. More generally, since we may assume that the members of primitive societies are rational, self-interpreting beings, they can after all be faced with the very questions we have been discussing – questions that will make all the more sense to them with the arrival of Western medicine and missionaries.

Consider, for example, Toren Monberg's recent evidence concerning not Australians and Trobrianders but the Polynesians of Bellona Island in the British Solomons, who have only lately been 'told by missionaries and British administrators that their beliefs through generations were "false" beliefs'[85] and were interviewed extensively about their beliefs, past and present, on the topic under discussion. Monberg's data appears clearly to support Spiro against Leach, at least with respect to this case. The Bellonese, he reports, believe that children come from the 'shade of the Gods' somewhere below the Eastern horizon and were implanted in the woman's womb by ancestral spirits: how this 'physically' took place was a matter of no concern to the Bellonese. Progeny were produced because the ancestors and deities were pleased with an alliance, not by or because of the man's copulation with a woman.

> According to all sources, copulation was considered a 'pleasant thing, joke, or game'. To the direct question of why humans copulated all informants said that it was because people liked it, it tickled, it was the habit of men and women. They moreover

[84] A.M. Hocart, *Social Origins* (Watts, London, 1954), p. 99. Cited by R. Needham in *Man*, n.s., 4 (1969), pp. 457–8.
[85] T. Monberg, 'Fathers were not genitors', *Man*, n.s., 10 (1975), p. 35.

added voluntarily that it was not until the advent of British government officials and missionaries that they heard about a relationship between copulation and pregnancy.

But, Monberg asks,

Was it really likely that we had here, in front of us, a patrilineal society which did not recognise the biological importance of a human genitor? All test questions put forward seem to indicate that this was really the case. Only once, in a group-interview with a number of males, one middle-aged informant said that 'we suspected that there might be some connection, because the penis went into the place where children are, but it was not an important matter at all, and we did not think about it'. Most of the other men present during the interview disagreed with this and said they had never thought of any connection between sleeping together . . . and pregnancy . . . before white man told them about this. 'How should we have known?', they added. [86]

(It is, of course, possible that they were all playing a huge joke on the anthropologist, but this possibility can surely be investigated.) Further test questions (about the significance of semen, birth control, likeness of children to mother or father, illegitimate liaisons, births of unmarried mothers, etc.) all yielded answers implying no physiological connection. Moreover, Monberg adds, the Bellonese could observe few mammals of considerable size, engaged freely in sexual activities but made little reference to them in myths, stories, songs and rituals, took them lightly and never linked them to procreation, which by contrast they took most seriously. Of course, Monberg admits they might always have known the facts of life deep in their hearts, but for this suggestion there is 'no empirical support'. [87]

Actually, Monberg's data establish (or render highly plausible) only that the Bellonese at least were ignorant of physiological paternity. But they do not establish what *sort* of ignorance this was, nor indeed what sort of a belief concerning conception they held to, nor indeed how they held to it. Was it cognitive and explanatory or were they rather not interested in explaining this phenomenon (i.e. how procreation occurs) – perhaps as against *why* it should happen to this particular couple? In this latter case to call them ignorant would be rather beside the point, or at any rate their point. Was their belief something that

[86] Ibid., pp. 35–6, 37, 37–8.
[87] Ibid., p. 40.

they could not question, without their entire system of belief and practice becoming incoherent, rather like the Zande's belief in witchcraft? Was it belief tied to specific situations and so on? But all these questions too, I maintain, are susceptible to empirical investigation. And if no given piece of evidence is decisive between alternative interpretations, some crucial mass of it will not fail to be so.

I have sought to make two points in this section. First, to suggest that in interpreting what people *do* when they 'believe' something is parallel to interpreting what they mean when they utter indicative sentences: it requires a strategic hypothesis whose application (once explanatory puzzles it raises have been solved) renders what they say and do intelligible. And second, to suggest, by working through a detailed example, that, in practice, contending interpretive strategies will raise different explanatory problems and appeal to different evidence, and will claim to account for all of it, but will win or lose in the face of some of it.

IV EXPLANATION: SYMMETRICAL OR ASYMMETRICAL?

I now turn to the question, which has divided writers on this topic, of whether the nature of beliefs, and in particular whether they are true or rational, makes a difference to how they are to be explained. The symmetry view is clearly set forth by Barnes and Bloor: historians of science and anthroplogists 'simply investigate the contingent determinants of belief and reasoning without regard to whether the beliefs are true or the inferences rational'. The asymmetry view is no less clearly enunciated by Hollis: 'true and rational beliefs need one sort of explanation, false and irrational beliefs another', with mixed explanations for the mixed cases.[88] Who is right?

In the first place, a certain kind of asymmetry is clearly implicit in what I said in the previous section about different explanatory puzzles arising from different interpretive strategies. An intellectualist approach, a symbolist approach and an approach based on the unintelligibility of the very distinction between the first two from the actors' (but not the interpreter's) point of view, each yields a different range of explanatory puzzles. Compare Spiro's questions with Leach's questions, and both with Evans-Pritchard's concerning the Azande's

[88] This volume, p. 23, 75.

beliefs in witchcraft. Or consider Clifford Geertz's account of the Balinese cockfight.[89] Here it clearly makes a decisive difference how the facts are interpreted – the 'thin' description of the facts being (1) that there was a single large central bet always made at even money and a vast host of small side-bets which were never made at even money but at odds ranging from 2–1 to 10–9, and (2) that the centre bet view was correct, in probability terms: underdogs and favourites won about equally often. Now, first, this (thin) description already sets an explanatory puzzle: why did the side-bettors go on betting in the way they did? And Geertz's interpretive answer, that what was really being wagered here was status, or rather the simulation of status, in turn gives rise to distinctive explanatory problems. So, generally, in one obvious sense, different interpretations of belief systems (even the thinnest) give rise to distinctive and different explanatory problems.

But suppose we focus again on propositional beliefs – sets of indicative sentences accepted as true. Does their truth value or the rationality with which they are held affect how we are to explain their being held? Consider the following six contrasts:

(1) One person believes that the sentence 'The candle is out' is true, and the indicated candle is out at the time. Another person, under the same conditions, believes that the sentence 'The candle is alight' is true.

(2) One Ancient Greek believes that because all men are mortal and Socrates is a man, Socrates must be mortal. Another strenuously believes that, nevertheless, Socrates is immortal.

(3) A Dorze tribesman believes that because it has always been known that there are dragons, they do indeed exist. A scientifically untrained modern Englishman believes that because scientists say there are electrons, they do indeed exist.

(4) A hack *savant* of the sixteenth century believes Ptolemy. A hack scientist of the seventeenth century believes Galileo.

(5) One member of a tribe believes that witchcraft and sorcery cause disease, and that it can be cured by magical means. Another tribesman believes that this is all hocus-pocus, preferring modern medical explanations and remedies.

(6) A scientist makes a revolutionary discovery. Others reject it, preferring to stick to the pre-revolutionary paradigm.

[89] C. Geertz, 'Deep play: notes on the Balinese cockfight', in his *The Interpretation of Cultures* (Basic Books, New York, 1973).

The first four contrasts are relatively easy to analyse, though (1) and (2) yield opposite results to (3) and (4). In the case of (1) and (2), asymmetry plainly holds. Simple observational beliefs such as (1) have the feature that the states of affairs which make them true suffice to explain why they are held, when they are true, assuming that various standard perceptual conditions and normal belief acquisition mechanisms are in operation. When they are false, the explanation must rather cite some disturbing factor – such as non-standard perceptual conditions or some abnormal physical or physiological condition of the believer. Of course, all sorts of physical, social, conceptual, linguistic, etc. conditions must hold in the first case, as in the second. But the point is that, in the second, they include disturbing and interfering factors which prevent the agent from acquiring, as he normally would, a veridical belief, and thus explain his false belief.

Similarly, in the case of simple inference, such as (2), the validity of the deductive move from premises to conclusion suffices to explain belief in it, given that a whole range of normal conditions hold (that the agent is conscious, understands what he says, is sincere, etc.). But if he gets it *wrong*, we need some further explanation – extreme stupidity, mental derangement, a religious trance, or the hypothesis that the inference is held to be a mystery or religious dogma – that could account for his conclusion.

So in cases (1) and (2), asymmetry holds. It rests on the distinction between normal and abnormal conditions, normality being *defined* as just that which obtains when a verifying condition or valid inference is sufficient to explain belief. That distinction is partly constitutive of what we take to be an agent, capable of holding beliefs (i.e. accepting them as true) and reasoning.

But what about (3) and (4)? Here, it would seem, symmetry holds. For in both cases, belief is on the basis of *authority:* that is, independent judgement on the facts of the matter or the reasons for the conclusion drawn is either suspended or not exercised – though judgement may well be made as to whether and why the source of authority is fit to be believed. In both (3) and (4), neither the truth value nor the reasons for the beliefs in question have a direct bearing on the explanation of why they are held, because in neither case does either of the parties hold them for the reasons which support them. They hold them for other reasons (which may indeed be very good ones) and these are symmetrically tied into configurations of social, cultural, political, etc., factors.

(5) and (6) represent 'hard cases'. On the one hand, we may be tempted to say that asymmetry holds, because otherwise the rational rejection of superstition and the progress of science would become unintelligible. Unless some people at least reject traditional and pre-scientific or disproved beliefs on rational grounds, could one make sense of the very ideas of scepticism or the rationalization of world-views or scientific progress? On the other hand, we know enough about the histories of both to know that the actors involved in these developments were very often motivated by the strangest reasons: consider the literature on conversions, or the known motivations, religious and political, of, say, Kepler, Boyle and Newton. Does either the truth or the rationality of beliefs affect their explanation in these cases?

The way forward here is to be more specific about what is to be explained. Consider first the question why a particular agent holds a particular belief. Why do particular tribesmen or peasants reject folk beliefs for modern applied science? Why did certain seventeenth-century scientists think their revolutionary beliefs true? In the first place, these are, plainly, highly theoretical beliefs, requiring deep conceptual, not to mention cultural, moral and psychological shifts: they are (to use Quine's image) deeply embedded beliefs often far removed from the observational periphery. Second, there appear to be no comparable normal belief-acquisition mechanisms that render certain verifying states of affairs sufficient explanations of their adoption. Third, they are often adopted and held for various diverse religious and political reasons – some of them apparently (to us) extraneous. In short, their being held may often be overdetermined, so that it is scarcely possible to tell which reason was decisive. (And indeed they may be held for *only* extraneous reasons – though this case is intended to be captured by cases (3) and (4)). So with respect to particular beliefs, no clear case for asymmetry seems feasible.

But suppose we now ask: what is the significance of the rejection of traditional folk beliefs in secularizing and modernizing societies, or the seventeenth-century Scientific Revolution? How are such transitions to be interpreted? One answer (though none is definitive) is that a detached, objective and absolute conception of knowledge was in effect isolated and made dominant in certain spheres – even if some of those engaged in the process had a deficient self-understanding of what they were doing. Understanding the world – with a view to explaining, predicting and controlling it – became, in Taylor's phrase, distinct from being attuned with it as a meaningful cosmos.

Now the relativist counter-move at this point is to see such transitions rather as confrontations between alternative, even incommensurable, ontologies and cosmologies, each with its own criteria of success. But consider the case raised by Rorty, and cited in our Introduction, of Galileo versus Cardinal Bellarmine.[90] Can anyone who has, for instance, read Bellarmine's letter to Paolo Antonio Foscarini (a Carmelite monk from Naples much impressed by Galileo's ideas) really see this as a clash of explanatory schemes, each offering an alternative understanding of the cosmos on the basis of alternative canons of rationality and standards of truth? Is it not obvious that the Cardinal was a master of *Realpolitik*, concerned as Giorgio de Santillana remarks, by signs of 'confusion in the ranks', his legal mind baffled by Galileo's proofs and dominated by 'his Aristotelian conditioning and his fear of "scandal" '.[91] As he wrote to Foscarini,

> to set out to affirm that the Sun, in very truth, is at the centre of the Universe and only rotates on its axis without going from East to West, is a very dangerous attitude and one calculated not only to arouse the Scholastic philosophers and theologians but also to injure our Holy Faith by contradicting the Scriptures . . . the Council of Trent forbids the interpretation of the Scriptures in a way contrary to the common opinion of the Holy Fathers . . . not merely the Fathers but modern commentators on Genesis, the Psalms, Ecclesiastes and Joshua . . . all agree in interpreting them literally as teaching that the Sun is in the heavens and revolves around the Earth with immense speed and that the Earth is very distant from the heavens, at the centre of the Universe, and motionless. Consider, then, in your prudence, whether the Church can tolerate that the Scriptures should be interpreted in a manner contrary to that of the Holy Fathers and of all modern commentators, both Latin and Greek.[92]

By contrast, Galileo, in his letter to the Grand Duchess (Madonna Cristina) attacking theologians made a clear plea for the new view of knowledge:

[90] See R. Rorty, *Philosophy and the Mirror of Nature* (Blackwell, Oxford, and Princeton University Press, Princeton, 1980), pp. 328–31.

[91] G. de Santillana, *The Crime of Galileo* (Heinemann, London, 1958), pp. 95, 103.

[92] Cited ibid., p. 99. Of course, Bellarmine's case was complex (he did after all

in all these propositions which are not directly *de fide* . . . it is in
the power of no creature whatever to make them true or false,
otherwise than they are *de facto*.[93]

To this Hacking might reply that Galileo was really advancing a new
'style of reasoning'. But this is to miss the point I am seeking to stress,
which is rather that he was discarding, for the purpose of understanding planetary motions, old *types* of reasoning – among them textual
exegesis, cosmic analogies and above all appeals to authority, scrip-
tual, ecclesiastical and political, and arguments of prudence. As Gellner in effect argues in his contribution to this volume, the Galilean
style stands for the route to knowledge itself. So the second question
must receive asymmetrical answers in cases (5) and (6), since the
self-evident explanatory success of the absolute conception of knowledge and the Galilean style is not dissociable from interpreting the
significance of the transitions in question.

The same holds for the third and final question we might ask: why
do modern scientific and technological beliefs in the end win out, both
within modernizing societies and in the history of our own? And here,
as Taylor well shows, the systematic practical and predictive success of
such beliefs in enabling people to control and manipulate their environments cannot simply be regarded as success internal to a *Weltans-
chauung*. It represents cognitive supriority that societies committed to
pre-Galilean modes of thought do not, and indeed, cannot fail to
acknowledge – though modern Western science may, nevertheless, be
rejected, as it was by anti-Westernizing literati in nineteenth-century
China.[94]

Of course, there is a dark side to the story of modern science, both in
its relentless impact on traditional, and indeed modern, forms of life
and in its disastrous ecological consequences. Much of modern science
(especially in the area of medicine) is much farther from the goals of
explanation, prediction and control, of consequences intended and
unintended, than its enthusiasts and true believers would ever care to
admit. And it would be hard to argue that its success was linked in any

---

believe in scriptural truth) but is it really plausible to see this as a rationally
unwinnable clash of styles of reason?
[93] Cited in ibid., p. 97.
[94] See J. R. Levenson, *Confucian China and its Modern Fate: a Trilogy*
(University of California Press, Berkeley and Los Angeles, 1968), vol. 1,
pp. 69–75.

simple way to survival value. For one thing, as a result of scientific discoveries and their systematic application, the survival of mankind itself is now in jeopardy. But the point I am seeking to make here is a much simpler one: that where modern science and technology win out, their doing so cannot be explained without reference to their indubitable predictive and manipulative successes relative to those of previous systems of belief.

V PERSPECTIVISM AND RELATIVISM

What then survives of the case for relativism, more particularly relativism of truth and of reason? The case against it as set out in this chapter and in this volume runs along two main lines. First, there is what one may broadly label the translation or bridgehead argument, mainly advanced here by Hollis and Newton-Smith, and elsewhere by Davidson. Barnes and Bloor claim that the accumulating evidence from anthropology and the history of science overwhelmingly supports thoroughgoing relativism; but from this argument it follows that, unless such relativism is denied, that evidence would never even show up. The second line of argument which we can broadly label, following Gellner, the 'Big Ditch argument',[95] focuses on the decisive emergence and systematic refinement and application of what has been variously described as the absolute Cartesian conception of knowledge, and the Galilean mode of reasoning, embodying the pursuit of objectivity (understood as perspective-neutrality). From this argument it follows that judgements of cognitive superiority of later over earlier phases of science and of scientific over pre-scientific modes of thought are not and cannot be relative to a particular conceptual or explanatory scheme. They are, on the other hand, clearly relative to the absolute conception of knowledge.

Which raises a further and deep question: what is the proper scope of the absolute conception of knowledge and the Galilean style of reasoning? Over which domains does it properly apply? This question

---

[95] See E. Gellner, 'Options of Belief' in his *Spectacles and Predicaments* (Cambridge University Press, 1979). It would, of course, be highly misleading to suggest that such ideas originated in the post-sixteenth-century world. They were already clearly worked out by the Greeks; the seventeenth century marks the beginning of their dominance and systematic application to the understanding and control of nature.

– itself too large to be more than broached in this final section to the final chapter of this volume – is already implicit in a couple of incidental remarks in Taylor's paper: that the 'dissociation of understanding and attunement achieves greater understanding *at least of physical nature*' and that the natural science model embodying such a dissociation 'has wreaked havoc in its successive misapplications in the sciences of man in the last few centuries. But this says nothing about its validity as an approach to inanimate nature.'[96]

Perhaps, however, it does say something about its validity as an approach to the understanding of animate nature or at least human affairs. I have so far identified the Galilean style of reasoning and the Cartesian absolute conception of knowledge. This, as Williams put it, is 'the conception of reality as it is independently of our thought and to which all representations of reality can be related' and it embodies the project of

> overcoming any systematic bias or distortion or partiality in our outlook as a whole, in our representation of the world: overcoming it, that is to say, in the sense of gaining a standpoint (the absolute standpoint) from which it can be understood in relation to reality, and comprehensibly related to other conceivable representations.[97]

Science methodically practised is the route to such a standpoint, yielding theories that are true in virtue of how the world is independently of any particular representation of it, or the meanings it might have for particular human subjects. Its constitutive ideal is objectivity, involving increasing abstraction and detachment from particular, internal and subjective points of view. As Thomas Nagel has put it, the 'attempt is made to view the world not from a place within it, or from the vantage point of a special type of life and awareness, but nowhere in particular and no form of life in particular at all'. The (unreachable) goal is to arrive at 'a conception of the world which as far as possible is not the view from anywhere within it'.[98]

But is this a fruitful or even a feasible approach or ideal for the sciences of man? Horton appears to answer this question in the

[96] This volume, p. 103. Emphasis mine.
[97] B. Williams, *Descartes: The Project of Pure Enquiry* (Penguin, Harmondsworth, 1978), pp. 66, 211.
[98] T. Nagel, *Mortal Questions* (Cambridge University Press, 1979), pp. 206, 208.

affirmative. For him the social sciences are less able than the natural sciences to make a plausible claim to cognitive superiority *vis-à-vis* traditional systems of belief because of a lack of general 'commitment to the goals of explanation, prediction and control' and the prevalence of 'rival visions of what is morally, aesthetically, or emotionally acceptable, with little in the way of shared criteria of "better" or "worse" to encourage any element of genuine reasoning'.[99] But perhaps the rivalry of such visions is as essential to the object as to the practice of the social sciences, perhaps 'prediction and control', though important in some fields of enquiry, are not always properly central to that practice, and perhaps 'explanation' can take markedly different forms unknown in and inappropriate to the natural sciences.

An alternative view to Horton's is implicit in Nagel's suggestion that 'not all reality is objective, for not everything is best understood the more objectively it is viewed. Appearance and perspective are essential parts of what there is, and in some respects they are best understood from a less detached standpoint.'[100] Often, the only 'objective', perspective-neutral description of the data will be the 'thinnest', least informative and socially relevant (though even this will embody interpretation).

Consider Clifford Geertz's famous story of sheep-stealing in 1912 Morocco,[101] whose thin description goes as follows:

> A Jewish merchant trading in an upland Berber tribe has his goods forcibly taken by some men from a neighbouring tribe. After being told by the local French commandant that he proceeded as his own risk, he tells the local tribe sheikh, that is of the tribe he trades to, of the event, and the sheikh mobilises his followers and they all go and take off the sheep herd of the neighbouring tribe. That tribe then rides out armed but after discussion with the sheep capturers the Jewish merchant selects five hundred of their sheep, after which, upon his return to his shop, the French commandant confiscates the sheep and throws the merchant in prison.

[99] This volume, p. 248.
[100] T. Nagel, 'The limits of objectivity' in *The Tanner Lectures on Human Values*, I (1980) edited by S. M. McMurrin (University of Utah Press, Salt Lake City, and Cambridge University Press, Cambridge, 1980), p. 78.
[101] In C. Geertz, 'Thick description: toward an interpretative theory of culture' in his *The Interpretation of Cultures*.

An interpretation of this story, according to Geertz,

> would begin with distinguishing the three unlike frames of interpretation ingredient in the situation, Jewish, Berber and French, and would then move on to show how (and why) at that time, in that place, their co-presence produced a situation in which systematic misunderstanding reduced traditional form to social farce. [102]

It would involve fitting together (at least) the sheikh's and the Jew's (differing) traditional perspectives and the commandant's colonial perspective, *from* the perspective of anthropological thought at the time of writing. More generally, as Geertz remarks, the proper model of explanation, or at least part of it, is 'thick description', essentially involving interpretations of actors' interpretations, where the observer is faced with 'a multiplicity of complex conceptual structures, many of them superimposed upon or knotted into one another, which are at once strange, irregular, and inexplicit, and which he must contrive somehow first to grasp and then to render'. It is, on this view, 'like trying to read (in the sense of "construct a reading of") a manuscript', the anthropologist's interpretation coming from a further (undetached) perspective. The anthropologist's business is typically to 'construct actor-oriented descriptions of the involvements of a Berber chieftain, a Jewish merchant, and a French solider with one another in 1912 Morocco'. [103] Here at least success does not consist in perspective-neutral description and explanation, nor is it obviously achieved by seeking 'objectivity' in this sense.

In what does it consist and how is it achieved? In my final paragraphs, I wish to pursue the thought shared by Nagel and Geertz, which I shall label 'perspectivism': namely, that at least some areas of social enquiry are inherently perspectival. By 'perspective' I shall mean a more or less closely related set of beliefs, attitudes and assumptions that specify how social reality is to be understood. They concern the appropriate field of observation, the proper domain of explanation (that is, where to seek it, and when to regard it as sufficient), the necessities and possibilities of social life and how the self and its relation to society is to be conceived and human interests identified;

---

[102] Ibid., p. 9. (The thin description quoted comes from Geertz's presentation at our Oxford seminar and is thinner than anything in his chapter.)

[103] Ibid., pp. 10, 15, 16.

and thus they involve moral and political judgments concerning the nature of the good and the proper goals of political action, and the proper means of achieving these.

Perspectivism can be formulated in either a weak or a strong form. In the weak form, it asserts that interpretation and explanation must make reference to actors' perspectives. (Of course, various further questions arise here. Must both *explanans* and *explanandum* be perspectival? Must the interpreter use the actors' concepts? etc.) In the strong form, it asserts that the interpreter's perspective cannot be divorced from the account he gives: that there can be no perspective-neutral interpretation and explanation.

Consider first weak perspectivism. This is of course already strong enough to run into conflict with many powerful traditions in social science, including psychology. Examples are: first, behaviourism, of various types; second, Durkheimian sociology; and third, those voting studies (of the Columbia rather than the Michigan school) which deduce voters' motivations from their socio-economic characteristics, and much of economics, such as the theory of the firm, which assumes, irrespective of evidence, that businessmen engage in profit maximization, and theorizing based on the notions of 'revealed preference' and 'rational expectations'. In the first case, the goal just is thin description and explanation. In the second, the methodological doctrine (though not the practice) of 'treating social facts as things' prescribed macro-explanations that abstract from actors' perspectives.[104] In the third, actors' beliefs and motivations are not investigated but *imputed*, for predictive and explanatory purposes, by a sort of Principle of Super-Charity ('Count them as believing what predicts their behaviour best').

The case for weak perspectivism begins from the observation that the social scientist's data – social actions, practices, norms and institutions – are not 'brute facts' but are meaningful for subjects whose shared understandings of their meanings are constitutive of them, essential to their being the realities they are. Such intersubjective meanings are essential to the very identification of social facts, such as say bargaining or crime or punishment or education or religious

---

[104] See my introduction to E. Durkheim, *The Rules of Sociological Method and Texts on Sociology and its Method,* newly translated by W. D. Halls (Macmillan, London, forthcoming).

observances or voting and, indeed, voting Democrat or Republican.[105]

Now weak perspectivism can itself take what we may call a 'soft' and a 'hard' form. Soft weak perspectivism claims that some types and fields of social enquiry are properly perspectival in this sense; hard weak perspectivism that all social enquiry must be. I knew of no general argument for the latter. There are doubtless some explanatory problems in the social sciences, say in migration theory, which can usefully abstract from the perspectival or what Max Weber called the 'meaningful' character of social life, though I doubt that there are many. Certainly, weak perspectivism would appear to have wide application in history and the social sciences.

Weak perspectivism does not of course in itself raise any questions concerning relativism. These arise only with strong perspectivism. This too can take a 'soft' and a 'hard' form – applying that is to certain areas and forms of social enquiry or to social enquiry as such. Once more, I know of no general argument for the hard version. But what of the soft version of strong perspectivism? It asserts, to repeat, that some areas of social enquiry yield interpretive and explanatory accounts that are always accounts from different interpreters' perspectives, that no account that is neutral between such perspectives is available.

What arguments might support this view? I can think of at least three, which I can only indicate here. First, as already argued above, in identifying beliefs and interpreting the sorts of beliefs they are, we use a model of the agent and his belief and desire network and apply a 'same practices hypothesis' that rely upon our self-understandings and in turn set distinctive explanatory problems for us to solve. Perhaps social enquiry is for this reason inescapably narcissistic: not only is the only access to the actor's perspective via the interpreter's perspective, but – and this is the spectre sceptically raised by Quine and Davidson – there may be no determinate 'fact of the matter' for him to discover. Or perhaps, less drastically, this might be true of only some domains of belief and action (say, in the ascription of utility functions or, as suggested above, in the decoding of 'mysterious' religious belief and practice).

Second, perhaps there are no *practical* ways of characterizing actors'

---

[105] See C. Taylor, 'Interpretation and the sciences of man', *Review of Metaphysics*, 25 (1971), pp. 3–51, and 'Understanding in human science', *Review of Metaphysics* 34 (1980), esp. p. 32.

perspectives that are not interpreter-relative, at least at the social level. In setting out his interpretation, the interpreter is engaging in a process of construction, selecting data and employing concepts in such a way as to 'make sense' to his readers. But his data are not 'brute data' and are always likely radically to underdetermine the story he tells or the analysis he gives. The historian or sociologist or political scientist or anthropologist is faced with assorted fragments of (already pre-interpreted) thought and behaviour, or the records of these, and the task of fitting them into plausible units of analysis (such as narrative sequences, or institutions, or political opinions, or belief systems). The contribution of the interpreter (not to mention of those who record and collect the data on which he relies) is poorly understood and likely to be considerable, but it also appears unavoidable if anything worthwhile is to be said about social facts beyond the micro-level of, say, conversation-sequences.

And, third, the concepts he employs will in many cases be 'essentially contested', that is, perspective-relative concepts, any given interpretation of which will depend upon background interests and assumptions, including moral and political judgements. Is there going to be any adequate explanation of, say, power relations, or political representation, or religious practice that does not employ the concepts constitutive of these very practices in one or another contested interpretation? If not, a stark choice exists: either a contested explanatory account, or an uncontested non-explanatory one. [106]

Finally, we must ask: if strong (albeit soft) perspectivism holds, does it carry relativist implications? Various considerations combine to limit such relativism as it implies. First, nothing said above implies that, relative to a given perspective, and its background interests and assumptions, interpretive and explanatory accounts will be incapable of truth. Interests, background assumptions and value judgements enter, not into the accounts themselves, but into their justification. [107] Second, even if perspective-freedom is impossible, various constraints operate upon every interpretation and explanation. Plainly, they must be open to, compatible with and refutable by (some level of) thinly-described data that is at least neutral between contending perspec-

[106] See my 'On the relativity of power' in Brown, *Philosophical Disputes;* and A. MacIntyre, 'The essential contestability of some social concepts', *Ethics,* 84, 1 (1973), pp. 1–9.
[107] I am grateful to Joseph Raz for making this important point clear to me.

tives. The data itself must be as distortion-free as possible – free both of the observer's influence and, more generally, of the distorting effects of power, generating both deception (telling the observer what he wants to hear) and self-deception. Practically, this will mean that, in cross-cultural studies, and indeed elsewhere, 'the student must feel he or she is answerable to and in uncoercive contact with the culture or people being studied'. [108] The data must be as systematically gathered as possible, relative to the explanatory purpose at hand. And the interpreter must be as reflexive as possible, maximally aware of his interpretive situation, without supposing that he can escape it. [109] Such awareness can enable him to relate perspectives, with their underlying assumptions, interests and values, to one another, thereby revealing the accounts they yield to be commensurable. Sometimes they are like architects' drawings, differing only in standpoint but united in interest and purpose (the normal case in the natural sciences), but often in the social sciences they differ with respect to these also, but are not for that reason incompatible, as *accounts* (even if the interests and purposes are) let alone incommensurable.

Such constraints are powerful. Their application yields perhaps the only 'objectivity' that is possible in much of social enquiry: not 'perspective-neutrality', but rather accounts that are not merely theory- but also perspective-relative, yet constrained by evidence that is as systematic and as reliable as possible, and relatable to other perspective-relative accounts. In applying them, one may explain from some perspective what could not be explained from no perspective.

[108] E.W. Said, *Covering Islam: How the Media and the Experts determine how we see the Rest of the World* (Routledge & Kegan Paul, London, 1981), p. 155.
[109] Compare Max Weber: 'We must . . . work out in the course of the discussion, as its most important result, the best conceptual formulation of what we here understand by the spirit of capitalism, that is the best from the point of view which interests us here. This point of view (the one of which we shall speak later) is, further, by no means the only possible one from which the historical phenomena we are investigating can be analysed. Other standpoints would, for this as for every historical phenomenon, yield other characteristics as the essential ones. The result is that it is by no means necessary to understand by the spirit of capitalism only what it will come to mean to *us* for the purposes of our analysis': *The Protestant Ethic and the Spirit of Capitalism*, translated by T. Parsons (Allen & Unwin, London, 1930), p. 47–8.

Bibliography

Barnes, B., *Scientific Knowledge and Sociological Theory* (Routledge & Kegan Paul, London, 1974)

  Interests and the Growth of Knowledge (Routledge & Kegan Paul, London, 1977)

  T. S. Kuhn and Social Science (Macmillan, London, 1981)

Beattie, J., *Other Cultures* (Routledge & Kegan Paul, London, 1964)

Berger, P., and Luckmann, T., *The Social Construction of Reality* (Doubleday, New York, 1966)

Bhaskar, R., *The Possibility of Naturalism* (Harvester Press, Hassocks, 1979)

Bloor, D., *Knowledge and Social Imagery* (Routledge & Kegan Paul, London, 1976)

Cole, M., and Scribner, S., *Culture and Thought: A Psychological Introduction* (Wiley, New York and London, 1974)

Collingwood, R.G., *The Idea of History* (Clarendon Press, Oxford, 1946)

Crick, M., *Explorations in Language and Meaning. Towards a Semantic Anthropology* (Malaby Press, London, 1976)

Davidson, D., 'On the very idea of a conceptual scheme', *Proceedings and Addresses of the American Philosophical Association*, 47 (1973–4), pp. 5–20.

  'Psychology as philosophy', in *Essays on Actions and Events* (Clarendon Press, Oxford, 1980)

Douglas, M., *Implicit Meanings: Essays in Anthropology* (Routledge & Kegan Paul, London, 1975)

Dray, W., *Perspectives on History* (Routledge & Kegan Paul, London, 1980)

Durkheim, E., and Mauss, M., *Primitive Classification*, trans. by R. Needham, Cohen & West, London, and University of Chicago Press, Chicago, 1963)

Evans-Pritchard, E.E., *Witchcraft: Oracles and Magic Among the Azande* (Clarendon Press, Oxford, 1937)

  Nuer Religion (Oxford University Press, Oxford, 1956)

  Theories of Primitive Religion (Clarendon Press, Oxford, 1965)

  History of Anthropological Thought, ed. A. Singer (Faber, London, 1981)

Fabian, J., 'Language, history and anthropology', *Philosophy of the Social Sciences*, 1 (1971), pp. 19–47

Feyerabend, P., *Against Method* (New Left Books, London, 1975)

  Science in a Free Society (New Left Books, London, 1978)

Foucault, M., *The Archaeology of Knowledge* (Tavistock, London, 1972)

Frazer, Sir J., *The Golden Bough: A Study in Magic and Religion* (abridged edition, Macmillan, London, 1922)

Gadamer, H. G., *Truth and Method* (Seabury Press, New York, 1975)

Geertz, C., *The Interpretation of Cultures* (Basic Books, New York, 1973)

Gellner, E., *Cause and Meaning in the Social Sciences* (Routledge & Kegan Paul, London, 1973)

Legitimation of Belief (Cambridge University Press, Cambridge, 1974)

Spectacles and Predicaments (Cambridge University Press, Cambridge, 1979)

Gipper, H., *Gibt es ein sprachliches Relativätsprinzip? Untersuchungen zur Sapir-Whorf Hypothese* (S. Fischer Verlag, Frankfurt, 1972)

Grandy, R., 'Reference, meaning and belief', *Journal of Philosophy*, 70 (1973), pp. 439–52.

Habermas, J., *Knowledge and Human Interests* (Beacon Press, Boston, 1971, and Heinemann, London, 1972)

Theorie des Kommunikativen Handelns (Surkamp Verlag, Frankfurt, 1981), especially Band 1, I, 3

Hacking, I., *Why Does Language Matter to Philosophy?* (Cambridge University Press, Cambridge, 1975)

Hallpike, C., *The Foundations of Primitive Thought* (Clarendon Press, Oxford, 1979)

Hamnett, I., 'Sociology of religion and sociology of error', *Religion*, 3 (1973), pp. 1–12.

Hesse, M., *Revolutions and Reconstructions in the Philosophy of Science* (Harvester, Hassocks, 1980)

Hollis, M., *Models of Man: Philosophical Thoughts on Social Action*, (Cambridge University Press, Cambridge, 1977)

'Witchcraft and Winchcraft', *Philosophy of the Social Sciences*, 2 (1972), pp. 89–103

Horton, R., 'African traditional thought and Western science', *Africa*, 38 (1967), pp. 50–71 and 155–87, reprinted in abridged form in B.R. Wilson (ed.), *Rationality* (Blackwell, Oxford, 1970)

'Paradox and explanation: a reply to Mr. Skorupski', *Philosophy of the Social Sciences*, 3 (1973), pp. 231–56 and 289–314

'Professor Winch on safari', *European Journal of Sociology*, 17 (1976), pp. 157–80

Jahoda, G., *Psychology and Anthropology* (Academic Press, London, forthcoming)

Jarvie, I., *Concepts and Society* (Routledge & Kegan Paul, London, 1972)

Kuhn, T., *The Structure of Scientific Revolutions*, 2nd edn (University of Chicago Press, Chicago, 1970)

The Essential Tension: Selected Studies in Scientific Tradition and Change (Chicago University Press, Chicago and London, 1977)

Lakatos, I., *The Methodology of Scientific Research Programmes* (Cambridge University Press, 1978)

Proofs and Refutations (Cambridge University Press, 1978)

Laudan, L., *Progress and its Problems* (Routledge & Kegan Paul, London, and University of California Press, Berkeley, 1977)

Lévy-Bruhl, L., *Les Fonctions mentales dans les societés inférieures* (Alcan, Paris, 1910)

The Notebooks of Lucien Lévy-Bruhl, trans. by P. Rivière (Blackwell, Oxford, 1975)

Lévi-Strauss, C., *The Savage Mind*, (Weidenfeld & Nicolson, London and University of Chicago Press, Chicago, 1966)

Lewis, D., 'Radical interpretation', *Synthese*, 27 (1974), pp. 331–4

Lukes, S., *Essays in Social Theory* (Macmillan, London, and Columbia University Press, New York, 1977)

MacDonald, G., and Pettit, P., *Semantics and Social Science* (Routledge & Kegan Paul, London, 1981)

MacIntyre, A., *After Virtue*, (Duckworth, London, and University of Notre Dame Press, Notre Dame, 1981)

'Is understanding religion compatible with believing', in B.R. Wilson (ed.), *Rationality*

'The Idea of a Social Science' in B.R. Wilson (ed.) *Rationality*

Needham, R., *Belief, Language and Experience* (Blackwell, Oxford, 1972)

Newton-Smith, W., *The Rationality of Science* (Routledge & Kegan Paul, London, 1982)

Nielsen, K., 'Rationality and relativism', *Philosophy of the Social Sciences*, 4 (1974), pp. 313–31

Popper, K.R., *Conjectures and Refutations: The Growth of Scientific Knowledge* (Routledge & Kegan Paul, London, 1963)

Objective Knowledge: An Evolutionary Approach (Clarendon Press, Oxford, 1972)

Putnam, H., *Meaning and the Moral Sciences* (Routledge & Kegan Paul, London, 1978)

Reason, Truth and History (Cambridge University Press, Cambridge, 1981)

Quine, W.v.O., *Word and Object* (Wiley, New York, 1960)

Ontological Relativity and Other Essays (Columbia University Press, London, 1969)

Rorty, R., *Philosophy and the Mirror of Nature* (Blackwell, Oxford, and Princeton University Press, 1980)

Sahlins, M., *Culture and Practical Reason* (University of Chicago Press, Chicago, 1976)

Skorupski, J., *Symbol and Theory: A Philosophical Study of Theories of Religion* (Cambridge University Press, 1976)

'Science and traditional religious thought', *Philosophy of the Social Sciences*, 3 (1973), pp. 97–115 and 204–330

Smith, J.Z., *Map is not Territory: Studies in the History of Religion*, (E.J. Brill, Leiden, 1978)

Sperber, D., *Rethinking Symbolism* (Cambridge University Press, Cambridge, 1975)

Strawson, P.F., *Individuals* (Methuen, London, 1959)

Taylor, C., 'Interpretation and the sciences of man', *Review of Metaphysics*, 25 (1971), pp. 3–51

Toulmin, S., *Human Understanding*, vol. 1 (Clarendon Press, Oxford, and Princeton University Press, 1972)

Turnbull, C., *The Mountain People* (Cape, London, 1973)

Turner, S., *Sociological Explanation as Translation* (Cambridge University Press, Cambridge, 1980)

Whorf, B.L., *Language, Thought and Reality* (M.I.T. Press, Cambridge, Mass., 1956)

Williams, B.A.O., 'The truth in relativism', *Proceedings of the Aristotelian Society* n.s. lxxv (1974–5), reprinted in *Moral Luck* (Cambridge University Press, Cambridge, 1981)

Winch, P., *The Idea of a Social Science and its Relation to Philosophy*, (Routledge & Kegan Paul, London, 1958)

'Understanding a primitive society', *American Philosophical Quarterly*, 1 (1964), pp. 307–24, reprinted in B. R. Wilson (ed.) *Rationality*

Wiredu, K., *Philosophy and an African Culture* (Cambridge University Press, Cambridge, 1980)

Wittgenstein, L., *Remarks on Frazer's 'Golden Bough'*, ed. R. Rhees (Brynmill, Notts. and Humanities Press, Atlantic Heights, N.J., 1979)

Wright, G.H. von *Explanation and Understanding* (Cornell University Press, Ithaca, 1971)

ANTHOLOGIES AND COLLECTIONS

Banton, M. (ed.), *Anthropological Approaches to the Study of Religion*, (Tavistock, London, 1966)

Barnes, B., and Shapin, S. (eds), *Natural Order. Historical Studies of Scientific Culture* (Sage, Beverley Hills and London, 1979)

Benn, S.I., and Mortimore, G.W. (eds), *Rationality and the Social Sciences* Routledge & Kegan Paul, London, 1976)

Borger, R., and Cioffi, F. (eds), *Explanation in the Behavioural Sciences* (Cambridge University Press, Cambridge, 1970)

Brown, S.C. (ed.), *Philosophical Disputes in the Social Sciences* (Harvester, Brighton, 1979)

Colodny, R.G. (ed.), *The Nature and Function of Scientific Theories* (University of Pittsburgh Press, 1970)

Dalmayr, F.R., and McCarthy, T.A. (eds), *Understanding and Social Enquiry* (University of Notre Dame Press, Notre Dame, 1977)

Douglas, M. (ed.), *Rules and Meanings: The Anthropology of Everyday Knowledge*, (Penguin Books, Harmondsworth, 1973)

Emmett, D., and MacIntyre, A. (eds), *Sociological Theory and Philosophical Analysis* (Macmillan, London, 1970)

Finnegan, R., and Horton, R. (eds), *Modes of Thought: Essays on Thinking in Western and Non-Western Societies*, (London, Faber and Faber, 1973)

Firth, R. (ed.), *Man and Culture* (Humanities Press, New York, 1970)

Hookway, C. and Pettit, P. (eds), *Action and Interpretation: Studies in the Philosophy of the Social Sciences* (Cambridge University Press, Cambridge, 1978)

Kippenberg, H.G., and Luchesi, B. (eds), *Magie: Die sozialwisenschaftliche*

Kontroverse über das Verstehen fremden Denkens (Surkamp Verlag, Frankfurt, 1978)

Kranz, M. and Meiland, J. w. (eds), *Relativism: Cognitive and Moral* (University of Notre Dame Press, Notre Dame, 1982)

Lakatos, I., and Musgrave, A. (eds), *Criticism and the Growth of Knowledge* (Cambridge University Press, Cambridge, 1970)

Lloyd, B., and Gay, J. (eds), *Universals of Human Thought: Some African Evidence* (Cambridge University Press, Cambridge, 1981)

Schoek, H., and Wiggins, J. (eds), *Relativism and the Study of Man* (Van Nostrand, Princeton, 1961)

Silverstein, A. (ed.), *Human Communication: Theoretical Perspectives* (Lawrence Erlbaum Associates, Hillside, N.J., 1974)

Wilson, B.R. (ed.), *Rationality* (Blackwell, Oxford, 1970)

Index